Praise for previous editions

"If you plan to explore Boston and Cambridge, by all means take Michael and Susan Southworth along! Their guide is surely the best of its kind on this continent. It tells you not only what you ought to know about America's most remarkable and varied collection of buildings, but also about the people and the culture that shaped these buildings and that these buildings, in turn, helped to shape."

—Wolf Von Eckardt, design critic, *Time* magazine

"The most comprehensive guide to Boston architecture ever published. . . . Yet for all its useful information, the *AIA Guide to Boston* is no dry, dense tome. The authors enliven their material with fascinating bits of history, culture, humor, and sharp opinion."

—Janice Harayda, *Boston Business Journal*

"It is addictive . . . a marvelously readable and informative book, which I read endlessly, go right through and then start over. Boston is a unique city of a sort rare in America, and the Southworths have done it full justice."

—Nash Kerr Burger, the *New York Times Book Review*

"Architectural buffs will here find a wealth of information on distinctive Bostonian structures and their histories."

—*Midwest Book Review*

"In this readable volume, the authors include anecdotes, social history commentary, and lucid building descriptions that will be useful to the professional and of interest to the informed layperson."

—*Library Journal*

"A truly great 'opus,' and *very* useful."

—Charles F. Mason Jr., curator of prints, Boston Athenaeum

AIA Guide to
BOSTON

Susan and Michael Southworth

THIRD EDITION

Guilford, Connecticut

All photographs © by Michael Southworth except as noted here and in the text: p. 69, Historic American Building Survey; p. 347, Shutterstock/Elena Elisseeva

Text design by Nancy Freeborn
Maps by XNR Productions Inc. © Morris Book Publishing, LLC

Library of Congress Cataloging-in-Publication Data

Southworth, Susan.
  AIA guide to Boston / Susan and Michael Southworth. — 3rd ed.
    p. cm.
  Rev. ed. of: The Boston Society of Architects' AIA guide to Boston. 2nd ed. © 1992.
  Includes bibliographical references and index.
  ISBN 978-0-7627-4337-7
  1. Architecture—Massachusetts—Boston—Guidebooks. 2. Boston (Mass.)—
Buildings, structures, etc.—Guidebooks. 3. Boston (Mass.)—Guidebooks.
I. Southworth, Michael. II. Southworth, Susan. Boston Society of Architects' AIA
guide to Boston. III. Boston Society of Architects. IV. Title. V. Title: Guide to Boston.
  NA735.B7S69 2008
  720.9744'61--dc22

                                                                    2007042837

Printed in China

10 9 8 7 6 5 4 3 2 1

Contents

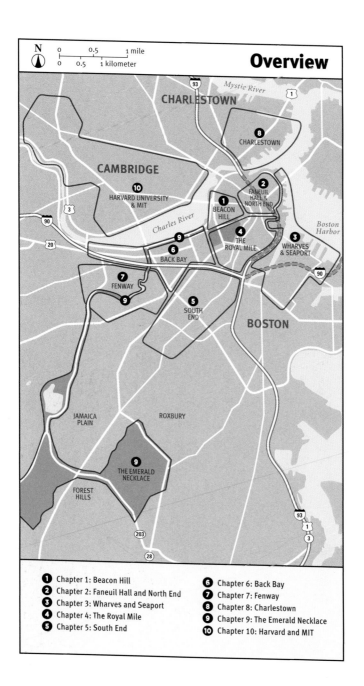

Overview

N

0   0.5   1 mile
0   0.5   1 kilometer

Mystic River

93 **1**

CHARLESTOWN

8
CHARLESTOWN

CAMBRIDGE

10
HARVARD UNIVERSITY
& MIT

2
FANEUIL
HALL &
NORTH END

1
BEACON
HILL

3
WHARVES
& SEAPORT

*Boston
Harbor*

3

90

Charles River

9

4
THE
ROYAL MILE

20

6
BACK BAY

90

7
FENWAY

9

5
SOUTH
END

BOSTON

JAMAICA
PLAIN

ROXBURY

9
THE EMERALD
NECKLACE

FOREST
HILLS

93
1
1
3

203

28

1 Chapter 1: Beacon Hill
2 Chapter 2: Faneuil Hall and North End
3 Chapter 3: Wharves and Seaport
4 Chapter 4: The Royal Mile
5 Chapter 5: South End
6 Chapter 6: Back Bay
7 Chapter 7: Fenway
8 Chapter 8: Charlestown
9 Chapter 9: The Emerald Necklace
10 Chapter 10: Harvard and MIT

Acknowledgments

Our years of historical research, interviews, and fieldwork on this book were inspired by a love of Boston and hope for preservation of its incomparable history while making a livable contemporary city. Looking critically at each building has left us more awed than ever by Boston and simultaneously more worried about the future of this national treasure. Can all of its best qualities be retained and enhanced for future generations? Our response was to offer a percentage of the royalties from our book to the Boston Society of Architects in support of their public education and advocacy of historic preservation.

We are indebted to the Beatrix Farrand Fund, which supported the landscape history research for this edition. To the many architects, landscape architects, planners, community leaders, and citizens we interviewed throughout the city, we are most grateful and cannot possibly list them all. The College of Environmental Design Library of the University of California, Bostonian Society, Boston Athenaeum, and Boston Public Library have been essential in the research. The Boston Landmarks Commission and Boston Redevelopment Authority have provided useful information. Of course, we thank Eran Ben-Joseph, Steve Rosenthal, Peter Vanderwarker, Will Watkins, and Sally Withington. Globe Pequot's former president Charles Everitt's enthusiasm was immediate and continues to this day; now it is editors Gillian Belnap and Jeff Serena who assisted us in publishing the third edition.

Introduction

"The Metropolis of this Colony, or rather of the whole Countrey"
—John Josselyn, *An Account of Two Voyages to
New-England,* London, 1674

Boston's architectural heritage is unique for every era, from 1630 to the twenty-first century. Since it had a head start and dominated the colonies throughout the pre-Revolutionary era, it is not surprising that Boston scored a number of architectural firsts. Beginning with the earliest colonial structures of wood and continuing with the later Georgian and Federal buildings of brick and stone, one can trace the history of this small peninsula through its architecture and its architects.

Boston-born Charles Bulfinch, America's preeminent architect of the late eighteenth and early nineteenth centuries, had a long career in architecture and planning here, as well as in Washington, D.C. Alexander Parris and other Boston architects developed the unique "Boston granite style," making use of the abundant local stone in warehouses and commercial buildings for the city's thriving commerce. The Back Bay, South End, and downtown were showcases for eclectic Victorian designs by nationally prominent Boston firms, including the most influential American architect of the century, Henry Hobson Richardson. Frederick Law Olmsted, the revered landscape architect, relocated his firm here from New York because he found Boston more sympathetic to his progressive ideas. Even Louis Sullivan, leader of the Chicago school, and Frank Lloyd Wright, Sullivan's devoted student, were influenced by their Boston years.

The city's leadership in architecture continued into the twentieth century with innovative work by local architects as well as international stars Aalto, Le Corbusier, Correa, Foster, Gehry, Gropius, Holl, Pei, Saarinen, Sert, and Vinoly. With more architects and architecture students per capita than any other American city, its preeminence seems secure. Boston has always been quick to adopt new ideas from throughout the world, but sometimes

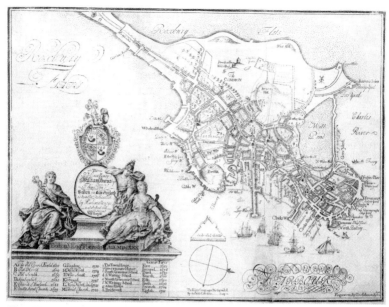

Map of Boston by William Burgess,1728

its leaders fell for undesirable fads. Sacrificing cherished neighborhoods to create superblocks, the boom mentality of mid-twentieth-century developments was resolutely indifferent to aesthetics.

Reacting to the horrors of mass clear-cutting through the city, preservation returned to the forefront for a few decades. Ambitious projects slumbered on drawing boards or struggled against myriad construction delays. But as the millennium drew to a close, Boston's leaders sought to create their legacies with *grands projets,* as Mitterand had in Paris. Big developments returned with a vengeance while "small is beautiful" receded. Across the nation megaconstructions spanned multiblocks. Nothing was bigger or more problematic than Boston's Big Dig, so well intentioned but blowing through its budget year after year as it fell further behind schedule. Even after the buoyant opening celebration, problems continued as the tunnels flooded and ceiling panels fell on passing cars.

Building tunnels was an old habit for Boston. The first was underwater, between downtown and East Boston, in 1904. Next came the Red Line, connecting Harvard to Quincy by burrowing under Beacon Hill, the Common, and downtown. The Green Line tunnels, Sumner, Orange Line,

Callahan, and finally the Ted Williams in 1995 followed. Like the Big Dig, they all unsettled Boston. Yet there was much to celebrate aboveground, as the city emerged like Punxsutawney Phil on Groundhog Day, able to see the Bay for the first time in fifty years.

Though the Big Dig and megabuildings were completed and fêted, the mood had already shifted. They had been overtaken by their polar opposite, the "green building" movement. The prevalence of energy-efficient and ecologically responsible design made the high-profile exceptions embarrassingly obvious. Artists for Humanity, the contemporary art center in South Boston, was the greenest institution in the nation for some years, inspiring others and demonstrating that green architecture doesn't have to be ugly.

More than any other American city, Boston has retained or adapted its physical past while allowing new landmarks to take root. Whether parsimony, sentiment, or foresight led them down this path, Boston emerged with the fine-grained, dense, and walkable environmental organization that is sustainable but unattainable in most other U.S. cities. Boston continues to successfully adapt streets and buildings from past centuries to life today. One must not be misled by the quaint old lanes and the rich treasure of historic buildings. Boston has the best of the old and the new.

Discover Boston Your Way

There are many ways to discover Boston. Some Bostonians habitually carry our guide and over years of late appointments or waiting for friends, they see everything in the book.

Boston can't be seen in a week or even a month. This third edition offers the people, history, and design of seven hundred places so visitors might focus on a few districts. Reading the chapter introductions will help you decide which areas of Boston fit your interests. Or you can flip through the book, stopping at whatever catches your eye. A simpler approach is to walk in any direction that appeals to you, stopping to read about a street, neighborhood, park, or building when you want to learn its age, who lived there, or its history. The maze of narrow seventeenth- and eighteenth-century streets is one of Boston's glories. With our guide in hand you can wander confidently.

Short on time? Choose a compact area such as Faneuil Hall and the

Blackstone Block, Boston Common and Public Garden, Harvard Yard, MIT's outdoor contemporary sculpture collection, Charlestown's Town Hill, or Copley Square where you can stand in one spot and just turn your head to see a half-dozen major sites.

Residents and visitors alike can spend a delightful morning or day walking a street from the first to the last site. Beacon Street, Broad Street, Commonwealth Avenue, Washington Street, HarborWalk, Main Street in Charlestown, and Brattle Street in Cambridge make wonderful strolls. Each season offers ample rewards for exploration on foot—brilliant autumn foliage in Charlestown's Winthrop Square, fresh fallen snow on Franklin Square, spring magnolias on Marlborough Street, and the shaded Riverway for languorous summer strolls.

If you are tired of walking, explore four centuries of Boston in your armchair!

Given ample time and the inclination to range widely, the Special Interest Tours take you through the region seeing single categories of sites such as Boston Urban Design, Contemporary Landmarks, or the work of Charles Bulfinch.

This guide is organized topographically by districts. Within each district or subdistrict, sites are arranged alphabetically by street and numerically by building address, except in the case of some very small districts where sites are arranged by proximity to one another. Sites identified with a locator number are keyed to the maps at the back of the book. In the index sites can be found under street address, name, and architect. Places of outstanding design interest are indicated with a $\overline{\text{m}}$, and historic landmark status is noted.

Why not begin today?

—Susan and Michael Southworth

BEACON HILL
National Historic District

Urban romantics fall in love with Beacon Hill. Walking up a cobblestone way or brick sidewalk, one enters the sepia-toned charm of a Henry James novel. Unlike Williamsburg or Disneyland, this is an authentic neighborhood where Boston's first settler, the Rev. William Blaxton, made his home in 1625. The southern slopes of Trimountain, much steeper and higher then, had their summits cut down and leveled two centuries later.

Newly contoured as a gently sloping hill dominated by the gold-domed state capitol, Federal, Georgian, Greek revival, and Victorian houses followed. With rare exceptions, the houses are brick, hugging brick sidewalks in a monochromatic palette that focuses attention on ironwork balconies, railings, and window guards, as well as myriad architectural details. Many houses have low doors to one side of their stately entrances, suggesting basement apartments inhabited by hobbits. In reality they open on low tunnels only big enough for a boy with a basket on his head to lead a cow to the rear kitchen garden—a requirement of the 1830s building code.

The Hill was the fashionable place to live until the 1870s, when the Back Bay was developing on a grander scale. Families left Louisburg Square, Chestnut Street, and Mount Vernon Street houses for French-influenced boulevards and mansard-roofed houses that were larger, lighter, and airier than the denser Beacon Hill. The period of decline was reversed in the mid-twentieth century, and Beacon Hill was suddenly *the* place to be once more.

The South Slope

Acorn Street

This cobblestone street is a charming remnant of early nineteenth-century life. Although it is one of the narrower streets remaining in Boston, the city's typical lanes were 4 feet wide and highways were 6 feet wide for most of two centuries. The flat-façade brick row houses have foundations as well as granite door and window lintels. These very desirable small homes were originally the residences of coachmen who served families in the nearby mansions and fine homes on Chestnut and Mount Vernon Streets.

Acorn Street

Beacon Street

Blaxton's Yellow Sweeting, the first named variety of apple in America, was cultivated here by Boston's first settler, the Rev. William Blaxton. When he wasn't tending his orchard, he might be seen riding through town on his saddled bull.

Considering Beacon Street's long, proud history, it is surprising to learn that its seventeenth-century name was "Poor House Lane." No doubt that was because of the old almshouse at the corner of today's Park Street. In 1708 the street was formally laid out and re-named after the signal lantern at the summit of the hill. Construction of the stately row houses came a century later, after the State House.

1 Boston Athenaeum
10½ Beacon Street
Edward Clarke Cabot, 1847–1849
Enlarged: Henry Forbes Bigelow, 1913–1914; later alterations by others
National Historic Landmark

:: The Boston Athenaeum is a proprietary library founded in 1807 on the site of Ralph Waldo Emerson's boyhood home. Before moving to its present location overlooking the Old Granary Burial Ground, it changed locations several times. Edward Clarke Cabot, who won a competition for its design in 1846, based his scheme on Palladio's Palazzo da Porta Festa in Vicenza, a work that was illustrated in a book held by the Athenaeum at that time, *Le Fabbriche e i Disegni di Andrea Palladio* by Ottavoi Bertotti Scamozzi. For years prior to this

Reading Room, Boston Athenaeum
© Boston Athenaeum

venture, Cabot had raised sheep in Vermont and Illinois. After his success in architecture, he served as the first president of the Boston Society of Architects, from 1867 until 1869.

The dignified façade of gray sandstone with rich patina is visually organized into two stories. Corinthian pilasters define the window bays, with double pilasters around the window of the central projecting bay in which the entrance is situated. Pedimented windows are set within the slightly recessed arches. The first floor is treated as a more massive basement story, with rusticated arches framing its windows.

Serene high-ceilinged interiors and labyrinthine stacks have provided the perfect setting for several generations of scholars and esthetes. Henry Forbes Bigelow added the impressive fifth-floor reading room. Especially appealing is its large central space under a coffered, vaulted ceiling, with many small sunfilled alcoves amid stacks of books and odd little stairways to the upper stacks. As David McCord wrote, it "combines the best elements of the Bodleian, Monticello, the frigate *Constitution*, a greenhouse and an old New England sitting room."

In earlier decades literary spinsters and old gentlemen went to the Athenaeum for an afternoon tea of bouillon with cheese sandwiches or sweet crackers, a tradition that remained unchanged for a century, as did the original charge of 3 cents.

The library houses many important historical collections, including George Washington's personal library. An early Athenaeum librarian, Charles Ammi Cutter, pioneered book classification systems for libraries. Some of the books are still organized in the Cutter system.

2 Chester Harding House
16 Beacon Street
1808
National Historic Landmark

:: Thomas Fletcher's four-story brick Federal house is a prestigious setting for the Boston Bar Association, the oldest legal organization in the country. The building's most famous resident was the artist Chester Harding.

Chester Harding House

3 Amory-Ticknor House

("Amory's Folly")
Beacon at 9 Park Street
Charles Bulfinch, 1803–1804
Altered: ca. 1815 and after 1885

:: Bulfinch's progressive design theories and public spirit were demonstrated over many decades. As a member of the Board of Selectmen, he persuaded the city to enact an ordinance regulating building height and style. It was applied to the east end of the Common when the lane was upgraded, removing the almshouse, bridewell (reformatory), workhouse, and granary.

The house built for merchant Thomas Amory on the site of the demolished almshouse was intended to set the standard for the new Park Street. Unfortunately, Amory lost many of his ships at sea and went bankrupt shortly before the housewarming. Since no one could afford to purchase the home, it became a boardinghouse for politicians. Lafayette occupied a floor during his stay in Boston in 1805. In 1806 the house was divided in half. Harvard professor George Ticknor took up residence in the Park Street side, and his name became associated with the house.

Today the once great mansion stands barely recognizable, although the basic brick volume and Adam entrance portico with fanlight and curving granite steps (one half is missing) are more or less intact. Many ground-floor shop extensions have been added, along with Queen Anne–style oriel windows and dormers on the upper floors. Though out of character, the Victorian predations

Half of the original horseshoe stairway of the Amory-Ticknor House was demolished for the protruding shop addition.

Claflin Building (William G. Preston, 1884), 20 Beacon Street

Union Club (ca. 1830–1840, remodeled, 1896), Park Street near Beacon Street

had a certain disheveled charm when they were filled with odd antiques, curiosity shops, and tearooms.

4 State House 🏛

24 Beacon Street
Charles Bulfinch, 1795–1797;
restored 1896–1898
Rear annex: Charles E. Brigham,
1889–1895
Wings: Chapman, Sturgis and Andrews,
1914–1917
Renovation: Shepley Bulfinch
Richardson and Abbott, 1993
National Historic Landmark

:: Charles Bulfinch, the foremost architect of the newly independent states, was born in 1763 into a wealthy Boston family. He attended Boston Latin and watched the Battle of Bunker Hill from the roof of his family's home on Bowdoin Street. After graduating from Harvard, he spent two years on a grand tour of Europe, as one would expect of the son of a prominent physician. He studied and admired the new English architecture, especially the neoclassic styles of Robert Adam and Sir William Chambers.

Returning to Boston, Bulfinch described the next several years as a "season of leisure, pursuing no business, but giving gratuitous advice in architecture." It was during this period that he designed two state capitols, three churches, two public monuments, a theater, a hotel, and twelve private homes! Although he was never well off financially during his Boston career, his contributions to the city were enormous. Besides his numerous fine buildings and ideas for civic improvement, he was chief of police and head of the Board of Selectmen for many years. Mayor Josiah Quincy wrote of Bulfinch: "During the many years he presided over the town government, he improved its finances, executed the laws with firmness, and was distinguished for gentleness and urbanity of manners, integrity and purity of character . . . Few men deserve to be held by the Citizens of Boston in more grateful remembrance than Charles Bulfinch."

One of his great contributions to the city, the state, and the country—for it was the most outstanding public building in America for decades after its construction—was the Massachusetts State House. Bulfinch prepared his first plan for it on his return from Europe in

State House

State House Annex

1787. His design was in the style of Sir William Chambers's 1778 Somerset House in London. Although Worcester, Plymouth, and the South End had been considered as a site, John Hancock's steep, rough pasture near the summit of Beacon Hill was purchased for the new State House. The design of the south (front) façade features a central projecting portico with colonnade of Corinthian columns (originally of solid Maine pine, but replaced with cast iron in 1960) supported on an arcade of brick arches. The gilded dome rests on a higher central pediment with brick pilasters beneath. Atop the dome is a lantern topped with a gilded pinecone, symbol of the abundant forests of Massachusetts. The north façade was similar to this, except pilasters were used instead of a portico colonnade.

The dome was originally whitewashed wood shingles. In 1802 the shingles were replaced with copper painted gray, installed by Paul Revere and Sons. In 1861 the dome was gilded and has remained so ever since, except during World War II when it was blackened again. Brick for the State House and most Boston buildings of the period came from Charlestown. In 1825 the red brick walls were painted white and thirty years later yellow, then white again in 1918 to match the new marble wings. (In Bulfinch's time it was common to paint the brick of more pretentious buildings if granite or marble could not be used.) Finally in 1928 the paint was removed, exposing the red brick.

Inside, one can still see most of Bulfinch's work in the first-floor Doric Hall under the dome, and in the Senate Chamber (originally the House of Representatives) and Reception Room (originally the Senate) on the second floor. The building has suffered numerous alterations, including a long rear extension built in 1889–1895. Six times the size of the original building, of yellow brick with gray trim, the extension must have looked absurd until the marble wings, added 1914–1917, obscured the view.

Bulfinch also designed statehouses for Connecticut (1793–1796) and Maine (1829–1832). President Monroe appointed him architect of the U.S. Capitol in 1817, a project that consumed Bulfinch for twelve years. His 1818 drawing of the Capitol building is exquisite, a three-domed, perfectly proportioned composition. Only the central portion of the west façade survives from his original design after the enlargements and alterations.

After decades of unpaid public service and unpredictable payments from private clients, these were comfortable years for Bulfinch and his wife on his annual federal salary of $2500. He died in Boston in 1844 at the age of eighty-one, fifteen years after his return from Washington.

5 Shaw Memorial
Beacon Street at Park Street
Augustus Saint-Gaudens, sculptor, with McKim, Mead, and White, 1897

:: The first Civil War regiments of freed blacks were formed in Boston. This me-

Shaw Memorial

morial by Augustus Saint-Gaudens honors the very first black regiment, which was led by Robert Gould Shaw. Shaw, the twenty-six-year-old son of an old Boston family, died in 1863 while leading his regiment's assault on Fort Wagner, South Carolina. The bas-relief memorial was dedicated in 1897 after thirteen years' work in the studio of Saint-Gaudens. Shaw is in high relief against his low-relief soldiers, but their faces were modeled in the round in the studio in preparation for the piece, so each of the black soldiers is a distinctive individual portrait. The monument was beautifully sited by McKim, Mead, and White opposite the State House on a small plaza overlooking the Boston Common. Broad steps on each side lead down to the Common.

6 George Parkman House
33 Beacon Street
Cornelius Coolidge, builder, 1825

:: The flat brick façade of this four-and-a-half-story house has been modified with the later addition of a delicate cast-iron verandah. George Francis Parkman lived here after the death of his father, Dr. George Parkman, who was killed in the 1850s by Harvard professor John White Webster in one of the grisliest and most publicized murders of the nineteenth century. Parkman—along with his mother and sister—withdrew from the public eye and lived in solitude in this house from 1859 until his death in 1908. Parkman felt a strong commitment to the public parks and bequeathed to the city his house and $5.5 million for maintenance of the Boston Common, which the house overlooks. It has been renovated for use by the city as a conference and reception center.

The brick house next door at 34 Beacon closely resembles the Parkman house. Number 25 is a 1926 building retaining only the first floor façade of the original house.

George Parkman House

7 John Phillips House

Beacon Street at 1 Walnut Street
Charles Bulfinch, 1804–1805
Altered: ca. 1830

:: John Phillips was Boston's first mayor, and his son, the reformer, abolitionist, and lecturer Wendell Phillips, was born here. Originally, the entrance was on Beacon Street, at the center of a five-bay Georgian façade resembling that of the Amory Ticknor house at the corner of Beacon and Park Streets. The entrance was moved to Walnut Street about 1830, greatly compromising the architectural integrity of the house. Nevertheless, it retains enough Bulfinch to be an important contribution to Boston.

Detail, Tudor Apartments

John Phillips House

8 Appleton-Parker Houses

39–40 Beacon Street
Alexander Parris, 1818
Addition: Hartwell and Richardson, 1888
National Register of Historic Places

:: This handsome pair of early Greek revival bowfront row houses has Ionic porticoes and wrought-iron balconies. It was here that Henry Wadsworth Longfellow courted and married Fanny Appleton. In 1888 a fourth floor was

Rippling façade, Tudor Apartments (S. J. F. Thayer, 1885–1887), 34½ Beacon Street at Joy Street

Entrance, Appleton-Parker Houses

added to both houses above the original cornice line. Now there are two cornices. Later the bow of the Appleton house was altered by the addition of an extra middle window on each of the four floors.

9 Somerset Club
42–43 Beacon Street
Alexander Parris, 1816–1819
National Register of Historic Places

:: The famous Boston painter John Singleton Copley had a house on this site and lived here until 1774, when he went to England. Four decades later Colonel David Sears built the two-story bowfront granite house that is the basis of the right half of the present structure. In 1832 the left half was added by Sears. Since 1872 it has been the Somerset Club, an exclusive private club (until recently for men only). After the club acquired the building, it added the third floor. The bows project more than the typical Boston bow and rise above the cornice line to create a separate volume. The rusticated garden wall distances the building from the street, increasing its monumentality.

10 Third Harrison Gray Otis House 🏛
(American Meteorological Society)
45 Beacon Street
Charles Bulfinch, 1805–1808

:: Harrison Gray Otis built three notable houses, all designed by Charles Bulfinch. Remarkably, all three are still standing today. This house in the Federal style was the last and largest of the three, and Mr. Otis remained here until his death in 1848. At the age of eighty, despite forty years of gout, he was said to breakfast on pâté de foie gras. Each afternoon ten gallons of punch were consumed from the Lowestoft bowl hospitably placed on the stair landing for those en route to the drawing room upstairs.

Somerset Club

Gate, Somerset Club

Third Harrison Gray Otis House

Samuel Eliot Morison, the Boston historian, wrote: "My great-grandmother, Emily Marshall Otis, died in childbirth in 1836. Her two little girls, Emily, my grandmother, Mary, who became Mrs. Alexander H. Stevens, and George (a childhood friend of Henry Adams), then lived in their grandfather Otis's mansion at 45 Beacon Street, where they were brought up under the care of a widowed aunt. My grandmother assured me that there was no plumbing of any description in that great house; all water had to be brought in from a well in the yard. She, Mary, and George were marched to the Tremont House once a week for a tub bath." Bathtubs were prohibited in Boston as late as 1842 because medical authorities said cockroaches lived in dirty water and died in fresh water; thus, bathwater was considered a menace.

The house was built on a foundation of stone taken from a neighboring powder house. The four-story façade is organized into five bays, and a portico with pairs of Ionic fluted columns defines the center entrance. The ground floor originally had recessed brick arches, like most Bulfinch houses. The tall triple-hung second-floor windows are ornamented with classical lintels supported on console brackets and with Chinese fretwork balconies, also used in the second Otis house at 85 Mount Vernon Street. A cobblestone courtyard leads to the carriage house, which is joined to the main house by a large servants' ell.

When the house was built, it was surrounded by English gardens and the Common on three sides, with the courtyard on the fourth. The Blue Hills were visible across Back Bay, which came to within 200 yards of the front door. These surroundings were lost in 1831, when Otis built a house for his daughter. The new house stood in his garden directly to the east and wrapped around his former bow window on the second floor.

The building is owned and occupied by the American Meteorological Society. The interior has been altered, but the exterior is largely intact.

11 William Hickling Prescott House
55 Beacon Street
National Register of Historic Places
54–55 Beacon Street
Asher Benjamin, 1808

:: Asher Benjamin added considerable distinction to this pair of bowfront brick row houses by his extensive use of Greek architectural motifs, notably the three-story wooden pilasters, the first-story colonnade with delicate columns, and the balustrade atop the cornice. The houses have fanlight doors and ornamental iron balconies on three floors. The second floor's tall slender windows are triple-hung sash.

The left-hand house, 55 Beacon Street, is Headquarters House for the National Society of Colonial Dames in the Commonwealth of Massachusetts. Between 1845 and 1849 it was the residence of William Prescott, who enter-

William Hickling Prescott House

tained the British author William Make-
peace Thackeray as his houseguest.
A pair of Prescott family eighteenth-
century swords inspired Thackeray's
The Virginians.

12 56–57 Beacon Street
Ephraim Marsh, 1819

:: These two houses may have been
the first built on Beacon Street with
bathrooms—which were rather inconveniently located in the front room of
the cellar. The construction contract
specified that "in the cellar there is to
be a bathing room in front into which
the aqueduct is to be led" and that
"the pump in the back yard is to have a
box to hang meat in." Compare the
bowfronts at 56–57 with those at 63–64
Beacon Street designed by the same architect a few years later. The paired entrances in this earlier set have flat
Federal-style doorways, each with a
fanlight and sidelights framing the door.
The Victorian oriel window with decorative iron filigree on the second floor of
number 57 is a later addition.

57 Beacon Street

13 King's Chapel Parish House and Rectory
63–64 Beacon Street
Ephraim Marsh, 1820s

:: A short time after completing the
very similar bowfront pair of houses at
56–57 Beacon Street, Ephraim Marsh
designed this pair with the newer Greek
revival–style portico entrances at the
extreme ends of the houses rather than
adjacent. To further emphasize the individuality of the houses, the portico on
the right has Ionic capitals and full sidelights framing the door, while the entrance on the left has Doric capitals and
a triglyph motif ornamenting the frieze.

The houses are notable for the purple colored glass in their windows.
Between 1818 and 1824 a glass manu-
facturer in England shipped glass with

King's Chapel Parish House and Rectory

this unusual hue caused by the transformation of the manganese oxide. Today authentic colored windowpanes survive only on these two houses and at 39–40 Beacon Street and 29A and 70B Chestnut Street. Modern purple glass imitations are sometimes installed elsewhere.

14 70–75 Beacon Street
Attributed to Asher Benjamin, 1828

:: Facing the Public Garden is a handsome row of light gray granite-front houses. The original pattern of three-story façades plus attic has been broken by three of the houses, and a picturesque small Victorian oriel was added to the second floor of number 70. The rusticated ground floor of each house has three arches with prominent voussoir patterns. Ornamental iron stair rails enhance the street scene. Distinguished though these houses appear, when the Mount Vernon Proprietors built them on the Mill Dam, they were very near the city dump. The common sewer emptied into the bay at what is now the corner of Beacon and Arlington Streets, and wharf rats made their home on the west side of the Public Garden.

70 Beacon Street

Wrought-iron stair rails, 72–73 Beacon Street

The Bull & Finch Pub in the basement of the Hampshire House at 84 Beacon Street was the setting for the long-running television program *Cheers*.

15 Deutsch House
Beaver Street at Beaver Place
Graham Gund Associates, 1983

:: On a street of former stables and carriage houses, this small corner house seems to grow out of the garden wall and has the air of a garden pavilion with its stucco walls clad in trellis and playful diamond and circle windows under the small gables. The second-floor addition was actually built above a tiny existing house.

Deutsch House © Steve Rosenthal

Cedar Lane Way

Branch Street

This narrow lane contains a unique mix of garages, carriage-house residences, and small private gardens glimpsed through gates. It was originally known as Kitchen Street because it served the rear entrances of the houses on Beacon and Chestnut Streets.

Cedar Lane Way

The charm of Beacon Hill lies not only in its historic architecture but also in its street pattern. The intimate pedestrian scale is as rewarding as it is rare in twenty-first-century America. Cedar Lane Way is a fine example of high-density, low-rise residential site planning, which does not depend on outstanding architecture to create a delightful small neighborhood. The tiny houses and gardens are entirely consistent with the diminutive scale of the site yet provide charming interior spaces.

Charles Street

Originally residential, Charles Street is now a pleasant shopping and service area for the adjacent neighborhood. Many of the houses retain residential uses on one or two upper floors, while the street level and often the old cellars have been converted to shops, restaurants, or offices. In keeping with its historic character, Charles Street has been noted for its antiques shops. Several of the small specialty shops have a long tradition of serving Beacon Hill families. The curve of the street around the base of Beacon Hill contributes greatly to the sense of the enclosed small-scale shopping street.

The greatest alteration to Charles Street occurred in the 1920s, when it was widened. Some houses on the west side lost their brownstone-trimmed brick façades and several feet of their front rooms. The east side retained most of its nineteenth-century architecture. Between Revere and Cambridge Streets are two groups of Greek revival row houses (81–85 and 121, 125–135 Charles Street).

16 Charles Street Meeting House

70 Charles Street
Asher Benjamin, 1804
Renovation: John Sharratt Associates, 1982
National Historic Landmark

:: Asher Benjamin designed this church two years before his Old West Church was built. The two brick Federal-style churches are similar, but this one is simpler. Both have rectangular towers serving as the primary façade and ceremonial entrance. The Charles Street Meeting House cupola is eight-sided and sits on a square projection above the tower.

The original congregation was the Third Baptist Church, which used the adjacent Charles River bank for its baptism ceremonies. Important antislavery speakers were heard from the pulpit, including William Lloyd Garrison, Wendell Phillips, Frederick Douglass, Harriet Tubman, and Sojourner Truth. In 1876 it became the African Methodist Episcopal Church, conveniently located for the black population on the north slope of Beacon Hill. When Charles Street was widened in 1920, the church was moved 10 feet west while its neighbors lost their façades. After the Great Depression the black congregation no longer lived on Beacon Hill, so the building was sold to the Unitarian-Universalist Church. When it was converted to office and commercial uses, it retained its essential external appearance.

Charles Street Meeting House

17 121, 125–135 Charles Street
1820s

:: These three-story Greek revival brick row houses show the character of Charles Street in the early nineteenth century. Today the houses have small shops on the first floors and in the basements and apartments on the upper floors.

Chestnut Street
Starting midway up the hill at Walnut Street and running down to the Charles River and Storrow Drive, Chestnut Street epitomizes the qualities for which Beacon Hill is noted. Ornamental iron balconies, kitchen yard gates, fences, a cast-iron hitching post, and early wrought-iron boot scrapers integrated into the delicate stair rails on

125–135 Charles Street

several of the houses provide interest for the passing pedestrian. Altogether, it is an urban design lesson in the harmonious use of varying ornamentation on row houses of restrained but excellent architecture. Without the thoughtful embellishments so splendidly illustrated on Chestnut Street, it might almost become monotonous. It is informative to compare the street with those of similar architecture in

Charlestown, which in general lack these embellishments. Before the filling of the Back Bay, Braman's Baths offered swimming lessons and hot and cold baths at the bottom of Chestnut Street.

18 Charles Paine Houses ⅲ
(Society of Friends)
6–8 Chestnut Street
Attributed to Charles Bulfinch, 1803–1804

∷ This handsome pair of mirror-matched houses (eventually joined internally) shares an entrance portico with horseshoe-curved steps. Originally each house had a side garden, but when Cornelius Coolidge, merchant and architect, purchased them twenty years later, he built houses in the side lots. The brown sandstone lintels over the first- and second-floor windows are in the reed pattern. Since 1957 it has been home to the Society of Friends.

19 The Swan Houses ⅲ
13, 15, and 17 Chestnut Street
Charles Bulfinch, 1804–1805
National Historic Landmark (number 13)

∷ Hepzibah Swan, a Boston heiress, built these Federal houses and the stables at 50, 56, and 60 Mount Vernon Street as gifts to her three daughters upon their marriages in 1806, 1807, and 1817. Her first daughter to be married was Mrs. John Turner Sargent, who moved into 13 Chestnut Street in 1806. The deeds carry Mrs. Swan's restriction that the roofs of the stables never be higher than 13 feet above the street, to retain the views of Mount Vernon Street from the Chestnut Street houses. A further restriction provides maintenance in perpetuity of a steeply sloped cattle ramp almost 9 feet wide from the stable yards to Mount Vernon Street so that the carriages and cattle of the three houses could go in and out. This survives intact.

Charles Paine Houses

Although Mrs. Swan had a Boston town house, she preferred to live in her elegant country house in Dorchester overlooking Dudley Street. Also designed by Bulfinch and built about 1796 (demolished ca. 1890), the house had a two-story round drawing room. Mrs. Swan's husband, Colonel James Swan, was involved in shaky financial dealings in Europe and in 1798 returned to France, where he was put in debtors' prison for the remaining twenty-two years of his life.

The houses are 25 feet wide, 50 feet deep, and four stories tall, plus basement and dormered attic. The simple brick façades are adorned with shuttered windows that reduce in height from the second story upward. The entry level of each house, defined by a granite foundation and a sandstone stringcourse at ceiling height, employs recessed arches around the ground-floor windows, a favorite Bulfinch treatment that serves to set off the more important second story of the house. The Adam-style entrance is defined by four slender fluted columns and a simple entablature. The door has sidelights. A front stair leads directly to the basement from the sidewalk.

The Swan Houses

Typical of Bulfinch, the interiors are simple, with ornament focused on the ceilings and mantels. In the original plan, still retained in number 13, the low-ceilinged entry level contains a reception hall with handsome stair on the left, a front dining room, and a large rear kitchen that overlooks the spacious garden. High-ceilinged double living rooms with classic but simple detailing and fine proportions are on the second-floor piano nobile, which has windows ornamented with wrought-iron railings. An arch with sliding double doors connects the double living rooms. The third floor contains two bedrooms, and the fourth floor has four servants' rooms with an attic space above. No Bulfinch house had a bathroom, but the pipeless privy was common. The introduction of the service stairway was in part to service the commode chairs in bedrooms or dressing rooms.

Julia Ward Howe, author of "Battle Hymn of the Republic," lived in number 13 for a short time and held meetings of the noted Radical Club there.

20 23–25 Chestnut Street
1809

:: Jeremiah Gardner built his charming house typical of Chestnut Street at number 23 together with its neighbor at 25. The Federal-style doorway with fanlight and sidelights is recessed within a portico *in antis* framed by fluted columns supporting Ionic capitals, architrave, frieze, and cornice. The Greek inspiration for the entrance is repeated in the cast-iron corner posts of the fence, which feature the Greek key-and-anthemion motif. The balcony on the second story uses an alternating pattern of anthemion, lotus buds, and an unusual star-in-circle for its cast-iron ornamentation.

21 27 Chestnut Street
Bellows, Aldrich, and Holt, 1917–1918
Renovation: Bullerjahn Associates, 1965

:: An architectural oddity, this massive four-story Gothic revival building is surprisingly compatible with the rest of Chestnut Street. Originally built as a theological school, it was converted to dramatic modern condominiums with high ceilings in 1965. While the setback limestone façade is an interruption of the brick context, the buttresses meet the façade line of the older Chestnut Street houses.

23–25 Chestnut Street

27 Chestnut Street

22 29A Chestnut Street
Charles Bulfinch, 1799–1800
Remodeled: ca. 1818

∷ The noted actor Edwin Booth, brother of John Wilkes Booth, lived here at one time. The Mount Vernon Proprietors, the wealthy developers of the south slope of Beacon Hill, began by building this house and sold it to Benjamin Joy. Like that of 55 Mount Vernon Street, also by Bulfinch, its façade is perpendicular to the street and overlooks a small side garden. The mid-Georgian design may be based on a similar house built by Thomas Leverton in 1769 in London's Bedford Square.
The bowfront has masonry unlike the rest of the façade and is thought to have been added after 1817 by Charles R. Codman. The extension at the back of the garden, now a separate dwelling, was built for Hopkinson's Boys' School, which occupied the buildings for a time.

29A Chestnut Street

23 Francis Parkman House
50 Chestnut Street
Cornelius Coolidge, 1830s
National Historic Landmark

∷ In the 1830s Cornelius Coolidge was actively involved as architect and builder of a number of Chestnut Street

Detail, Chestnut Street

Francis Parkman House

Ironwork, Chestnut Street

houses on the south side of the street, of which this is one. The noted American historian Francis Parkman lived here from 1865 until 1893.

24 Harvard Musical Association
57A Chestnut Street
West Cedar Street section, 1827

:: Art and music societies proliferated in Boston in the nineteenth century. In 1837 several Harvard graduates founded the Harvard Musical Association to provide a focus for musical gatherings and to encourage Harvard College to establish a department of music. In 1900 the organization purchased this building for its musical men's club, many of whose members had formerly been in the Harvard University Band. On the second floor is a fine concert hall for their musical evenings. Baked beans and beer followed by Welsh rarebit (no dessert) made up the traditional menu for the substantial preconcert suppers. The association established the first music library in the country. Note the ornamental iron lyre inset in the brick wall on West Cedar Street.

Joy Street
Joy Street is one of the oldest streets in Boston and dates from 1661. It was originally two streets, Belknap's Lane on the north slope and George Street on the south slope. Not until 1803 were they joined across Myrtle Street when the ropewalks were dismantled. In 1851 the George Street section was renamed after an apothecary, Dr. John Joy, who had acquired two acres of land on George in 1791 and was thus the primary property owner. Dr. Joy's third house was built in 1822 on his George Street property but facing Mount Vernon. This house, number 32 Mount Vernon, was purchased by Dr. Samuel Gridley Howe and his wife, Julia Ward Howe, in the 1870s.

Window, Chestnut Street

Harvard Musical Association

25 Louisburg Square ⅲ
Plan: S. P. Fuller, 1826; houses built 1834–1848

:: For many people, the private cobblestone street and small park of Louisburg Square epitomize Beacon Hill. Charles Bulfinch had designed a larger semicircular green with a crescent of houses curving around the uphill side. It was an advance on his 1793 Franklin Place design, which had first introduced the garden square, but was too ambitious for the Mount Vernon Proprietors. The much simpler Fuller plan was completed in 1826, but sales of the lots and

Louisburg Square

construction of the row houses lagged behind Mount Vernon Street.

By 1844 most houses were finished when the owners met to arrange maintenance of their garden and street. Since the oval was a visual ornament, not a recreational space, they voted to enclose it with an iron fence. There was no gate until 1929. The initial simple arrangement of eighteen elm trees and lawn has seen several tree species, seventeen different shrubs, flower beds, and a fountain come and go.

While the park has changed considerably, the houses, at least on the outside, remain largely unchanged. On the west side of the square, the houses are mainly bowfronts with areaways providing light into the front basement rooms. In contrast, on the east side, finished later, only a few shallow swells interrupt the flat façades. For most of the twentieth century, the Episcopal Society of St. Margaret occupied the three houses at the northeast corner

of the square. The sisters lived plainly and quietly. Sometimes they hung laundry on the roof, observed by the authors from a nearby garret apartment. Celebrity owners drastically altered the interiors of several houses, bringing the ultimate in luxury to the core of puritan Boston.

The Louisburg Square Proprietors were the first home association in the country. The records of their meetings have been maintained through all the years. They taxed themselves to maintain their sidewalks, street, and park, sharing the firewood when the trees were trimmed. Christmas Eve caroling with bell ringers and candles in windows started here in the late nineteenth century.

26 1 and 3 Louisburg Square
1846–1847

:: This pair of bowfront houses is ornamented with elaborate cast-iron balconies at the second story. Noteworthy wrought-iron serpents have twisted tongues and tails forming flagpole holders. Number 2, across Louisburg Square, was built at the same time.

1 and 3 Louisburg Square

27 4 and 6 Louisburg Square
1842

:: In contrast to the rest of the west side of Louisburg Square, numbers 2, 4, and 6 are flat-façade buildings, with number 2 the largest of all. The Federal revival pair at 4 and 6 have tall windows and cast-iron balconies on the second level. William Dean Howells lived at number 4 while he was editor of the *Atlantic Monthly*. Number 6 was the original home of the elite Number Six Club for MIT undergraduates.

28 Louisa May Alcott House
10 Louisburg Square
1835

:: After Louisa May Alcott's literary success, she purchased this house and moved her penniless parents and sisters here from 20 Pinckney Street. Her imaginative but impecunious father, Bronson Alcott, died in the house just before Louisa herself succumbed. Like numbers 8–22, the Alcott house is a three-story bowfront plus dormered attic. Originally all these houses had dining rooms in the basement kitchen level with windows looking up toward the sidewalk. Most of the houses have been considerably altered inside.

29 14–20 Louisburg Square
1836

:: On February 15, 1852, Jenny Lind, the "Swedish Nightingale," was married at 20 Louisburg Square to her accompanist, Otto Goldschmidt. The house belonged to Samuel Ward, the representative of Jenny Lind's London bankers and the brother of Julia Ward Howe. The marriage marked the completion of an American tour that earned P. T. Barnum a $500,000 profit. The ever-resourceful Barnum had neither seen nor heard the Swedish soprano when he signed her at fees that were enormous for those days. For a year

Entrance, 8 Louisburg Square

before the tour, Barnum ran a national publicity blitz based largely on his imagination. By the time Jenny Lind arrived in America, Barnum had succeeded in arousing the American public to a frenzy of excitement about this unknown singer.

Mount Vernon Street 🏛
Henry James said of Mount Vernon Street that it was "the only respectable street in America." Originally called Olive Street, it sweeps majestically from the Bowdoin Street side of the State House, through the passage beneath the Annex, past the fine residences built by the Mount Vernon Proprietors, and down the hill toward the Charles River. The group of wealthy investors included Harrison Gray Otis, Jonathan Mason, Charles Bulfinch, Benjamin Joy, and Mrs. James Swan. Otis had wangled eighteen acres of pasture from John Singleton Copley's agent for the bargain price of $1,000 per acre, despite Copley's horrified but tardy protests from England.

The Mount Vernon Proprietors began building in 1799 and did not complete the development of the land until 1848. Like many developers after them, they demolished fine buildings—in this case, large old Federal mansions. Charles Bulfinch designed a few of the houses built by the group and has a total of twelve houses remaining on Beacon Hill. For more than three decades after Bulfinch, Greek revival remained the predominant architectural style on Beacon Hill. Blending beautifully with the older Federal houses, it resulted in a harmonious neighborhood that is widely admired.

Beacon Hill Memorial Column

30 Beacon Hill Memorial Column

Mount Vernon Street behind the State House
Charles Bulfinch, 1790–1791
Rebuilt: 1865, 1898
Ashburton Park
Carol R. Johnson & Associates, Inc., 1990

:: The summit of Beacon Hill, first called Sentry Hill, was originally 60 feet higher than it is today and was roughly in the area of the State House Annex. In 1634 a beacon on a wooden pole was placed at the top of the hill by the general court "to give notice of any danger." It remained there until one windy November night in 1789, when it blew down.

The young Charles Bulfinch proposed to replace it with a monument to the American Revolution, a classical column such as those he had seen in Europe. On his own he solicited donations to construct the 60-foot monument. It had a gilded eagle atop a Doric column made of plaster on brick, set on a stone pedestal that had four commemorative plaques. Interested parties claimed that the column soon began to deteriorate, but it stood for two decades until John Hancock's money-hungry heirs purchased the hill. They destroyed the monument and leveled the summit to provide fill for the Mill Pond at the foot of the hill. The result was fifty acres of new land.

In 1898 the column was reconstructed, 60 feet lower and 100 feet to the east of its original position. Until 1990, when a new underground garage was built, the column stood awkwardly in the State House parking lot. With the cars moved underground, the column now stands in Ashburton Park.

31 Lyman-Paine House

Mount Vernon Street at 6 Joy Street
Alexander Parris, 1824

:: At the busy intersection of Mount Vernon and Joy Streets is this solid four-and-a-half-story house with lovely private garden bordered by an unusual wrought-iron fence with wavy bars. Its unpretentious façade with some asymmetrical elements is pleasing but unusual for this period on Beacon Hill. Exterior ornament is largely focused on the Greek revival entrance on Joy

Street. With neighbors such as the State House, Little, Brown, and Company, and the Appalachian Mountain Club, the serenity within the house is a surprise. The garret apartment has wonderful views over Beacon Hill and the Boston Common. This house and the one next door at 18 Mount Vernon Street were interconnected and owned by the same family from the time of construction until 1943.

32 28, 30, 32, and 34 Mount Vernon Street
1822

:: Number 32, Dr. John Joy's house, was sold to Dr. Samuel Gridley Howe and his wife, Julia Ward Howe, author of "Battle Hymn of the Republic," in the 1870s. They entertained notable people on a regular basis, among them General Ulysses S. Grant and the writer Bret Harte, who was served a hearty breakfast that included broiled chickens, English bacon, and buckwheat cakes.

Dr. Howe is best remembered as the founder of the Perkins Institution for the Blind. Less well known is his role as the organizer of the Committee of Vigilance to protect fugitive slaves. On September 26, 1846, Dr. Howe wrote to forty abolitionist acquaintances informing them that they had been selected as members of the committee to prevent

28–34 Mount Vernon Street

the return of any fugitive slaves who had sought safety in Massachusetts. The Committee of Vigilance had a distinguished career, with records of aid given to more than 300 fugitive slaves, most of whom were men. The money for all the activities of the committee came from its prominent Boston members. Often the committee paid for railroad and boat fares to take the fugitives to safety in the Maritime Provinces.

Not only did the Committee of Vigilance aid runaway slaves who had taken the initiative to escape, but also if word came to them of slaves being held in any ship in the harbor, a daring rescue was sometimes undertaken. The committee printed and circulated abolitionist sermons, provided legal defense for any fugitive slave in jeopardy, and pressed for legal changes within the government.

33 37 Mount Vernon Street
1805

:: Flemish bond brickwork, rarely used after the early nineteenth century, is found in this four-story house with a brownstone stringcourse and granite foundation. A "header" brick—the

Lyman-Paine House

short end of the brick—is laid alternating with the long side—the "stretcher" side of the brick. Each row is identical, but the order is offset so that an interesting pattern results.

34 John Callender House 🏛
Mount Vernon Street at 14 Walnut Street
1802

:: John Callender's "small house for little money" was built on land purchased from Dr. Joy and was one of the first houses on Mount Vernon Street. The lot cost Callender $2,155, and he spent between $5,000 and $7,000 on the construction of the house in 1802. Its Federal-style brick sheathed in butt-joined boards is typical of the period. The Mount Vernon Street side was the original entry façade of the house, but in 1821 the elevation of Walnut Street was lowered by the city, so a fine large retaining wall had to be built for the garden. Callender decided to move the entrance to Walnut Street at the lower level, leaving an uncharacteristic Federal façade on Mount Vernon Street. Someone later added the curious oriel window. The large garden in the rear has street access through an arched passageway.

35 40–42 Mount Vernon Street
1850

:: Augustus Hemenway demolished an 1822 mansion in order to build this large brownstone pair. After many years as the World Peace Foundation, it was converted to condominiums.

36 44, 46, and 48 Mount Vernon Street
1820s

:: These dignified smaller houses typify much of the south slope of Beacon Hill. Each house has a recessed entry with fanlights and leaded sidelights

John Callender's "small house for little money"

Entrance, 46 Mount Vernon Street

providing gracious introductions to the first-floor hall, parlor, and dining room. The basements have inconspicuous front entries with steep descending steps and child-size doors.

37 Swan Stables
50–60 Mount Vernon Street
Charles Bulfinch, 1804–1805

:: The stables, later converted to dwellings, were built by Hepzibah Swan to accompany the houses for her three daughters at 13, 15, and 17 Chestnut Street. They are restricted by deed to a height of 13 feet. The cattle ramp remains in its original condition, ready to serve as carriage and cattle access for the Swan houses.

Swan Stables

38 Mason Houses
51–57 Mount Vernon Street
(Nichols House Museum, 55 Mount
Vernon Street)
Charles Bulfinch, 1804

:: Jonathan Mason, one of the Mount
Vernon Proprietors, commissioned
Bulfinch to design this series of houses
for his daughters. Originally both 55
and 57, which stepped back, faced
Mason's gardens and his Bulfinch-
designed mansion to the west (demolished). Number 57 had a side entrance
like that of 55, but when a house was
built directly to the west in 1837, cutting off its view, the entrance was
moved to face the street and the 8-foot

Nichols House Museum

space between the houses was filled with an extension.

Daniel Webster lived in number 57 from 1817 to 1819, and Charles Francis Adams lived there from 1842 to 1886. His sons, Charles Francis Adams II and Henry Adams, author of *Mont-Saint-Michel and Chartres,* spent their boyhoods here.

Except for number 55, all of the houses have been greatly altered; in 55 only the entrance portico is not original. Miss Rose Nichols—writer, landscape architect, niece of Augustus Saint-Gaudens, and true Beacon Hill eccentric—was the last resident of 55. Her sister, Mrs. Arthur Shurcliff, started Beacon Hill's Christmas Eve tradition of handbell ringing in Louisburg Square. When Rose Nichols died at the age of eighty-eight in 1960, she left her house and furnishings to the public as a museum, the only private house museum on Beacon Hill.

39 59 Mount Vernon Street
Edward Shaw, 1837

40 67–83 Mount Vernon Street
1836–1837

:: Jonathan Mason built a large stone mansion designed by Bulfinch on the north side of Mount Vernon Street with stables behind it on Pinckney Street. When he died in 1836, both the mansion and the stables were torn down and the Greek revival houses numbered 59 through 83 were built on the vacated land; numbers 61, 63, and 65 were rebuilt later. The gracious 30-foot setback distinguishes this block from any other on Beacon Hill. Mason and his fellow Mount Vernon Proprietor Harrison Gray Otis had agreed to maintain this setback on their adjoining properties.

Number 59 has the restrained dignity of the Greek revival style in its four-story bowfront plus attic with

59 Mount Vernon Street

61 Mount Vernon Street

handsome Ionic portico *in antis* supported on Ionic columns. Number 61 has a flamboyant and impressive cast-iron fence of large scrolled vines with anthemion-and-lotus motifs supported on massive lotus posts. The gate, largely of cast iron, is designed to fit within the carved granite posts. Number 77 houses the venerable Club of Odd Volumes, whose small membership is limited to distinguished book collectors, publishers, and writers. Sir Winston Churchill was given a luncheon here by his American publishers, the Boston firm of Houghton Mifflin. The iron balcony on the 1835 William Ellery Channing House at 83 is in the "Bulfinch" design.

41 70–72 Mount Vernon Street
Richard Upjohn, 1847
Renovation: Bullerjahn Associates, 1965

:: John and Nathaniel Thayer left their rural life in Lancaster, Massachusetts, where their father was a minister, to make their fortune as Boston bankers. Needing houses, they commissioned Richard Upjohn to design this massive adjoining pair. After their deaths the buildings served for many years as the Boston University Theological School and were connected to the Gothic revival structure at 27 Chestnut Street. In 1965 the Mount Vernon and Chestnut Street buildings were renovated as apartments. Preservation-conscious Beacon Hill residents prevented the buildings from being razed by a developer who planned to erect a new apartment building.

In scale, materials, and detailing, these houses bear no resemblance to the rest of the street. The first-floor windows are twice the height of those of the neighboring houses, and the first two floors could contain nearly three floors of a typical Beacon Hill house. Projecting entrance bays with quoins, tall recessed round arches, and projecting balconies on brackets define each end of the façade. Third-floor windows have heavy projecting stone lintels on brackets. The large second-floor windows appear to be later alterations, replacing narrow windows like those on the other floors. The interiors were gutted at the time of the renovation.

42 Second Harrison Gray Otis House 𝕀𝕀𝕀
85 Mount Vernon Street
Charles Bulfinch, 1800–1802
Remodeled: Peabody and Stearns, 1882
National Register of Historic Places

:: In the second house designed for Otis, Bulfinch attempted to establish the character for the rest of the development by the Mount Vernon Proprietors on John Singleton Copley's land. His vision of Mount Vernon Street lined with grand freestanding mansions on spacious landscaped grounds did not materialize. This house remains the exception to Beacon Hill's dense development.

As in many other Bulfinch works, the ground-floor windows are set

70–72 Mount Vernon Street

Second Harrison Gray Otis House

Cobblestone drive, 85 Mount Vernon Street

within recessed arches. Unlike other houses, these tall windows house the principal rooms. Window size decreases on each floor until the third-floor windows are only small squares. Strong ornamental features enliven the façade: iron railings are in a Chinese fretwork pattern, two-story Corinthian pilasters define the end bays, and a stringcourse separates the principal floor from the other levels. A balustrade circles the entire roofline above the cornice, and an octagonal cupola surmounts the roof.

A cobblestone drive leads to the entrance and to the rear stable, a separate dwelling. The original entrance was on the other end of the house, where the bow window is now located. Otis lived here only until 1806, when he sold the house to the widow of a Salem merchant for $22,984. One twentieth-century owner was a frugal elderly lady. She lived alone in the large house but spent most of her time in a single third-story room, its floor covered with linoleum. The only heat came from a small freestanding gas heater.

43 Stephen Higginson House
87 Mount Vernon Street
Charles Bulfinch, 1804–1809

:: Between 1804 and 1806 Bulfinch was involved in at least eighteen building projects, in addition to being head of the Board of Selectmen and chief of police for Boston. He bought this property and that next door at number 89 and built twin houses on it, which he then sold to banker Stephen Higginson Jr. (number 87) and to Connecticut mill owner David Humphreys (number 89). The houses were set back to conform with the 30-foot setback of the Otis house at 85 Mount Vernon Street. Elaborate tall windows grace the second-floor parlors. Placement of the entrance in the second bay of the first floor allowed creation of two rooms in addition to the entrance hall.

More than twenty craftsmen were involved in the Mount Vernon Street houses, including ornamental plasterer Daniel Raynerd and woodcarver Simeon Skillin, who also carved the State House capitals. The ornamental plaster and woodwork are most evident in the parlors on the second floor.

Number 87 was for many years the home of General Charles J. Paine, yachtsman and America's Cup defender. It is now the headquarters for the Colonial Society of Massachusetts. Number 89 was demolished and replaced with a Victorian house, which was renovated half a century later in a twentieth-century neo-Georgian style.

44 "Sunflower House"
130 Mount Vernon Street
1840
Renovation: Charles Luce, 1878

:: Charles Luce had some fun when he transformed a small 1840 house into a whimsical cottage. The stuccoed first floor and garden wall are painted bright yellow in gay contrast to the red English-style tiles on the second floor. The huge carved sunflower under the half-timber gable is hardly the traditional Tudor flower. The projecting entrance is centered beneath the Tudor revival jetty supporting the overhanging second story on the Mount Vernon Street façade.

A large ornamented dormer penetrates the roof of the River Street side.

Henry James lived nearby at 131 Mount Vernon Street.

45 Church of the Advent 🏛

Mount Vernon Street at Brimmer Street
Sturgis and Brigham, 1875–1888
Lady Chapel interior: Cram and Goodhue, 1894

:: The congregation of the Church of the Advent was founded in 1844 in the old West End. It brought the Oxford Movement to Boston and was considered very high church. In 1883 they moved into this brick and stone Gothic revival church with Perpendicular influence. Its art and liturgy caused a sensation in Puritan Boston and made it something of a tourist attraction in the later nineteenth century. The tower has angle buttresses and a spire of brick and stone with gablet-topped lucarne windows on each face. It houses one of the finest sets of carillon bells in the country. At the base of the tower are clustered chapels, forming a delightfully complex frontage along Mount Vernon Street.

The highly ornamented interior spaces were designed for religious ceremony. Tall striped Gothic arches rest on striped columns, while several rows of light-colored stringcourses accentuate the form of the apse. The high altar, designed by Sturgis, and the screen above it by Sir Ernest George and Harold Peto were both given to the church by Isabella Stewart Gardner ("Mrs. Jack"), one of the more colorful parishioners. As penance for one of her more flamboyant escapades, it is said that she was required to scrub the church steps during Lent.

The stained-glass windows include work by the English makers Kempe, Clayton and Bell, and Christopher Whall. The Lady Chapel interiors, executed in 1894, were the first important

"Sunflower House"

Church of the Advent

religious interiors by Ralph Adams Cram and Bertram Goodhue and illustrate Cram's concern with making ornament serve the larger purposes of the architecture and its ceremonial functions. The attractive garden of the church rectory is sometimes open to the public.

46 Samuel Eliot Morison House

Mount Vernon Street at
44 Brimmer Street
1850s

:: Dozens of public liveries and private stables were located between Charles Street and the river. "The horsey end of town" was Samuel Eliot Morison's description of the neighborhood where he lived from the time he was born until his death in 1976. Morrison himself was certainly "horsey," commuting to Harvard on horseback and lecturing to his classes in jodhpurs. He spent more than five decades at Harvard, first as a student and then as a history professor. After World War II horses were excluded from the streets, so he wore his naval uniform on campus. Even then he wouldn't let Radcliffe women into his classes. His idiosyncrasies made him a prominent figure both on campus and in Boston.

Pinckney Street

The street is named for Charles Cotesworth Pinckney, sent by President John Adams to discuss high seas piracy with French Foreign Minister Talleyrand. When a bribe was demanded just to secure a meeting, Pinckney's response is often quoted as, "Millions for defense, but not one cent for tribute." Henry David Thoreau lived in an apartment at 4 Pinckney for two years as a young child. At various times Louisa May Alcott lived in rooms at 20, 43, and 81 Pinckney.

With its steep slope diving toward the Charles River and its frontage on Louisburg Square, Pinckney Street has always been known for its fine views. The repeating bowfronts cascading down the hill are striking, particularly at sunset.

Because of the ropewalks running the length of Myrtle Street, Pinckney long served as the edge of the dignified south slope. On the north side of the ropewalks, Beacon Hill developed a bo-

Samuel Eliot Morison House

hemian character. By the twenty-first century bohemians were rare among the costly condominium conversions.

47 Middleton-Glapion House 🏛

5 Pinckney Street
ca. 1795

:: A 1,925-square-foot lot in this location was sold to George Middleton and Louis Glapion for thirty pounds in 1786. A 1791 assessor's note mentions a "small house by south side ropewalk." In 1792 Middleton and Glapion were each taxed for half a house. The 1798 federal dwellings tax listed a house "345 square feet, one story, four windows." Today it is a two-story clapboard house with an added attic dormer. How much of the one-story house remains in the present structure is unclear, but the two off-center doors and larger single window on the left match the earliest references. It may be the oldest house on Beacon Hill.

Middleton was a black coachman and commander of the Revolutionary Bucks of America. He was a natural leader, founding the African Society and leading a petition drive in 1800 for an African public school. Louis Glapion was a French mulatto barber who plied his trade in the one long room that was his half of the house.

48 Hidden Houses
9½ and 74½ Pinckney Street

:: In the eighteenth and early nineteenth centuries, it was not unusual to construct secondary dwellings with no street frontage. Several remain behind Pinckney Street houses. They are entered through tunnel-like passages called "sally ports." Number 9½ Pinckney has three hidden houses on its courtyard.

49 17–19 Pinckney Street

:: This Federal-style three-story frame house stands perpendicular to the street, like many houses of the period (including number 21 next door). It faces an intimate courtyard that it shares with 19 Pinckney, its clapboard neighbor at the rear of the site. Number 17 has prominent corner quoins, a flat Federal entrance with fanlight and sidelights, and a Victorian oriel on its narrow street façade.

Middleton-Glapion House

50 20 Pinckney Street

:: This modest house was the first Beacon Hill home of the Bronson Alcott family. They later moved to the Louisburg Square house purchased by daughter Louisa May Alcott.

51 "House of Odd Windows"
24 Pinckney Street
Renovation: William Ralph Emerson, 1884

:: Ralph Waldo Emerson's nephew, William, designed this house with extraordinary individuality. From its rooftop eyelid window to the small square window sharing the door lintel, every window in the house is different but exquisitely proportioned and placed. Emerson predated Robert Venturi by

17 Pinckney Street

"House of odd windows"

almost a century in his "complex and contradictory" renovation of this former carriage house.

52 Pie-Shaped House
56 Pinckney Street

:: Although this house has a typical street façade suggesting no less spaciousness and grandeur than its neighbors, the interior reveals a surprise that is quite charming. The house gradually narrows to a point!

53 House with Hidden Chamber for Fugitive Slaves
62 Pinckney Street
1840

:: A number of houses on Beacon Hill were stopping points on the Underground Railroad, including this brick row house built for George S. Hillard, law partner of Charles Sumner. Many white abolitionists in Boston housed fugitive slaves, when it became too hazardous to board them among black Bostonians. Although Hillard was a federal commissioner and thus obligated to uphold the Fugitive Slave Act, he and his wife, Susan, sheltered and employed numerous fugitive slaves. Most famously, these ardent abolitionists protected William and Ellen Craft when agents of their master came looking for them in Boston.

While making repairs to the house in the 1920s, workmen discovered a small attic space in the ell accessible through a concealed trap door in a closet. Although the space had no windows, it had provisions for ventilation and was large enough to hold several people. Two tin plates and two iron spoons were found, perhaps remains of the last meal eaten there.

54 Boston English High School
Pinckney Street at 65 Anderson Street
1824
Renovation: Graham, Meus, 1983–1984

:: This cruciform school building was influenced by the work of Charles Bulfinch and Asher Benjamin and uses relieving arches above the second-story windows. It served as the first building of the English High School until 1844, when the Phillips School, a grammar

Pie-Shaped House

English High School

school named after the first mayor of Boston, John Phillips, moved in. The school accepted both black and white boys and was the first integrated school in Boston. In 1861 the Phillips School moved, to be replaced by the Sharp School, a public school. In the late twentieth century, the building was recycled as twelve condominium units.

55 86 Pinckney Street
1840

:: For two decades at the end of the nineteenth century, this was the home of the free black barber John J. Smith and his family. Until then they boarded in various houses on the north slope. Smith's wife, Georgiana, was active in the movement to desegregate Boston's schools, and their daughter Elizabeth was one of the first African-American teachers in the integrated public schools.

56 7, 9, and 11 West Cedar Street
Asher Benjamin, ca. 1825

:: These restrained brick row houses by Asher Benjamin contribute enormously to the elegance of West Cedar Street. Benjamin designed and built number 9 as his own residence. A cast-iron balcony railing with beveled scrolls and ribbed leaves beautifully ornaments the tall second-story windows of numbers 7 and 9.

57 36 West Cedar Street
ca. 1820

:: A pair of brick stringcourses is the only cornice on the three-story-plus-attic house with side entry. Its height and small square windows on the third floor are typical of its era. The double-height windows reveal the parlor level. One of its earliest occupants was the Rev. Thomas Paul. A free black born in New Hampshire, he was pastor of the African Meeting House for more than two decades at the beginning of the nine-

Ironwork, 7–9 West Cedar Street

teenth century. Reverend Paul died of tuberculosis in this house in April 1831 at the age of fifty-eight, two years after ill health ended his preaching.

58 61–63 West Cedar Street

:: Primus Hall started a school for children of color in his home, then at the rear of these two lots. Elisha Sylvester, a Harvard undergraduate, was the instructor. A yellow fever epidemic in 1800 caused it to close, but it reopened a year later in a carpenter's shop behind 2 Smith Court. Hall was motivated to establish his private school when George Middleton's petition for an African public school was denied by the Massachusetts legislature.

The North Slope

Many people associate Beacon Hill with the wealthy "Boston Brahmins," yet it has always had a diverse population. The north and south slopes had very different characters through accidents of development and the complicated street pattern. Though it is a grid, the varying widths, lengths, and slight bends yield only three streets crossing both the north and south slopes. For decades the ropewalks were barriers to any communication between the slopes.

The south slope is epitomized by Louisburg Square, the quiet and lovely Chestnut Street, and the larger and busier but immensely dignified Mount Vernon Street, so revered by Henry James. The north slope has splendid views and Smith Court, with the oldest houses on the Hill.

59 Mission Church of St. John the Evangelist 🏛

35 Bowdoin Street
Solomon Willard, 1831

:: A harmonious row of brick bowfront houses along Bowdoin Street forms a solid boundary defining the northeast side of historic Beacon Hill. The focus is this English Gothic revival church of handsome rough dark granite blocks. The back side seen from Temple Street is almost as striking as the front. The heavy square crenellated tower has quatrefoil windows. The church was originally built for the Congregational Society led by Harriet Beecher Stowe's father. In 1883 it became the Church of St. John the Evangelist, the mother church for the Cowley fathers of the Society of St. John the Evangelist and the highest Episcopal Church in Boston. The artist Gyorgy Kepes designed the contemporary stained-glass window visible at the entrance.

Mission Church of St. John the Evangelist

Cambridge Street

As its name tells us, the street leads to Cambridge from the North End. Because the street's width was doubled in 1926, the only historic building remaining on the north side is the Otis house, which was moved 40 feet back.

The old West End was isolated by the extensive destruction to widen Cambridge Street. Three decades later it was demolished, and redevelopment began on one of the first federal urban renewal projects. Few remnants survive of the old West End, with its teeming street life and intimate lanes lined by three- and four-story brick row houses and tenements. It was a neighborhood that, like the North End, was the first American home for countless families of immigrants. Before her marriage to Nathaniel Hawthorne, West Street resident Eliza Peabody established a foreign language bookstore and lending library there. A generation of sociologists studied the impact of the redevelopment on the people who were forced to relocate, and much current social-planning theory has its roots here.

60 Longfellow Bridge

Cambridge Street
Edmund March Wheelwright, 1907

:: On his visit to St. Petersburg, Russia, Wheelwright admired the eighteenth-century tower bridges that French engineer Perrone constructed over the Neva. Returning to Boston, he designed the "pepperpot" bridge. It carries MBTA trains, autos, bicyclists, and pedestrians, offering wonderful vistas up and down the Charles River.

61 Suffolk County Jail

Charles Street at Cambridge Street
Gridley J. Fox Bryant, 1851
National Register of Historic Places
Incorporated into Charles Street Hotel
Cambridge Seven Associates, Inc., with Ann Beha, 2007

Suffolk County Jail

:: In this jail's early decades, prisoners rioted if they were served lobster too often each week. The gentry wouldn't have it at all. Lobster was so cheap and plentiful that it was considered food fit only for servants and prisoners.

The first jails built in a number of U.S. cities were cruciform in plan, imitating this one. Though it lost the east wing in the late twentieth century, it originally had four symmetrical four-story hipped-roof wings radiating from the central octagonal pavilion. The west wing was the sheriff's home and office, hospital, and chapel. In 1901 the north wing was enlarged mimicking Bryant's design, and in 1920 the west wing was doubled, again duplicating the architect's detailing. Made of Quincy granite, the prominent corner quoins and keystones above the windows add to the gravity of the building.

When it was considered too antiquated, the former jail was converted to the lobby and restaurant for a hotel. Most of the guest rooms are in the fifteen-story addition adjacent to the former jail.

62 George R. White Memorial Building
off Cambridge Street on Fruit Street
Coolidge Shepley Bulfinch and Abbott, 1939

:: This Massachusetts General Hospital building was designed one year after the architects' 784 Memorial Drive. Both are art deco–international style. The White Memorial Building is of light gray brick with stepped massing and faceted projecting bays. Its distinctive form made it a widely recognized city landmark. Designed to be functional and modern, it avoids historicism, in contrast to much of the firm's work of the period.

63 Bulfinch Pavilion and Ether Dome ⅲ
Massachusetts General Hospital, near Cambridge Street and Fruit Street
Charles Bulfinch, 1818–1823
Altered: 1844 and later
National Historic Landmark

:: In 1816 Bulfinch was sent by the hospital board to examine several hospitals in New York, Philadelphia, and Baltimore. In 1817 an award of $100 was offered to the designer of the best plan for a hospital to be built specifically of Chelmsford granite cut at the state prison in Charlestown. Bulfinch won the commission, which was his last in Boston. Alexander Parris, who was to become an important Boston architect, prepared the working drawings.

The building, influenced by the work of Robert Adam and John Soane with its central columned portico and wings on a rusticated granite base, employed the most progressive ideas of the time and was widely admired. The operating theater with seating for observers was beneath a skylit dome. The first public demonstration of ether as an anesthetic was conducted here in 1846.

On the floors below the operating theater were administrative offices, the apothecary, and, on the lowest floor, the kitchen, bathing room, and laundry. Cantilevered stairways of solid granite were similar to those of University Hall at Harvard and are one of the few interior

Bulfinch Pavilion and Ether Dome

features that survive intact. Wings contained wards and private rooms for patients totaling one hundred beds. In the basement, furnaces supplied heat to the upper floors through air flues. Pipes supplied water throughout the building.

Today nineteenth-century medical instruments and documents are exhibited in the building, but most of the space is still used for hospital purposes. The building is substantially altered and has been surrounded by a jumble of unsympathetic structures, making it diffi-

cult to find. The south elevation is the least changed, but the wings have been extended and the pediment altered. One of the best views of the dome is from the top of Anderson Street at Pinckney Street on Beacon Hill.

Nancy Schön's 2004 *Nursing Sundial* in the Bulfinch Lawn recognizes the timelessness of round-the-clock nursing. Three bronze figures dressed as Greek goddesses portray the history of nursing. The earliest (smallest) woman carries a lamp, lighting the beginnings, and specifically refers to Florence Nightingale. The middle woman holds a book, portraying the educational emphasis of today's nurses. The third woman represents the global reach of nurses. At the base of the gnomon is the MGH nursing cap.

64 First Harrison Gray Otis House 🏛

141 Cambridge Street
Charles Bulfinch, 1795–1796
Restoration: began in 1916 and continued intermittently
National Historic Landmark

∷ This is the first of three grand houses Bulfinch designed in the ten-year period 1795–1805 for Harrison Gray Otis, a Massachusetts senator, third mayor of Boston, and flamboyant socialite. The Federal design is based on the William Bingham house Bulfinch saw when he was in Philadelphia in 1789, a house that, in turn, was derived from one in London.

The elegant brick façade is symmetrically organized around the central bay containing entrance and stair hall. Above the entrance, which was added after 1801, is a Palladian window with pilasters, and on the third floor a lunette. Each story is defined by a brownstone stringcourse. The floor plan is arranged in the colonial manner with two rooms on each side of the central stair hall and the kitchen in an ell. Third-floor ceilings are exceedingly low, barely over 6 feet.

In the 1830s the house was used as a ladies' Turkish bath. Then it became a patent medicine shop, followed by a ladies' boardinghouse. It was in a terrible state by 1916, when restoration work was begun. In 1926 Cambridge Street was widened, forcing the house to be moved back 40 feet. The original expansive front terrace and carriage approach were reduced to barely enough room for the front steps.

The house is owned by the Society

Shriners Hospitals for Children Burns Institute, Odell Associates

First Harrison Gray Otis House

for the Preservation of New England Antiquities. Computer color analysis produced a bright palette of colors in the restoration. Bostonians accustomed to the somber faded tones were startled to see them replaced by vivid hues.

65 Old West Church 🏛

Cambridge Street
Asher Benjamin, 1806
National Historic Landmark

:: In 1737 a wood-frame church was built on this site. During the British occupation the church became a barracks until 1775, when it was razed by the troops who suspected that the steeple was being used by Revolutionary sympathizers to signal the Continental troops in Cambridge. Not until three decades after the Revolution was this handsome red brick Federal church built on the site.

As in Asher Benjamin's earlier Charles Street Meeting House, the entrances and cupola are placed on a three-and-a-half-story projecting block. Four two-story brick pilasters, highlighted with white wood trim, define three entry doors. The third level of the tower is ornamented with pairs of Doric pilasters that support a triglyph frieze. Beneath the square wood cupola are swag-ornamented clocks on both the short and the long sides of the tower. The church has a fine Fisk tracker-action pipe organ.

Old West Church

66 2–6 Derne Street
ca. 1846

:: On this very short street, three narrow Greek revival houses offer a contrast with the huge State House that overshadows them. Victorian cast-iron balconies were added to the second stories to ornament the flat brick façades. In the twentieth century the houses were subdivided into offices and apartments.

Embankment Road

With the completion of the Charles River Dam in 1910, this street was laid out on filled land and changed the character of the area. Charles River Square and West Hill Place were built on a former coal yard. The two squares of brick Federal revival houses relate harmoniously to historic Beacon Hill architecture. Each group focuses on its own inner space rather than on the large-scale river and Esplanade.

Annie Fields (wife of James T. Fields, who was proprietor of the famous Old Corner Bookstore) entertained Charles Dickens during his Boston visit in the lovely garden behind her house at 148 Charles Street (demolished). The garden contained shrubs planted by Henry Wadsworth Longfellow. In *Not Under Forty* Willa Cather told of Annie Fields, the great hostess who was especially fond of artists, writers, and actors. Annie's garden remains in a much altered form and, although private, is visible from Embankment Road adjacent to West Hill Place.

Hancock Street

Hancock Street is unique in having large and significant buildings by Charles Bulfinch framing both ends of its two-block length. Walking up Hancock Street, one sees the State House, while walking down the street the first Harrison Gray Otis house is the focus. Perhaps inspired by its fine architec-

tural examples at each end, the street has many worthy houses in the Federal, Greek revival, and even Egyptian revival styles. The row of seven narrow Federal houses at numbers 11–23 were built about 1808. On the upper block of the street between Myrtle and Mount Vernon Streets, several of the mid-nineteenth-century houses have attractive cast-iron balconies based on the anthemion motif.

67 Home of Charles Sumner
20 Hancock Street
1805
National Historic Landmark

20–22 Hancock Street

68 22 Hancock Street
1805

:: This pair of three-bay brick Federal houses features Greek revival porticoes. Number 20 was the home of Senator Charles Sumner from 1830 until 1867.

69 31–37 Hancock Street
Attributed to Jonathan Preston, 1859

:: The marble façades of these houses set back from the property lines are a great surprise on Beacon Hill. The four houses share a continuous mansard roof with a handsome pedimented dormer in the attic of each one. A projecting stringcourse separates the third story from the second story with its oriel windows. Leading to the raised entry level is a stair with ornamental cast-iron rail.

70 32–34 Hancock Street
James McNeely, 1974

:: The first contemporary façade
within the Beacon Hill Historic District,
34 Hancock Street replaces a house destroyed by fire in 1967 and is connected
with the renovated house at 32 Hancock. Because of its lower ceilings, the
recent building is able to squeeze five
floors into the same height occupied by
four of the older one. A single elevator,
stairway, and fire escape serve both
buildings, which together house twelve
two-bedroom, two one-bedroom, and
three studio apartments. The newer
building employs traditional Beacon Hill
brick, but an angular bay projection and
large unpaned windows declare its
modernity.

71 57 Hancock Street
ca. 1875

:: This curious French Second Empire
house has a very lively façade of three
five-story bays and a classical revival
entrance portico. Each story is identified by a stringcourse, and the most
prominent windows on the second and
third stories are pedimented. The entire
composition may be flamboyant, but
the left bay reveals attention to detail
in the elegant chamfered corner. The
mansard roof with dormers capping the
bays uses the Egyptian pylon form. This
unusual design feature leads to the
designation of the house as one of the
few Egyptian revival houses in the
country. The house grandly announces
the entry to Myrtle Street.

72 Joy Street Horse Stables
40–42 Joy Street
1830–1840

:: Two brothers built this pair of identical brick stables to avoid disputes.
After the end of the horse-and-buggy
era, the stables served as the Brick
Oven Tavern, then as a theatrical playhouse, and finally as art studios. Until

31–37 Hancock Street

Ironwork, Hancock Street

Egyptian revival dormers

the late twentieth-century renovation, the original horse stalls, horse feeders, and trough remained on the first floor, as well as a huge winch for raising carriages to the second floor.

Joy Street Horse Stables

73 Abiel Smith School
46 Joy Street
Richard Upjohn, 1835

:: This was the first schoolhouse built for black children. It served children from the North End as well as the north slope of Beacon Hill. Abiel Smith, a wealthy merchant, had been a prime supporter of the school before it moved into the African Meeting House. When he died in 1815, he left $4,000 for the building of a school for African children. For twenty years interest from his bequest supplemented the city's support for the school's budget until the city added $2,500 to the building fund and hired the architect. Upjohn was paid $50.

Abiel Smith School

After black citizens' demand for integrated schools was mandated by the state legislature in 1855, it became a primary school for children of all races aged four to seven. Later it was a city warehouse. In the twentieth century the building was the James E. Welch Post 55 American Legion and Ladies Auxiliary.

74 74 Joy Street
1862
National Historic Landmark

:: For many years this French Second Empire Victorian building was Police Station Number 3. The third-story mansard attic, quoins, and overhanging cornice with wooden supporting brackets are its most prominent features.

Smith Court, off Joy Street ⅲ
Smith Court became a center of the black population in Boston in the early nineteenth century, when the African Society encouraged blacks to leave the

74 Joy Street

North End for better residences. In 1829 the city directory of employment listed 224 black citizens in a wide variety of jobs, including many sailors and barbers.

In the mid-nineteenth century Walt Whitman was impressed by the very different status "black persons" had in Boston than in New York. Commenting especially on their employment in important office positions, he cited an official in the State House and a black lawyer named Anderson who lived in Chelsea and had one of the biggest practices in Boston. Whitman also wrote about the very natural way in which blacks went to any public place such as a restaurant and were served with politeness and with no indication it was out of the ordinary.

James Scott House

75 Joseph Scarlett House
2 Smith Court
1853

:: Foundation stones from the 1803 wooden tenement that it replaced were recycled in this house. The site is rich in African-American history from the abandonment of the ropewalk in 1803 until this brick house was built. Originally a two-story structure, the third level was added after 1884. Later the side entry arch was crudely blocked up.

76 James Scott House
3 Smith Court
1800
National Historic Landmark

:: For many years the building served as a black rooming house, and under the ownership of James Scott, fugitive slaves were taken in. Bricklayers William Lancaster and Benejah Brigham built the three-story Federal structure. The two-story ells on each side were added later. The front and sidewalls are clapboard, but the rear is windowless brick. The center entrance and third-floor small square windows are typical of the period

elsewhere but are rare on Beacon Hill.

James Scott purchased the house in 1865 but had been a tenant here since 1839. In 1851 he was arrested for leading the mob that freed fugitive slave Shadrach Minkins from federal marshals. Scott was released. His more famous fellow tenant from 1850 to 1857 was William Cooper Nell, journalist, author, and active abolitionist with the Boston Vigilance Committee. Nell's best-known book is *Colored Patriots of the American Revolution*.

77 5 Smith Court
ca. 1825–1835

:: This austere three-story clapboard house boasts an interesting offset window pattern.

78 7 Smith Court
ca. 1802–1811

:: The roofline alterations and late oriel modify this very early north slope house.

79 Holmes Alley House
7A Smith Court
1799

:: The frame house behind 7 Smith Court is the only remaining house of the early row that lined the eight-foot wide lane for most of the nineteenth century. It was one of the first houses built on the vacated land of a short ropewalk that paralleled Belknap's Lane. A mariner and a hairdresser purchased the house in 1800 and immediately subdivided it. In 1826 and 1833 David Beal, the Smith Court grocer, bought the two halves of the house. Most of the tenants continued to be short-term.

80 African Meeting House
8 Smith Court
1806
National Historic Landmark

:: The African Meeting House was built by blacks to use as a church. There has been some conjecture that Asher Benjamin participated in the design of the building, both because he often employed blacks and because the brick structure makes use of the inset relieving arches familiar on his Charles Street Meeting House. In 1808 a schoolroom was funded by Abiel Smith, and Primus Hall's school relocated here from the carpenter's shop next door. In 1812 the city accredited the school and budgeted $200 a year for its operating expenses. Two decades later it was overcrowded and was belatedly replaced by the Abiel Smith School.

William Lloyd Garrison founded the New England Anti-Slavery Society here on January 6, 1832. Meanwhile, the congregation adopted different names; first they became the African Baptist Church and then in the 1850s the Independent Baptist Church. As the black population increased and moved on to Phillips Street, the Charles Street Meeting House became the African Methodist Episcopal Church.

In the late nineteenth century, blacks were attracted by the availability of better housing in the South End and Roxbury and began leaving first

African Meeting House

Smith Court, then Phillips Street. By 1925 a new influx of Irish and Jews found shelter in the areas vacated by blacks. The African Meeting House was sold to the Hassidic Jewish Congregation Anshe Lebawitz, which followed its congregation to Beacon Hill from its previous location at 188 Hanover in the North End. In the 1970s the building was purchased by the Afro-American Museum.

81 Holmes Alley
End of Smith Court, between Joy Street and South Russell

:: Holmes Alley is entered through a passage off South Russell Street and then runs through the middle of the block until it connects with Smith Court. Scarcely wider than 2 feet, it was recorded as one of the hiding places for fugitive slaves during the abolitionist era. At the beginning of the nineteenth century, there was a row of small frame houses, probably one story, where now there are backyards. The one Holmes Alley house remaining is 7A Smith Court, behind number 7.

Holmes Alley, a site in the Underground Railroad

Myrtle Street

Myrtle Street rides the crown of the hill like a spine between the north and south slopes, displaying mixed characteristics. At its west end are Greek revival row houses, while the center has back entrances to Revere Street tenements. From their top floors or roofs, many of its tenements have long views over the Charles River, Government Center, and the south slope because of the street's high elevation.

The area between Myrtle and Revere streets is approximately the width of the three ropewalks that extended from Hancock past Grove until 1803. They made it impossible to cross Beacon Hill at any point between Bowdoin and West Cedar. Because of this barrier, while distinguished homes were built on the south slope, the north side had a distinctly different social history, rich in ethnic diversity.

When the ropewalks were dismantled in 1803, the slopes were connected

Myrtle Street

on two additional streets—Anderson and Belknap's Lane, together with George Street, eventually renamed Joy Street. Development of the north slope became more intense as its accessibility increased.

At the west end Myrtle Street turns north to Revere Street rather than continuing downhill to West Cedar, expressing the historic insularity of the two sides of Beacon Hill. They remained very different into the twentieth century, with low-income elderly, young professionals, students, and artists on the north slope. Convenient corner markets and services were prevalent on the north side but shunned on the south side. When condominiums and renovations came to both areas, the hill became more socially homogeneous with each decade.

Phillips Street

During its significant abolitionist history this was Southac Street, later renamed in honor of antislavery activist Wendell Phillips. It was lined with lodging houses where fugitive slaves lived, their bills paid by the Committee of Vigilance, which was founded by Dr. Samuel Gridley Howe of the south slope. These buildings were demolished and replaced at the end of the nineteenth century.

82 John P. Coburn Houses
2 Phillips Street
Asher Benjamin, 1844–1845

83 3 Coburn Court
off the passage between 24 and 28
Phillips Street
before 1830

:: In the early nineteenth century,
small houses were often constructed
behind the principal dwelling on the
north slope of Beacon Hill. The raised-
entry two-story house at 3 Coburn
Court is one of the few remaining. John
P. Coburn bought it in 1835 and lived
there until 1844. It stayed in the Coburn
family until 1889. A decade after buy-
ing the small rear yard dwelling, he
hired a prominent architect and built an
impressive house on Phillips at the corner of Irving. It remains the most distinguished home on the street, with
double end-wall chimneys and a cast-
iron gallery along the entire second
floor.

Coburn, a free black probably born
in Massachusetts, was treasurer of the
New England Freedom Association that
assisted fugitive slaves, but he was not
a member of the Boston Vigilance Committee, which was predominantly
white. He provided one-third of the
bond money for James Scott and was
arrested on the charge of aiding the escape of Shadrach Minkins. Everyone
was acquitted.

Walter Muir Whitehill suggests that
Coburn and his brother-in-law, "the
handsomest quadroon of his day," ran
a private gambling club in the house at
2 Phillips, but 3 Coburn Court seems a
much more likely site for gambling.
There were always boarders or tenants
sharing the house on Phillips, including
Coburn's sister and brother-in-law, the
sometime waiter and hairdresser.

With the wealth accumulated from
his successful clothing shop on Brattle
Street in the North End and perhaps

The Vilna Shul

from the mythical gaming club, John P.
Coburn bought several other houses on
the north slope, including 71 Joy in
1866, probably for his son, Wendell T.
Coburn.

84 The Vilna Shul
16 Phillips Street
Max Kalman, 1919
National Historic Landmark

:: This synagogue was originally built
with a narrow Gothic revival entrance
of twin spires framing a crenellated
cornice over a drop arch but was rebuilt
in 1919. Founded in 1814, it is one of
the oldest Jewish congregations in
Boston, having reached its peak with
the move to Beacon Hill of many Jews
from the North End.

85 66 Phillips Street
before 1842

:: Calvin Fairbank, whose memoirs
were published in 1890, began rescuing
slaves in 1835 before entering Oberlin
College. Despite two convictions for vi-
olations of Kentucky's slave laws and
imprisonments in the Kentucky State
Penitentiary (1845–1849 and 1852–

66 Phillips Street

The three-story red brick Federal row house has a side entry passing through a vestibule between the outer and inner doors, an arrangement typical of the 1840s. The mansard attic is a later addition.

86 Primus Avenue and "Flower Lane"
off 82 Phillips Street
Clarence H. Blackall, 1920s (Primus Avenue)

:: Primus Avenue was called Wilberforce Place in 1843. Clarence Blackall designed the charming terraced lane of

Primus Avenue

1864), he transported forty-seven slaves to freedom. Fairbank was ultimately pardoned by the Governor and took up residence in the utopian community of Florence, Massachusetts.

In 1844 Fairbank ferried Lewis Hayden, his second wife, Harriet, and stepson across the Ohio River to freedom. William Lloyd Garrison brought them to Boston and hired Hayden to help the abolitionist movement as a speaker. In 1847 he moved his family into the boarding house at 66 Phillips Street joining six other families. The Warren Insurance Company owned the house and rented it out to fugitive slaves and free men from 1846 until 1853 when it was sold to Francis Jackson, a prominent abolitionist, in response to the Fugitive Slave Act. In 1865, with the Civil War over, Jackson's will assigned the house to Harriet Hayden.

After moving to Phillips Street, Hayden opened a used clothing store at 107 and later 121 Cambridge Street. He succeeded in raising the $650 reimbursement for his former master.

Hayden is famous for his involvement on behalf of fugitive slaves William and Ellen Craft, William Jones, and Shadrach Minkins.

"Flower Lane"

duplex apartments in the 1920s. Opposite Primus Avenue is "Flower Lane," a narrow and dark midblock passageway made appealing by plantings and a gas lantern.

Revere Street Lanes 🏛

In the street's early history, the sheds of the Myrtle Street ropewalks occupied the south side from Irving to beyond Grove. On the north side, development focused away from the industrial street onto charming little lanes. Rollins, Goodwin, Sentry Hill, and Bellingham, preserved together, offer a rare comprehensive view of early nineteenth-century working-class streetscapes.

87 Rollins Place and Goodwin Place
27 and 73 Revere Street

:: Rollins Place, at 27 Revere Street, is one of four charming cul-de-sacs that stem from Revere Street. Two-story red brick Greek revival row houses built by John Rollins in 1843 line this place, but the focus of attention is the two-story wooden Ionic portico, which concludes the vista at the end of the place. What a charming white house, what a surprise on Beacon Hill! What family lives behind those shuttered windows so genteel, so withdrawn from the public way? In fact, the white portico is nothing but a false façade. The extravagant architectural tromp l'oeil is an Italian Baroque trick but in the style of Charleston, South Carolina. This architectural fantasy creates diversion for passersby—a surprising bit of artifice in the bastion of Boston propriety.

Goodwin Place, at 73 Revere Street, is lined with three-story brick Greek revival row houses.

88 Sentry Hill Place
79 Revere Street

:: This little lane was named May Street Place in 1844. An iron gate and gas lamp announce the entrance to the

Rollins Place

Sentry Hill Place

cul-de-sac. The last two narrow brick three-story Greek revival houses both have two-story frame ells that conclude the vista of the lane in a successful way.

89 Bellingham Place
85 Revere Street

:: Bellingham Place was named for Governor Richard Bellingham in 1847. Its east side is lined with narrow three-story brick Greek revival row houses. On the west side is a two-story-plus-mansard-roof house that has another full story at the level of West Cedar Street below. This clapboard house is another reminder of the early frame houses that previously fronted on these lanes. The garden glimpsed at the end of the lane and the ivy-clad walls add greatly to its attraction.

Bellingham Place

90 Joseph Ditson House
43 South Russell Street
ca. 1797

:: One of the oldest houses still standing on Beacon Hill, this Federal three-story brick house was freestanding when it was built about 1797. Joseph Ditson was the father of the music publisher Oliver Ditson.

On the upper part of the street there are two groups of mid-1840s Greek revival row houses, 42–58, and the charming small houses at 21–35 South Russell Street.

91 Temple Walk

:: Converted to a pedestrian street in 1977, Temple is the convenient path between the State House, Hurley Building, Brooke Courthouse, and North Station beyond. Added to this foot traffic are the students coming and going from Suffolk University, which dominates the upper portion of the west side of the street. Federal and Greek revival row houses line both sides of the street. Most of these have been renovated or restored. Until 1952 a pair of wooden houses built ca. 1787 stood at 44 and 46 Temple Street, where a parking lot opens up a view of the fine masonry wall of the Mission Church of St. John the Evangelist.

Temple Walk

FANEUIL HALL
AND NORTH END

Faneuil Hall District

Boston's modern Government Center and North End flank the colonial-era Mill Pond. At high tide, water swept through Mill Creek to the Charles River. By damming the mouth of the tidal inlet, a pond was captured. Mills along contemporary Causeway Street were powered by rising and falling tides, grinding wheat and corn into flour and meal.

Bridges at Hanover and North Streets crossed Mill Creek (today Blackstone Street), connecting the primary colonial areas. Between the two bridges was Creek Square, a seventeenth-century center of commerce and still at the center of some of Boston's oldest landmarks. The Boston Stone, Ebenezer Hancock house, and Faneuil Hall are a stone's throw from the Government Center of the 1960s that replaced the Dickensian lanes of the nineteenth-century Scollay Square.

1 Blackstone Block ⏤
National Register of Historic Places
Boston Landmark

∷ Three centuries of Boston architecture are found in the Blackstone Block, from the early eighteenth-century Capen House to the late twentieth-century hotel. Marshall Street, Scott Alley, Salt Lane, Marsh Lane, Creek Square—the narrow winding lanes of Boston's earliest days—seem right out of Dickens. At Creek Square a stone that had been used to grind paint

Boston Stone

pigments became the marker from which distances to and from Boston were measured. Benjamin Franklin spent much of his boyhood in and near these seventeenth-century streets. His father's chandlery shop was nearby, next to a stream that carried waste from butchers past the Blackstone Block.

2 Union Oyster House
(originally Capen House)
Blackstone Block, 41 Union Street
ca. 1713–1717

:: An oyster house has been here since 1826. Before then it had been the dry-goods shop and home of the Capen family, and in 1798 the home of tailor James Amblard, above whose shop the Duke of Chartres lodged and taught French to Boston merchants. (He returned to London in 1800, later to assume the French throne as Louis Philippe.) On the second floor Isaiah Thomas printed the *Massachusetts Spy*, an early newspaper of the Whig Party, from 1771 to 1775. The three-story building has a gambrel roof with dormers. The Union Street façade is of Flemish bond brick with dentil cornice, stringcourse, and segmental arch windows at the second floor.

3 Ebenezer Hancock House 🏛
Blackstone Block, 10 Marshall Street
ca. 1767
Boston Landmark

:: John Hancock's brother, Ebenezer, may have built this house, since he was a mason and bricklayer. During the Revolution, Ebenezer was paymaster for the Continental army, which was paid here in 1779. In style the house is similar to the Union Oyster House at 41 Union Street, with Flemish bond brick, second-floor stringcourse, and segmen-

Scott Alley

Union Oyster House

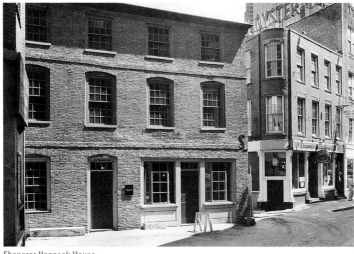
Ebenezer Hancock House

tal arch windows. The first floor was remodeled as a store before the close of the eighteenth century.

4 Millennium Bostonian Hotel
Blackstone Block, 26 North Street
Mintz Associates, 1980–1982

:: To put a hotel on this small remnant of seventeenth-century Boston might seem a disastrous idea, yet the result is surprisingly successful. All of the old streets were retained, including the narrow Scott Alley, Salt Lane, Marsh Lane, and Creek Square, which give views into the hotel as they wind through the block. The impact of the hotel is small-scale considering its 150 rooms. A three-story curving brick

Italian market

façade along North Street conceals an off-street vehicle entrance and court-yard. The narrow six-story 1889 building by Peabody and Stearns at 24 North Street was integrated into the hotel and contributes to the sense of several small structures. The unornamented brick is appropriate to the simple commercial structures within the block.

Government Center Master Plan
I. M. Pei and Partners, 1960

Government Center was carved out of the historic but seedy Scollay Square. Over several decades, buildings for city, state, and federal offices with private office and retail space, parking, and public transit were developed around a plaza. Major historic landmarks and views were protected in the master plan. The Sears Crescent and steaming teakettle were preserved, as were views from various points on the plaza of Faneuil Hall, the Old State House, Old North Church, and the U.S. Custom House Tower. New buildings were limited in height, bulk, setbacks, open space, and spatial relations with other buildings. The focus was City Hall. Pedestrian links were provided to

Washington and State Streets via Washington Mall, to One Center Plaza, Faneuil Hall, the market area, and a "walk to the sea."

Government Center's redevelopment was an abrupt change in the scale and character from the historic city and its high-density, low-rise building form that had served Boston well for centuries. Planned for large celebrations and demonstrations, the plaza was too large and undefined. It did not have the elegant form that makes it appear inevitable as the great Italian piazzas do even centuries after their creation.

5 Boston City Hall ⅲ
City Hall Plaza
Kallmann, McKinnell, and Knowles with Campbell, Aldrich, and Nulty, 1961–1968

:: Though under threat of demolition at the dawn of the twenty-first century, the award-winning City Hall had established its architect's reputation and inspired similar buildings across the nation. From the pigeonholes of city bureaucracy to the dramatic concrete forms of the mayor's office and council chambers looming over the entrances, the powerful expressionist form communicates the working of city government. Monumental gathering spaces both inside and outside provide the setting for celebrations, performances, ceremonies, exhibitions, and political rallies. The top-heavy massing and overhanging sunscreens recall the sculpted form of Le Corbusier's convent at La Tourette. The rugged interiors of concrete, brick, and glass seem indestructible, as they should be for public buildings, but present a challenge to any demolition crew.

6 Sears Crescent
City Hall Plaza
1816
Renovation: Don Stull Associates, 1969
National Register of Historic Places

:: The most successful edge of City Hall Plaza hugs the Sears Crescent and its small granite neighbor, the Sears Block, along the old street line. The curving brick façade forms a perfect backdrop and is compatible with its aggressive neighbor, City Hall, while recalling the historic form of the area. The six-story central brick building is flanked by a pair of five-story wings with wooden attics above their brick machicolation and cornice. The façade rests on an open base of granite posts and lintels, providing generous light, views, and access to the ground floor.

Next door, the small 1848 Sears Block sports a remnant of old Scollay Square, the famous steaming 227-gallon teakettle. The most beloved sign in Boston, the 1873 kettle was cast for the Oriental Tea Company at 57 Court Street, where it hung until 1967.

Boston City Hall

Sears Crescent

The steaming tea kettle

7 Faneuil Hall ⛪

Faneuil Hall Square
John Smibert, 1740–1742; rebuilt 1762
Rebuilt and enlarged: Charles Bulfinch, 1805–1806
Restoration: 1898–1899; Goody, Clancy & Associates, Inc., 1992
National Historic Landmark

:: John Smibert, an artist, designed the original Faneuil Hall in the style of an English country market, with an open ground floor and an assembly room above. The building was a gift of French Huguenot merchant Peter Faneuil (probably pronounced *funnel* in his time). After a fire, the building was rebuilt in 1762 along the same lines.

By Bulfinch's time, Faneuil Hall was becoming too cramped for the rapidly growing city, so he prepared a clever design that retained its colonial character but doubled its width and added a third floor. This increased the height of the assembly hall and provided space for the Ancient and Honorable Artillery Company in the attic. Four bays were added to the original three, the cupola was moved to the Dock Square end of the building, and the open arcades on the ground floor were enclosed. The building's original dormers were changed to barrel-shaped ones, relating to the bull's-eye windows in the pediments. Brick pilasters in the Doric order are on the first two floors, and the new third floor was given the Ionic order. Pilasters are paired at each corner. Inside, Bulfinch added galleries on three sides of the meeting hall and numerous decorative elements, including the swag panels between the old and new windows on the east and west walls.

In 1898–1899 the hall was entirely rebuilt using noncombustible materials. Colonial Bostonians frequently put weather vanes on the tops of churches and government buildings. This one is a copper-gilt grasshopper.

As decreed in Faneuil's gift, the meeting hall is forever to be used for discussion of public affairs. Here suffragettes advocated the vote for women, and abolitionists declaimed against slavery. To this day candidate debates and public forums are regularly held in the upstairs hall.

Faneuil Hall

8 Faneuil Hall Marketplace

Faneuil Hall Square
Renovation: Benjamin Thompson and Associates, 1976–1978
Quincy Market
Alexander Parris, 1824–1826
National Historic Landmark

:: Quincy Market, named after Mayor Josiah Quincy, who conceived it as an extension to the Faneuil Hall markets, was the largest single development yet undertaken in Boston. Today it is the centerpiece of Faneuil Hall Marketplace. In Mayor Quincy's own words: "A granite market house, two stories high, 535 feet long, covering 27,000 feet of land, was erected at a cost of $150,000. Six new streets were opened, and a seventh greatly enlarged, including 167,000 feet of land, and flats, docks and wharf rights obtained to the extent of 142,000 square feet. All this was accomplished in the center of a populous city, not only without any tax, debt or burden upon its pecuniary resources, but with large permanent additions to its real and productive property."

Architect Alexander Parris, like many of his contemporaries, had a penchant for the Greek revival style. He had also designed the Cathedral Church of St. Paul in the same idiom. When built, the handsome structures of Quincy granite were at the harbor's edge at the town dock. Meat and produce merchants' stalls lined the long market halls, and at the center was a rotunda. Despite the traditional style, the original structure employed several innovations, including cast-iron columns, iron tension rods, laminated wood ribs for the copper-covered dome, and the first large-scale use of granite and glass in the manner of post-and-beam construction.

The successful restoration-recycling of the old markets has been widely admired and emulated but did not come about easily. After considerable encouragement and negotiation, the enterprise went ahead and became the Rouse Company's biggest success. Later, they used a similar approach in Baltimore's Harborplace, New York's South Street Seaport, New Orleans's River Walk, and elsewhere.

The markets still function in much the way they did when they were built, with individual merchants lined up in stalls displaying and selling their

Faneuil Hall Marketplace © Steve Rosenthal

Horse-drawn carriages and live street jazz in Faneuil Hall Marketplace

goods, though there is certainly more variety and intensity of activity today than ever before. The pushcarts, too, follow the historic precedent of the old Haymarket. Faneuil Hall Marketplace is aging into an integrated part of Boston's history.

9 Marketplace Center
Near Faneuil Hall at 200 State Street
WZMH Group, 1983–1985

:: This project masked the intrusive elevated expressway until it was torn down, then it provided a gateway to the Rose Kennedy Greenway. The three-story retail base contains shops and offices. Offset on a portion of the base is a tower, whose awkward location was dictated by the desire to minimize its visibility from Faneuil Hall Marketplace. Its height was limited to sixteen stories to maintain the dominance of the Custom House Tower in the district.

10 Kevin White and James Michael Curley Statues
Carmen Park, Congress Street near Faneuil Hall
Lloyd Lillie, sculptor, 1980, and Pablo Eduardo, sculptor, 2006

:: Boston has never forgotten its beloved mayor James Michael Curley, and in these sculptures he becomes a permanent part of the street life across from City Hall. His Irish political machine was derided by Francis W. Hatch, a Yankee of poetic bent, who quipped: "Vote often and early for James Michael Curley." In 2006 the redoubtable Curley was joined by a statue of former mayor Kevin White striding purposefully along the sidewalk with a coat flung over his shoulder.

Marketplace Center

James Michael Curley statues

Kevin White statue, Pablo Eduardo, sculptor, 2006 © Peter Vanderwarker

Holocaust Memorial

11 The New England Holocaust Memorial

Carmen Park, Congress Street near Faneuil Hall
Stanley Saitowitz, 1995

:: A black granite path leads visitors to a series of six glass towers, one for each of the major Nazi extermination camps. The square towers suggest the furnaces' chimneys and trap steam rising through grates from dark smoldering holes evoking the gas chamber experience. Six million numbers are etched in glass, representing the tattoos of those killed in the camps, as well as the Nazi ledgers.

12 Government Center Garage

New Sudbury Street
Kallmann and McKinnell with Samuel Glaser and Partners, 1970

:: This dramatic garage carries on the brutalist concrete style of City Hall by the same architects, but with completely different means. Built of precast concrete components stacked up almost like Lincoln Logs, bold sun-catching elements are juxtaposed with deep voids. Two floors of offices were added on top in the late 1980s.

13 Richard Haas Mural

101 Merrimack Street
Building: The Architects Collaborative, 1990
Mural: Richard Haas

:: The focus of this contextual office building is a six-story trompe l'oeil mural by Richard Haas. Most of one wall of the multilevel central interior space is a mural suggesting a domed glass pavilion. A small fountain at the base provides sound to reinforce the image. Haas's painted details enhance the central space, producing a winter garden effect without the chore of maintaining real palm trees and tropical plants.

Richard Haas mural at 101 Merrimack Street © 1990 Nick Wheeler

14 Charles F. Hurley State Service Center
19 Staniford Street
Paul Rudolph, Shepley Bulfinch Richardson and Abbott, Pedersen and Tilney, M. A. Dyer, Desmond and Lord, 1970

:: In a tour de force demonstrating the sculptural possibilities of concrete, Paul Rudolph created his own landscape for a large government complex using his trademark corduroy concrete. The long stretches of terracing, deep overhangs, and cylindrical towers form a twentieth-century evocation of a European piazza. It establishes its own strong vocabulary without attempting to relate to its diverse neighbors. Sunscreens mask the endless office windows, stairways become sculptural flights, and paving swirls in sinuous curves of small terraces. Semicircular bench bays provide extensive seating along most of the sidewalk frontage. For lack of funds the focal tower was never built.

107 Merrimac Street, a flatiron building in the Bulfinch Triangle near North Station

Charles F. Hurley Building

15 Edward W. Brooke Courthouse
24 New Chardon Street
Kallmann McKinnell & Wood
Architects, 1999

:: After decades, the triangular end of this site was completed by the courthouse, closing off the unfinished arm of the adjacent Rudolph building. Where the two meet along a narrow lane, there is a startling juxtaposition of the darker rough concrete of Rudolph's building pushing against the pale sleek skin and square columns of the courthouse's high arcade.

The county courthouse contains eighteen courtrooms with an administrative level available for future additional courtrooms when needed. Three separate circulation systems segregate the public from staff and prisoners. This internal complexity is not apparent in the composed façade. A fly roof sweeps up to a sharp point and deeply overhangs a row of windows.

Edward W. Brooke Courthouse

16 One Center Plaza
City Hall Plaza
Welton Beckett and Associates,
1966–1969

:: The architecturally unremarkable One Center Plaza echoes the crescent of row houses it replaced. The street entering the plaza was replaced with a stairway and escalator connection, cutting the visual link from the former Scollay Square to the John Adams Courthouse.

17 John Adams Courthouse
Pemberton Square
George A. Clough, 1896
Enlarged: 1906–1909; Desmond and Lord, 1936–1939
Renovation: Childs Bertman Tserkares, 2005
National Register of Historic Places

John Adams Courthouse

:: Old Pemberton Square, developed in the 1830s, was inspired by Bulfinch's superb tontine crescent at Franklin Place. Though a pale imitation, it was an attractive residential crescent of brick row houses enclosing a small

View of Pemberton Square, 1885 Boston Athenaeum

park. Construction of the 1896 Court-house destroyed the flat side of the square. The remaining houses survived until the 1960s Government Center redevelopment.

The French Second Empire façade is articulated to suggest a smaller build-ing of three or four stories plus attic. Above the rough granite base, smooth-faced arches and pilasters rise to a heavy cornice and entablature. The pale green two-story mansard roof, a later addition, has three different styles of dormers. The central entrance pavil-ion relates to the end pavilions in form

and features a Roman-numeral clock surmounted by a broken pediment with cartouche in the tympanum. Inside, a grand space with allegorical figures by Domingo Mora provides a common focus for the different floors.

18 Suffolk University Somerset Street Residences
10 Somerset Street
Cannon Design, 2003

∷ Squeezed in next to the old Pember-ton Square is a nineteen-story dormi-tory with an atrium that harvests daylight and acts as a solar collector.

19 Garden of Peace

behind 100 Cambridge Street on
Somerset Street
Brown, Richardson & Rowe, 2004

∷ A stone stream spirals up around
a grass mound. Names of homicide
victims are inscribed on individual
river stones. The ibis sculpture represents hope.

Garden of Peace

North End

Before the Revolution the North End
was the fashionable area of Boston and
the site of the mansions of Lt. Gov.
Hutchinson, Sir Henry Frankland, and
Governor Phips. Nearly an island, it was
connected to the mainland by bridges
over Mill Creek. Although it had only a
few houses and a windmill in the early
1700s, by the end of the century it was
the most densely populated section of
Boston. Wharves had been built in
every possible location, all but obliter-
ating the original shoreline.

The area never really recovered its
earlier status after the Revolution, however, since a number of Loyalists who
had been among its leading residents
were forced to abandon their property
and fled to Halifax, Nova Scotia. Although most of the early settlers were
Puritans, a settlement of Afro-Americans
on Copp's Hill had given that area the
nickname "New Guinea." Throughout
the nineteenth and early twentieth centuries, successive waves of immigrants
moved into the North End, and later to
the West End and Beacon Hill. Beginning with the potato famine in 1824,
the Irish came, followed in the 1860s
and later by eastern European Jews,
then Portuguese and Italians. In this
context Eben Jordan founded his department store chain and John F.
"Honey Fitz" Fitzgerald began his
career in politics.

Today the North End is an explorable
labyrinth of narrow activity-filled
streets with attentive residents and
laundry hanging out of upper windows.
This is the area Jane Jacobs praised in
the early 1960s for its street life and
sense of community, when urban renewal was destroying other such
neighborhoods across the country. It is
a close-knit Italian community with
strong traditions and fierce pride, despite creeping gentrification. Streets
are lined with shops selling fine Italian
imported foods, cafés with delicious
gelati and cappuccino, pasta and pastry
shops, and fresh-produce markets.

Storefront social clubs, some of
which are funeral brotherhoods, play an
important part in the life of the neighborhood. Each club has a patron saint,
usually the patron of the members'
hometown in the old country, and spon-
sors a summer street *festa* honoring
the saint. These colorful street festivals
are famous North End events that attract admiring participants from all
parts of the city. Confetti, balloons, and
dollar bills are thrown down on the pro-
cessions from windows above the decorated streets as the statue of the
honored saint is carried on the shoul-
ders of the club members. From the
statue hang streamers to which people
pin money for charity in the name of the
saint. The street life, social traditions,
and political sentiments of the North
End create a strong and vital community.

John F. "Honey Fitz" Fitzgerald,
grandfather of John Fitzgerald Kennedy,
was born on Ferry Street in 1863. He
spoke so frequently and fondly of the

Ferry Street

"dear old North End" that the neighborhood's residents came to be called the "Dearos." The name was adopted by the Irish political and social organization led by Fitzgerald. Rose Fitzgerald Kennedy, daughter of Honey Fitz and mother of President Kennedy, was born at 4 Garden Street a few blocks away and is buried at St. Stephen's Church on Hanover Street.

Hanover Street

From the early settlement of Boston, Hanover was the route linking the North End with the rest of the peninsula. Today it is the commercial spine of the neighborhood, lined with Italian shops and restaurants. Two department store tycoons started their businesses on Hanover Street. Eben Jordan, who came from Danville, Maine, with $1.25 in his pocket, opened a small dry-goods store at 168 Hanover. Eventually it became the major New England department store Jordan Marsh Company. A few years later Rowland H. Macy of Nantucket opened a similar store a few doors away. It prospered and grew into the national R. H. Macy's. Hanover Street was a sadder place during the Great Depression, when bread lines were a daily occurrence.

20 North End Branch Library
off Hanover Street at 25 Parmenter Street
Carl Koch and Associates, 1965

∷ In his design for the library, Carl Koch considered the cultural background of the Italian residents of the North End. The interior is treated as a courtyard or piazza, a common element in the architecture of Italy. The library has a 14-foot-long model-diorama of the Doge's Palace in Venice, sculpted in plaster by Miss Henrietta Macy, a North End kindergarten teacher who spent much of her life in Europe and died in Venice in 1927.

21 St. Stephen's Church 𝍖
(originally New North Church)
Hanover Street at Clark Street
Charles Bulfinch, 1802–1804
Restoration: Chester F. Wright, 1964–1965
National Register of Historic Places

∷ Of the five churches Bulfinch built in Boston, only this one remains. It is a staggeringly intricate composition of recessed brick arches, lunettes, Ionic

St. Stephen's Church

pilasters, entablatures, balustrades, urns, pedestals, scroll brackets, pediments, engaged columns, and an octagonal cupola. Somehow he managed to keep this assemblage under control. The interior side aisles and galleries are expressed in the façade by lower recessed wings flanking the central entrance under a tower thrust to the front in the manner of English architect James Gibbs.

The Rev. Francis Parkman, father of the noted historian, was minister here from 1813 until 1849. To serve the Catholic immigrants arriving in the North End, the Unitarian church was sold to the Roman Catholic diocese in 1862 and renamed St. Stephen's. The weather vane was removed and a spire constructed over the cupola. In 1870 the church was moved back 16 feet to accommodate the widening of Hanover Street.

22 Paul Revere Mall 🏛

("The Prado")
off Hanover Street opposite
St. Stephen's Church
Arthur Shurtleff, 1933

:: The Paul Revere Mall is carved out of the densely built-up North End and links two landmarks, St. Stephen's Church and the "Old North" Church. The irregularly shaped space is effectively defined by brick walls, which minimize the backs of apartment buildings. Bronze plaques commemorate local people and events. Two rows of trees strengthen the linear space, providing shade and a visual contrast with the hard surfaces of neighborhood streets too narrow for trees. Year-round the Prado, as it is called by North Enders, bubbles with activity. Children play while their mothers or grandmothers look on, men huddle over tables playing checkers or cards, and tourists parade through.

Paul Revere Mall

This mall is the best pedestrian approach to Old North Church. One passes Cyrus Dallin's 1885 (not cast until 1940) equestrian statue of Paul Revere amid the outdoor life of today's North End. At the head of the mall is the restored Clough house and a good view of the back of Old North Church. As one ascends the stairs the space squeezes in, presenting views of small gardens and the side of the church. Then it pinches in again at the church's front entrance, tight against narrow Salem Street. Certainly the mall's designer, Arthur Shurtleff, had in mind the wonderful spatial sequences of Venice and other Italian cities when he conceived this.

Regrettably, some significant old houses were destroyed for the mall, including five early eighteenth-century houses built by Ebenezer Clough.

North Square

The triangular granite plaza off North Street is rich in history and still has some of the flavor of colonial Boston in the Revere and Hichborn houses, blended with the nineteenth-century Mariners' House and the apartments of today's Sicilian and Italian residents. In the eighteenth century Boston's two grandest houses were on North Square, called Clark's Square then. William Clark, merchant, had a three-story brick house with twenty-six lavish rooms, and nearby, facing the garden court, was John Foster's house, later occupied by Governor Hutchinson. On Moon Street just off the square was the house of the Rev. Samuel Mather.

At the head of the square was the church of the Mathers, the 1677 Second Church of Boston, called "Old North." It was destroyed by the British for firewood in 1776. There is substantial evidence that this was the church from which Paul Revere was warned of the approaching British, but the matter has never been settled conclusively.

Across from the Paul Revere house is Rachel Revere Park, a playground named after Paul Revere's second wife, the mother of eight of his sixteen children. A bit farther down North Street at Richmond Street is the oldest sign in Boston, dating from 1694. It is at the third-story level of the northeast corner and is inscribed with the initials W, T, S. They are the initials of Timothy Wadsworth and his wife, Susannah, granddaughter of Nicholas Upsall, who owned the Red Lyon Inn at this corner.

North Street was originally called Ann Street, and by the early nineteenth century it had become a rowdy place, known for "the nymphs of Ann Street." After it was cleaned up in the 1850s, it was renamed North Street.

23 Mariners' House
11 North Square
1838

:: The Mariners' House is dedicated to the service of seamen. The dignified structure of four stories plus dormered attic is in the Federal style. On its roof is an octagonal lantern, or cupola, presumably built so the seafaring residents of the house could keep their eyes on the sea. The six-over-six-paned windows have granite lintels and sills.

24 Paul Revere House 🏛
19 North Square
ca. 1677; extensively rebuilt mid-eighteenth century
Restoration: Joseph E. Chandler, 1907–1908
National Historic Landmark

:: The oldest frame house in Boston was built shortly after the great 1676 fire where Increase Mather's house had been. The land behind it was large enough for a garden or stable and had the unsanitary combination of well and privy, the cause of much disease. Rear lots were often sold off and built upon, with the small back houses linked to the main streets by a maze of tiny passageways.

North Square, Mariners' House

Paul Revere House

a reproduction of the original early eighteenth-century English wallpaper discovered during restoration beneath seventeen layers of paper. Behind the house is an attractive garden with pump.

Salem Street

Beginning in the 1850s, Salem Street was the center of the North End community of eastern European immigrants, mainly Jewish. The song "My Name Is Solomon Levi" tells of a man who has a clothing store on Salem Street. This was the Washington Street of the North End, with many clothing, tailoring, fabric, and lace shops. Today the street is demonstrably ethnic, with Italian grocery stores, butchers, and bakeries. Happily, it has changed little in recent decades. Sophie Tucker lived at 22 Salem Street as a child.

Typical of the houses of the period, it was a small frame structure, close to the street, with an overhanging second floor, or jetty. The low-ceilinged dark rooms cluster about the massive central chimney. Small leaded windows provide light and view. Several of the Reveres' furnishings may be seen inside.

Paul Revere, descendant of Huguenots named Revoire, purchased his house in 1770, when it was already nearly one hundred years old. During the three decades he owned it, he fathered sixteen children; produced copper engravings, cannons, church bells, and false teeth; and was a leading gold- and silversmith.

26 North Bennet Street School
Salem Street at 39 North Bennet Street
1881

:: In 1881 educator and social worker Pauline Aggassiz Shaw established the North Bennet Street Industrial School in this mansard-roofed three-story brick structure to help the North End's immigrants develop job skills. Today the

25 Pierce-Hichborn House 🏛
29 North Square
1710
Restoration: 1950
National Historic Landmark

:: Nathaniel Hichborn, Paul Revere's cousin, lived next door to the Reveres in this brick house built in 1710 by Moses Pierce, a glazier. The three-story house is laid in the early American bond of three stretcher courses for every header course. Stringcourses separate the floors. Windows are framed with brick relieving arches. On the ground floor are the kitchen and parlor, each with a large fireplace. The floors have the original pine boards of varying widths up to 20 inches. Walls are papered in

Pierce-Hichborn House

Salem Street Italian market

school offers courses in cabinetmaking, carpentry, piano technology, violin making and repair, bookbinding, and locksmithing.

27 Christh Church 🏛
("Old North")
193 Salem Street
William Price, 1723
National Historic Landmark

∷ Christ Church, or "Old North," is the oldest church building and the second Anglican parish in Boston. Built of brick in the style of Sir Christopher Wren, it is thought to have been modeled after St. Andrew's-by-the-Wardrobe in Black-friars, London. Its bricks were made in Medford, and the timber came from the area of York, Maine.

The 175-foot, three-tier steeple houses a peal of eight bells, cast by Abel Rudhall of Gloucester, England, in 1744. They are the oldest church bells in America and are still rung today. At age fifteen Paul Revere formed a guild of bell ringers with six friends. The steeple has twice been toppled by hurricanes, first in 1804, after which it was rebuilt from a drawing by Charles Bulfinch, and again in 1954. The original weather vane by Deacon Shem Drowne, a colonial craftsman, still tops the spire.

Inside, the bright airy space, painted white since 1912, offers tranquility and purity contrasting sharply with the complex and animated maze of shadowed brick streets outside. The high box pews were owned by parishioners and were designed to keep the warmth of hot coals or bricks placed on the floor on wintry days. The gleaming brass chandeliers were gifts of Captain William Maxwell and were first lighted on Christmas Day 1724. At the rear gallery ticks a clock made by two parishioners, Avery and Bennett, in 1726.

Doorway, 18 Cooper Street

Christ Church ("Old North")

Each year on the eve of Patriots' Day, lanterns are hung in the belfry by descendants of Paul Revere or Robert Newman to commemorate the night of April 18, 1775, when Revere rode on horseback to warn Lexington and Concord of the approaching British forces. Eighteen years earlier the steeple had been the launching pad for the first flying man in America, John Childs, who in 1757 leaped from the tower with an umbrella-like contraption strapped to his back and landed safely several hundred feet away.

The controversy over whether this is the real Old North Church or whether it was in fact Second Church on North Square has never been fully put to rest. Since the end of the Revolution, the celebrations have been here.

Several peaceful small gardens cluster about the back of the church, including the Washington Memorial garden and an herb garden. The ironwork was made by inmates of the old state prison in Charlestown.

28 Copp's Hill Burial Ground 🏛
off Salem at Hull and Snowhill Streets
National Register of Historic Places

:: From Copp's Hill Cemetery one has excellent views of Boston Harbor, Charlestown, Bunker Hill, the Navy Yard, and the USS *Constitution*. The cemetery is the oldest in the North End, the first burial probably having occurred in 1660. It is estimated that there have been more than 10,000 burials here, including 1,000 blacks. Boston's first black colony, called "New Guinea," was located on Copp's Hill at the northeastern base.

The western portion of the cemetery was reserved for blacks, slave and free, and has a monument to them placed in that section by the Masons. Among the many notables buried here are the Mathers—Increase, Cotton, and Samuel—as well as Thomas Hutchinson and John and Andrew Eliot. Strolling among the old slate gravestones, the visitor will find some stones scarred by the British soldiers who used them for target practice during the siege of Boston. Since then stones have been moved about, and in later centuries builders took them for repairs to nearby houses.

"Pope Day" was a raucous Boston celebration of Guy Fawkes' plot to blow up the British Parliament and King and install a Catholic monarch. "Remember, Remember, the Fifth of November" was the old British doggerel shouted rather than sung on that day. Competing mobs from the North End and South End

Copp's Hill Burial Ground

gathered around bonfires on Copp's Hill and the Common. They set off toward each other bearing effigies of the Pope, Devil and Catholic Pretender. After the mobs met, the winners of the brawl returned with the opponents' effigies to sacrifice in their bonfire.

29 44 Hull Street
ca. 1800

:: This house has the distinction of being the narrowest house in Boston, with a width of about 10 feet and only one window per floor facing the street.

30 Copp's Hill Terrace
off Salem Street across from Copp's Hill Burial Ground
National Register of Historic Places

:: A fine granite promontory off Charter Street, at the edge of the cemetery, leads down to Commercial Street and the waterfront. Nearby Jackson Avenue, a charming pedestrian lane, also leads down to the waterfront. From its ramparts one finds views of the Bunker Hill Monument, USS *Constitution* and Charlestown Navy Yard, Boston Harbor, and Copp's Hill Cemetery. It was near here that the famous molasses disaster occurred in 1919. A huge two-and-a-

Ironwork detail, Copp's Hill Terrace

half-million-gallon tank of molasses burst, releasing a tidal wave that took with it buildings and people. Twenty-one people were killed in the spill, and the area smelled of molasses for decades.

Nearby, at the corner of Commercial and Foster Streets, Paul Revere had a foundry where he cast church bells. The USS *Constitution* ("Old Ironsides") was built at Constitution Wharf at 409 Commercial Street. Its keel was laid in 1794, and it was launched in 1797. Near 379 Commercial Street the North Battery was erected in 1646 to defend Boston.

31 Dodd House
190 Salem Street
1804

:: The Dodd house was built on land that was part of Sir William Phips's estate and originally overlooked Governor Phips's garden. The Dodds were the last of the old North End families to remain in their family home. They were also the last to do their cooking in the fireplace. When stoves replaced fireplaces, the Dodds went up to Hanover Street and ordered one, but after returning home and thinking about it, they decided the new gadget was not for them and canceled the order.

The basement contains a bricked-up archway that is said to have connected

44 Hull Street

with a mysterious tunnel to Copp's Hill. Possibly it connected with the legendary tunnel of Captain Gruchy, a smuggler, privateer, and deacon of Old North Church, who used his tunnel to avoid taxation on goods he stole at sea. Gruchy lived in the old Phips home.

20 Unity Court

32 20 Unity Court
LDA Architects, 2000

:: To create a dramatic town house in the North End tradition, three façades of the building were restored. The south façade was removed and replaced with large areas of glass, providing spectacular views of Old North Church. The interior was opened to provide multistory spaces.

33 Clough House
21 Unity Street
ca. 1715
National Register of Historic Places

:: Ebenezer Clough, a master mason and one of the Sons of Liberty who participated in the Boston Tea Party, built this house and was one of two masons who laid the brick of Old North Church. It is one of the few early eighteenth-century houses remaining in Boston. Window and door lintels are finely executed in brick, with raised brick panels over the first-floor windows and carved brick detail over the door. Originally the house was two stories with a gambrel roof and dormers, but over the years the roof was raised to make a full third story.

By 1962 the property was in poor condition and had been divided into six apartments with a butcher shop on the ground floor. Old North purchased and restored the house in 1972, cleaning the original brick and restoring the fireplaces, wainscoting, and English oak staircase with pendant acorn drops.

The house next door, one of a row of six built by Clough, was owned by Benjamin Franklin and occupied by his two sisters. It was demolished when the Paul Revere Mall was built.

Clough House

WHARVES
AND SEAPORT

In the seventeenth and eighteenth centuries, Boston was the preeminent merchant port of the colonies. From its hilltop site, Fort Point protected the inner harbor. Wharves multiplied and expanded as clipper ships sailed as far as China in pursuit of trade. Venturing through the North Sea to Saint Petersburg, Boston captains found abundant sailcloth, tar, and hemp. Soon dozens of ships rechristened with Russian names plied the route with goods from Imperial Russia to Russia Wharf. Ice was shipped to the West Indies, Persia, and Australia.

Nineteenth-century Boston grew so rapidly in population and trade that it could not build wharves or land fast enough. Responding to the need, the Boston Wharf Company filled the tidal marsh across the Fort Point Channel with rubble cleared from the 1872 fire and built masonry warehouses. The Mount Washington Bridge connected them to the west side of the channel. By 1930 there were a half-dozen bridges crossing the channel—Summer Street (1899), Northern Avenue (1908), Broadway (1914), and Congress Street (1930).

Stables, liveries, and hay and straw purveyors kept the horse-drawn traffic moving. A steady stream of wagons carted molasses, wool, coffee, spices, dry goods, ice, and fish from wharves to warehouses or markets.

Overhead, coal shuttled along a gantry while wheelwrights and black-smiths added smoke and noise to the maelstrom. Glassworks, iron foundries, and machine shops produced lanterns, cannons, boilers, and the first elevators.

From the colonial barriers and forts built for protection against roving brigands through a series of landfills moving ever outward and construction of long wharves, the radical changes never stopped along the waterfront. The galloping development of the water's edge in the eighteenth and nineteenth centuries was followed by abrupt abandonment in the twentieth century as shipping declined with the departure of textile mills from New England.

When political leaders turned their attention to the empty water-front, stunning old wharf buildings were torn down and their foundations used as vast open-air parking lots. The most destructive decade in Boston's history had arrived. With wanton disregard for the seaport that had been the source of great prosperity since colonial times, wholesale destruction ensued. Many cities in the U.S. and Europe had forfeited their waterfronts. The giant scar that was the Central Artery was only one of the outrageous indignities visited on Boston in the 1950s and early 1960s.

The construction of the elevated Fitzgerald Expressway seemed to seal the fate of the waterfront. Controversial from its beginning, it destroyed 20,000 households and shops and proved to be an unsightly barrier between the North End, the waterfront, and the rest of Boston. Completed in 1959 with no federal safety standards, its frequent and abrupt access ramps, narrow lanes, and sharp curves were a traffic engineer's nightmare. And it was too congested. With no room to increase capacity aboveground, the only solution seemed to be putting the traffic under the city. As well as knitting the old Shawmut peninsula back together, the Big Dig opened up a vast stretch of public open space. Ironically, it was named the Rose Fitzgerald Kennedy Greenway, honoring the daughter of "Honey Fitz," who had bestowed his name on the cause of all the trouble.

Completion of the Big Dig in 2006 after fifteen years and $15 billion made the Wharves and Seaport the new frontier for condominiums and offices. But some had pioneered in the area decades earlier. In the 1960s several architects began renovating forgotten wharf buildings as apartments. Atlantic Avenue was rerouted to accommodate a waterfront park. Government Center and Faneuil Hall Marketplace reestablished a link to the harbor under the freeway.

Too often American cities have turned their backs on their waterfronts. For an unhappy period Boston did, too, but with the completion of the Big Dig, it has the most accessible waterfront. HarborWalk, the 47-mile waterfront walk along the Massachusetts Bay, is the best way to see the wharf and seaport districts.

Wharf District

Since the 1960s, despite the barrier of the Fitzgerald Expressway, a substantial population came to live and work in renovated wharf buildings. The appeal of contact with the harbor and the architectural splendor of the early granite finger piers drew tourists as well.

Atlantic Avenue was constructed in 1870 between the ends of T Wharf and Commercial Wharf on a stone seawall. Dirt from Fort Hill was dumped into the basin, preparing new land. The center of Charles Bulfinch's incomparable India Wharf was razed to allow Atlantic Avenue to pass through.

1 Pilot House
1–10 Atlantic Avenue
1863
Renovation: Carl Koch, 1971

:: This small brick wharf building with arched windows was built by the

Pilot House

Eastern Railroad during the Civil War. It was renovated as apartments and a restaurant.

2 One Lewis Wharf
off Atlantic Avenue
Skidmore, Owings & Merrill, 1982

:: This office building is oriented to the harbor with primarily glass façades on the south and east. Cantilevered sunscreens permit solar heat gain in winter but shade the offices from the summer sun, while providing visual interest on an otherwise solid mass. A brick screen wall with tinted precast concrete bands faces the street.

3 Lewis Wharf
28–32 Atlantic Avenue
Richard Bond, 1836–1840
Renovation: Carl Koch and Associates, 1965–1969, 1971

:: Lewis Wharf, one of the first wharf buildings to be renovated for residential use, is constructed of Quincy granite and heavy timber. The original gabled roof has been greatly altered and now accommodates two floors of apartments. Until about 1868 the building extended west as far as the site of a brick shop building, formerly a Sunoco station, designed by Anderson, Notter Associates. In the eighteenth century John Hancock's warehouses were located on Hancock Wharf on the north side of Lewis Wharf. Opposite the head

Lewis Wharf

of the wharf was the North End Coffee House until 1783.

Edgar Allan Poe's macabre tale "The Fall of the House of Usher" is said to be based upon actual events that took place on the site of Lewis Wharf in the eighteenth century. Two lovers—a sailor and the young wife of an elderly man—were trapped in their trysting place, a mysterious underground tunnel, by the avenging husband. It has been said that when the old Usher house was torn down in 1800, two embracing skeletons were found at the foot of some steps behind a rusty iron gate.

4 Prince Building
45–69 Atlantic Avenue
Renovation: Anderson, Notter, Feingold, 1966–1969

:: Originally the Prince Macaroni factory, this structure was one of Boston's first conversions of industrial space into apartments. The simple reinforced-concrete structural system is clearly expressed on the exterior with new recessed window balconies defined by white fins. The irregular plan of the building allowed a variety of unit types.

5 Commercial Wharf
84 Atlantic Avenue
Isaiah Rogers, 1832–1834
Renovation: east half, Halasz and Halasz, 1968–1969; west half, Anderson, Notter, Feingold, 1971

:: Isaiah Rogers, a leader in the design of monolithic granite buildings, had worked for Solomon Willard, another influential designer in granite. Rogers was also architect of Boston's first luxury hotel, the 1828 Tremont House. This fine wharf building uses Quincy granite both decoratively and structurally. Window and door lintels and jambs and a stringcourse above the first floor are of smooth cut granite, while the walls are rough with more massive blocks on the first floor.

Prince Building © Hutchins Photography, Inc.

Commercial Wharf

The building is now in two parts, one on each side of Atlantic Avenue, which cut through its middle about 1868. The mansard roof on the eastern section was added at that time. A dignified classical entrance with an inset clock above it is centered on the narrow end of the western half of the building. Two doors flanking the entrance have simple carved lintels with stylized pediments cut into them, later obscured by signs and window alterations. The simplified pediment form appears on all the lintels of the upper floors. Both buildings have been subjected to roof and façade alterations, but the strength of the original design is still apparent.

The Big Dig

In the mid-twentieth century, politicians made mistakes that were so massive and ill-considered that the city suffered the consequences for decades. The Fitzgerald Expressway was one of the first urban expressways, and nearly every mistake possible was made in its conception. It mercilessly cut through the historic core of Boston, separating the North End and waterfront from the rest of the city. No attempt was made to mitigate the intrusive structure through design.

Correcting the damage by undergrounding more than 7 miles of highways and ramps posed mammoth engineering challenges. While trains, subways, and vehicular traffic continued to circulate above, massive underground engineering work went on at depths of 100 feet or more. Tunneling under central Boston required threading a path through relocated utility lines, the "Presidents Road" shipping channel into Boston Harbor, and all previous tunnels. To stabilize the tunnels, the ground was artificially cooled below thirty-two degrees, hardening it against the powerful vibrations coming from below. Where the ground wasn't

frozen, buildings settled and cracks appeared. The new tunnel acted as a dam that unintentionally disrupted the water table of Back Bay and Bay Village.

But digging also brought an archeological boon, unearthing many artifacts from early Boston. Long-gone topographical features emerged, including Paddy's Alley and the old Mill Pond, which had been filled soon after 1800. Most dramatically, the removal of the elevated highway opened up a vast stretch of land for the Rose Kennedy Greenway.

Rose Kennedy Greenway

6 North End Park
Crosby Schlessinger Smallridge with Gustafson Guthrie Nichol Ltd, 2007

7 Wharf District Park
EDAW, Inc, 2007
Streetscape: CWDG, 2007

8 Chinatown Park
Carol R. Johnson Associates with May Sun, 2007

:: Even before the newly created land was redeveloped, the visual opening was important. The wharves, seaport, and Old North Church became visible from Government Center and the Custom House district for the first time in half a century. North End Park reaffirms the bridge linking the early North End over Mill Creek to the Blackstone Block and Creek Square. Wharf District Park links the city with the sea, focusing on the wharves from Christopher Columbus Park to Rowe's Wharf. At the southern end of the Greenway, Chinatown Park features plantings and elements significant in Asian culture.

9 Christopher Columbus Waterfront Park
Atlantic Avenue
Sasaki Associates, 1976
Renovation: Halvorson Design Partnership, 2002

:: When Atlantic Avenue was rerouted from the water's edge, space was created for a four-and-a-half-acre park, designed to complete the "walk to the sea" that commenced at the State House on Beacon Hill. The focus of the park is a cobblestone plaza at the water's edge, extending from the re-built seawall to the waterfront promenade. A long arched wisteria trellis defines the main space and connects the subareas of the park. Materials reflect the waterfront character of the area—brick, granite, cobblestones, and wood. The furniture continues the nautical theme with bollards linked by anchor chain and lighting resembling ship's lanterns. The park is intensely used by neighborhood residents, tourists, and workers. The Big Dig required some adjustments and rethinking of the park to relate to the Rose Kennedy Greenway.

Christopher Columbus Waterfront Park

10 Long Wharf 🏛
202 Atlantic Avenue, at the end of State Street
1710
National Historic Landmark

:: Long Wharf originally extended from near the Old State House along what is now State Street far out into the harbor. Constructed by Captain Oliver Noyes, it was lined with warehouses and served as the focus of Boston's great harbor. At the wharf's head in the eighteenth century was the Bunch of Grapes Tavern. The painter John Singleton Copley spent his childhood on the wharf, where his mother had a tobacco shop. Nineteenth-century landfill projects cut its length in half, and the construction of the Central Artery in the 1950s dealt another blow.

11 Custom House Block
off Atlantic Avenue on Long Wharf
Isaiah Rogers, 1845–1847
Renovation: Anderson, Notter, Feingold, 1973

:: As in his earlier Commercial Wharf building, Isaiah Rogers designed the Custom House Block primarily of granite. The forceful ground level is constructed of massive posts and lintels of single chunks of stone. A central block with pyramidal roof rises one story above the four-story building to define the arched center entrance. The brick rear façade is of utterly different character, with several gabled windows. It was here that Nathaniel Hawthorne served as customs inspector.

12 Chart House Restaurant
(formerly Gardner Building)
60 Long Wharf
1763, 1812
Renovation: Anderson, Notter, Feingold, 1973

:: Long Wharf was originally built up with colonial brick warehouses similar

Gardner Building

Park and Atlantic Avenue. The lower floors of the building contain function rooms and a 225-car garage. On the main floor, three five-story spaces serve as lobbies, lounges, and public function areas. The building rests on about 500 precast, prestressed concrete piles, 14 inches square and with an average length of 90 feet, bearing on bedrock. Its bolted steel frame is designed for earthquake loads.

to this one, the only remaining building. The simple but solid structure has a slate roof and six-over-six-paned windows with shutters and granite lintels and sills.

13 Marriott Long Wharf Hotel
Atlantic Avenue at 296 State Street
Cossutta and Associates, 1980–1982

:: The linear form of the Marriott Long Wharf Hotel relates to the thrust of the original wharf, and its simple massing and use of brick vaguely recall the early warehouse buildings. The stepped form rises to heights that vary from 49 to 104 feet, relating in scale to its neighbors, the smaller Chart House, and the larger Custom House Block. It is set back on the south and east sides to open views to the Chart House from Waterfront

14 New England Aquarium and Central Wharf
250 Atlantic Avenue
Cambridge Seven, 1969, 1973, 1979
Addition: Schwartz/Silver Architects, 1999

15 IMAX Theater
E. Verner Johnson & Associates, 2001

:: Charles Bulfinch designed the original Central Wharf buildings, completed in 1817, a row of four-story brick structures nearly 1,300 feet long. A small fragment of the wharf survives on Milk Street.

The New England Aquarium now occupies part of the site. The core of the aquarium is a concrete box housing a three-story, 40-foot-diameter tank surrounded by a ramp that rises through the four-story central space. Glass and metal additions crawl up and

Marriott Long Wharf Hotel © Steve Rosenthal

New England Aquarium

IMAX Theater, New England Aquarium

over the aquarium, obscuring most of the original concrete structure. Extreme angles and asymmetrical punched-out window bays arrived in Boston before Gehry's Stata Center at MIT. Silver metal sheathing in a ripple pattern relates to the cool northern water of the Boston harbor.

The adjacent IMAX Theater echoes the materials, sloped walls, and multiple corners.

16 Aquarium Station
Atlantic Avenue
1904
Expansion: Ellenzweig Associates, 2003
Mural: Jun Kaneko, 1993

:: The first underwater subway station in the United States was modernized in conjunction with the Big Dig project. Each of the new head houses responded to its context: granite on State Street, brick adjacent to Long Wharf. Connecting the new entrances required doubling the length of the platform.

17 Harbor Towers
off Atlantic Avenue at 65–85 East India Row
I. M. Pei and Partners, 1971

:: One of the most ambitious projects in the country at the beginning of the nineteenth century, India Wharf included more than a half mile of wharves, warehouses, and stores running from India Wharf along India Street to State Street. Bulfinch's fine 1807 India Wharf buildings stood here until the last section was razed in 1965 to make way for Harbor Towers. In contrast to the historic long, low forms of brick, granite, and timber extending like fingers into the harbor, Pei's towers introduced a new form and scale to the Boston waterfront. Apartments in the forty-story towers of cast-in-place concrete are organized pinwheel fashion about a central core. Concrete balconies stack up to create a zipper-like sculptural relief against the flat grid of the façade. The stainless-steel sculpture at the base is by David von Schlegell (1972).

Harbor Towers

India Wharf before 1868 Historic American Buildings Survey

18 Rowe's Wharf

Atlantic Avenue near Harbor Towers
Skidmore, Owings & Merrill, Chicago,
1987

:: In the seventeenth century there
were a number of fortresses along the
waterfront. On this site the Boston
Sconce battery was built in 1666 by Maj.
Gen. John Leverett. Overlooking it, on
Fort Hill, stood the barracks. The modern

Rowe's Wharf complex benefits from
strict site-specific urban design rules, including height limitation, view preservation, continuous public pedestrian
frontage along the water, and public
water shuttle and commuter boat facilities in a prominent part of the site.

The vaguely traditional red brick
complex of three eight-story stepped
structures resembles finger piers. The

HarborWalk at Rowe's Wharf

massive arch recalls on an exaggerated scale Bulfinch's 1807 India Wharf. An octagonal domed glass pavilion is the water shuttle waiting room. The promenade along the water on two levels links water commuters to financial district destinations and joins the continuous pedestrian HarborWalk.

19 Commercial Block
126–144 Commercial Street
Attributed to Gridley J. Fox Bryant,
1856
Renovation: Mintz Associates, 1978

:: A dignified granite façade rises from a simple trabeated first floor. Rusticated pilaster-like verticals strengthen the corners, while stringcourses and a bracketed cornice organize the façade horizontally. Architectural historians have praised Boston's granite warehouses. Sigfried Giedion felt the Commercial Block in particular was an important influence on the work of H. H. Richardson. A floor was added above the roofline.

20 Christopher Columbus Plaza
145 Commercial Street
Mintz Associates, 1977

:: Sponsored by the Ausonia Knights of Columbus of the North End, this 151-unit housing project for the elderly was developed with the participation of community groups and the Massachusetts Historical Commission. Its unpretentious brick volumes, penetrated by simply detailed large windows, relate in height to the surrounding buildings and allow the animated rooflines of the North End and St. Stephen's and Old North Churches to be seen from Waterfront Park. Because of the very different scale on each of the streets surrounding the project, an effort was made to relate each façade to the character and scale of its particular street.

As is typical in the North End, the building hugs the street, but a semiprivate courtyard is created in the center. On the fifth floor a greenhouse and solarium overlook the park.

Commercial Street

Commercial Block

21 Union Wharf

323 Commercial Street
ca. 1846
Renovation: Moritz Bergmeyer, 1979
National Register of Historic Places

:: The somber dignity of Boston's granite warehouses is nowhere better expressed than in Union Wharf. Its rough
granite is utterly straightforward and
without artifice. The building's masonry
walls with iron-shuttered windows
speak for themselves, and its name is
boldly set in granite in the pediment.
The stone blocks of the ground floor are
of a larger scale than in the upper
floors. Unfortunately, brick dormers
were added when the building was still
a warehouse, seriously compromising
the original form. A string of brick row
houses was added to the wharf by the
same architect who did the renovation.

Union Wharf © Steve Rosenthal

22 Lincoln Wharf Condominiums

357 Commercial Street
1901
Renovation: The Architectural Team,
1987

:: This former MBTA power plant has
been converted to low- and moderate-
income housing. Units are organized
around an interior atrium.

Lincoln Wharf Condominiums

23 McLauthlin Building 𝕚𝕚𝕚

120 Fulton Street
possibly Daniel Badger, ca. 1864
Renovation: Moritz Bergmeyer, 1979

:: The first cast-iron-façade building in
New England, the McLauthlin Building
is reminiscent of the work of James
Bogardus in New York. Besides being
fire resistant and easily fabricated,
cast-iron façades made possible large
windows for interior lighting. The
façade is divided into six bays, and on
the second through fourth floors, each
bay holds two arched windows with
fanlights. Pilasters and small columns
alternate across the façade, and each
floor is defined by a projecting string-

McLauthlin Building

course. A cornice tops the fifth floor. The sixth floor is awkwardly squeezed into a mansard roof. Until the late twentieth century, the building was occupied by its original owner, the McLauthlin Elevator Company. It is now condominiums. Compare this with another famous cast-iron building, the Richards Building.

24 Mercantile Wharf
33–81 Mercantile Street
Gridley J. Fox Bryant, 1856
Renovation: John Sharatt and
Associates, 1976

:: Architect Gridley Bryant, son of the builder of the Bunker Hill Monument, also designed the State Street Block opposite the Custom House. Mercantile Wharf is an example of the late "Boston granite style" and closely resembles the nearby Commercial Block built one year later. Stringcourses run beneath the windows of each floor, while a substantial bracketed cornice defines the top of the mass. Each three-window bay is expressed by rusticated verticals, similar to pilasters but without capitals. The ground floor with its large arched openings is particularly impressive. The shallow arches with keystones rest on slender granite posts, supporting the façade.

Ships' chandlers, sail makers, and riggers were the original occupants of the building, but today it has been recycled as a shopping galleria with apartments surrounding a six-story space. The exterior has been well preserved, the major change being the windows, which were originally six-over-six-paned sash. It is admirable that this wharf conversion has maintained the rooflines, whereas most others have added decks and dormers.

Custom House District
National Historic District

In the early nineteenth century, the Custom House was at the center of Boston economic life. Situated at the head of Long Wharf (now State Street), it surveyed the harbor, then bordered by India Street. A few reminders of Boston's mercantile past survive in the district, including parts of Charles Bulfinch's rows of brick warehouses and stores on Broad Street and Central Wharf, as well as several outstanding examples of granite warehouses. While the Custom House tower dominated the Boston skyline for many decades, it has been upstaged by megaprojects of the 1980s.

Broad Street 𝕚𝕚𝕚
Broad Street was laid out by the Broad Street Association according to the plans of Charles Bulfinch shortly after 1805. Several of the Federal-style four-and-a-half-story buildings from that development survive. The Broad Street Association included Harrison Gray Otis, Francis C. Lowell, and Rufus G. Amory, under the leadership of the indefatigable developer Uriah Cotting. Today this is one of the most impres-

Detail, Mercantile Wharf

sive but fragile historic streets in Boston, an important remnant of early nineteenth-century commerce.

25 The Architects Building
50–52 Broad Street
Charles Edward Parker, 1853
Renovation: Ken DeMay, Peter Forbes, Dennis Rieske, Brigid Williams, 1989
Boston Landmark

:: One of the few structures to survive the Great Fire of 1872, this granite building with mansard roof has rock-faced rustication on the second, third, and fourth floors. Windows of the upper floors have bracketed lintels, while those of the ground floor have semicircular arches with prominent keystones. Originally the building was used as a warehouse, and later it held offices and various businesses. Granite-faced buildings began replacing the Federal brick buildings on Broad Street in the mid-nineteenth century, significantly changing the scale of the street and dwarfing the remaining Federal architecture. In 1988 the building was purchased and renovated by the Boston Society of Architects, with the financial backing of Jung/Brannen Associates and the entire building industry, for use as the headquarters for the BSA and the building industry.

The Architects Building

72 and 80 Broad Street

26 72 Broad Street
from designs of Charles Bulfinch, 1805–1807
Boston Landmark

:: This is one of the early nineteenth-century remnants of Bulfinch's plan for new warehouses and stores to replace the old wharves that had developed here in a rather helter-skelter fashion during the seventeenth century. The brick structures have flared lintels with small square windows on the top floor in the Federal manner. Beneath the hipped roofs were brick dentil courses,

and stringcourses of granite separated the floors. Other buildings of the Bulfinch development survive, although several have been extensively altered, at 5, 7–9, 63–65, 64–66, 67–73, 68–70, and 102 Broad Street.

This one survives as part of the 80 Broad Street development.

27 Batterymarch Building

89 Broad Street and 60 Batterymarch
Street
Henry Kellogg, 1928
Boston Landmark

:: An early art deco building that both
breaks and makes the rules, the Batterymarch Building has the solid block
mass at street level, but instead of car-
rying sheer walls up ten or fifteen stories before terracing in with typical art
deco giant steps, the base is an unin-
timidating two stories. The third-story
open arcade is a decorative device for
defining and framing the open courts as
it connects the three elegant, narrow
brick towers, which are actually connected at the back. Vertical dividers
projecting between ranks of windows
emphasize the height of the towers. At
the top, the forms of the towers change,
with chamfered corners and stepped
end bays. The building suggests New
York's Beekman Tower (originally the
Panhellenic Hotel), built about the
same time, which even employs the
same two-story-plus-arcade base. After
nearly a century as an office building, it
too became a hotel.

One of the most intriguing design
innovations of the Batterymarch Building is its use of color. The brick is

Batterymarch Building

shaded from dark at the base to progressively lighter tones toward the top,
thus increasing the building's impression of height. If one stands near the
base and gazes directly up at one of the
towers, it seems to recede into the sky.
Architects' renderings of art deco buildings frequently showed the tops of
towers ringed with clouds, emphasizing
their height. The color shading of the
Batterymarch Building is a literal real-
ization of the shading and coloring used
on these drawings, although inappropriate masonry repairs have weakened
the effect.

28 99–105 Broad Street

1854
Boston Landmark

:: Here is an important example of
early slab-granite construction. Prominent stringcourses and a deep-bracketed
cornice highlight the smooth granite
façade of these large warehouse
buildings.

29 109–139 Broad Street

1870

:: Segmental arches cut from single
slabs of granite form the lintels for both
the large ground-floor windows and
doors and the upper windows. Rock-
faced rustication has been used, with
each story defined by a stringcourse of
smooth granite. The top floor is an attic
with three-sided dormer windows. Between numbers 105 and 109, old Half
Moon Lane leads past a sensuously
curved brick wall to the Chadwick Lead
Works and its brick tower, which was
used to make lead shot.

30 20 and 21 Custom House Street

Bruner/Cott & Associates, Inc., 1988,
1989

:: These two buildings were the first
to be developed in response to the
Boston Redevelopment Authority's 1986
guidelines. Modest in size, style, and

99–105 Broad Street

115 Broad Street

109–139 Broad Street

20 and 21 Custom House Street © Peter Vanderwarker

design, they are built of granite like many of their notable neighbors. A one-block pedestrian-scaled street passes between them.

31 Chadwick Lead Works
184 High Street
William Preston, 1887

:: From the square tower attached to the rear of the Chadwick Lead Works, molten lead was dropped, forming shot in the course of its fall. The front façade is notable for its bold three-story arches topped by a cornice of closely spaced windows and corbelled parapet. Spandrels between the arches are treated decoratively, the lower one of herringbone brickwork bulging out along with the windows, and the top one dotted with bumps.

32 Central Wharf Buildings
146–176 Milk Street at India Street
Attributed to Charles Bulfinch, 1816–1817

:: Central Wharf was built following designs of Bulfinch. Originally it contained fifty-four buildings, as well as a seamen's chapel, and extended beyond the expressway to the wharf where the New England Aquarium now stands. Only eight of the original wharf buildings survive, in various degrees of alteration. The original Federal-style buildings were four stories tall and three windows wide and had hipped roofs.

295 Franklin Street

146–176 Milk Street

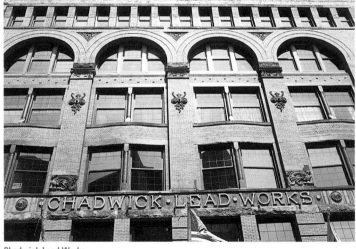

Chadwick Lead Works

33 Grain and Flour Exchange Building 🏛

177 Milk Street
Shepley, Rutan, and Coolidge,
1891–1893
Boston Landmark

:: H. H. Richardson's successors designed the Grain and Flour Exchange using many of the ideas he had employed in his wholesale store for Frederick L. Ames, built in 1882 at Kingston and Bedford Streets. The rounded corner of the site is dramatized by the conical roof surrounded by a string of pointed dormers topped by finials. The sixth and seventh floors are suspended from the roof structure and are now used as an architectural office. The Milford granite exterior is organized into several tiers with two ranges of arches, the large lower order encompassing three floors. The small clustered arches of the top floor act as a cornice.

Grain and Flour Exchange Building

34 Richards Building

114 State Street
ca. 1867

:: Because Boston was well developed before the nineteenth century, cast-iron architecture never achieved the popularity here that it did in some younger cities. During the era of cast-iron construction, there were still far more granite than cast-iron buildings built in Boston. Since the 1820s, granite had suited the city's need for solidity and permanence.

The lower five floors of the façade of the Richards Building were fabricated in Italy and bolted together after they reached Boston. Later the Italianate arcades were surmounted with a pair of two-story oriel windows when the mansard attic was removed and

Richards Building

two additional office floors were
added.

35 Cunard Building
126 State Street
Peabody and Sterns, 1901

:: The Cunard Building deftly uses ornament to express the company's nautical business. Between the second and
third floors a Vitruvian scroll band
strongly suggests waves with a head of
Neptune at each end. Bronze anchors
support the lighting brackets at the entrance. Cunard's transatlantic service
was inaugurated on July 4, 1840, with
a fourteen-day voyage from Liverpool to
Boston.

36 MBTA Traction Power Substation
136 State Street
Ellenzweig Associates, 2003

:: Behind the discreet limestone, granite, and aluminum façade, major power
and ventilation machinery goes unno-
ticed by all but the keenest observers.

MBTA Traction Power Substation

37 Custom House ⅲ
State Street at India Street
Ammi Burnham Young, 1837–1847
Tower addition: Peabody and Stearns,
1913–1915
Boston Landmark

:: Built at the nineteenth-century
water's edge, the new Custom House
was ideally situated on State Street,
which had long served as the primary
route from the wharves to the Old State
House, the banks, and Washington
Street. State Street, called King Street
until the Revolution, was an important
street in seventeenth-century Boston.
The original Custom House was a four-
faced Greek temple with fluted Doric
columns of granite weighing forty-two
tons each. The interior rotunda had a
skylit dome, but the tower was built
over this in 1913.

Although Boston had a 125-foot
height restriction, the federally owned

Custom House

Custom House property was not subject
to city height limits. Thus Boston's first
skyscraper was built, a sixteen-story
landmark that was a shock to the city.

38 State Street Block 🏛

177–199 State Street at 1 McKinley
Square
Gridley J. Fox Bryant, 1858

∷ McKinley Square is dominated by
the enormous dark granite mass of the
mid-nineteenth-century State Street
Block, which originally was much
longer, stretching down to the waterfront. The rock-faced rustication of the
upper floors is ornamented by the contrasting smooth granite stringcourses
between floors and by segmental
arches with keystones over the windows. The central pavilion displaying
the carved name of the building has a
massive broken segmental pediment in
front of the two-story mansard roof. A
granite globe is centered in the window
framed by the pediment. Assorted additions have been made above the cornice, including the mansard.

State Street Block

Leather and Garment District

Lincoln, Utica, and South Streets
National Historic District

Though leather fabricators and tanners
also located on the other side of the
Fort Point Channel, including the 1887
United States Leather Company building at 313 Congress Street, this area
retained the name even after all the
leather-related companies had departed. The Great Fire of 1872 destroyed almost 800 buildings, many
associated with merchandising and
manufacturing in Boston. Lincoln and
South Streets are lined with five- and
six-story warehouse and factory buildings constructed over three decades
after the fire. Handsome compositions
of Romanesque arches and carved
stone ornament a number of buildings.
The strength of the district lies in the
continuity of the brick façades and the
handsome rhythm of the windows, as
well as the uniformity of building

height, massing, material, and frontage
line.

The old home of the shoemaking
and leather-tanning industries declined
into marginal uses and sweatshops

South Street, Leather and Garment District

until the area experienced a renaissance in the 1980s. Its uncluttered warehouse spaces were converted to art galleries, artists' studios, and luxury loft conversions. High-style restaurants arrived to cater to artists and collectors who were attracted to the area. Artifacts of early New England leather and garment companies were exhibited in some shop windows, providing a link to the district's past.

South Station clock pediment © Susan Southworth

39 Lincoln Street Garage
125 Lincoln Street
1956, 1959
Addition: Brian Healy Architects, 1999

:: This hybrid structure portrays late-twentieth-century urban economic history, from a one-story garage to early supermarket, multilevel parking with small ground-level shops, and, finally, Internet start-ups. Rather than hiding the structure's evolutionary layers behind a unified façade, the intention was to display them in an archeological sense. The renovation left four decades of careless add-ons in place while adding a high-style office penthouse. After the Central Artery was undergrounded, the garage became the dominant edge between Chinatown and the Leather and Garment district.

Fort Point Channel

National Historic District

For most of its history, the Fort Point Channel area was an industrial and warehousing district strategically located at transportation intersections. Originally it was a transfer point from wagons to channel barges or ferries. With the coming of railroads in the 1830s, commerce shifted to rail, and a new compact industrial area with substantial buildings of brick and stone developed on the South Boston side of the Channel. In the twentieth century it linked commuter rail, Amtrak, bus, subways, and major interstate highways.

As the century advanced, artists

Lincoln Street Garage © Dan Bibb

moved into empty warehouses near the Fort Point Channel. Eventually others followed, as the warehouses had become hip. Rents increased and loft spaces were converted to pricey condominiums, driving out those who had rescued the district. Artists organized campaigns and put up posters to protest changes that excluded them. The district survives nearly intact, with the industrial structures converted to offices, galleries, museums, and loft apartments or condominiums.

40 **Artists for Humanity (AFH) EpiCenter**
288–300 A Street
Arrowstreet, 2004

:: Founded in 1991 by Susan Rogerson to serve "at-risk" youths, Artists for Humanity teaches the techniques and tools of business and art. Inner-city teens are empowered to explore their worlds and selves through the visual arts. They then offer their vision and skills to the community. Painting, sculpture, silkscreen, photography, and graphic design studios as well as gallery and event space are combined in a green building.

The sustainable features include low-flow faucets, rainwater harvesting, natural ventilation via a night airshaft rather than refrigerant-based cooling, high-performance walls, daylighting, low-emissivity windows located by energy criteria, and a 49-kilowatt photovoltaic array with surplus power sold back to the power grid. Recycled and salvaged materials were used throughout construction, including abandoned train rails and Crown Victoria windshields from junked police cars. The center was built on a tight budget and operates economically due to its energy self-sufficiency.

41 **Vent Building**
500 Atlantic Avenue
Wallace Floyd Associates, 2002
Hotel and condominiums: Elkus/Manfredi Architects, 2005

:: Like the other six ventilation stacks for the Big Dig, it processes air for the vast tunnel network of highways through downtown Boston and connecting to the airport. This vent stack differs in having a hotel and condominiums wrapped around it in an unusual application of air-rights development. The engineers had to overcome vibrations from both the vent and the tunnel directly under the building.

42 **Russia Wharf**
530 Atlantic Avenue, 270 and 286 Congress Street
1899
Renovated 1980

:: Three late-nineteenth-century seven-story buildings occupy the former site of Russia Wharf. In the eighteenth century Massachusetts traded with

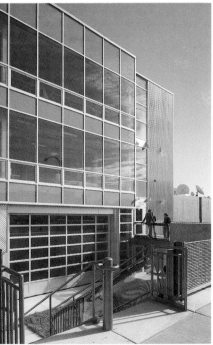

Artists for Humanity EpiCenter © Richard Mandelkorn

Russia, primarily through Cronstadt, the port of St. Petersburg. Though the clipper ships thronging the port flew their American flags, many carried Russian names: *Volga, Czarina, Cronstadt, Petersburg, Peterhof, Tsar, Ladoga,* and *Strelna.* Quills for pens, candles, soap, sailcloth, hemp for the rope makers, and tar from Smolny Dvor landed at Russia Wharf. So active was the trading relationship that Russia's first embassy in the United States was established in Boston in 1809.

43 Federal Reserve Bank of Boston
600 Atlantic Avenue
The Stubbins Associates, 1977

∷ The long-span floors of the tower are supported on tall, slender end pylons, which, in turn, straddle a low U-shaped mass housing public areas and high-security banking operations. The top of the low-rise block contains recreation and employee facilities, which have access to a landscaped roof garden. The aluminum skin was selected in part to reduce solar heat gain. The projecting aluminum spandrels of the tower both serve as sunshades and

help reduce the downdraft problem characteristic of tall buildings, thus making the ground level more comfortable for pedestrians.

The entrance area features a "water court" with a pool and an 18-foot-high, 140-foot-long waterfall running along the gallery-exhibition area. The structure readily adapted to stringent new security requirements after 2001. Halvorson's Dewey Square plaza deftly integrates defensive measures in an inviting public space.

44 South Station
Atlantic Avenue at Summer Street
Shepley, Rutan, and Coolidge, 1899
Renovation: Skidmore, Owings & Merrill; The Stubbins Associates; Stull and Lee, Inc.; Prellwitz/Chilinski, 1989
National Register of Historic Places (South Station Headhouse)

∷ South Station stands on the site of a 1668 house that became the Bull Inn in 1689. The station has been the focus of Dewey Square since its construction. In the early twentieth century, it acquired a chapel, movie theater, and bowling alley, all in the art deco style. Josep Lluis Sert prepared a design for a re-

Federal Reserve Bank © Peter Vanderwarker

South Station

placement station, which was abandoned when the old headhouse acquired landmark status.

The 1899 headhouse survives. Its curved corner façade of classical aspirations nicely joins Summer Street and Atlantic Avenue. Above the two-story entry arches rise three-story Ionic columns topped by a balustrade and entablature with center pediment. The eagle and clock provide a final flourish.

South Station was renewed in the 1980s and provides convenient connections between rail, subway, and bus in a lively public setting that is within walking distance of Boston's historic core. The old structure was restored on the outside and completely renovated on the inside, and a new west wing was added in the style of the original building, even incorporating pink granite from the same quarry in Connecticut that had been used ninety years earlier. The Food Court shops and stands serve commuters and workers in surrounding office buildings. Having lunch while watching the trains arrive and depart just outside the expansive glass wall and listening to the train announcements might tempt diners to try a train journey.

45 Boston Children's Museum
300 Congress Street at Fort Point Channel
Morton D. Safford, 1889
Renovation: Cambridge Seven and Dyer Brown Associates, 1975
Expansion: Cambridge Seven Associates, Inc., 2007

Children's Museum

:: This former wool warehouse on the 1882 Nickerson Wharf has served well as a museum for children. The large, simple open spaces with rough character easily absorb school and family groups. The giant milk bottle was a drive-in snack bar from the 1930s, relocated here to serve as an eye-catching symbol for the museum.

46 One Financial Place
Dewey Square
Jung, Brannen Associates, 1983

:: This was the first structure in Boston clad with a precast concrete rain-screen system (developed in Canada) that uses the pressure-equalization principle to minimize water penetration.

47 South Postal Annex
Summer Street at 15 Dorchester Avenue
Renovation: Perry, Dean, Rogers and Partners, 1980

South Postal Annex

:: Lying beside the Fort Point Channel, the metal-clad South Postal Annex recalls a streamlined ocean liner of the 1920s. Until 1980 it was faced with brick. Refacing with insulating panels reduced its energy consumption.

48 Summer Street Bridge
1899

:: Each of the Fort Point Channel bridges used a different engineering solution to open for navigation. This one retracted diagonally in two sections.

Summer Street Bridge

South Boston Warehouses 🏛

Boston's Soho is located in the warehouses south of the Fort Point Channel on A, Binford, Broadway, Congress, Melcher, Midway, Summer, and Wormwood Streets.

The substantial, richly formed turn-of-the-twentieth-century warehouses of this district, including nearby Congress Street, are largely the work of Morton D. Safford. Particularly appealing is the curving Melcher Street, which dips down one full level to cross under Summer Street at A Street, leaving its imprint on the wonderful curved forms of 253 and 259 Summer Street. Harmonious continuous façades tightly define the curvature of the transition from Summer Street.

49 263 Summer Street
Morton D. Safford, 1905

:: The rounded corner of 263 Summer Street elegantly leads into Melcher Street. It is one of the many warehouses built on Summer Street by the Boston Wharf Company, which can be identified by the egg-and-dart roundel in bronze affixed to each building with the date and B W CO in raised letters. Safford was Boston Wharf's architect for twenty-four years. His work can be readily identified not by one architectural style but by his template, which gives the district its handsome regularity. The inevitable monotony of large warehouses is relieved by the flourishes he added to the top and the bottom of the street façades: projecting cornices, arches, or Gibbs surrounds as seen here on the third floor.

Wool Traders' Warehouses

50 250, 256, and 262 Summer Street
Morton D. Safford, 1899

51 280 Summer Street
Morton D. Safford, 1898

52 300 Summer Street (at the A Street overpass)
Morton D. Safford, 1898

Melcher Street Warehouses

Beginning in the late nineteenth century and continuing for several decades of the twentieth century, a number of wool traders were located on Summer Street, supplying textile mills in Lawrence and other New England mill towns. The demolished 1882 Dorr Building was the first wool warehouse built in South Boston. The Union Wool Building (George F. Shepard, 1917–1919) at 425 Summer Street claimed to have the largest wool storage facility in the world. Above its entrance was a handsome ram's head keystone, lost with the demolition of the warehouse in 1999.

Three warehouses at 250, 256, and 262 Summer Street share façade detailing. At 300 Summer Street the eighteen-bay, seven-story Francis Willey Company building is the most architecturally elaborate wool warehouse still standing of the ninety that were constructed over four decades. Double Romanesque arches announce the entrance and ring the entire sixth floor under a projecting cornice. By the late twentieth century it was filled with architects and art galleries as well as the studios of dozens of artists. The first Open Studios day was in 1980. Vintage shops, restaurants, clubs, and Internet services soon followed.

53 Court Square Press Condominiums
9 West Broadway
1906
Renovation: John Cunningham, 2004

:: In the mid-twentieth century a financial document printing company took over the MacAllen factory building. Five decades later the limestone-trimmed brick factory was incorporated into a complex of loft condominiums and modern town houses. During demolition of smaller adjacent buildings, a portion of the original factory was destabilized and then rebuilt. Old brick elevator shafts in the surviving factory

were retained and became small studies or closets.

54 Bay State Brewery and Malt House
West First Street near A Street
1862

:: Ice-making and steam engines brought large-scale commercial brewing. Breweries and alehouses were located near the Fort Point Channel and South Boston waterfront before Massachusetts's 1869 Prohibitory Liquor Law. Upon repeal there was an explosion of new breweries—by 1890 there were twenty-seven, many in Roxbury. An exception was Frank Jones, the New Hampshire brewery magnate. He bought the Henry Souther brewery in 1875 as part of his expansion into new territories and businesses. His steamship, the SS *Frank Jones,* began calling at South Boston in 1892.

55 Factory Buildings Trust
Wormwood, Binford, and A Streets
1895–1930

:: These buildings (including the former Atlantic Machine Screw building) house Boston's first artists' loft cooperative. The 222-foot Wormwood smokestack serves as the icon.

Seaport District

South Boston was annexed to Boston in 1804 but was connected across the Fort Point Channel only by a ferry until 1899. Irish dock and factory workers settled near their employment, giving "Southie" its famous ethnic character. Simple bars and diners served the longshoremen and fishermen beer from nearby breweries.

While Boston's eighteenth- and nineteenth-century wharves still have a human scale, the Seaport district is all about big. Twenty-first-century construction along South Boston's waterfront followed the suburban financial model. Developers were given the responsibility for streets, utilities, and open space. Monster buildings on scattered superblocks may feel like 1960s retro, but the huge scale started here long before then with the early twentieth-century Fish Pier and army warehouse.

56 Northern Avenue Bridge
at the mouth of the Fort Point Channel
William Pratt Jackson, engineer, 1908

:: The last working drawbridge on the Fort Point Channel, an iron turntable bridge, closed to vehicles in 1997. It was the final crossing constructed to link South Boston to the neck. Northern Avenue was realigned to the Evelyn Moakley Bridge.

57 John Joseph Moakley Federal Courthouse and Harborpark
Fan Pier at Seaport Avenue
Pei Cobb Freed & Partners, 1998

:: Fan Pier occupies the former rail yards, where spurs radiated out in the form of an open fan. A wide cobblestone and brick promenade continues the HarborWalk along its waterfront. Harborpark is landscaped with trees and plants indigenous to New England.

The Moakley Federal Courthouse embraces Boston Harbor through its curved slant-back stadium frontage. Twenty-one Ellsworth Kelly paintings were commissioned for the rotunda and galleries. In contrast to its glassy waterside, the courthouse presents a granite-trimmed brick façade to South Boston. The district's congressman was instrumental in obtaining federal funding for the Big Dig as well as the courthouse that bears his name.

58 The Institute of Contemporary Art/Boston
100 Northern Avenue
Diller Scofidio + Renfro with Perry Dean Rogers Partners, 2006

:: With hysterical praise and a MacArthur Foundation "genius" grant before they produced anything, Boston expected more from this New York firm. Though the main gallery appears to hang over Boston Harbor, it stops at the water's edge. Dangling from it precariously, like a falling drawer, is the Mediatheque. Below that a grandstand greets the HarborWalk and continues indoors as the theater. Despite glass by the mile, the museum is largely inward-looking. The floor-to-ceiling glass walls on the gallery level were to be covered

The Institute of Contemporary Art/Boston © Peter Vanderwarker

with microscopic vertical lenses to blur the view outdoors in an artistic way. Only strenuous objections by the ICA board prevented that expense and left open the panoramic harbor views.

This building is a surprise in the era of sustainable architecture. South American hardwood, overindulgence in glass, an inefficient shape, and massive elevator-cab dimensions contrast starkly with the other major art institution in the neighborhood, the ultra-green Artists for Humanity EpiCenter. The stairway to the gallery is small and inconspicuous to encourage use of the glass-walled elevator. The architect Elizabeth Diller described the building as "almost like porn," unintentionally evoking the reality of its energy porn.

Museums want to be iconic. Since its inception in the Back Bay, the ICA has led the city in its commitment to contemporary art. Relocating from a recycled fire station in a transit-rich environment, the ICA has built a highly symbolic replacement.

59 **South Boston Maritime Park**
D Street at Northern Avenue
Halvorson Design Partnership and Machado and Silvetti Associates, 2004

:: The wedge-shaped park incorporates four sequential experiences: the lawn, pergolas, a pavilion, and the garden. Literature and songs associated with the sea, tidal lights, nautical

Maritime Park © Halvorson Design Partnership

measurements, planting beds in triangular sail shapes, and weather signals all contribute to the maritime theme of the park. At risk for saline infiltration and exposed to wind and salt spray, the park design responded with sustainable materials and captured roof runoff to feed the water table, grasses, ground covers, and shrubs that thrive in ocean settings. Together, Maritime Park and the earlier Eastport Park sculpture garden are the major public open spaces in the Commonwealth Flats neighborhood of South Boston.

60 **Eastport Park**
World Trade Center, Seaport Boulevard/ Northern Avenue
Halvorson Design Partnership, 2000
Sculpture: David Phillips and Judy McKie

:: Two years after the sculpture garden opened and despite Massachusetts Chapter 91 requiring public access in waterfront development, Fidelity Investments hired a British landscape architect to develop a redesign that would discourage public use of Eastport. Artist David Phillips went to court to prevent destruction of Craig Halvorson's people-friendly design but ultimately lost.

61 **Boston Convention and Exhibition Center**
415 Summer Street
Rafael Vinoly Architects, PC, with HNTB Architecture and thirty consultants, 2004

:: Cantilevers are in. While the nearby Institute of Contemporary Art cantilevers a glass box, here Vinoly projects an enormous tongue shape that shadows an acre of forecourt and glass lobby. Looming over Summer Street, it is intimidating. Some of the whalelike 2,000-foot-long convention center occupies the former site of wool traders' warehouses.

Boston Convention and Exhibition Center © Peter Vanderwarker

62 Tug *Luna*
berthed at Commonwealth Pier (Henry
F. Keyes, 1911), renamed World Trade
Center
Seaport Boulevard/Northern Avenue
1930
National Historic Landmark

:: The first diesel-electric tugboat was
the last wood-hulled harbor tug,
demonstrating the transitional role of
Luna. Following a decade of commercial harbor service in highly visible
flaming red-orange paint, she was req-
uisitioned by the U.S. Navy to launch
warships, assemble convoys, and rescue ships in distress in coastal waters.
After sinking, she lay in the Charles
riverbed for a year before she was
raised and restoration began.

63 Boston Fish Pier
1212 Northern Avenue
Henry Keyes, 1912–1914

:: When it opened, the *Fishing
Gazette* trumpeted the pier as "the
largest, most complete and sanitary
building in the world devoted exclusively to the handling of fish." With the
largest ice plant and its own power
plant, it guaranteed Boston's preemi-

nent position as a fish market. Fish
was shipped out on rail lines adjacent
to the pier from forty-four wholesale
companies located here.

By the 1970s the enormous U-
shaped structure was abandoned except for the remaining fish processing.
Renovated to incorporate third-floor
office space and the Exchange Conference Center, while retaining its historic
ambience, it attracted back major fish
industries and the fish auction to stand
as the oldest continuously working fish
pier in the United States.

64 Albanian Orthodox Cathedral
of St. George
523 East Broadway
Samuel J. F. Thayer, 1872
National Register of Historic Places

:: The Hawes Unitarian Church was
named for its founder, John Hawes,
whose 1805 house is at 568 East Fifth
Street. The Albanian congregation acquired it in 1950 and added the iconos-
tasis necessary for Orthodox services.

Fan S. Noli established an Albanian
Orthodox church in 1908 when a Greek
Orthodox church outside Boston re-
fused burial to an Albanian nationalist.
The Besa-Besen (Oath of Loyalty) Soci-

ety had recently been organized to promote Albanian nationalism in the United States. Albanians continued to immigrate to Boston into the twenty-first century, reinforcing the city's position as the country's center of Albanian history and population. The Orthodox liturgy was first heard in the Albanian language, not in Albania, but in two local churches in the twentieth century.

65 Boston Design Center
One Design Center Place
(formerly Boston Army Supply Base),
660 Summer Street
U.S. Army Corps of Engineers, 1918
Renovation: Earl R. Flansburgh & Associates with Stubbins Associates/Interior Design Group, 1986

:: Originally built to warehouse tanks and trucks, this building was engineered for tremendous live loads. The largest military warehouse in the world at that time, it is an impressively long structure with 1.5 million square feet of floor space. Adapted as a showplace for the design and contract furnishings industry of New England, it contains showroom space, professional offices, and seminar and conference rooms. The narrow west end facing downtown Boston was redesigned, adding an entry plaza and giant segmental pediment to announce the entrance.

66 John F. Kennedy Library 𝕚𝕚𝕚
Columbia Point
I. M. Pei and Partners, 1977–1979
Landscape design: Kiley, Tyndall, Walker with Mrs. Paul Mellon
Exhibit design: Chermayeff and Geismar Associates
Stephen E. Smith Center
Pei Cobb Freed & Partners, 1991

:: After ten years of controversy and consideration of eight different sites, this dramatic site on Columbia Point overlooking open sea was chosen for the Kennedy Library. The simple forms of a nine-story white pyramid connected to the two-story cylinder by a parallelogram and the gray glass form of the 110-foot-high Presidential Pavilion make a strong symbolic statement. The visitor is led from the reception lobby overlooking the glass pavilion to an exhibition lobby and two auditoriums seating 300 people each. Leaving the auditoriums, visitors descend to the lower-level exhibition area and finally enter the large glass space frame with its expansive view of the bay.

A 1991 addition, the Smith Center, provided a large function room, classroom, and archives. Kennedy's sailboat, *Victura,* is displayed on the granite Bay Plaza. The point is planted with flora associated with Cape Cod: pines, dune grass, bayberry, and rugosa roses.

Boston Design Center © Steve Rosenthal

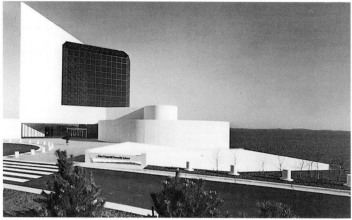

John F. Kennedy Library © Nathaniel Lieberman

67 Harbor Point

1 Harbor Point Boulevard, Dorchester
Reconstruction: Mintz Associates
Architects/Planners, Inc with Goody,
Clancy & Associates, 1990

:: This former harbor mudflat had a
long negative history. It was a garbage
dump, then a World War II prisoner-of-
war camp before it became the notorious Columbia Point public housing.

Transformation of failed public housing into successful communities has not
happened often, but Boston explored
the possibilities of this kind of recycling
in several locations. Rescuing New England's largest and most troubled project
started with demolition of most of the
vacant buildings. Abandoning the 1950s
scheme of twenty-seven nearly identical
oppressive buildings that ignored the
dramatic setting on Boston Harbor, a
new street grid and central tree-lined
mall was inserted. New housing was
oriented to harbor views and remaining
buildings were renovated, resulting in
1,283 units of mixed-income housing.
The final step in disassociating from the
past was a new name.

Harbor Point © Anton Grassl/Esto

THE
ROYAL MILE

In the English Colonies in America, governors ruled with the absolute authority bestowed by the King's Charter. Returning to London in 1674 after eight years in the Crown Colony, John Josselyn reported that Boston was "the Metropolis of this Colony, or rather of the whole Countrey…Their streets are many and large, paved with pebble stone…."

Outside Boston, the Colony's roads were rugged footpaths at best until 1700. Worse, the only land approach to the city was through windy tidal marshes. Arriving at the town gate weary and drenched with salt spray, the grim welcome was a gallows. Beyond it the fortified stone and brick gate sat on a rammed earth parapet.

Once admitted inside the gate, the aspect changed to an engaging array of shops and homes, closely built. The farmer with a land dispute, a merchant seeking a charter, or the wife of a convicted felon seeking reduction of his penance still had a mile to rehearse the petition, but they might easily have been distracted by amazing displays on all sides.

The ancient thoroughfare linking Province House with the town gate at the neck of the Shawmut peninsula survives as Washington Street, which is still lined with historic landmarks. Though the stocks and whipping post of Puritan Boston are gone, the Old State House survives. Inns and taverns that lined the lane in early Boston have disappeared, but housing is returning in the form of luxury towers.

While Washington Street has always been a busy commercial street, nearby Tremont Street was more ceremonial, with the Royal Custom House, the King's Chapel, and the Old Granary Burial Ground. In Victorian times Tremont became the center for entertainments including lecture halls, concert halls, and theaters. The Boston Museum, a gaudy multimedia display of curiosities, attracted throngs of people—including the awestruck young P. T. Barnum—to its building on Tremont Street between Court and School streets. From 1837 until 1899 Lorenzo Papanti taught Bostonians to waltz in his dance hall, famous as America's first spring-floored ballroom.

Downtown

Bromfield Street

A staging post for coaches was located here, conveniently near the royal governor's mansion. In the nineteenth century, as the stable yards were replaced by fine masonry buildings, the street's name was changed from Rawson's Lane. A hotel named Bromfield House stood next to 30 Bromfield.

1 28–30 Bromfield Street 🏛
1847–1848
Boston Landmark

:: Boston has many fine granite buildings from the first half of the nineteenth century, yet this one stands out for its stark perfection. Smooth granite Doric pilasters define the windows in a façade of enormous vitality. The attic has bold dormers giving views in three directions. Surely the original street-level façade was equally masterful but, alas, is long gone.

28–30 Bromfield Street

Detail, 28–30 Bromfield Street

2 Wesleyan Association Building

32–36 Bromfield Street
Hammet and Joseph Billings, 1870

:: Next door to the extraordinary 28–
30 Bromfield Street is this more conventional but fine French Second
Empire five-story building, also of granite. The central pavilion has a roof projecting above the mansard roof. The
second floor has bracketed lintels over
segmental arch windows. Both buildings face Province Street and the
Hutchinson Building, where the official
residence of the royal governor of the
Massachusetts Bay was built in 1679.
After the Revolution it was renamed
Government House. Only its garden
steps survive on Province Street.

Boston University's school of theology, formerly the Boston Theological
Seminary, was established at 36 Bromfield Street.

Wesleyan Association Building

Hutchinson Building, 32–54 Province Street

3 10 School Street

Kallmann and McKinnell, 1972

:: This site is oddly shaped and small,
precluding regular geometry. Moreover,
it faces two eighteenth-century landmarks: Old South Meeting House and
the Old Corner Bookstore. While making no attempt to emulate its important
neighbors, it does them no harm.
Rather, its bold openness and simplicity contrast with their solid decorated
masses. The award-winning design is
a brawny concrete structural skeleton
radiating from the center. Following
the curve of the lot, a glass wall is set
back behind the columns, exposing the
full interior to the street. Built for a
bank, it successfully adapted to a large
book emporium.

Cutting away the corner of School
Street opened views to the historic
landmarks across a triangular plaza.
At its center is a memorial to the Irish
famine.

10 School Street

4 Old City Hall

45 School Street
Gridley J. Fox Bryant and Arthur
Gilman, 1862–1865
Renovation: Anderson, Notter
Associates, 1969–1970
National Historic Landmark

Old City Hall

:: The first public school in America, Boston Latin, was built here in 1635, giving School Street its name. Statues of two of its prominent graduates, Benjamin Franklin and Josiah Quincy, stand before the elaborate French Second Empire City Hall that replaced an earlier one by Bulfinch. The base of the banded rustication supports two levels of pilasters and arched windows. An exuberant central pavilion rises several floors above the basic mass. A fine cast-iron gate and fence stands at the property line.

Many Bostonians remember the opulent interiors, with black-and-white marble floors and imposing staircases of iron and oak. The second-floor hall of aldermen, generously proportioned at 44 feet square with a 26-foot ceiling, had noteworthy ornamentation. On the fourth floor the Common Council Chamber had galleries on three sides. Unfortunately, the interior was considerably altered to accommodate modern offices and a restaurant.

5 Kirstein Business Branch

Boston Public Library
School Street at 20 City Hall Avenue
Putnam and Cox, 1930

Kirstein Business Branch

:: Despite its broad-sounding name, City Hall Avenue retains the narrow seventeenth-century scale of Boston's early streets. Now a pleasant pedestrian lane, it connects School Street with Court Street and the Government Center beyond. At its midpoint is the Kirstein Business Branch of the Boston Public Library, a Georgian revival brick box.

The façade is appropriately based on the central pavilion of Bulfinch's fine tontine crescent, built on Franklin Street in 1793–1794 and demolished about 1858. Pairs of Ionic pilasters and engaged columns supporting the entablature frame the central Palladian window. The segmental arch in the crescent was an open passageway. The rooms above it were built by Bulfinch as a gift to the Boston Library Society and the

Massachusetts Historical Society. Acting as both architect and developer, Bulfinch's idealistic generosity proved financially disastrous to him and his family.

6 Parker House
60 School Street

:: Boston's venerable hotel stands on the second site of the Boston Latin School. The first Parker House was built in 1855. After several enlargements, it was completely rebuilt in 1927.

Most of Boston's late nineteenth- and twentieth-century notables seem to have congregated where the Parker House roll and Boston cream pie were invented. The literary stars who regularly met here count everyone from Ralph Waldo Emerson to Henry Wadsworth Longfellow. Charles Dickens, Samuel Clemens, and Willa Cather stayed here for extended periods, and Edith Wharton used it as a setting in *The Age of Innocence*. There were even celebrity employees: Ho Chi Minh worked in the kitchen and Malcolm X was a busboy.

7 26–38 Summer Street
1874
101 Arch Street
Hoskins Scott Taylor & Partners, Inc., 1989

:: The Summer Street façade is the remnant of one of the commercial palaces built by dry-goods and clothing businesses after the Great Fire of 1872. Constructed of red brick with sandstone trim and decorative terracotta, it is an elaborate example of the panel brick style.

In the 1980s it was slated for demolition to make way for a tower. The compromise resulted in a "historic skirt" incorporating restored façades of the brownstone Gothic revival 101 Arch Street and cast-iron Long's building around a midblock tower. To create a

26–38 Summer Street and 101 Arch Street

larger site, a narrow old street was eliminated. The tower's lobby features the rough brick Bussey Place facade of Long's 1873 building with its five-story cast-iron spiral fire escape as a work of art. The tower can be identified on the skyline by its giant clock, postmodern pediment, and deco revival surface motifs.

The "odd-top" concept was imported from San Francisco. Eye-catching devices on the tops of new towers were intended to create an imageable skyline.

8 King's Chapel iii
58 Tremont Street
Peter Harrison, 1749–1754
National Historic Landmark

:: From King's Chapel one can see Old North Church in the North End beyond the 1960s City Hall. The vista linking these three important Boston landmarks was created intentionally as part of the urban design plan for Government Center. King's Chapel, founded in 1686 to serve British officers, first occupied a small wooden structure on the same site. The first Anglican church in Puritan Boston, it was quite unpopular with the colonists.

In 1749 the present building, designed by Peter Harrison, an architect from Newport, Rhode Island, was begun. Construction was financed largely by Charles Bulfinch's grandfather, who wanted to strengthen the Church of England in Boston. Other notable works by Harrison include the Redwood Library, Touro Synagogue, and Brick Market in Newport, and Christ Church in Cambridge. Harrison, who was known as a loyalist, later became a crown official in New Haven, where his house was wrecked by the Connecticut equivalent of the Sons of Liberty.

A fine example of American Georgian architecture, King's Chapel was conceived in the style of James Gibbs's churches such as St. Martin's in the Fields in London. Due to a lack of funds, the elaborate steeple was never built. To avoid disrupting services, the new building was built around the old one, which was then dismantled and tossed out the windows! Built of dark Quincy granite, the church has 4-foot-thick walls, surmounted by a hipped roof. The rectangular mass has two stories of arched windows on the north and south and a Palladian window on the east. Harrison's wood colonnade of Ionic columns was added around the square tower in 1785–1787.

Inside, pairs of large Corinthian columns, each carved from a single tree, project in front of the galleries. The main floor is divided into family pews that were owned or rented and were originally decorated according to the tastes of their owners. One canopied pew was reserved for the royal governors and later for important Americans such as George Washington. Slaves sat in the rear gallery on the cemetery side of the church, and condemned prisoners had a special pew to the right of the main entrance, where they came to hear a sermon before being hanged on the Common.

The fine tracker-action organ was

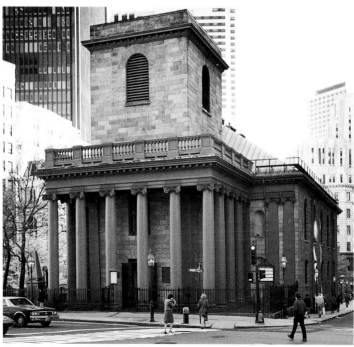

King's Chapel

built by Charles Fisk in 1963 and looks much like the church's 1756 English organ, said to have been played by Handel. The seventeenth-century pulpit is the one remnant of the earlier church. The largest bell was cast in England and hung in 1772. When it cracked, it was duplicated by Paul Revere, and it is still rung before every service.

After the evacuation of Boston by the British, few Anglican families remained. Under the leadership of James Freeman, a lay reader, King's Chapel (called Stone Chapel after the Revolution) became the first Unitarian church in America in 1789.

The cemetery adjacent to the church, dating from 1631, is the oldest in the city. Governors John Winthrop and John Endicott lie buried here. It is a setting in Nathaniel Hawthorne's *The Scarlet Letter,* and the 1704 stone of Elizabeth Pain suggested Hester Prynne's gravestone. In the heraldic banner on its left corner one can identify several letters, including an *A*.

9 73 Tremont Street
Winslow Wetherell, 1896
Renovation: Childs, Bertman, Tseckares, 1990

:: During the renovation of this prominent office building, the original large outdoor light court was filled in and the interior was completely rebuilt with a two-story lobby. The architects were sensitive to the building's surroundings; no historic narrow streets were eliminated and no tower was shoehorned in.

10 Tremont Temple
76 Tremont Street
Clarence H. Blackall, 1896

:: The famous early Boston theater, Tremont Temple, was built here in 1828. The theater presented many well-known actors and orators, including Charlotte Cushman, Fanny Kemble, Daniel Webster, and Edward Everett.

Tremont Temple

Jenny Lind sang here during her celebrated American tour. The current office and church complex carries a reminder of that temple at the top of its façade, which also has Venetian aspirations in its diamond-patterned stonework.

Another example of the temple-topped tall building may be found in the Danker and Donohue parking garage at 341 Newbury Street, which uses a simple suggestion of the Greek prototype.

11 David J. Sargent Hall, Suffolk University Law School
120 Tremont Street
Tsoi Kobus and Associates, 1999

:: This postmodern building has a façade dominated by a swelling semicircle supported on a colonnade. On the

Sargent Hall, Suffolk University Law School © Peter Vanderwarker

first floor the Adams Gallery provides space intended for public exhibits.

12 Orpheum Theater
Hamilton Place, off Tremont Street
Snell and Gregerson, 1852
Altered: Little and Browne, 1900; Arthur Vinal, 1904; and Thomas Lamb, 1915

:: The Old Music Hall, renamed the Orpheum Theater, was an important center in Boston's musical history. Boston University's college of music, the New England Conservatory, the Handel and Haydn Society, and the Boston Symphony Orchestra all began here. Tchaikovsky's first piano concerto had it world premiere in the Music Hall. Many other works had their American premieres here, including the second symphony of Brahms, which provoked much of the audience to walk out. Prominent Bostonians, however, stayed to hear the outrageous new music and were accused of being "Brahmins," later expanded to "Boston Brahmins." The name stuck, perhaps making this the origin of the term.

The 2,000-seat theater was extensively altered in the early twentieth century, becoming Boston's first cinema in 1915. Its organ went to Methuen's Memorial Music Hall, and the statue of Beethoven went to the lobby of the New England Conservatory. Later in the century it reverted to a performance theater for the Opera Company of Boston and others.

13 Old Granary Burial Ground 🏛
Tremont Street near Park Street
1660

:: Passing through the Egyptian-style granite gateway designed by that multitalented man, Solomon Willard, one enters one of the most illustrious cemeteries in the country, nestled among the tall nineteenth-century buildings that surround it. Not only Paul Revere but Samuel Adams, Gov. John Hancock,

Benjamin Franklin's parents, Peter Faneuil, and Robert Treat Paine lie buried here, along with many other patriots and victims of the Boston Massacre. The cemetery is named after the granary that once stood next to it on the site of Park Street Church.

Old Granary Burial Ground and Park Street Church

Granite detail, Old Granary Burial Ground

14 Park Street Church 🏛

Tremont Street at Park Street
Peter Banner, 1810

:: To make way for the church, it was necessary to demolish the 1738 granary, a long wooden structure designed to hold 12,000 bushels of grain in case of scarcity. Next to it on Park Street was the workhouse, a two-story 120-foot-long building that accommodated idlers, tramps, and vagabonds and kept them busy working.

The English architect Peter Banner adapted a Christopher Wren design for the steeple, which rises 217 feet. The church has always emphasized evangelism and missions; it founded the Hawaiian church that was responsible for the establishment of many other churches in the remote Pacific islands beginning in 1819. Several Boston families sent sons there to make their fortunes or to serve as missionaries. It was in Park Street Church that William Lloyd Garrison gave his first speech against slavery and where "America" was first sung. The location of the church came to be known as "brimstone corner" because of the zeal of its Congregational preachers. Also contributing to the name was the fact that gunpowder was stored in its basement during the War of 1812.

In the early twentieth century, a flower shop and tearoom were installed in the basement facing out on the Common.

15 Cathedral Church of St. Paul

Tremont Street near Winter Street
Alexander Parris, 1820
National Historic Landmark

:: Overshadowed by commercial buildings towering on each side, the Episcopal cathedral is a dignified gray granite Greek temple with an Ionic portico of Potomac sandstone. Bas-relief figures were never carved in the blank tympanum. The interiors are equally austere

Cathedral Chuch of St. Paul

and commanding. Ralph Adams Cram remodeled the chancel along classical lines in 1913–1927. Parris designed St. Paul's five years before Quincy Market, where he also saw fit to employ a temple façade, despite the utilitarian function of the market building.

Washington Street

Cornhill, Marlborough, Newbury, and Orange—the several original names assigned to the mile-long thoroughfare by the colonial governor had royal associations. The Earl of Marlborough stayed in Cole's Inn in 1637 and gave his name to the segment closest to the Governor's Palace. After the Revolution the street was given one name in honor of George Washington's 1789 Boston visit. In the nineteenth century Boston's "Fleet Street"—a concentration of publishers, booksellers, and newspapermen—clustered near the Old Corner Bookstore. Boston's publishers drifted away but the buildings remain and Nathaniel Hawthorne's *Twice Told Tales* brings Province House and other Washington Street landmarks back to life.

16 Spring Lane
off Washington Street

:: The Winthrop Building preserves one boundary of old Spring Lane. To modern eyes this is an intimate pedestrian way, but its dimensions were generous in Boston's seventeenth and eighteenth centuries. For more than two centuries, Bostonians came here to draw their water from a spring.

Mary Chilton, the only *Mayflower* passenger to leave Plymouth for Boston, lived on Spring Lane until her death in 1679.

17 Winthrop Building ⬛
276–278 Washington Street
Clarence H. Blackall, 1893
National Register of Historic Places

:: The ancient Spring Lane and Water Street dictated the Winthrop Building's slender curving form. It makes an incomparable contribution to the streetscape. Though discreetly applied, there is a wealth of ornamentation on this sliver building, including egg-and-dart moldings, pateras, and terra-cotta bands in the spur pattern on the third

Winthrop Building and Spring Lane

and fourth floors. This is probably Boston's first entirely steel-framed office building. It is best viewed from Water Street, looking uphill toward its narrow end and curving side.

18 Old Corner Bookstore ⬛
(formerly Thomas Crease House)
285 Washington Street
ca. 1718
Renovation and addition. 1828
Restoration: Francis N. Cummings Jr., 1960–1964
National Register of Historic Places

:: Before the notable literary history of this site began, the home of William Hutchinson and his controversial wife, Anne, stood here. Anne Hutchinson arrived in Boston in 1634, enthralled by the charismatic John Cotton, a Puritan divine. She became a self-made preacher and believed God revealed to her who among the colonists were pious and who were not. Many prominent Boston landowners and merchants supported her absolutist theology of the elect of God. She had the protection of the royal governor until Sir Henry Vane was succeeded by Governor Winthrop. He prosecuted her despite her popularity and wealthy husband. In 1637 she was excommunicated and banished for religious heresy. Her husband died in Rhode Island. Anne and six of her children were scalped by Siwanoy Indians in what is now the Bronx, New York.

The large Hutchinson home was destroyed in the fire of 1711, and a few years later (probably in 1718), an apothecary named Thomas Crease built the present house of rose red brick with a deep gambrel roof. The main room at street level was his apothecary shop, entered from Washington Street. A garden on the School Street side of the property gave access to his residence above. Several subsequent owners carried on their business in the shop and lived upstairs until it became the Old

Old Corner Bookstore

Corner Bookstore in 1828. A young publisher renovated the house, adding shop windows similar to those now present and the rear extension where the garden had been. He put his presses in the extension and a bookshop in the original apothecary shop.

Never again was the house lived in, but it had various commercial enterprises associated with publishing, most notable of which was that of Ticknor and Fields, the publishers of Longfellow, Lowell, Whittier, Holmes, Hawthorne, Thoreau, Emerson, Tennyson, Browning, Thackeray, Dickens, and Harriet Beecher Stowe. It was also here that the *Atlantic Monthly* became the most famous periodical of the day. The *Boston Globe* restored this important eighteenth-century landmark, to keep its history alive.

19 Old South Meeting House 🏛
Washington Street at Milk Street
Joshua Blanchard, builder, 1729
National Historic Landmark

:: A handsome spire of wood surmounts the balustraded square brick tower of the Wren-influenced Old South Meeting House, Boston's second-oldest church. (The oldest is Old North Church.) Originally this was the site of the garden of John Winthrop. It was here that the town meetings leading to the Boston Tea Party and the Revolution were held.

In 1670 the first meetinghouse of the South Church was built on the site, and Benjamin Franklin was baptized here in 1705, across the street from his

Albert Paley's forged iron gate, Old South Meeting House

Old South Meeting House

birthplace at 17 Milk Street. After the British occupation, the church was left in such poor condition that the congregation was unable to use it for five more years. It narrowly escaped destruction in the Great Fire of 1872, which stopped just short of it. Again in 1876 it came close to demolition for commercial development but was saved in the nick of time through a public appeal for funds to purchase the property. The Old South Association has operated Old South Meeting House as a monument and a museum of its role in American history since that time. The congregation has met in the New Old South Church in Copley Square since 1875.

20 Boston Post Building
Washington Street off 17 Milk Street
Peabody and Stearns, 1874

:: This building occupies the site of Benjamin Franklin's birthplace, which stood here until 1810, when it was destroyed by fire. The architects integrated a bust of Franklin, made to resemble stone, into the elaborate cast-iron façade.

21 Boston Transcript Building
322–328 Washington Street
Gridley J. Fox Bryant, 1873

:: In the late nineteenth century, "booksellers' row" was in this area and had the atmosphere of London's Fleet Street. Two newspaper publishers stood side by side, the *Boston Tran-*

script and the *Boston Post* at 17 Milk Street. The Boston Transcript Building is a mansard-roof granite structure with corner quoins and the suggestion of end pavilions on its Milk Street façade. Each floor is defined by projecting stringcourses.

22 Washington Street Downtown Crossing
Washington Street between Milk Street and Temple Place
Street improvements: Arrowstreet, 1975–1978

:: Fires plagued downtown Boston from its earliest days. Finally in 1803 a law was enacted requiring all buildings 10 feet or more in height to be made of brick or stone and roofed in slate or tile. Nevertheless, there were still conflagrations, the most spectacular being the great fire of November 1872, which destroyed a huge area bounded by Washington, Broad, Milk, and Summer Streets. Nearly the entire Washington Street district was built after the 1872 fire.

Several centuries of change on this pre-Revolutionary street eliminated almost every convenience for the throngs of shoppers on foot. By the 1970s the

Boston Post Building

Boston Transcript Building

shopping area had become architecturally complex, and the simplistic, automobile-oriented suburban shopping centers seemed awesome competition. The downtown renewal program limited vehicular traffic and focused on accommodating pedestrians. The departure of Jordan Marsh and Filene's created the impetus for rethinking Washington Street in the twenty-first century.

23 426 Washington Street
Daniel Burnham and Company, 1912
National Register of Historic Places

:: This was the last major building by the outstanding midwestern city planner and architect of the early 1900s, Daniel Burnham. The basically simple façade organization of corners, cornice, and base outlining the mass and providing a frame for the window infill reflects the influence of the Chicago school. The design emphasis was on bringing light into the store interior through the plentiful windows, although later alterations have blocked most of them. Burnham's gray-and-green terracotta ornamentation is far more traditional than his design conception. The subtle curve of the Summer Street façade enriches the street space.

When this was the Filene's Building, the store pioneered the discount marketing of overstock and previous-season merchandise in its Filene's Basement. Tales were told of luxury items bought the week of the final automatic markdown. All unsold goods were donated to charity.

24 450 Washington Street
Perry, Shaw and Hepburn, 1948–1951

:: Although built during the reign of the international style, this department store building displays distinct postmodernist tendencies in its medley of themes. Federalist window frames separated by roundels are plastered on the steamship-like brick mass. The delight-

Carillon, Filene's Building

450 Washington Street

ful corner at Summer and Chauncy Streets is the best part of the building. A three-story cylindrical window made up of small panes penetrates the concave brick corner wall. The concave corner is repeated at a smaller scale in the set-back mass and top band of windows. All is unified by the canopy as it sweeps around the corner. After Jordan Marsh closed, it became a Macy's.

25 Locke-Ober Café ▥
3 Winter Place off Winter Street
Founded May 1875
National Register of Historic Places

:: In the mid-nineteenth century Winter Place was lined with attractive row houses, parts of which remain. Louis Ober took over a new restaurant at

Locke-Ober Café main dining room in 1876 Courtesy Locke-Ober Café

number 4 in 1868. After arriving here with his parents, Ober, a French Alsatian, had tried many occupations—including barbering, taxidermy, and bookselling—but never before had he been associated with a restaurant. In 1875 he purchased the house where his restaurant occupied the cellar and the adjacent 3 Winter Place, renovated them both, and expanded his restaurant. Eben Jordan, founder of Jordan Marsh Department Store and a regular patron of the restaurant, loaned him the money, and the new establishmnet was opened under the name of Ober's Restaurant Parisien.

Ober and his family took up residence in the upper floors of the two houses. The restaurant prospered and grew in reputation, and a second renovation was undertaken in 1886, when all of the grandeur of the first floor that remains today was installed: the carved mahogany, the extraordinary German silver tureen and platter covers on counterweights, the brass fittings, and the leather-upholstered chairs.

In 1892 a competitor, Frank Locke, opened a restaurant at numbers 1 and 2 Winter Place. Two years later Ober abruptly sold his restaurant to liquor dealers and devoted himself to his many real-estate holdings. Locke's new restaurant was lavish in its decoration and furnishings: mirrors, glass, myriad electric lights twinkling everywhere, paintings, carved mahogany, plush and damask, and a waterfall! Over the entrance hung a large, intricately scrolled lock with FRANK inscribed on it, which inspired the lock-shaped sign of today.

Just two years later Locke died, and the same liquor merchants who had taken over Ober's restaurant now bought the extravagant competition next door and combined the two. A Parisian manager, Emil Camus, was hired but left Boston in 1896, only to return in 1901 and buy Locke-Ober's. He ran the restaurant in his imperious, taciturn style until 1939, establishing many of the menu items still enjoyed today.

Financial District

Unlike the old commercial centers of most American cities, Boston's financial district has not experienced wholesale destruction. It is the old seat of financial wisdom for the entire country. In the early nineteenth century, most Boston banks were located on State Street, where the city's commerce was first conducted. Since the seventeenth century, conservative New England trust funds have been managed on these streets.

It was particularly difficult for the authors to select sites for this book from the old mercantile, financial, and government areas, where many fine buildings represent two centuries of history. The most significant asset of the district is its complex pattern of streets surviving from the seventeenth and eighteenth centuries. The narrow, irregular streets focus on "squares" (usually triangular in shape) such as Winthrop, Church Green, Post Office, and Liberty Squares. Instead of following an abstract geometric concept such as a rectangle, the pre-Bauhaus architecture hugs the streets, creating odd-shaped buildings and wonderful townscape. It is exciting to wander through the area, following one's intuition, enjoying spatial sequences that are full of surprises.

Boston Brahmins invested heavily in cultural and educational institutions, which explains why Boston has more colleges and universities per capita than any other city. As technological innovations grew out of these farsighted investments, Boston pioneered venture capital and mutual funds as the next step in modernization.

Church Green
National Historic District

26 Church Green Building
105–113 Summer Street
Attributed to Jonathan Preston,
ca. 1873
Boston Landmark

:: The triangular intersection of Summer and Bedford Streets acquired the name of Church Green because of the fine granite church designed by Charles Bulfinch that stood from 1814 until 1868 where the Church Green Building is today. In 1838 E. C. Wines of Philadelphia voiced his impression of Summer Street: "Another pleasant feature of Boston is the many green and shady front yards which relieve and refresh the eye, as you wander through its winding streets. More or less of these are met with in every part of the city; but Summer Street, on both sides, is lined with them from one end to the other. This, to my taste, is decidedly the handsomest street in Boston. Town and country seem here married to each other . . ."

After the 1872 fire, the South Boston horse railway depot remained in Church Green, but residents left the area. It was rebuilt for business.

Church Green Building

27 Bedford Building

99 Bedford Street
Cummings and Sears, 1875–1876
Renovation: Bay-Bedford Company,
1983
National Register of Historic Places

:: The Bedford Building is a cornucopia of Ruskinian Gothic elements executed in red granite, white Tuckahoe marble, and terra-cotta panels. Finials crown each gable, and checker-work elliptical arches surmount the bays on the third floor. Windows are articulated with pilasters. The high first floor of rusticated blocks imitates a fortress, and the corner tower presents a clock.

Detail, Bedford Building

Detail, Bedford Building

28 Angell Memorial Park

Congress Street
Earl R. Flansburgh and Associates and
City Life Boston, 1982

:: The primary focus of the redesigned Post Office Square continues to be the Angell Memorial Fountain, designed by architects Peabody and Stearns as a watering spot for horses in 1912. The fountain is a memorial to George Thorndike Angell, a founder of the Society for the Prevention of Cruelty to Animals. A secondary focus is a "creature pond" made up of assorted bronze animals. Circular bands of paving radiate from the two foci, framed by a circle of inward-looking granite benches. The outer edges are bordered by greenery and long benches formed of steel rods, which are oriented to face the streets. The park is the result of several years' work by artists, designers, and the city. Four adjacent property owners maintain it.

29 Post Office Square Park ⅲ

Park structures and garage: Ellenzweig
Associates, Inc., 1990
Landscape design: The Halvorson
Company, Inc., 1991

:: Although a fifty-story tower designed by Edward Larrabee Barnes was proposed here, Post Office Square Park instead became a peaceful glade in the heart of the financial district on the site of a dismal old parking garage. Seven levels of underground parking accommodating 1,400 cars are buried beneath the park; the discreet, narrow entry ramps have retaining walls topped with cast-iron fencing. The garage excavation, 80 feet below grade, used an unusual "top-down" construction technique, as in a mining operation. After they completed the top level, they excavated and built the subsequent garage levels below.

Escalator access to the garage is in glass gazebos that look almost too delicate to withstand the fierce Boston winters. Other glass and lattice gazebos shelter a café and flower stand. No avant-garde minimalist tortured landscape here—people felt at home in the park from the day it opened. Among the plants are six specimen trees on permanent loan from the Arnold Arboretum. An open pergola, manicured grass, and precise border plantings create a lighthearted domestic style that is decidedly welcoming. The design gives special attention to accommodating users at peak lunchtime hours and offers a variety of seating arrangements for both individuals and groups.

Post Office

30 Post Office 🏛

Congress Street at Angell Memorial Park
Cram and Ferguson with James A. Wetmore, 1929–1931

∷ One of Boston's best art deco buildings, the Post Office exhibits several features typical of the style. Its windows are organized vertically into recessed slits between granite strips that soar skyward. As the top stories are approached, the hard mass of light gray granite softens with elaborate geometric steps and ornament. The ornamentation is a combination of geometric devices and stylized plant forms.

Window grille, Post Office

Post Office Square Park © Halvorson Design Partnership

The art deco style originated in Paris, the term deriving from the French *arts décoratifs,* and was the conscious rejection of all historic style and form. Its practitioners restricted themselves primarily to surface features and did not rethink the entire basis for architecture, unlike the founders of the international style.

31 Ames Building 🏛
1 Court Street
Shepley, Rutan, and Coolidge, 1889
National Register of Historic Places

:: The massive, solid appearance of the Ames Building is a reflection of its masonry bearing-wall construction, 9 feet thick at the base and decreasing as it rises. It is the second-tallest such structure in the world, and for several years it dominated the Boston skyline. The Romanesque revival motifs made famous by H. H. Richardson dominate the façade of this building carried out by his successors, Shepley, Rutan, and Coolidge, after Richardson's death in 1886. Three three-story Romanesque arches organize the lower stories,

which form a base for the upper levels. The middle five stories are unified by four arches that have no relation to the rhythm of the large arches below. The top two stories form a massive cornice, with a string of arched windows that almost create the effect of corbelling.

32 26 Court Street
Edward T. P. Graham, 1914

:: Banded rustication provides a base of suitable scale for the monumental classical revival office building. The entrance façade's enormous, six-story, engaged fluted Corinthian columns become pilasters on the side façade and support an equally gigantic architrave, frieze, and dentil cornice. Atop the cornice, four Amazons in flowing Greek drapery by sculptor Roger Noble Burnham once stood.

26 Court Street

Ames Building drawing by D. A. Gregs, ca. 1889 © Shepley Bulfinch Richardson and Abbott

33 Wigglesworth Building 🏛
89–93 Franklin Street at Winthrop Square
N. J. Bradlee and W. T. Winslow, 1873
Renovation: Shepley Bulfinch Richardson and Abbott, 1984
National Register of Historic Places

:: The five stories of this brick building undulate and turn, following the old

Lamp, 100 Franklin Street

Wigglesworth Building

Franklin Place *Massachusetts Magazine,*
February 1794

lanes and forming a dynamic definition of the public space. The curves of the façade are emphasized by the string-courses of the second, third, and fourth floors.

34 New England Press Building
off Franklin Street at 1 Winthrop Square
William Ralph Emerson and Carl
Fehmer, 1873
Renovation: Childs, Bertman, Tseckares
Associates, 1974

:: Henry Cabot Lodge was born in his grandfather's house on Winthrop Square in 1850. In the mid-nineteenth century Winthrop Square became an

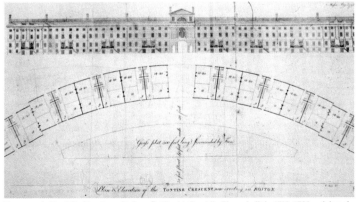

The curve in Franklin Street results from Bulfinch's Franklin Place, built in 1793–1794 and demolished about 1853. Massachusetts Magazine, February 1794

New England Press Building © Hutchins Photography, Inc.

important center of dry-goods merchandising. Not only was Beebe located at 1 Winthrop Square, but in the 1860s Eben Jordan and his partner had a six-story wholesale and warehouse building on Devonshire Street in the square. In 1872 the great fire started just behind the Beebe store on Summer and Otis Streets. After the fire, Beebe immediately hired Ralph Waldo Emerson's architect nephew and Carl Fehmer to design his new store on the same site.

The granite-faced result is quite unusual in its use of corner pavilions, which entirely overwhelm the low pediment marking the center of the façade. The cornice above the third story almost comes as a separation between two entirely different buildings, so dramatically do the two parts differ. The top two floors recall the visual tricks Emerson played with the "house of odd windows" and the Boston Art Club. The bracket falling down over the top edge of the pediment is extremely odd, and the low mansard roof behind it, which crouches between the taller hipped-roof pavilions, stranger still. The center column is almost unheard of. Emerson's work was daringly unconventional, and his playful attitude

toward architectural traditions astonishingly contemporary.

35 State Street Trust Building
Franklin Street at 75 Federal Street
Thomas M. James, 1929

36 101 Federal Street
Kohn Pederson Fox, 1988

:: The 1929 art deco jewel at 75 Federal Street presented a striking profile against the sky, a skewed stepped mass crowned by a gilded pyramid. It was an example of the willingness of developers to work effectively with the odd-shaped sites of Boston's financial district. But in the late 1980s the Boston Redevelopment Authority permitted the elimination of narrow streets such as Snow Street to create larger parcels. An L-shaped parcel was assembled here to accommodate the tower at 101 Federal Street, conceived

75 Federal Street

101 Federal Street © Cervin Robinson

as three crenellated shafts and joined on the first eleven floors to 75 Federal.

The fenestration of the limestone façade of 101 Federal Street takes its cues from its distinguished neighbor. The surface appliqué of raised circles and linear ocean-liner motifs in brushed aluminum does not compete with the low-relief figurative and floral bands concentrated between the second, third, and fourth floors of 75 Federal Street. Inside, the original art deco lobby of 75 Federal remains the star. Golden yellow and black marble are coupled with stunning gold and black elevator doors, with elevator control panels and signs lettered in the Broadway Engraved style.

37 United Shoe Machinery Building ⅲ

High Street at 138–164 Federal Street
Parker, Thomas, and Rice, 1928–1930
National Register of Historic Places
Boston Landmark

:: The house in which Trinity Church rector Phillips Brooks was born stood on this land before the large trapezoidal art deco building was built. It was the first art deco skyscraper in Boston and influenced the design of subsequent

Telephone Building, Cram and Ferguson, 1947

buildings in both Boston and New York City. Sitting on a base of limestone and black granite, the complex mass is clad in brick, stone, and metal. The various vertical blocks step back progressively toward a central tower capped by a truncated pyramid of tile. Boston's height-restriction law was revised in 1928 to allow taller buildings, provided they were stepped back in this fashion to allow more sun to reach street level. The elaborate art deco metalwork still survives in the lobby.

38 MBTA Operations Control Center

45 High Street
Leers Weinzapfel Associates
Architects, 1994

:: Growing from five stories to ten while operations continued on-site was the kind of tricky project these architects effectively undertook. A stylish new façade united the added floors to the original building it encloses.

United Shoe Machinery Building

MBTA Operations Control Center

39 125 High Street
Jung/Brannen, 1991

∷ This building meets the sky with a stepped top and the ground with an exterior arcade. The twin towers echo the art deco style, from the interior lighting fixtures and stair rails to the variations on diamonds and squares in the granite and gray-green metal façade decorations. Between the towers is an eight-story skylit atrium with space-frame glass roof and retail shops. This superblock development includes the reassembled workshop of Alexander Graham Bell, a renovated nineteenth-century building on Purchase and Oliver Streets, and a fire station.

40 International Place
High Street at Fort Hill Square
Philip Johnson and John Burgee, 1985, 1992

∷ From 1632 through the end of the eighteenth century, this was the location of one of the forts that defended the city from attack by sea. In the early 1800s the site developed into an attractive square surrounded by brick row houses, much like Monument Square in Charlestown today. From the park atop the hill merchants such as Thomas Handasyd Perkins and Harrison Gray Otis watched ships entering the harbor. By the 1850s, in response to the demand for housing from immigrant workers, property owners subdivided their homes into rooming houses and apartments. Conditions became so crowded and unhealthful that in 1866 the city began clearing the entire area for redevelopment for commercial use, and by 1872 the 80-foot-high Fort Hill itself was leveled.

Today International Place stands on an irregular 2.6-acre site that was part of Fort Hill. Crammed onto one of Boston's most historic sites, this 2,000,000-square-foot complex is a highly visible representative of the worst of the overdevelopment of the 1980s. Although the architects attempted to break down the mass into smaller units, a great failure was in not understanding the street space and how to humanize the buildings at the ground level. The façade of endlessly repeated Palladian windows with false mirror-glass arched tops is a travesty of the form. The project stimulated so much opposition and debate in the later 1980s that zoning and design review for downtown Boston was eventually modified.

41 International Trust Company Building
45 Milk Street
William Gibbons Preston, 1893
Enlarged: 1906
National Register of Historic Places
Boston Landmark

∷ The fire of 1872 stopped at the intersection of Milk and Devonshire Streets but burned part of the five-story iron building that stood on this site. The foundation and internal structure left standing were used in this 1893 building. The third, seventh, and eighth floors are horizontally organized by

International Trust Company Building

means of a series of arched windows, while the fourth, fifth, and sixth floors are unified vertically by attenuated engaged columns and decorative trim around the window groups. At the center is a shallow inset bay window of three stories. The eclectic façade is further decorated by Beaux Arts–style figures representing Commerce, Industry, Security, and Fidelity carved by Max Bachman.

42 Liberty Square
Earl R. Flansburgh and Associates, 1989

43 Appleton Building
110–114 Milk Street
Coolidge and Shattuck, 1924–1926
Renovation: Irving Salsberg, 1981
National Register of Historic Places

:: Liberty Square is a prime spatial asset of the old financial district, a human-scaled space tightly defined by historic buildings. The buildings form a charming ensemble framing this tiny intersection of six narrow seventeenth- and eighteenth-century streets. The old winding streets provide a sense of enclosure and create unexpected vistas, such as the view of the Batterymarch Building.

The Appleton Building's rounded

corner between Batterymarch and Kilby Streets dominates the square. The building is named for Samuel Appleton, a leader in the Boston insurance industry. The classical revival façade is

Liberty Square

Appleton Building

appealing in its simplicity. Window openings are organized into tiers, and three bands of small windows function as friezes and subdivide the façade. The largest window openings encompass two floors and add variety to the treatment.

Liberty Square was named at the end of the eighteenth century when a 60-foot liberty pole was set up to commemorate the Stamp Act riots that took place here in 1765. The area had been a center of Tory businesses, including the London Bookstore and British Coffee House, so it was a natural choice as the location of the new office for the king's stamp master. While the pre-Revolutionary era is no longer apparent, Liberty Square today retains a sense of its nineteenth-century character and a suggestion of its long importance in the financial and political concerns of the nation.

In the 1980s the city agreed to memorialize the October 1956 Hungarian Revolution, adding the 18-foot figural sculpture by Gyuri Hollosy to the 1,300-square-foot triangular park. The Hungarian revolutionaries tore the communist insignia out of the flag, leaving the hole represented in the sculpture.

44 Langham Hotel

250 Franklin Street at Pearl Street
R. Clipston Sturgis, 1922
Renovation: Jung, Brannen Associates, 1981
National Register of Historic Places
Boston Landmark

:: A 330-room hotel was inserted into the shell of the Renaissance revival Federal Reserve Bank, preserving and restoring selected spaces and elements such as marble door frames and mantelpieces, bronze-arched windows on the lower level, the painted dome ceiling and gold-leaf vaults in the foyer, and murals by N. C. Wyeth. Four extra floors of hotel rooms were added.

45 Richardson Block

109–151 Pearl Street
William G. Preston, 1873
National Register of Historic Places

:: Even though different owners built each building in this row, the entire block was designed as a unit. Built shortly after the Great Fire of 1872 that destroyed much of downtown Boston, it is a rare example of a marble-façade commercial block. The storefronts consisted of cast-iron piers with granite lintels but have been mistreated. Each of the upper stories is treated in a different manner; all feature incised ornament. The block was built for use by the leather industry, and until 1872 Pearl Street was a world center for boot and shoe manufacturing.

Richardson Block

William G. Preston designed several other Boston buildings, including the Museum of Natural History, the oldest section of the Hotel Vendome, and the International Trust Company Building.

46 Old State House 🏛

State Street at Washington Street
1712–1713, 1748
Altered: Isaiah Rogers, 1830
Restoration: George A. Clough, 1881–1882
Renovation: Goody, Clancy & Associates, Inc., 1991
National Historic Landmark
Boston Landmark

:: From the mid-seventeenth century onward, the old Town House and the State House that replaced it were the center of business and political life for the colony. The earliest marketplace of Boston was established on this site even before the building of the old Town House, which housed the market in its open first floor. As early as 1634 the stocks and whipping post of Puritan Boston were here. In 1772, just two years after the Boston Massacre occurred in front of the building, the first stagecoach to New York left from this important focus of Boston activity. In the nineteenth century it was festooned with advertisements and not treated as the inviolable historic masterpiece it is today.

Despite the tall office buildings around it, the Old State House remains the focus of State Street. Its most notable features include an ornate three-tier windowed tower, a segmental pediment over Corinthian pilasters, bull's-eye windows, and a gambrel slate roof concealed by stepped pedimented façades. Under the lion and unicorn, symbols of the crown, the Declaration of Independence was first read to Bostonians from the ceremonial balcony on July 18, 1776.

47 28 State Street
Edward Larrabee Barnes with Emery Roth and Sons, 1969

:: On a prominent site between the Old State House and the 1960s City Hall is Boston's first sleek, ultra-simple office tower. The base and top of the granite-faced structure are sculpted with shadowed openings, terraces, and arcades. The shaft's taut skin is severely detailed in glass and stone.

Old State House

48 Stock Exchange Building and Exchange Place

53 State Street
Peabody and Stearns, 1889–1891
Façade restoration and tower: WZMH Group, 1981–1984
National Register of Historic Places
Boston Landmark

:: The Stock Exchange Building stands on the site of the historic Bunch of Grapes Tavern, which was at the head of Long Wharf in the eighteenth century, the water's edge being near Kilby Street then. The tavern was the favorite meeting place of the patriots before the Revolution and was reputed to serve the best bowl of punch in Boston. The first Masonic lodge in the country was formed at the tavern in 1733, and in 1786 the Marietta Company, pioneer in the development of the Midwest, was organized there. Nearby was the first Boston house of John Winthrop (1588–1649), who was governor of Massachusetts for twelve years.

The main floor of the Boston Stock Exchange Building by Peabody and Stearns was a replica of the old counting house. Developers later bought the site intending to demolish the Exchange Building and replace it with a 1,000,000-square-foot tower. Preservationists protested but succeeded in only rescuing a 60-foot L-shaped portion of the pink granite façade facing State and Kilby Streets. The new tower, sheathed in a grid of reflective glass, is linked to the remains of the old building by a five-story atrium. An existing monumental marble staircase from the ground to the second floor is the focus of the restored space.

The project is an example of a nationwide wave of façade preservation, often at the expense of the substance of the building. The battle between the most profitable use of land and the retention of visible links with the past continues.

49 99 Summer Street

Goody, Clancy & Associates, Inc., 1986

:: This is one of many 1980s high-rise buildings that have tried to respect the historic scale and character of the street façades by setting the high-rise mass in the center of the block. The gray granite façade was inspired by the attractive row of nineteenth-century five-story buildings, as were the window proportions and the granite cornice lines. Even the hugely exaggerated pedimented dormers encompassing the upper floors derive from those of the historic five-story buildings at the base. But here the analogy is lost because of the enormous jump in scale. When 99 Summer Street is seen together with the old Church Green Building, the older structure is refined and comfortable in comparison to its overfed cousin.

50 125 Summer Street

Kohn, Pederson, Fox, 1990

:: This highly visible tower is a prime example of the "historic skirt" style of preservation and is one of the best arguments for it. The new tower takes its architectural cues from the restored historic façades at its ankles and tries to sit primly behind them by retaining enough roof over each façade for verisimilitude. The four five-story brick and granite commercial buildings dating from the 1870s were well worth saving. Each of the faces of the tower

99 and 125 Summer Street at Church Green

responds differently to its surroundings. Most striking is the 80-foot-diameter apsoidal form facing South Station. The granite and cast stone façade is liberally decorated with pediments, pilasters, cornices, moldings, and bay windows. While one normally experiences culture shock when entering a "façade wrap" or "historic skirt" lobby, the designers of 125 Summer Street happily settled on a nineteenth-century European-style interior arcade lined with shops.

Theater District

National Register of Historic Places

For more than a century this has been the theater district, but in the eighteenth century this area of Washington Street was lined with wharves. In fact, Josiah Knapp's wharf at the intersection of Washington and Stuart Streets was so close to the street that pedestrians complained about the bowsprits of his vessels obstructing the highway.

The first theaters were built near the 1852 Music Hall. Over the next decades a dozen theaters were built several blocks south on Tremont, Washington, and Boylston Streets. The district was so well identified and densely populated with theaters that there was a connecting network of underground passages and lobbies. In bad weather, patrons could walk from theater to theater without ever going out of doors. Boston's many theaters attracted famed actors from England and the Continent to its stages.

In 1900 there were thirty-one theaters in Boston with a total of 50,000 seats, but they were threatened by competition from coin-operated video machines, or "nickelodeons," the forerunners of movies that launched the careers of Sam Goldwyn and the Warner brothers in Boston. The nickelodeon ultimately meant the demise of many theaters not only in Boston but also across the country. With the closing of theaters, Boston actors began the flight to Hollywood in the 1920s. Some legitimate theaters, such as the Majestic, Plymouth, and Copley, were turned into movie houses, and D. W. Griffith's *Birth of a Nation* premiered in 1915 in the Tremont Theatre.

Today the district is active, with full seasons of plays, musicals, operas, and ballets on a number of historic stages. While New York City systematically demolished its best old theaters, Boston has cherished its architecturally significant collection of early theaters.

51 Procter Building
100–106 Bedford Street
Winslow and Wetherell, 1897
Boston Landmark

:: Certainly this is the most exuberant commercial building in Boston! It would almost be simpler to list the ornamental elements that are absent. The small cream-colored building is decorated with a frieze, a cornice, arches, finials, and cresting along the roofline, forming a delightful composition that is entirely unified despite the complex mixture.

Procter Building

52 Liberty Tree Block

Washington Street at Boylston
1850
Boston Landmark

:: On the second floor was one of the
many ballrooms constructed in the mid-
nineteenth century in Boston. The
ground floor held shops. The building's
owner, David Sears, commissioned ship
carvers Winsor and Brothers to create
the third-floor bas-relief that gave the
building its name. It represents the famous elm tree where the Sons of Liberty gathered. So powerful was the
symbol that the British cut down the
tree in 1775.

Boylston Building/China Trade Center

53 Boylston Building/China Trade Center

2–22 Boylston Street
Carl Fehmer, 1887
Renovation: The Architectural Team,
1987
National Register of Historic Places
Boston Landmark

:: The sandstone façade of this handsome building is dominated by Romanesque arches in three sizes. After
renovation, it helped improve the character of the former "combat zone."
Regrettably, however, it replaced
Bulfinch's market.

54 Young Men's Christian Union

48 Boylston Street
Nathaniel J. Bradlee, 1875
National Register of Historic Places
Boston Landmark

:: Growing out of an 1851 Harvard student group, the Christian Union moved
to Boston to serve a wider population.
Boston once had many of these Ruskin
Gothic buildings, but most have been
demolished. The tiers of pointed arches
are accentuated with stone voussoirs
and moldings in alternating colors. The
gable over the complex entrance composition is ornamented with crockets.

Young Men's Christian Union

The building originally had a tall clock
over the entrance.

55 "Piano Row"

Boylston Street between Tremont and
Charles Streets
National Historic District

:: "Piano Row" was the center for
piano building and music publishing in
Boston, indeed in the entire country, in
the nineteenth and early twentieth centuries. Besides the Steinert Building,
other piano buildings on Boylston Street
include the Wurlitzer Company at num-

ber 100, the E. A. Starck Piano Company Building at 154–156, and the Vose and Sons Piano Company at 158–160. The Mason and Hamlin Building at 146 Boylston Street has been demolished.

56 Colonial Theatre
106 Boylston Street
Clarence H. Blackall, 1889–1900
Interior decoration: H. B. Pennell

:: The prestigious Colonial Theatre, Boston's oldest theater to survive intact under the same name, has been the setting for countless theatrical debuts, from Sigmund Romberg and Irving Berlin to the Ziegfeld Follies and Rodgers and Hammerstein. The combination of a theater with an office building was a sophisticated idea that beautifully integrates prime street frontage for use as shops and lobbies for the theater and offices. Beyond the rather narrow street entrance are lavish gold theater interiors combining elaborate paneling and bas-reliefs executed by the John Evans Company with ceiling and wall murals.

Clarence H. Blackall made many important and lasting contributions to Boston architecture, including his fourteen theaters, the Winthrop Building and several other buildings. Blackall was a senior partner in the Boston firm of Blackall, Clapp, and Whittemore.

57 Steinert Hall
162 Boylston Street
Winslow and Wetherell, 1896

:: The oldest piano showroom in the country is housed in the six-story limestone and brick Beaux Arts–style façade with terra-cotta ornament and a copper cornice. The concert hall, Steinert Hall, now closed because of water damage, was a restrained Adam-style auditorium with fluted Corinthian pilasters separating round arches.

Tavern Club, Boylston Place

58 Boylston Place

:: Boylston Place is a remnant of the mid-nineteenth century that today finds itself a heavily used pedestrian access to the Transportation Building. Boylston Place is identified as the location "where football was born." A student of Mr. Dixwell's Private School organized the first game in 1860, using for a ball a rubber sphere that is in the collection of the Society for the Preservation of New England Antiquities.

The unusual brick building at 3 Boylston Place, built in 1888, has cast-iron ornaments on its arches and shallow copper oriel windows. An iron gateway to Boylston Place by artist-blacksmith Dmitri Gerakaris provides a fitting entry to the world of theater. A bronze frieze includes the musical dog, cat, rooster, and donkey from the tale of the Bremen Town Musicians. Lyres with a keystone of piano keys and theater masks span the arch. A 4-foot Tavern Club bear in top hat, tails, and evening cape stands at the gate holding back the folds of a steel curtain. Other motifs include the Swan Boats and bridge from the Public Garden, as well as ducklings from *Make Way for Ducklings*.

59 Tavern Club
4 Boylston Place, 1819
5–6 Boylston Place, 1844

:: The venerable Tavern Club has occupied its charming historic quarters in three brick row houses connected by a stucco structure over a carriageway since 1887. Number 4 is a Federal house with fanlight and side lights at its entry door, and numbers 5 and 6 are early Victorian row houses with oriel windows and dormered attics. The club's private performances of musicals and hilarious plays with club members as cast and backstage crew have been famous among generations of Bostonians. The presence of the club in this extremely urbane little corner of the theater district reinforces the character and special nature of the district.

60 Tufte Center for Performance and Production, Emerson College
10 Boylston Place
Elkus Manfredi Architects, 2005

:: An eleven-story addition to the Majestic Theatre contains a thrust stage theater, television studios, costume and stage design studios, schoolrooms, faculty offices, and an art gallery.

61 15–17 Essex Street
Attributed to Cummings & Sears, 1875

:: This handsome Romanesque revival building had flats on the upper two floors and commercial space below. For three decades Stern & Company, a sewing machine dealer, was here. A restaurant, then liquor store followed, and for too long it was empty and seemingly abandoned.

62 Transportation Building
Park Square
Goody, Clancy & Associates, 1983

:: The best thing about the Transportation Building is the way it hugs the bend of Stuart Street. In many other

Tufte Performance and Production Center
© Hedrick Blessing

15–17 Essex Street

areas Boston's unique street pattern has been negated by insensitive development that has imposed regular geometry onto the irregular fabric.

63 Jacob Wirth's 🏛
31 Stuart Street
Greenleaf C. Sanborn, 1844–1845
National Register of Historic Places
Boston Landmark
These simple dormered bowfront row houses are an important reminder of the mid-nineteenth-century architectural context that has disappeared from this area. The restaurant and bar, a

Jacob Wirth's

Boston institution, seemingly offer the same German sausage and sauerkraut menu and service in the same atmosphere as when they opened their doors in 1868. It is a rare opportunity to experience a genuine nineteenth-century restaurant interior that makes no compromise for the sake of modernity.

64 Emerson Majestic Theatre
219 Tremont Street
John Galen Howard, 1901–1903
Restoration: Elkus Manfredi Architects, 2002
Boston Landmark

:: The Majestic Theatre was particularly known for musicals and light opera. A lobby of Numidian marble was buried beneath an unfortunate redecoration, but the grand Rococo theater interior survives. Above the marquee, the exterior is extravagant and elaborate gray terra-cotta. Fluted engaged columns with composite capitals dominate the façade. Festooned windows are surmounted by oculi and high-relief masked faces as keystones. Beneath the balustrade a Vitruvian scroll band is executed in terra-cotta. The interiors were the first to use electric lighting creatively. Glass globes are integrated into the richly sculpted arches of garlands that enclose the auditorium.

The architect, John Galen Howard, founded the University of California School of Architecture in Berkeley. He had studied at MIT and the École des Beaux-Arts and worked under H. H. Richardson and McKim, Mead, and White. Eben Jordan, son of the founder of Jordan Marsh, built this theater as well as Jordan Hall and the demolished Boston Opera House. The theater was restored for Emerson College's performing arts programs.

65 Wilbur Theatre
246 Tremont Street
Clarence H. Blackall, 1914
National Register of Historic Places
Boston Landmark

:: The Wilbur Theatre combines Georgian, Federal, and Greek revival motifs. The building is topped by a cornice and balustrade with discreet Adam-style bas-relief and name panels. Three tall

Emerson Majestic Theatre
© www.brucetmartin.com

Wilbur Theatre

arched windows with iron balconies and carved tympanums appear on the second floor above the three classical pedimented entrances with Ionic columns *in antis*. The intimate 1,000-seat theater has had its share of important premieres, including the pre-Broadway trials of Thornton Wilder's *Our Town* and Tennessee Williams's *A Streetcar Named Desire* with the young Marlon Brando and Jessica Tandy. The interior makes economical use of space, with an attractive lower lobby that now serves as a café.

66 Shubert Theatre
265 Tremont Street
Hill, James, and Whitaker, 1908–1910
National Register of Historic Places

:: The small, elegant façade is beautifully proportioned and detailed with a Palladian window, carved tympanum, and modillion cornice. The wrought-iron and glass marquee was reinstalled when the original marble façade was replaced with limestone at the time of

Shubert Theatre

the 1925 widening of Tremont Street. The theater was named after Sam S. Shubert, eldest of three brothers in the theater business. He is often called the "founder of the independent theater movement." This theater's illustrious dramatic history has included performances by Sir Laurence Olivier, John Barrymore, Maurice Evans, and Sir John Gielgud.

67 Wang Center for the Performing Arts
(originally the Metropolitan Theater)
268 Tremont Street
Blackall, Clapp, and Whittemore, 1923–1925
Renovation: Jung/Brannen, 1982
National Register of Historic Places
Boston Landmark (interior)

:: The Metropolitan Theater, renamed Music Hall, was conceived and built as a true movie palace several years before Radio City Music Hall in New York City. The intention was to attract well over 4,000 people to each of four variety and film showings every day. Four lavish Louis XIV marble lobbies organized the flow of ticket holders and departing patrons, keeping them entertained all the while. Besides gazing at the opulent rose jasper pillars, marble doorways, and 1,800-pound gold-plated chandeliers, patrons could amuse themselves with bridge games, table tennis, dancing, billiards, and other activities until the next show began.

In 1932 a stylish art deco restaurant called the Platinum Salon was added. The theater was a miniature city that even had its own medical station in case of emergency. An immense Wurlitzer organ, an orchestra that rose out of the pit on an elevator, a corps de ballet, a one-hundred-voice chorus, and stars such as Jack Benny and Burns and Allen provided stunning reviews prior to the film showing, all for 35 cents, 75 cents on weekends. As the

Wang Center for the Performing Arts, the stage was enlarged in the late twentieth century to accommodate national and international opera, ballet, and theater companies.

68 Charles Playhouse
76 Warrenton Street
Asher Benjamin, 1838–1839
Renovation: Cambridge Seven, 1957–1966
National Register of Historic Places

:: Built as the Fifth Universalist Church in 1839 and later used by the Hebrew Temple Ohabei Shalom and the Scotch Presbyterian Church, this Greek revival structure took up a theatrical life only in the late 1950s. The pediment is supported on brick pilasters and two central Ionic columns on the second and third levels. The granite ground floor was built as two stores to provide rental income to the church.

69 Modern Theatre
523 Washington Street
Levi Newcomb and Son, 1876
Renovation: Clarence H. Blackall, 1913
Boston Landmark

:: The Modern Theatre, one of Boston's first movie theaters, was inserted into an already existing Victorian Gothic furniture store and warehouse built thirty-seven years earlier. The small theater seated 800. It had no stage and was designed with special concern for its acoustics with the assistance of Wallace Sabine, the Harvard professor who first applied scientific principles to the study of sound and space. The interiors were executed in the Renaissance style. The entrance façade features a large entry arch, originally open, framed by Corinthian pilasters with entablature. The first talking film, *The Jazz Singer,* was premiered at the Modern Theatre in the late 1920s.

Charles Playhouse

Modern Theatre

70 Opera House
539 Washington Street
Thomas Lamb, 1928

:: Benjamin F. Keith, for whom this theater was originally named, introduced the term *vaudeville* and the notion of continuous, wholesome entertainment at low prices. By the time of his death, he had a chain of more than 400 theaters. Part of Keith's success was due to his opulent theaters, which attracted respectable society and later became the model for movie theaters. The flamboyant Spanish baroque façade in terra-cotta is only a

Opera House

taste of what follows in the vast high-ceilinged lobby with its several levels of galleries and sixteen Italian marble columns weighing seven tons each. The auditorium is equally impressive and quite well preserved. The Opera Company of Boston used the theater for a number of years.

71 Paramount Theatre
549 Washington Street
Arthur Bowditch, 1930–1932;
restoration 1999
Boston Landmark

:: The theater was built exclusively for films, with a large Wurlitzer organ that could be raised to stage level for entertainment before the movie. The façade is dominated by a "moderne" sign, which was particularly effective when illuminated at night. Much of the deco marquee was removed. The art deco interiors have inlaid woodwork of polished Oriental walnut and African ebony with geometric aluminum and gold decorations. Many of the design motifs were used in other Paramount theaters across the country.

72 Hayden Building

681 Washington Street at La Grange
Street
Henry Hobson Richardson, 1875–1876
Restoration: Bruner/Cott, 1995
*National Register of Historic Places
Boston Landmark*

:: This too-long-neglected gem by
Richardson is in his characteristic
Romanesque revival style, using rusticated masonry except on the top floor.
There the simple brownstone slabs
contrast with the row of semicircular
arches uniting the third and fourth
floors and the wide segmental arch
spanning the second floor.

73 Human Nutrition Research Center

U.S. Department of Agriculture
711 Washington Street
Shepley Bulfinch Richardson and
Abbott, 1982

:: Part of the Tufts–New England
Medical Center, this high-rise research
facility contains a unique combination
of laboratories, housing for twenty-eight
volunteers who live at the center for six-
to twelve-month periods, recreational
facilities that include a swimming pool,
and extensive animal-research areas.

74 Boston Floating Hospital

New England Medical Center
Washington Street near Kneeland
Street
Perry, Dean, Rogers and Partners, 1982

:: The Rev. Rufus Tobey conceived the
Boston Floating Hospital in 1892. Tobey
had noticed how mothers fled the hot
tenements and took their young children to the harbor to refresh them in
the cool ocean breezes. By 1894 he had
raised enough money to launch a ship
that would cruise about the harbor in
the summer, exposing the children to
sunshine and sea air and providing
them with free medical care. Besides
the young patients, the Floating Hospi-

Paramount Theatre marquee

Hayden Building

tal had doctors, nurses, and often parents on board.

A larger ship was acquired in 1905.
When it burned in 1927, the institution
moved onshore. It has been a leader in
pediatric medicine since its founding
and originated the concept of family
participation in the care of the hospital-
ized child, as well as play programs and

the "whole child" approach to hospitalization. Although no longer waterborne, the hospital appears to float, supported by four truss arches spanning Washington Street.

75 Josiah F. Quincy School and Community Center
885 Washington Street
The Architects Collaborative, 1976

:: The original Josiah Quincy School was at 90 Tyler Street. This campus was conceived as an urban village. Its terraced rooftops form piazzas for play areas while a pedestrian street runs diagonally through the site, linking two neighborhoods. All of the community and shared facilities are located along this path. The school's four open-plan subschools are clustered around a media center and central support facilities. A porcelain enamel frieze derived from children's drawings decorates the exterior.

Chinatown 🏛

Beach, Hudson, Oxford, and Tyler Streets
National Historic District

The first Chinese in Boston came from California's gold rush. By 1875 some worked briefly in North Adams factories during a strike. When they lost their jobs at the end of the strike, they took the train into Boston and settled in this area near South Station. Ping On Street was the site of the city's first Chinese settlement.

A large Chinese gate is the formal entrance to Chinatown on Beach Street. Other signs of Asian culture can be found in the district's architectural motifs: Look for fu dogs, bronze Tao bas-reliefs, feng shui mirrors, decorative posts on upper floors, Wen-ti Tsen's mural, and a pagoda roof terrace on the top of the Chinese Merchants Association Building at the corner of Hudson and Stuart Streets. The Chi-

Josiah F. Quincy School © Steve Rosenthal

Gateway, Chinatown

nese restaurants on Tyler Street have flamboyant façades, and on the other streets many shops display Chinese groceries, fresh fish, spices, produce, pots and pans, and colorful clothing.

Chinatown has grown geographically and culturally and is now a focus for a variety of Asian cultures. Vietnamese grocery stores and the China Trade Center have changed the atmosphere of Washington Street in the former "combat zone," and Asian decorative arts shops have spread into the leather district.

76 **Old Josiah Quincy School**
90 Tyler Street
Gridley J. Fox Bryant, 1847

:: It was here that Horace Mann created the first school separated by grade with a separate classroom for each. When the school relocated to its Washington Street campus, the building became a community center for Chinatown. Later the Quong Kow School relocated here from the former garment factory at 18–20 Oxford Street that it had occupied from 1931 to 1984.

Bay Village

Boston Architectural Conservation District

The mudflats of Bay Village became buildable in 1825 with the construction of a dam near Fayette Street. The neighborhood's streets were laid out in the 1820s and 1830s. Fayette was the first street and had the first houses. Francis Lowell Cabot owned the largest lot in 1821, but it was cut in half by the building of Tremont Street. By midcentury many carpenters and artisans for Beacon Hill homes had built their own modest but finely crafted homes here. The original inhabitants of the area included housewrights, painters, ink makers, harness and rope makers, blacksmiths, surrey makers, sail makers, upholsterers, paperhangers, salt merchants, tin workers, toll gatemen, cabinetmakers, and musical instrument makers. It was known as the Church Street district, after the 1827 Presbyterian Church built on Church Street between Piedmont and Winchester Streets.

In the 1860s the neighborhood was unsettled. Sanitary problems caused by the filling of the Back Bay made it necessary to raise nearly 500 houses and commercial buildings. The first floors were raised to 18 feet above sea level and the backyards to 12 feet.

The colorful history of the area was enhanced during the 1920s, when there were known to be many speakeasies here. As the adjacent area to the north became a thriving theater district, actors and musicians flocked to the

neighborhood. Film distribution companies joined them. The name Bay Village was acquired in the late twentieth century and seems to fit its pleasant short streets of small brick houses.

The world-renowned Haynes Flute and Piccolo Company at 12 Piedmont Street is a twentieth-century continuation of the tradition of artisans in the area. Edgar Allan Poe may have been born at 62 Carver Street in 1809 while his parents were boarding in the house of H. Haviland, since demolished.

1 Bay Street

77 1 Bay Street
1830s

:: The only remaining house on Bay Street is this tiny but charming ivy-covered two-and-a-half-story house. Built on land once owned by Ephraim Marsh, it is a good example of carpenters' work of the 1830s. This small street inspired the new name of Bay Village after the historic name, Church Street district, had lost its appeal. Originally there were four brick houses on the east side of the street and six wood houses on the west.

Fayette Street Row Houses

78 First Corps of Cadets Armory iii

130 Columbus Avenue at Arlington Street
William G. Preston, 1891–1897
National Register of Historic Places
Boston Landmark

:: The First Corps of Cadets, which financed and built the armory, was a private military organization founded in 1741 to guard the governor of the Massachusetts Bay Colony. Reorganized in 1776, the corps was commanded by John Hancock. Its members served valiantly as patriots in a number of battles in the Revolution. During the Civil War and the First World War they continued to serve as a unit, and in 1940 they were inducted into the National Guard. In its role as a National Guard unit, the First Corps of Cadets no longer focused its activities on the armory. It stopped using the building altogether in the late 1960s, when the armory was taken over by the University of Massachusetts and used as a library.

The imposing and quite convincing rusticated granite castle dominates the intersection. It was located in this strategic military position in the center of the city population, near the railroad lines, and with visual communication to the State House for signaling. The structure is outfitted with the necessities of medieval defense, which must have fascinated the Victorians, considering the number of castlelike armories across the country. It has a six-story crenellated tower with machicolation and loop windows for arrows, and a winged dragon. Steel shutters were protection against musket fire. The drawbridge has corbel towers for "flank defense." But the moat it crosses is actually a light well for the basement drill hall.

After a period of neglect, the armory's drill hall began a new life as an exhibition hall, then a restaurant.

First Corps of Cadets Armory

79 Youth's Companion Building

195–217 Columbus Avenue and 140–144 Berkeley Street
Hartwell and Richardson, 1892
National Register of Historic Places

:: Built of brick and red sandstone, this building is in the Richardson Romanesque style. The façade is organized in

Youth's Companion Building, 195–217 Columbus Avenue

48–50 Melrose Street © Steve Rosenthal

tiers, and the windows are grouped in bays. The monumental entry portal with a deeply recessed entry beneath a coffered archway is reminiscent of similar entrances in Louis Sullivan's Chicago work. The Youth's Companion, founded in 1827, was published here. It was a weekly publication intended to entertain young people and to instill the values of education, work, thrift, and morality.

80 **48–50 Melrose Street**
1915
Renovation and addition: William Rawn Associates, 1985

:: The original two-story film studio was built when Bay Village was the center of Boston's film industry. The renovation added two residential floors with window size, placement, and style similar to the original façade. Subtle deviations were introduced: a small balcony and the grouping of arched windows that illuminate an interior two-story space. The façade contributes to the entire street without trying to imitate its Federal-style neighbors. The resulting mixed-use building is better than the original.

Salada Tea Building, Stuart Street entrance

81 **Salada Tea Building**
Stuart Street at Berkeley Street
Densmore, Le Clear, and Robbins, 1929

:: The elephants on the bronze doors of the Stuart Street entrance to the Salada Tea Building have long delighted children and adults alike. Sculpted by Caesar Caira, they were cast by the Gorham Company from a design by Henry Wilson, an English artist, and depict scenes from the tea trade. The doors won a silver medal at the Paris Salon in 1927. Elephant heads project in bas-relief from the capitals of the pilasters, and elephants in profile form the frieze above the doors. Above the frieze is a broken pediment with cyma reversa (double curve) molding. The classically inspired building appears to be a massive square block, but in fact it is triangular in plan.

SOUTH END

Boston Landmark District
National Historic District

In the eighteenth century the South End was ocean cove and tidal flats except for a narrow natural causeway along the Neck, as the approach to Boston was called. As talk of landfill began in 1801, Charles Bulfinch drew a plan for a neighborhood of oval gardens, treed streets, and row houses. Extensive land-making did not begin for three decades, and by then the Bulfinch plan had been set aside in favor of haphazard development.

To entice reluctant buyers, the city introduced developer incentives, reviving the abandoned Bulfinch idea of garden squares but without his organizational structure. Each time lots didn't sell on a newly plotted street, the city created an oval garden, with iron fencing, trees, shrubs, flower beds, a fountain, benches, paved formal walkways, and an arbor. This explains the curious randomness of the South End garden parks. Curves and jogs in long-established principal streets resulted in some irregular blocks. Since oddly shaped lots were the most difficult to sell, the city laid out rectangular lots around the perimeter of those blocks. The leftover parcels in the center became private open space, as in Montgomery Park and Carlton Park.

By the 1870s the streets of uniform row houses were occupied. The South End experienced a brief period of social prestige, especially Washington Street and Chester Square, which had the showiest houses. All the garden ovals were carefully tended. But in a few years the wealthier residents left for the newer Back Bay. The Panic of 1873 was hard on the South End, putting many speculatively built homes into foreclosure. Banks then sold them at bargain prices, further depressing real estate values.

At the same time thousands of new Irish immigrants needed housing. From the 1870s until the 1970s, the South End welcomed immigrants, factory workers, and others earning low wages. The bowfronts were converted to lodging houses and rented rooms. Basement diners served meals to residents who lacked any kitchen facilities. By the turn of the twentieth century there were not only Irish, but also Jewish, Italian, Chinese, Greek, Polish, Syrian, and Lebanese residents. Lithuanian Bernard Berenson and Lebanese Kahlil Gibran arrived with their immigrant parents as the neighborhood became more diverse. It was a dynamic period, incubating many institutions, including synagogues, a settlement house, Boston University Medical School on East Concord, and Boston College on Harrison Avenue.

By 1900 African Americans were relocating here from Beacon Hill, beginning an important new chapter in the history of labor, civil rights, and the arts. Jazz clubs abounded, and boardinghouses catered to musicians. Sleeping-car porters and domestics organized themselves, achieving landmark advancements. Dr. Martin Luther King Jr. lived on Massachusetts Avenue while attending Boston University and led his first march to Boston Common from the South End.

Urban renewal continued its destructive wave begun elsewhere in Boston in the 1950s, designating the South End blighted in 1963. That allowed the city to demolish 25 percent of the neighborhood, leaving in its wake empty wastelands or new projects that were unrelated to the Victorian heritage. Though many blocks of row houses were left intact, the garden ovals were modernized with simple fencing, unattractive lighting, and street furniture. Insensitive as the urban renewal was, in combination with the investment in the vast Prudential Center, the South End began attracting the middle class. When gentrification arrived in force, lower-income residents were increasingly squeezed out.

Massive public investment at the end of the twentieth century respected the neighborhood's Victorian origins. Putting the South End back together made it prestigious once more. Nowhere was the rebirth more dramatic than along Washington Street, the old cart track up the Neck.

---

1 Magna Building
49 Berkeley Street
1872–1873
Renovation: Boston Architectural Team,
1974–1975

:: This building was built for the Twenty-eighth Congregational Society of Boston, a Unitarian Church founded by Theodore Parker in 1845. Since then it has had many uses, including schools, a Jewish community center, and the Magna film company. It was then converted to apartments and commercial space.

A large hall originally on the second and third floors is expressed on the façade by a center window where the Star of David was added. The pronounced center pavilion rises above the wings. Exaggerated dormers pierce the mansard roof. The second story is notable for the shouldered architraves above the windows, while the third story features groupings of round-arched windows.

2 Site of Dover Street Station
Between Berkeley and Oak at
Washington Street
1899–1901

:: The elaborate copper-and-wood elevated station that stood here exemplified Victorian industrial architecture at its most charming. It served the first mass-transit line across the neck of the Shawmut peninsula. Nearby, the old Dover Street bridge had a floating bathhouse, the first public bathhouse in the country. There one could have a

Magna Building

towel, soap, and shower for 2 cents.

The town gate and gallows were located near here, a harsh welcome to anyone approaching Boston on foot or on horseback. Fortifications were built in 1710 of stone and brick with a parapet of earth. Guns included two twenty-four-pounders and eight nine-pounders. An earlier barrier had stood between what are now Dedham and Canton Streets, where seven men protected the settlement from Indians in the early 1630s.

3 Braddock Park
1870s

:: The last of the garden squares developed in the South End was called Berwick Park until 1918.

4 Pine Street Inn
60 Bristol Street
Edmund March Wheelwright, 1894
Renovation: Childs, Bertman, Tseckares,
and Casendino, 1980

:: Edmund March Wheelwright was
Boston city architect for a time and
worked successfully in several styles.
His many other Boston projects include
Horticultural Hall and the Longfellow
Bridge.

This former fire station was based
on the Palazzo Vecchio in Florence,
Italy. The medieval Italian fortress–
style design features a fine tower of
yellow brick with crenellated turret supported on machicolated projections.
The tower was used for drying hoses. A
smaller-scale, denser machicolation
forms the cornice of the five-story brick
building. The structure has been renovated to house the Pine Street Inn,
which provides food, shelter, and social
services to homeless men and women.

The inn stands adjacent to the site
of Crafts Wharf, where coal, lumber,
brick, and other building materials were
unloaded in the nineteenth century
for construction in the South End and
Back Bay.

Clarendon Park
Clarendon Park is an area of the South
End comprising Appleton, Warren,
Chandler, Lawrence, and Gray Streets.
It has been suggested that these attractive small-scale versions of Beacon
Hill houses were built to house servants of the prominent Beacon Hill families for whom the streets are named.
The predominant style is two- or three-
story brick with stone lintels, recessed
side entrances, and occasional oriel
windows and dormers. They make delightful single-family homes today.

5 Boston Ballet
Clarendon Street at Warren Street
Graham Gund Associates, 1991

:: This postmodern brick box was built
to house studios and practice rooms.
Bold window shapes characteristic of
Gund are scattered playfully on the
façade with cookie-cutter scallops and
a half-moon balcony on top. Four cast-
stone roundels at the entrance level illustrate the history of the Boston Ballet.

Pine Street Inn

Boston Ballet

Lawrence Street in Clarendon Park

6 No. 2 Clarendon Square
2 Clarendon Street
1868
Renovation: Notter Finegold +
Alexander, Inc., 1988

:: The former Clarendon Street Baptist
Church is one of a number of South End
churches that have become condominiums or apartments after being victim-
ized by arsonists or abandoned by their
shrinking congregations. It was here
the Blind Asylum movement originated
and the Chinese Sunday School was

founded in 1887. A new cast-iron fence
was added as part of the renovation.

7 Union United Methodist Church
485 Columbus Avenue
Alexander R. Estey, 1872

:: The congregation of the Universalist
Church was organized in 1817 in a
building on School Street. Like many
other churches, it followed its congregation to the South End, constructing
this building in 1872. The Gothic revival
country church of Roxbury puddingstone is a landmark for Columbus Avenue and Rutland Street. The angle
buttresses and fine broach spire of
stone are similar to that of another
Estey design, Church of Our Saviour
(Maclaurin and Rogers). Estey was also
architect of the original Emmanuel
Church.

8 Harriet Tubman House
United South End Settlements
566 Columbus Avenue at Massachusetts
Avenue
Stull Associates, 1974

:: The South End House was established in 1892 by Robert Woods to
serve the residents of the district that
had become almost exclusively lodging

No. 2 Clarendon Square

Union United Methodist Church

houses. In 1901 its name was changed. The headquarters for the United South End Settlements was built at a corner that was much in need of an activity and visual anchor on the site of the Hi Hat jazz club. The building is named after Harriet Tubman, "Moses of the South," who was a runaway slave and an organizer of the Underground Railroad.

9 Harriet Tubman Park
Columbus Avenue at Warren and West Newton

:: C. Cunningham's 1999 bronze bas-relief depicts Harriet Tubman (1820–1913) leading other slaves to freedom. Not satisfied with her own escape, she returned to the South nineteen times to bring others out on the Underground Railroad. On the same triangular park is the rededicated 1913 Emancipation Monument by Meta Veux Warrick Fuller.

10 Allan Crite Square
Columbus Avenue at West Canton and Appleton Streets
1986

:: The pedestrian zone honors the prominent artist of South End life near his home and research institute.

11 Concord Square
1860s

:: Because the city installed the garden after some lots had been sold and several houses had been built, only a narrow slice of land was available. A single row of trees was planted in 1866 and 1868, moving from Tremont toward Columbus Avenue as the houses were built and occupied. Identical brick bowfronts were built in contiguous groups. Depending on the developer, they are three or four stories plus dormered attics. All the front stairs originally had elaborate cast-iron balustrades. These squares exemplify small-scale English planning in contrast

Harriet Tubman House, United South End Settlements © Stull Associates

to the French organization of large-scale relationships as seen later in the laying out of the Back Bay.

12 Tent City
130 Dartmouth Street
Goody, Clancy & Associates, 1988

:: Tent City's name commemorates neighborhood residents who camped here in 1968 to protest the lack of affordable housing in the South End as it gentrified. It became a precedent for the city's later "linkage" projects, in which funds were siphoned off "high end" development to serve neighborhood needs—until the development bubble burst and developers had to be enticed with guarantees.

The design of Tent City attempts to relate to both the scale of Copley Place and the South End neighborhood by stepping down from twelve stories to four-story town houses. Twenty-five percent of the units were reserved for low income and 50 percent for moderate income; the balance are market-rate units.

13 Dartmouth Place
off Dartmouth Street

:: Off Dartmouth Street is this quiet cul-de-sac of brick row houses with second-story oriel windows and recessed entries a few steps above the street. The houses face the rear gardens of the Appleton Street houses.

14 Lawrence Model Lodging Houses
79, 89, and 99 East Canton Street
Charles K. Kirby, 1874–1875
109 East Canton Street: William F.
Goodwin, 1892
National Register of Historic Places

Lawrence Model Lodging Houses

:: These four buildings are the oldest remaining examples of philanthropic housing in Boston, built in accordance with the will of Abbott Lawrence to provide "Model Lodging Houses . . . to be let to poor, temperate and industrious families . . . at reasonable rents." Lawrence, who died in 1855, was a leading Boston industrialist and philanthropist and founded the textile city of Lawrence, Massachusetts. As ambassador to the Court of St. James in 1849–1852, Lawrence may well have seen the first model dwellings for the poor built by the Birkenhead Dock Com-

pany in 1847. Such housing was later built for the prince consort by the Society for Improving the Condition of the Labouring Classes and displayed at the Great Exhibition in London in 1851; Lawrence participated in planning the American section of the Great Exhibition.

Each of the buildings has a name: Lawrence, Abbott, Bigelow, and Groton. The five-story structures are built of brick in a simplified French mansard style and contain twenty apartments each. The interior stairways are entirely of cast iron with lattice-patterned risers. The quartet offers an instructive contrast to the nearby twentieth-century public housing.

Dartmouth Square condominiums, the former Rice School, renovated by Arrowstreet, 1985

15 Sculpture Courtyard
500 Harrison Avenue

:: Historic industrial artifacts from surrounding nineteenth-century mills are deployed as sculptures.

16 West End Street Railway Central Power Station
540A Harrison Avenue
William G. Preston, 1889–1892

:: This complex of brick gable-roofed sheds is handsomely detailed with arches and corbels. In 1889 the West End Street Railway had 9,000 horses and more than 1,500 wagons in a transportation system covering Boston and adjacent towns. Henry Whitney had already decided to experiment with electric streetcars. Closed streetcars were a great improvement, especially in cold weather. They replaced the horsecar lines when he built the largest electri-

West End Street Railway Central Power Station

Immaculate Conception Rectory

cal traction system in the world to supply the power. After 1899 the station supplied power to the Boston Elevated Railway. When it was replaced by a power station on East First Street in South Boston, it served as a maintenance facility.

17 Immaculate Conception Rectory
761 Harrison Avenue
Louis Weissbein, 1858–1860

:: Boston College was founded in this imposing brick building with classical ornamentation. The windows on the first story are set within recessed arches and have prominent keystones. On the second and third stories the windows are capped with pediments of contrasting styles. The center of the façade is adorned with a gabled pavilion the full height of the façade, with a projecting Corinthian portico over the entrance. Both the college building and the church next door have a bold cast-iron fence with arch-and-circle motif capped with an inverted-arch cresting.

18 Immaculate Conception Church/ Jesuit Urban Center
771–775 Harrison Avenue
Patrick C. Keeley, 1858–1861

:: The Irish immigration into Boston and the South End brought with it the need for new Catholic churches. Patrick C. Keeley designed many of these for the diocese, including the gigantic Cathedral of the Holy Cross. Here he has freely combined classical, Renaissance, and Georgian themes. Ionic pilasters ornament the corners and frame each of the three entrance portals of the granite church. The central Palladian window and all the tall arched windows feature the Gibbs surround of blocks of stone punctuating the jambs. The side façade is particularly animated, with Ionic pilasters and seven tall windows with the Gibbs surround. The central pavilion projecting from the

Immaculate Conception Church

façade is unusual in placing a broken pediment in front of a larger pediment.

In 1987 Boston preservationists were outraged when the church leaders suddenly ripped out much of the historic interior to accommodate offices. The Boston Preservation Alliance prepared petitions to the Vatican and to the Boston Landmarks Commission to preserve the interior, and a group of preservation leaders worked with the church over several months to develop a compromise solution. As a result the church interior retains some important features.

19 Boston City Hospital
818 Harrison Avenue
Gridley J. F. Bryant, 1862–1864

:: Boston City Hospital was built as a symmetrical group of brick buildings with dormered mansard roofs. The central focus for the grounds was the administration building, with its Ionic pilasters, a raised formal stair of white marble, and two domes. Curving arcades connected the central building with medical and surgical pavilions, boiler house, laundry, isolating wards, outpatient clinic, morgue, and kitchen. Some sections of the original hospital remain here and there within the hodgepodge of later construction, but the classical architectural composition is gone.

20 Chester Square
Massachusetts Avenue
1850–1851
Destroyed: 1952

:: Where today there are six lanes of traffic, in the nineteenth century there was a spacious park where children tended by nursery maids rolled hoops or sailed boats in the fountain. The square has lost not only its fountain and white-aproned nursery maids, but much of its beauty and serenity as well.

Boston City Hospital, original building *King's Handbook*

This, the largest of the linear gardens, was a 400-by-164-foot oblong with rounded ends. Twenty-foot-wide malls extended beyond Tremont and Shawmut Avenues. Strolling paths were laid out in a large figure-eight pattern centered on the fountain. Trees, shrubs, and flower beds were planted, and four large gates were installed to keep out all but the immediate neighbors. The city even copied the Louisburg Square fencing and lampposts in an effort to import the prestige of that address.

All this was done before anyone came to live in Chester Square. In contrast to Franklin Place and Louisburg and Pemberton Squares, all the South End garden squares were created at city expense to entice reluctant buyers to the area. Despite the sales incentives, barely half the lots sold at the city's auction. After significant price reductions, they did sell. By 1860, the new houses were among the most opulent residences in the entire South End, and only a few empty lots remained on Chester Square.

Flat-fronted houses with lanterns are flanked by bowfronted houses that step out to enclose the curves of the former park. When it was built, the street was not a thoroughfare, for Massachusetts Avenue did not yet cross the Charles River into Cambridge.

21 John Farwell House
558 Massachusetts Avenue,
Chester Square
1860

:: John Farwell, a sea captain and abolitionist, hid fugitive slaves in his house, which had a hidden staircase and tunnel for that purpose. On the first floor was a large double salon with dining room behind. The butler's pantry was adjacent to the dining room and above the street-level kitchen. Above the main floor were a sitting room at the rear and a library at the front of the house. The top two floors were bedrooms.

22 Rutland Square
1860s

:: Rutland Square is a narrow park, just a slice down the center of the street with trees and grass enclosed by an iron fence. The Italianate bowfront houses do not step back to enclose the square, yet the slender park creates an important focus and identity for the block, accomplishing far more as green space than its meager size would add to the roadway. The houses and park are more modest versions of those in the large South End squares. Yet like the others, it is city property and was created and maintained by public funds and foundation grants. Its development matched neighboring Concord Square.

23 Blackstone Square Elementary School
380 Shawmut Avenue
Stull Associates, 1976

:: An upper-level "street" connects the five autonomous houses of the Blackstone School, which are expressed in the building's form. It also provides access to central facilities, including a media center, science center, cafeteria, community clinic, auditorium, music and seminar rooms, and gymnasium.

24 The St. George and The Columbia
St. James Street at Franklin Square
Hacin + Associates, 2001

:: Both buildings combine market rate with affordable condominium units for their client, Tent City. Architecturally, they sought inspiration from the massing and scale of earlier Franklin Square buildings. By clinging to the sidewalk they restore the enclosure of this side of the square.

Blackstone Square Elementary School
© Peter Vanderwarker

Reed Block and Thayer Pedestrian Street

Cyclorama Building

25 Reed Block
Thayer Street off Harrison Avenue

∷ The handsome brick Reed Block has granite lintels and sills on the upper-level windows. The large window and door openings of the first floor are framed in rock-faced granite posts and beams. Two cast-iron posts are placed between every pair of granite posts. The six-over-six-paned windows of wood contribute to the dignity of fine nineteenth-century industrial buildings such as these. To create an enclave of galleries, Thayer Street was land-scaped and paved with parallel brick paths at two levels.

26 Cyclorama Building
Boston Center for the Arts
539 Tremont Street
Cummings and Sears, 1884
National Register of Historic Places

∷ The large steel-trussed dome of the central building in this complex origi-nally housed the enormous 400-by-50-foot cyclorama painting of the Battle of Gettysburg, which attracted throngs of people. It is now exhibited in Gettys-burg, Pennsylvania. Boston's famous prizefighter John L. Sullivan also fought here. From 1923 to 1968 the structure served as the flower market. The highly decorative kiosk on the plaza was a cupola on a now demolished 1850s orphanage in Roxbury by Gridley J. F. Bryant.

27 St. Cloud Hotel
567 Tremont Street
Nathaniel J. Bradlee, 1870
Renovation: Arrowstreet, Inc., 1987

∷ This French Academic–style building stood vacant for several years before the Boston Center for the Arts reno-vated it, along with the adjacent 1879 Mystic River Bridge Building, as retail space and condominiums. A penthouse was added to the St. Cloud Hotel, and three stories were added to its neighbor. The tall, elegant first-floor retail areas with black cast-iron columns serve a vibrant neighborhood.

St. Cloud Hotel

28 Villa Victoria

Tremont, Shawmut, West Dedham, and West Newton Streets
John Sharratt Associates, 1972–1982

:: Villa Victoria is the result of collaboration between a far-sighted architect and a Puerto Rican neighborhood that fought demolition and displacement by urban renewal. After many years' work and the total involvement of the community in the planning and development process, the result was affordable housing for 3,000 residents in more than 600

Typical entrances, 690–692 Tremont Street

Tremont Street

units. The nineteenth-century street grid was replaced with two loops in a superblock, importing the suburban cul-de-sac. Town houses and mid-rise and high-rise structures offer choices integrated with shops and recreation space. The tile mural celebrates the life of a fighter for Puerto Rican independence.

29 Taino Tower
640 Tremont Street
1872
Reconstruction: Communitas, Inc., 1991

:: The congregation that built a brick Romanesque revival church here in 1872 began on Shawmut Avenue in 1845. At about the same time, H. H. Richardson designed his Romanesque Brattle Square Church (now First Baptist Church), also with a square campanile-like tower. The tower here had a short spire with pinnacles when it was built. The strong form of the tower is now capped by machicolation with loop windows punctuating its faces. A blind arcade runs above the three round entry arches.

The church was hit by arsonists and stood vacant for several years. It was reconstructed as affordable housing incorporating the old tower and part of the entrance façade.

30 New Hope Baptist Church
740 Tremont Street
Hammat Billings, 1862

:: Roxbury puddingstone was used in this unusual Gothic revival church with two towers, each with a spire, lancet windows, and buttresses. To add to the architectural ambiguity, two entrances and two nave forms are melded together.

Shawmut Congregational Church before the fire *King's Handbook*

New Hope Baptist Church

31 Piano Craft Guild

(originally Chickering Piano Factory)
791 Tremont Street
Edwin Payson, 1854
Renovation: Gelardin, Bruner and Cott, 1974

:: The expansive Chickering Piano Factory was built with massive timber posts and beams and a skin of brick punctured with hundreds of windows. Jonas Chickering's 400 employees produced sixty pianos a week in this steam-powered factory. Besides Chickering, Spencer's Repeating Rifles was here, manufacturing weapons for the Civil War.

The 1974 recycling of the building as artists' housing was one of the earliest and largest mill conversions in Massachusetts. One hundred seventy-four residential units for both living and working were created. Emphasis was on open, rough spaces with low rents suited to artists' needs. Public areas, including a gallery, mailroom, laundry, and commercial spaces, are clustered around the entrance.

32 Union Park ⅲ

Garden and lots, 1850
Houses, 1854–1859

:: Union Park is one of the loveliest green spaces in the South End and was the first square in the neighborhood to be completed. Two fountains, flowers, mature trees, and an iron fence make a lush foreground for the large Victorian brick row houses. The façades that step forward to enclose the park heighten the sense of a special place. The ornamental ironwork is noteworthy, especially the simple modern pattern at 23–25 Union Park and the Victorian cast-iron fence, balcony, and stair rail at 43 Union Park, which are found in many nineteenth-century ironwork catalogues.

In a sudden rush, most of the houses were sold between 1885 and 1890. There was almost a frenzy to get out of the South End by then.

Piano Craft Guild © Bruner/Cott

Chickering Piano Factory Courtesy Bostonian Society

33 Row Houses
1–34 Union Park Street

:: Just beyond an attractive triangular park with Victorian cast-iron fence is a long and striking row of brick flats. Upper-level windows have stone lintels composed of prominent stepped voussoirs. Entries are recessed, with large semicircular stilted arches with prominent keystones. Separate doors to each building's basement, first floor, and upper floors are contained within its archway.

34 Site of Female Asylum until 1910
1008 Washington Street

:: Boston had a tradition of social service institutions created and run by women, such as the Women's Educational and Industrial Union in two houses on Boylston Street facing the Public Garden and the Student's House at 96 The Fenway. Before either of those, the Female Asylum was founded in 1800 to care for orphaned girls.

The Washington Street El
The Washington Street El, built in 1899–1901, was one of the first elevated train lines in the country. Noisy, dirty, and a blight to the area through which it clattered, it nevertheless provided a scenic ride, with views across rooftops and down into gardens. It was demolished when the Orange Line was

Union Park

Union Park Houses

1–34 Union Park Street

Washington Street El (demolished)

rerouted along the Southwest Corridor.

The demolition of the Washington Street El resulted in an overly wide, empty-looking street, demanding a green boulevard of trees down the center. Neighborhood activism brought considerable public investment in a rebuilt roadbed, widened sidewalks paved in brick, Victorian lighting standards, history kiosks, and transit shelters. Shabby Washington Street emerged glamorous, its boarded-up old buildings restored and desirable again.

Condotopia

From the beginning, the South End was a focus of civic concern and investment. Sometimes this focus was damaging, as in the mid-twentieth century urban renewal bulldozing of vast stretches of brick row houses. The land stood vacant or was rebuilt in unsuitable midcentury styles.

Despite some previous traumatic transitions, more change was brewing in SOWA (south of Washington) at the turn of the millennium. With the Silver Line came a whole new look for Washington Street. Suddenly, expensive condominiums and lofts sold out before they were even built. The hot condo market threatened to overwhelm the neighborhood, which had been eco-

nomically diverse for more than a century. Affordable housing was incorporated into the development plans to maintain the neighborhood's existing population while increasing it.

Many of the mid-rise condominium buildings were loft units, including Laconia Lofts (2000), The Savoy (2002), Willows Passage Lofts (2002), 160 East Berkeley Street (2004), and Gateway Terrace (2005). Often they incorporated abandoned buildings or adopted local materials and detailing to better fit into the South End.

35 160 East Berkeley Street
off Washington Street
Hacin + Associates, 2004

:: Two-level apartments were accomplished by using a skip-stop corridor system like that first seen in Boston in the Fenway Studios.

36 Laconia Lofts
1200 Washington Street
Hacin + Associates, 2000

:: The design borrowed materials from the district's historic mill buildings and added a flying canopy above the roof deck to create a very identifiable silhouette. Inside are a combination of affordable artists' live/work spaces and market-rate lofts.

37 The Savoy
1280 Washington Street at Savoy
1890
Restoration and addition: Hacin + Associates, 2002

:: Though the nineteenth-century building had gone through significant alterations by the time the St. Vincent de Paul shop closed there in 1999, the façade was incorporated into the new mid-rise mixed-use structure. Also constructed in 2002 was Willows Passage Lofts on the site of the mid-nineteenth-century Hotel Continental.

Gateway Terrace © Hresko Associates

The Lofts at 160 East Berkeley Street
© Richard Mandelkorn

Laconia Lofts

38 Cathedral of the Holy Cross
Washington Street at Union Park Street
Patrick C. Keeley, 1867–1875

:: As the diocese grew rapidly in the mid-nineteenth century, the Cathedral of the Holy Cross on Franklin Street became inadequate. The archbishop then built this cathedral, the largest Catholic church in the country at the time. In fact, it is as large as Westminster Abbey. Situated in the South End, where large numbers of Irish Catholic immigrants had settled, it is on the site of the old town gallows. It is 364 feet long and 120 feet high and accommodates 3,500 people seated or 7,000 standing. The Gothic revival complex of Roxbury puddingstone consists of the sanctuary and its chapels, the vestry, and the chantry with its own small organ. The mansion of the archbishop was also here at one time. The two towers were intended to have spires, but these were never built.

39 Blackstone and Franklin Squares
Washington Street at West Newton Street
S. P. Fuller, 1825
Renovated: 1911, 1960s, 1980s

:: Boston emerged without a single example of a Bulfinch crescent, and this was the last and largest lost opportunity. As unpaid chairman of the Board

Blackstone Square

Cathedral of the Holy Cross *King's Handbook*

of Selectmen, he submitted a "Plan of the Land on the Neck" in 1801. Bulfinch's oval park had crescents of row house lots facing and enclosing the garden. Once again, as in Beacon Hill's Louisburg Square, it was Fuller who drew up a more rudimentary plan to replace Bulfinch's graceful vision. This pair by Fuller is two squares with diagonal paths crossing in the center, where each square has a fountain.

40 Row Houses
Washington Street at West Newton Street, on Blackstone Square

:: The former elegance of Blackstone Square is reflected in this row of brownstone houses with unusually fine façades of pedimented formal windows. Pilasters frame the doors, and the cornices are heavily bracketed.

41 Franklin Square House
Washington Street at 11 East Newton Street
Maturin M. Ballou, 1868
Renovation: Boston Architectural Team and Archplan, 1976

:: When built as the St. James Hotel, this was one of the most luxurious hotels in Boston. It had reading and smok-

Franklin Square House

ing rooms, clubrooms, ladies' and gentlemen's parlors, a telegraph office, billiard rooms, and two steam-powered elevators. Since the social position of the South End neighborhood never reached expectations, however, the hotel suffered. In 1882 the 400-room hotel was taken over by the New England Conservatory of Music. In the twentieth century it was converted into apartments for senior citizens. The large brick building is in the French Second Empire style, with central and corner pavilions, mansard roof, and quoins defining each of the pavilions.

Behind Franklin Square House is what remains of the South Burying Ground. In 1810 it was a potter's field where the poor were buried without gravestones. Across Washington Street from the cemetery was O'Donnell's Gymnasium, where John L. Sullivan trained to become a prizefighter.

42 Minot Hall
1721–1735 Washington Street
1859
Renovated: Hresko Associates, 1998

:: The recovery of this architecturally unique landmark is very welcome. The deeply scooped mansard roof has three forward chimneys. Its refined brick façade is composed of double-arched inset panels framing tiers of four windows each. The third-floor hall is reflected in the double-height windows. The ballroom originally had gilded mirrors and a musicians' balcony. The street-level shop fronts were reconstructed in period style.

43 Fragments of Deacon House
1667 Washington Street
Charles Lemoulnier, 1848

:: Fragments of the most extravagant house ever built in the South End still stand at the end of a gated walk between two newer buildings. Peter

Rutland Washington Community Garden

Minot Hall

Minot Hall, detail © Blind Dog Photo

Parker built the house for his daughter and son-in-law, Mr. and Mrs. Deacon. It was decorated in the greatest elegance he could import from France. Among the furnishings were the eighteenth-century carved and gilded panels from the Hotel de Montmorency in Paris that are now exhibited in the Museum of Fine Arts. The original entrance to the house was on Concord Street through double gates guarded by a porter's house, which gave access to the court-yard and porte cochere. Within the house were an imposing entrance hall with a gallery at the upper level, draw-ing room, ballroom, dining room, and boudoir.

While the couple was visiting Eu-rope, Mr. Deacon died, and although Mrs. Deacon returned to Boston to live in her grand house, it never again pos-sessed the gay and glamorous atmos-phere of earlier years. After the death of her father, the house and its contents were sold at auction in 1871. In the 1880s it became an art school and later a dance hall. The last time the authors saw the ballroom, with its columns, gallery, and frescoed ceiling, it was being used for paint storage.

Deacon House in 1850s *Gleason's Pictorial Drawing Room Companion*, 28 January 1854

44 Allen House
1682 Washington Street
John J. McNutt, builder, 1859

:: This beautifully restored brownstone mansion reveals its first owner in the unexpected mixture of elements, from lion's paws on the porch columns and windows to oriels popping out unexpectedly under elaborate mansard central gables with pear-shaped windows, corner quoins, and a rusticated basement level. Aaron Allen was a furniture dealer and borrowed ornamentation from furniture of the period for his lavish home.

When Allen moved to the waterside of Beacon Street in 1871, the house became the Central Club. Ten years later the Central Club, too, moved to the Back Bay. In 1894 the house was sold to the Catholic Union of Boston, which added a bowling alley in the basement and an auditorium in the rear. For decades it seemed unloved. Cheap shacks were tacked onto the front, and the domed lantern disappeared from the roof. At its lowest point it was boarded up and abandoned—hard to imagine as it now stands with a fine lantern and cresting.

45 Porter Houses
Washington Street at East Springfield Street
1806
Renovation: Hacin + Associates, 2001

:: The exterior of this very old attached pair of houses was reconstructed after almost two centuries of hard use and alterations. The interiors were adapted to contemporary use.

West Brookline Street
West Brookline Street has a strong and harmonious pattern of brick bowfront row houses with paired entrances and front steps. Several of the small front gardens have attractive Victorian iron fences.

Allen House

Porter Houses © Richard Mandelkorn

46 Concord Baptist Church
West Brookline Street at 190 Warren Avenue
1869

:: In the 1870s many Baptist congregations moved to the South End. This brick church features a portico of three pointed arches and pointed arch win-

Concord Baptist Church

dows. A large octagonal clerestory is centered above the auditorium.

West Canton Street

Brick bowfronts with projecting wood cornices line the street where a number of South End lodging houses were first converted back into single-family residences in the 1970s. At number 197 a contemporary ornamental iron fence is a design by the authors for Victorian Boston houses. Its simple curves and alternating spacing of verticals can be executed economically with today's materials and technology.

47 All Saints' Lutheran Church
85 West Newton Street near
Tremont Street
1899

:: This rather austere German Gothic–style church of buff-colored brick features a square tower with angle buttresses and a shingled spire above a belfry with plate tracery. A small octagonal tower at the right side of the entrance has a smaller spire. Albert Schweitzer once played an organ concert in this church.

48 Pullman Porter House
218 West Springfield Street
ca. 1860

:: In the 1920s black porters slept here on their days off. Meetings of the Brotherhood of Sleeping Car Porters were held on the parlor floor.

49 Langham Court
26 Worcester Street
Goody, Clancy & Associates, 1991
Garden court: Halvorson Design
Partnership, 1991

:: This mixed-income housing development occupies one acre with a five-story block fronting on Shawmut Avenue and four-story blocks articulated like town houses on West Springfield and Worcester Streets. Concealing the

West Canton Street

All Saints' Lutheran Church

Langham Court

parking underground made possible the landscaped garden court that gives Langham Court its distinction. It occupies part of the site of the demolished 1870 Commonwealth Hotel, later renamed the Langham Hotel.

50 **Worcester Square**
Garden and lots, 1851
Houses, 1861–1864
Garden renovation: 1980s

:: In the nineteenth century Worcester Square was the jewel of the South End. This perfectly proportioned garden square was terminated by the colonnaded and domed Boston City Hospital, creating an impressive architectural composition. Symmetrical mansarded bowfronts with identical high balustraded entrances formed unbroken rhythms embracing the garden and side carriage lanes.

To provide more space for cars, the garden lost 14 feet of its width. The fine nineteenth-century iron fence was dismantled. While the garden is narrower, the 15-foot fountain basin was removed and replaced with a much larger one in the 1980s. The 25-foot basin completely altered the proportions of the landscape design. In place of the tiered Victorian cast-iron fountain is a modern sculpture with several low jets in the basin. Removing the original granite basin was antithetical to landscape preservation but might

have been justified by substituting a smaller one to fit the reduced dimensions of the garden.

The houses have been altered as well. The double basements made conversion to lodging houses or other multifamily partitioning easy. Some scalloped stairways have been destroyed, as well as doorways and mansard rooflines. Nevertheless, the remains of Worcester Square's quiet dignity can be felt.

Roxbury Neck

The Neck connected pre-Revolutionary Boston with the rest of the colony. At the mainland end the Neck widened out gradually from the swampy causeway to become solid land. This narrowest part of Roxbury was closely associated with the South End from the time of the first landfills. Today the South End flows seamlessly into this corridor with major arterials and public transit.

51 **Roxbury Community College**
1234 Columbus Avenue
Stull and Lee, Inc., 1987

:: This linear arrangement of red brick gable-roofed buildings serves a student body of 1,500. The major buildings are the Student Center, the Academic Core, Media Arts, and Administration.

52 **Madison Park High School**
75 Malcolm X Boulevard
Marcel Breuer and Tician Papachristou, 1974–1978

:: The old Madison Park neighborhood of Roxbury was cleared to provide a ten-acre site for the Madison Park High School, built as a "magnet school" to attract students from all parts of the city into voluntarily integrated education. The interconnected buildings housed some of the most outstanding

Worcester Square

Roxbury Community College © Ben E. Watkins

facilities of any high school in the country at the time. The gymnasium building includes three swimming pools and a rowing tank. The performing arts building includes a music department with a fine organ, harpsichord, concert grand piano, numerous harps, and sound-proofed practice rooms. The media arts component includes a complete television station with full capabilities to videotape, edit, and broadcast throughout the school.

Swimming pool, Madison Park High School © Gatje, Papachristou, Smith

The architectural solution is a precast concrete–faced group of tightly linked buildings somewhat fortresslike in appearance. There are six interconnected components: an administration/library building with mechanical services and main kitchen, two classroom buildings, a gymnasium, a science center, and a shop/drama building.

Madison Park Town Houses (John Sharratt Associates, and Glaser, De Castro, Vitols, 1975–1983) © Nick Wheeler

53 **Hubert H. Humphrey Occupational Resource Center**
55 New Dudley Street
Shepley Bulfinch Richardson and Abbott, 1980

:: In contrast to the fortresslike high school next door, the Occupational Resource Center is more open. A pedestrian mall allows students and visitors views into each work area through glass partitions. Eight types of work environments for vocational training are provided, including television studio, bank, automotive shop, retail store, supermarket, and restaurant.

Hubert H. Humphrey Occupational Resource Center © Nick Wheeler

Boston Police Department Headquarters
© Peter Vanderwarker

Dimock Community Health Center © John Grummitt, Platt Anderson Freeman Architects

54 Boston Police Department Headquarters
1 Schroeder Plaza, Roxbury Crossing
Stull and Lee with Primary Group, 1998

:: Suggestions of Le Corbusier's 1932 Swiss Pavilion might be imagined in the blue glass archway and first-floor inset.

55 Cary Cottage
Dimock Community Health Center
55 Dimock Street
Cummings and Sears, 1872
Renovation: Platt Anderson Freeman Associated Architects, 2005
National Historic Landmark

:: On a small picturesque hill of scattered puddingstone outcroppings, the first hospital run by women was established as the New England Hospital for Women and Children. Over the next decades a number of hospital structures surrounded the original cottage, converting the nine-acre site into a campus-style group of medical buildings. All have been renovated or restored and adapted to contemporary needs, except the 1890 power plant by Cummings and Sears that still operates.

BACK BAY

National Historic District

The Back Bay and South End neighborhoods are the largest surviving examples of Victorian architecture in the United States. In contrast to the South End's many garden squares and informal street patterns, the Back Bay has a formal grid conceived on a French model with no garden squares. Its highly structured street pattern offers visual rewards through symmetry and allows the richness of the architecture to dominate. The focal open space is the wide grassed boulevard down the center of Commonwealth Avenue, whose length compares with the promenade vistas of grand French chateaux.

Despite the variety of Victorian styles and elements, controls on height, setbacks, and materials created the harmonious streetscape. Each house contributes to and benefits from the cumulative effect. As one progresses from Arlington through the alphabetically arranged cross streets to Hereford and on to the Fens, the glorious parade of architectural styles reveals the history of Victorian taste through the second half of the nineteenth century.

Filling the Back Bay tidal flats became inevitable when the Cross Dam (along Massachusetts Avenue) and Mill Dam (along Beacon Street) were unsuccessful as sites for mills due to the sluggish flows. The captured

Back Bay Victorian Promenade

stagnant water at the foot of Beacon Hill gave off a stench so offensive it could not be ignored. The gigantic operation took thirty years. Trains ran every forty-five minutes from West Needham with 2,500 cubic yards of gravel—the equivalent of two house lots—a day. By 1870 there was land as far as Dartmouth Street. Not until the late 1880s had filling reached the Fens.

Among the many architects offering plans for the new land, Arthur Gilman, an admirer of French architecture, was selected. Architect George Snell and landscape gardeners Copeland and Cleveland contributed suggestions to the final design of Commonwealth Avenue. Back Bay was an immediate success, though some locations were more desirable than others. Wags claimed that Beacon Street had the old rich and Marlborough had the old poor, while the new rich resided on Commonwealth Avenue and the new poor on Newbury Street!

Back Bay in progress, 1872 Boston Athenaeum

George Santayana, philosopher, novelist, and poet, lived at 302 Beacon Street (now demolished) as a boy. In *Persons and Places* he described Back Bay life in the 1870s:

> The water in 1872 still came up to Dartmouth Street and to what is now Copley Square. Among the provisional features of this quarter were the frequent empty lots, ten or fifteen feet below the level of the street. These lots were usually enclosed by rough open fences, often broken down at the corners, from which a short cut could be made diagonally to the next street; and by this we schoolboys were quick to profit, for a free run on rough ground amid weeds and heaps of rubbish . . . Our twin houses had been designed to attract the buyer, who might sell his bargain again at a profit if he didn't find it satisfactory; and this was precisely the ground on which my mother was persuaded to buy her house, not expecting a financial crisis and a sudden but prolonged disinclination on the part of the consumer to buy anything that he didn't need. The advantages in our house were in the first place social or snobbish, that it was in Beacon Street and on the better or fashionable waterside of that street; which also rendered every room initially attractive, since it had either the sun if in the front, or the view if in the rear . . . The grand attraction of the water view was marred by two counter-effects discovered eventually by enthusiastic purchasers . . . Under your nose was a mean backyard, unpaved, with clothes or at least clotheslines stretched across it . . . Under your nose too—and this was the second counter-effect—rose now and then the stench from mudflats and sewage that the sluggish current of the Charles and the sluggish tides that penetrated to the Basin did not avail to drain properly.

Outstanding architects of the late nineteenth century designed Back Bay houses that spared no effort and no expense. They became models for home design across the country. Most Back Bay houses are 25 or 26 feet wide and four or five stories plus basement. The typical floor plan has a side entrance and a stair hall, leading into the first-floor front drawing room and rear dining room and pantry. On the higher-ceilinged second floor, the piano nobile, were the formal drawing room and library. Above that were one or two floors of family bedrooms. Servants' quarters were at the top, under the mansard roof, in the French manner. Kitchen and laundry facilities were in the basement. From the beginning most houses had furnaces, but these were quite inefficient and heated only the first two floors. Upper floors relied on fireplaces with coal grates. By the mid-1870s many houses had gravity hot-water heating systems throughout the entire house.

While some neighborhoods gentrified, Back Bay de-gentrified after the Great Depression. Many families were forced to sell their homes, which were too grand and too expensive to maintain. Developers converted some into apartments; others became schools or dormitories for the city's numerous colleges. Often this process was very destructive. Kitchens, bedrooms, and bathrooms were sometimes added to each floor by chopping up the grand old rooms and tearing out plaster and wood ornamentation. Palatial staircases were boxed in or totally eliminated. Valuable wood paneling was painted or ripped out to expose brick walls, thus reducing acoustical privacy between buildings. Other houses became lodging houses, with the new owners occupying several of the original formal rooms and renting out the rest of the house to elderly or working people. Happily, most of these retained their original architectural character, although often in a somewhat shabby state.

With the condominium craze of the 1970s, developers once again hit the neighborhood. They ripped out elaborate French moldings, walnut and mahogany doors, plaster ceiling and wall ornament, and period hardware. Wood-framed windows were replaced with inappropriate aluminum frames. Suburban-style roof decks, wedged into every possible corner, increased the sale value of units but destroyed the French mansard roofscape. While façades survived, there was no mechanism to preserve the Back Bay's incomparable interior architecture. Huge profits were made while violating the architectural heritage. Yet despite a few wayward high-rise buildings, the large-scale design of the district was strong enough to survive as one of the loveliest neighborhoods in the country.

Back Bay

1 1–3 Arlington Street

Attributed to Gridley J. Fox Bryant, 1861

:: Arlington Street originally presented a handsome continuous mass of five-story brownstone houses with mansard roofs from Beacon Street to Boylston Street. Built in the French academic manner then current in Paris, these three houses are massed together to give the impression of a single monumental edifice. The center house is slightly set back and the two end houses frame it with their projecting mansard roofs. Each story has a different window treatment expressing the relative importance of each floor, with tall, heavily pedimented windows on the second-floor drawing rooms and small arched dormers on the top-floor servants' quarters. The stone of the ground floor is rusticated in contrast to the smooth finish of the upper floors.

2 8 Arlington Street, 1870

9–11 Arlington Street, 1861
11 Arlington Street renovation: Perry, Dean, Rogers and Partners, 1982

:: Although somewhat altered on the exterior and greatly altered inside, the group of four houses at 8–11 Arlington still provides the kind of architectural continuity the developers of the Back Bay had in mind. Like 1–3 Arlington Street, these four separate houses are treated as one mass.

The *Atlantic Monthly*, first published in 1859 by William D. Ticknor and James Thomas Fields and originally located above the Old Corner Book Store on Washington Street, was at 8 Arlington from 1920 until the 1980s. Among its notable founders were James Russell Lowell, Ralph Waldo Emerson, Henry Wadsworth Longfellow, and Oliver Wendell Holmes.

3 Harbridge House

12 Arlington Street
Arthur Gilman, 1859–1860

:: The grandest of the surviving houses on Arlington Street, this five-story mansion in the French-Italian academic style is faced in smooth Nova Scotia sandstone. The projecting central entrance bay contains the entrance portico with oriel window above. Its architect, Arthur Gilman, also designed the Arlington Street Church.

8–11 Arlington Street

Harbridge House

In 1893 Mrs. J. Montgomery Sears, patron of the arts and social figure, joined this house to the immediately adjacent 1 Commonwealth Avenue in order to accommodate her growing art collection and to make a palatial music room on the second floor. The entrance of the Commonwealth Avenue house was removed. Mrs. Sears's notable visitors included pianist Ignace Paderewski and violinist Fritz Kreisler, as well as Prince Henry of Prussia and painter John Singer Sargent, who painted a portrait of Mrs. Sears and her daughter in the house. The sixteen Tiffany windows date from 1898 to 1933.

4 Ritz-Carlton Hotel

15 Arlington Street
Strickland, Blodget, and Law, 1927
Addition: Skidmore, Owings & Merrill, 1981

:: For generations this was a quintessential Boston institution, neither glamorous nor imposing. Of late it wants to be both. Regency blends with art deco in low-relief fans over the second-story windows and the lobby's plasterwork ceilings. Art deco murals and other details in the café were removed during the 1985 redecoration. Art deco never predominated in Boston, but Strickland, Blodget, and Law used the style effectively in several other buildings: the Katharine Gibbs School at 0 Marlborough Street (the 1929 Junior League Building) and two storefronts at 69 and 83 Newbury Street.

5 Arlington Street Church ⅲ

Arlington Street at Boylston Street
Arthur Gilman, 1859–1861
National Register of Historic Places
Boston Landmark

:: Arlington Street Church, the first building in the Back Bay, is considered the "mother church" of Unitarianism in America. William Ellery Channing,

Arlington Street Church

noted Unitarian minister and abolitionist, served here for many years. His statue stands at the corner of the Public Garden facing the church. The church reestablished its political activist roots with antiwar protests against the Vietnam and Iraq wars.

Influenced by the work of English architects James Gibbs and Christopher Wren, the building is topped by an elaborate tower of many levels. The simple brownstone exterior is organized by two-story pilasters capped by a deep entablature. The pedimented front portico contains a tall round-arched entrance flanked by single unfluted Corinthian columns. Inside, the interiors recall the light, airy white spaces of many New England churches. The sixteen Tiffany windows date from 1898 to 1933. Some of Solomon Willard's interior carvings for Bulfinch's Federal Street church (demolished) are preserved here and display a rudimentary knowledge of the Gothic style. Willard was the multitalented designer of the Bunker Hill Monument.

6 118 Beacon Street
Little and Browne, 1907

:: Reminiscent of McKim, Mead, and White's Pickman house at 303 Commonwealth Avenue built twelve years earlier, this grand classical revival bowfront house of granite is occupied by Fisher Junior College. The broad bow with center entrance is unusual for Back Bay architecture. Some of the interiors retain their elaborate plasterwork, moldings, and pilasters. The original grandeur of the house is apparent in the hall's dramatic coiled marble staircase.

7 Gibson House Museum and Victorian Society, New England Chapter ⫿⫿
137 Beacon Street
Edward Cabot, 1860
Boston Landmark

:: Here the visitor has a rare opportunity to see the interior of a Back Bay row house just as it was left by its last occupant, Charles Hammond Gibson, who established it as a museum. The nineteenth-century interiors are intact and reflect the typical middle-class Back Bay house of the period. This and the house next door at 135 Beacon were built together by related families, the Russells and the Gibsons. Although the exteriors are nearly identical, the interiors are quite different.

8 147 Beacon Street
1861

:: The strange asymmetrical locations of the corner windows on the third and fourth floors give the front corner bedrooms sliver views of the Public Garden and Common. Forty years later the entrance was lowered to the ground level and moved to the Berkeley Street side, creating a bigger garden in front of the house and the convenience of immediate entrance from the street.

118 Beacon Street

Gibson House Museum

9 Fuller Mansion, Emerson College Abbott Library
150 Beacon Street
Alexander Wadsworth Longfellow, 1904

:: Isabella Stewart ("Mrs. Jack") Gardner's father built her a house here in 1861. In 1880 the Gardners bought the adjacent house at 150 Beacon and connected it with their own house to make space for a music room. It was here that John Singer Sargent painted Mrs. Gardner's famous portrait and she assembled the greatest private art collection in Boston. In 1902 she moved to her newly completed "palace" in the Fenway.

E. S. Draper demolished both houses in 1904 and built the double-width Italian Renaissance revival house that became the residence of Alvan T. Fuller, governor, congressman, founder of Fuller Cadillac Company, and art collector. Its rusticated ground floor and two-story fluted Ionic pilasters embrace the second and third floors. A handsome high wrought-iron fence with stone gateposts adds to the monumental effect.

148 Beacon Street

10 Brownstone Gothic House
165 Beacon Street
1869

:: Victorian Gothic never took hold in Boston as it had in England. This house is one of four examples in the Back Bay, the others being at 76 and 80 Commonwealth Avenue and 117 Marlborough Street. Only the first- and fifth-floor windows are actually pointed; the rest have flat tops with pointed arches and tracery infill panels above. The top-floor gingerbread gable is reminiscent of many wooden Victorian cottages.

11 Goethe Institute
170 Beacon Street
Ogden Codman, 1900

:: Built of light sandstone in the Italian Renaissance revival manner for E. H. Gay, this house somewhat resembles the Fuller mansion at 150 Beacon Street. Arched windows appear both on the rusticated first floor and on the second floor with its window balustrades. The heavily ornamented interiors are still visible in the foyer and first-floor rooms. The house was designed as a setting for Mr. Gay's extensive collection of Chippendale furniture, the story

Fuller Mansion

154 Beacon Street

Goethe Institute

of which is told in Gay's book *Chippendale Romance*.

The first floor was executed in the English style of the early eighteenth century and features elaborate plasterwork done by Italian workmen over a two-year period. The fine doors are of flame mahogany and have brass hardware from France. A music room was in the front and joined the library in the middle of the floor. The dining room was in the rear.

The second floor was in the Adam style of the late eighteenth century and had a handsome game room overlooking the river with a billiard table and exceptional English doors dating from 1785. A bedroom was in the front. The upper floors are substantially altered to serve as the German Cultural Center for New England, a branch of the Goethe Institute in Munich.

12 180 Beacon Street
S. J. Kessler, 1965

:: All of the design standards established by the Back Bay's fine Victorian architecture were violated with this building's height, bulk, and extensive use of metal and glass. Ornament is studiously avoided, and the elegant, cool entry court is uncharacteristically walled off from the street. Although successful on its own terms, it is one of the buildings that sounded the alarm and helped reinforce the preservation of historic Back Bay architecture.

13 241 Beacon Street
1868

14 242 Beacon Street
Sturgis and Brigham, 1881

:: Julia Ward Howe lived at 241 Beacon Street after the death of her husband, Dr. Samuel G. Howe. Godfrey Lowell Cabot and his wife, Maria, lived at 242 Beacon Street. Mr. Cabot was the foremost member of the Watch and Ward Society, a bastion of virtue that battled sin and corruption. It was primarily the upright Godfrey Lowell Cabot who inspired the old jingle:

> *And this is good old Boston*
> *The home of the bean and the cod*
> *Where the Lowells talk only to*
> *   Cabots*
> *And the Cabots talk only to God.*

15 266 Beacon Street
Shaw and Hunnewell, 1886

:: An early example of Italian Renaissance in the Back Bay, this 40-foot-wide house built for Elizabeth Skinner organizes the upper façade with two-story fluted pilasters and a strong cornice topped by a balustrade with urns that conceal the set-back top floor. The foundation stones have a vermiculated surface. The same firm designed a similar but less interesting house a year later at 412 Beacon Street.

16 270 Beacon Street
Richard Tucker, 1956

:: A house by McKim, Mead, and White originally occupied this site, while next door at 274 Beacon was a large house by H. H. Richardson. The current apartment complex has considerable design interest and, despite its innovations, fits well into its context.

Perhaps the most original and essential feature is the open piazza that passes through the entry level, terminating with a view to the Charles River and unifying the entire design. The projecting bowfronts are in the Back Bay vernacular but are executed in a simple manner with large expanses of glass. Ornament is found in the stepped corners, the bas-relief panels above the entrance, and the bold entry pylons and ironwork. The rear elevation is different but equally appealing—a rarity in the Back Bay, which usually ignored the rear façades. A small parking garage with turntable was ingeniously worked into the rather small site.

270 Beacon Street

17 New England College of Optometry
422 Beacon Street
Little, Browne, 1899
424–426 Beacon Street
Julius H. Schweinfurth, 1904

∷ Julius Schweinfurth, architect of two other Back Bay houses (43 and 304 Commonwealth Avenue), won a Rotch Fellowship that allowed him to study European architecture firsthand. Some of his European sketches are in the collection of the Boston Athenaeum. His knowledge of French styles is evident in the rich façades of these paired houses with their handsome balustraded mansards, high-relief stonework, and ornamental iron railing. They are unified in their ground-floor treatment, balcony, balustrade, mansard, and fourth-floor windows. The 7-foot disparity in their widths is handled expertly, with complementary windows on the second, third, and fifth floors. Compare these houses with the pair at 128–130 Commonwealth, which was remodeled in the French style one year later. The added fire-escape balconies are a serious blemish.

New England College of Optometry

Shell cornice, 448 Beacon Street

18 448 Beacon Street
Andrews and Jacques, 1889

:: A handsome sandstone cornice carved with the shell motif adorns this chateau-inspired mansion. Besides the cornice, its main attractions are its round corner tower and its materials— yellow brick and red stone—which are unusual for the Back Bay.

Entrance and oriel window, 12 Hereford Street at Beacon Street

19 Church Court
Beacon Street at Massachusetts Avenue
Graham Gund Associates, 1983
Landscape design: Carol R. Johnson Associates, Inc.

:: A spectacular fire in mid-1978 ravaged the Mount Vernon Church designed by Walker and Kimball in 1891. Portions of the ruins were melded into an L-shaped building to make forty-two condominium units. Most of the apartments overlook the Charles River, but several are oriented to the courtyard located where the sanctuary had been. Town houses are built into the tower, entrance portico, and side wall of the ruins. In contrast to the mellow textured and ornamented stone of the original church, the 1980s construction is outfitted in gay pastels.

20 Hotel Cambridge
483 Beacon Street
Willard T. Sears, 1898

:: Architecturally this is one of the most successful of the large Back Bay apartment hotels. The bulk of Hotel Cambridge is organized by means of a two-story rusticated base and by a mansard roof that unites the top two

Church Court © Steve Rosenthal

floors. Most of the windows of the top floors are grouped in two tiers of dormers topped on each side by a pediment bearing the H-C monogram of the building. Compare this with another but less successful apartment hotel by the same architect, The Marlborough, one block away.

Hotel Cambridge

21 The Charlesgate Hotel
535 Beacon Street
J. Pickering Putnam, 1901

:: Major apartment hotels were built at the turn of the twentieth century fronting the exquisite Charlesgate, Olmsted's first landscape design in Boston. The naturalistic basin and landscaped banks offered idyllic views to the residents. Romantic bridges and winding paths attracted strolling Bostonians. The 1951 Bowker Overpass obliterated Charlesgate Park, replacing it with a raised highway.

J. Pickering Putnam, also architect of Haddon Hall, studied architecture at the École des Beaux-Arts as well as at the Royal Academy of Architecture in Berlin. Here his imagination reveled in assorted bays, oriel windows, bartizans, and towers. A finely carved Romanesque entrance arch is reminiscent of Louis Sullivan, its intricate plant forms intertwined with the name of the building. Even in the 1920s, when other Back Bay apartment buildings had begun to decline in social status, this one was still desirable. Today it is a dormitory.

The Charlesgate Hotel

Boylston Street
In the early twentieth century, prominent jewelers located in stylish art deco shops on Boylston Street. The venerable Shreve, Crump and Low moved to 330, where stylized pilasters, column capitals, and grillwork combined the zigzag with plant motifs. Inside, the decorated columns and silvered ceiling gave the merchandise a special panache. Down the block at 384,

Entrance archway, Charlesgate Hotel

Former Museum of Natural History

Bigelow Kennard had an equally elaborate art deco storefront with entablature and cut stonework. The original projecting sign of Bigelow Kennard is in the Museum of Fine Arts.

Ancient Fish Weir
During the excavations for the subway station on Boylston in 1913 and for the New England Mutual Life Insurance building in 1939, 65,000 sharpened wooden stakes were found at a level 31 feet below the current street level. The 4-foot-long birch and white pine stakes retained bits of horizontal woven wattling that would have connected them. Archeologists concluded that they formed a part of an ancient fish weir, possibly used between 2,000 and 3,600 years ago by the aborigines of New England.

One section of the excavated weir is located in the northeastern part of a block bounded by Stuart Street and St. James Avenue on Berkeley Street, and another is under Boylston Street between Berkeley and Clarendon Streets. A diorama model showing a reconstruction of the fish weir may be seen in the lobby of the New England. The Peabody Museum at Harvard also has an exhibit

devoted to the use and construction of fish weirs.

22 Former Museum of Natural History
Boylston Street at 234 Berkeley Street
William G. Preston, 1862

:: In 1814 a group of Boston gentlemen banded together to share their natural history specimens and books. Stimulated by mutual enthusiasm, their united collections grew rapidly. The Linnaean Society of New England evolved into the Boston Society of Natural History. Overwhelmed by the size and curatorial demands, they offered their fine collection to Harvard with clear conditions. When Harvard failed to care for the collection, the remains were returned to the society.

The society rebuilt their library, and by 1840 had 660 of the most valuable volumes from three centuries. In 1848 they purchased a building on Mason Street. Again the collection swelled with gifts from the Boston gentlemen. In 1860 the state legislature bought the Mason Street building from the society and granted land on Berkeley Street.

This French Academic–style museum

and library was built for its collections. Two-story brick pilasters with Corinthian capitals encase the building and rest on a high rusticated sandstone ground floor. Animal heads were carved in the keystones on the ground-floor arches, but these have been removed. For more than a century, the society published natural science research of great significance. That ended in 1946 when its library and then the building were sold. It became the Boston Museum of Science and usurped all the parkland on top of the Charles River dam. The building was converted to commercial uses.

The first MIT building, also designed by Preston, was located next door and bore a strong resemblance to this building. It is hard to imagine that even in 1872 nothing had been built west of the MIT building on Boylston Street.

23 Warren Chambers Building
419 Boylston Street
Ball and Dabney, 1896
Renovation: Childs, Bertman, Tseckares, and Casendino, 1982–1984

:: Warren Chambers was Boston's premier doctors' building, featuring the latest concepts in office layout and services for the period. The imposing Renaissance revival façade of brick and marble is highlighted by a coffered triumphal arch entrance with bronze gates. The lobby continues the grandeur in golden and dark green marble.

After many decades, the building had become outdated. In the 1980s the façade was restored and interiors were renovated. In the 1982 film *The Verdict*, Paul Newman's office shows the pre-renovation interiors. The authors' office was above his, with yellow parachutes strung across the ceilings to warm the harsh florescent lighting and silver airplane wing–shaped drafting tables.

Warren Chambers Building, 419 Boylston Street

24 Berkeley Building
420 Boylston Street
Codman and Despradelle, 1905
Renovation: Notter, Finegold & Alexander, 1988
Boston Landmark

:: The advantages of steel-frame construction are explored in this early twentieth-century Beaux-Arts-influenced office building. Its walls are mainly glass and metal curtain wall organized into a variety of windows unified vertically by slender arches of glazed white terra-cotta. The cornice rises a full story to demarcate the entrance bay; the steel supports for this bit of stage scenery can be seen from farther down Boylston Street. The original ground-floor treatment has been largely obliterated by unsympathetic alterations.

25 222 Berkeley Street at Boylston Street
Robert A. M. Stern, 1991

Berkeley Building

26 500 Boylston Street

John Burgee Architects with Philip
Johnson, 1988

:: This pair of buildings evolved from
one of Boston's famous urban design
battles of the 1980s. Originally the entire block was to have been occupied
by twin towers, each with a forecourt,
like the one eventually built at 500
Boylston by Johnson and Burgee. Community opposition was so intense, however, that the developer agreed to hire
another architect. The commission for
the other half of the site went to Robert
A. M. Stern, known for his eclectic
house designs. The result is both
heavy-handed and intrusive at the
street level. Yet when viewed on the
skyline, the pair is modest in size compared to both the John Hancock towers.

The Johnson/Burgee building at 500
Boylston is a staid neoclassical revival
style that has been compared to a
1930s Philco radio. The hulking mass

has compromised the view of Trinity
Church from Copley Square. The large
forecourt on Boylston Street is far too
grand. Even worse is the way in which
it ignores the microclimate. The space
is almost always in shadow, and it
traps high winds the tower draws into
the space. On St. James Street, however, it is a real improvement.

The red brick and limestone Stern
building is highly mannered. It repeats
motifs found all over Boston—acanthus leaves, monstrous urns, and gold
capitals inside. A tiny gold State House
dome sits over the Boylston Street entry
portico. Oriel windows are sprinkled
here and there to recall the wonderful
rippling glass bays of the demolished
Coulton Building that stood here. Inside
there is a vaulted, skylit "winter garden" framed by shops and four levels
of offices.

27 The New England

501 Boylston Street
Cram and Ferguson, 1939–1942

:: Of this building, designed for the
New England Mutual Life Insurance
Company, poet David McCord quipped:

> *Ralph Adams Cram*
> *One morning said damn,*
> *And designed the Urn Burial*
> *For a concern actuarial.*

500 Boylston Street

The design was actually done by Cram's partners and is said to have greatly displeased Cram. The large granite mass with its small cupola contains highly stylized references to colonial architecture and perhaps is at its best inside the auditorium, bank lobby, and main entrance hall. However conservative its appearance, the structure was innovative in its engineering and rests on a floating foundation. Dioramas of the Indian fish weir that was discovered during excavations for the building may be seen in the lobby.

28 Boston Center for Adult Education
5 Commonwealth Avenue
Thomas and Rice, 1912

:: For the Back Bay, this is a very recent house, built in 1912 by Walter C. Baylies, a Boston textile industrialist. It replaces an earlier house dating from 1861, which was identical to the house next door at number 3. Designed in an Italianate style, the 1912 house has two symmetrical bows flanking a center entrance and rising three stories, while the top floor, with its small square windows and swag panels, sits back behind the third-floor cornice.

Ballroom entrance, Boston Center for Adult Education

One of the Back Bay's most glamorous ballrooms, reminiscent of the Petit Trianon at Versailles, was added about 1913 and has a separate entrance through the tall wrought-iron gate. A stable was located behind this façade before it was rebuilt as a ballroom. The first floor of the house contained the library, parlor, dining room, pantry, and ballroom. Bedrooms were on the upper floors, and the kitchen and laundry were in the basement. Much of the ornament and interior finishes are intact, marred only by the addition of classroom lighting and furnishings.

29 20–34 Commonwealth Avenue
Bryant and Gilman, 1861

:: Each of the houses is only 19 feet wide, but a very strong and harmonious effect is created by the repetition of oriel windows against the plain brick façade and a continuous mansard roof with deep cornice. There is some variation in treatment of doors and windows without ill effect on the whole composition.

30 25–27 Commonwealth Avenue
1861

:: Samuel Hooper, congressman and merchant, built 25 and 27 Commonwealth Avenue as a three-story home. It is the only house in the Back Bay with a large corner yard and set-back side entrance. In 1883 it was divided into two houses.

31 Haddon Hall
29 Commonwealth Avenue
J. Pickering Putnam, 1894

:: Haddon Hall caused quite a stir when it was built because of its eleven-story height. Eventually, height restrictions were tightened on the rest of Back Bay, restrictions that obviously have been violated a few times since. The building was designed as luxury apartments, and it is an oddity in more

Hooper Mansion, 25–27 Commonwealth Avenue

Entrance, 25 Commonwealth Avenue

Haddon Hall

than its height. Unlike most buildings in the Back Bay, it is of yellow-tan brick and brownstone. Each floor is demarcated with brown stringcourses, which are appealing in the way they ripple over the bays on the Commonwealth Avenue end. The triangular bay is a delight.

32 43 Commonwealth Avenue
Julius Schweinfurth, 1902
Ground-floor renovation: Michael & Susan Southworth, 1974

:: The four Schweinfurth brothers all became architects, influenced, no doubt, by their father's architectural ornament business. Julius was hired by Peabody and Stearns in 1879, becoming their chief designer before leaving to start his own practice in 1887. Beyond the buildings bearing his name, he was responsible for significant Peabody and Stearns architecture of the 1880s. This house characteristically displays his powerful manipulation of the European architectural vocabulary he acquired while traveling on a Rotch scholarship. It is one of the first steel-framed houses in Boston.

Zigzagging around the furnace room, elevator machinery, and utility areas, the authors converted the original kitchen and maids' rooms for their residence and reconstructed the traditional rear kitchen garden.

33 62–66 Commonwealth Avenue
Henry Williams, 1872

:: Three separate houses were conceived together to form a grand composition. The center house rises a full story higher with its tall mansard roof ornamented with iron cresting. The oriel window also rises an extra story. The flanking houses are mirror images of each other. Horizontal stringcourses of stone unify the façade.

Art deco entrance, 56 Commonwealth Avenue

Animated Georgian revival bowfronts, 58–60 Commonwealth Avenue

62–66 Commonwealth Avenue

34 First Baptist Church 🏛

Commonwealth Avenue at Clarendon Street
Henry Hobson Richardson, 1870–1872
National Register of Historic Places

:: Originally built for the Brattle Square Unitarian congregation, which had decided to sell its 1772 colonial meeting-house, this was H. H. Richardson's earliest use of Romanesque forms.

Although he was to become one of Boston's most famous architects, Richardson was born far from Boston on Priestley Plantation in St. James, Louisiana, in 1838. His original intention was to enter military service, but because of his stutter, his wealthy parents encouraged him to pursue another career—fortunately for American architecture. After graduating from Harvard, Richardson headed for Paris. He was admitted to the École des Beaux-Arts in 1860 and remained there for seven years, studying European architecture and developing his skills as a designer. While he was in Paris, the American Civil War cut off his funds from home, forcing him to work as a draftsman by day and to study at night.

The new church for the Brattle Square congregation was Richardson's first important commission. Like many Boston churches of the period, it is built of Roxbury puddingstone laid in random ashlar. Its plan is basically cruciform. The monumental tower, almost free-standing like an Italian campanile, is (as Richardson himself felt) the most innovative and successful part of the building. The square tower, topped by a decorative frieze and corbelled arches that are, in turn, surmounted by a low-peaked overhanging roof, is one of the majestic forms on the Boston skyline. It is best viewed from Commonwealth Avenue Mall.

The frieze is notable, for it was modeled by Bartholdi (the Statue of Lib-

First Baptist Church

erty sculptor) in Paris. Italian workmen carved the frieze after the stones were set in place. It depicts the sacraments, and the faces are said to be likenesses of noted Bostonians of the time such as Longfellow, Emerson, Hawthorne, and Sumner. The trumpeting angels on the corners who look down over Back Bay have earned the building its nickname, "Church of the Holy Bean Blowers." The trumpets were originally gilded.

The Romanesque feeling of the church is conveyed by many round corbels, windows, and arches in the tower and by the portico arches. The theme is further developed in the beautiful

windows based on a circle motif. It is interesting to note that Charles F. McKim, who was nine years younger than Richardson and later to become renowned as designer of the Boston Public Library and numerous other public edifices, worked on this project as a draftsman.

Four years after the new church was completed, the Brattle Square congregation dissolved, unable to bear the heavy costs of the new building. For several years it stood empty, and there was even thought given to tearing it down, perhaps leaving the tower standing alone. But in 1881 the First Baptist Church, fleeing its former quarters in the declining South End, came to the building's rescue. They solved the acoustical problems of the sanctuary by adding galleries in 1884 to reduce echoes.

35 121 Commonwealth Avenue
Cummings and Sears, 1872

:: The Ruskin Gothic style was characterized by abundant decorative and colorful elements that together make a picturesque ensemble. Two colors of brick, two of slate, stone, wood, wrought iron, and polychrome tile are used. The bay window is treated almost like a tower, with an ornamented peak that projects out from and above

Ruskin Gothic House, 121 Commonwealth Avenue

the mansard roof. Two years later the same architects designed New Old South Church on Boylston Street, which also explores a variety of surface decoration.

36 128–130 Commonwealth Avenue
S. D. Kelley, 1882
Renovation: Arthur Bowditch, 1905

:: As on Beacon Street, the sunny north side of Commonwealth Avenue was preferred, but many stunning houses were built on the south side, including these two. Elaborate stone facades in the Baroque style of Paris's École des Beaux-Arts were added to these houses twenty-three years after they were built. The style was more popular in New York than in Boston, which has only a handful of examples. The wrought-iron fence, gate, and balconies of number 130 are particularly fine. Bowditch also designed the Stoneholm at 1514 Beacon Street in Brookline, one of the most elaborate apartment buildings in the Boston area.

Beaux-Arts façades, 128–130 Commonwealth Avenue

37 Chilton Club
152 Commonwealth Avenue
Peabody and Stearns, 1870

:: The Chilton Club, founded in 1910, is of greater significance socially than architecturally. It is named in honor of

Mary Chilton, the only *Mayflower* passenger to leave Plymouth and live in Boston. She married John Winslow, and they built a house in Spring Lane, where she died in 1679.

Like the fabled Boston hat handed down for generations, the building is serviceable, sturdy, unpretentious, and rather plain. The club was for many years the female counterpart of the exclusive men's club, the Somerset. It has three entrances originally intended for different social levels: the Commonwealth Avenue entrance was for members only, the Dartmouth Street entrance was for members with guests, and the alley was for servants and deliveries. Life for many women of Boston society was structured around their clubs, of which several still exist. Traditionally, sewing circles were the core of clubdom, a new one formed from each year's flock of debutantes.

38 Ames-Webster Mansion 🏛
Commonwealth Avenue at
306 Dartmouth Street
Peabody and Stearns, 1872
Enlarged: John H. Sturgis, 1882
Restoration: Childs, Bertman, Tseckares, Casendino, 1969

:: Built for congressman Frederick Ames and enlarged ten years later for Oakes Ames, the house has some of the most elaborately ornamented interiors in the Back Bay. Sturgis enlarged it in 1882 by adding a four-story monumental tower with a commanding mansard roof and a chimney ornamented with pediments and bas-reliefs. Next to this he created a new entrance and porte cochere with fine wrought-iron gates.

Inside, a grand hall was created, 63 by 18 feet with an 18-foot ceiling, paneled in richly carved oak woodwork. At the end of the hall a grand staircase rises beneath a skylit dome of stained glass by John La Farge, surrounded by the murals of the French painter Benjamin Constant. Guests arriving for par-

Ames-Webster Mansion

Wrought-iron gate, Ames-Webster Mansion

Hall, Ames-Webster Mansion © Robert Perron

ties drove into the porte cochere and took the elevator to the second floor, where they removed their coats, then made a grand entrance descending the broad staircase into the glittering hall.

The Commonwealth Avenue side features an elaborately worked wrought-iron fence of spiral posts and intertwined floral vines and a two-story projecting plant conservatory.

39 Hotel Vendome

160 Commonwealth Avenue
William G. Preston, 1871 (corner building)
J. F. Ober and R. Rand, 1881 (main building)
Renovation: Stahl Bennett, 1971–1975

:: The French Second Empire former Hotel Vendome was built at the then exorbitant cost of $1 million. It boasted of many luxuries, including private bathrooms, fireplaces, and steam heat. In 1882 it was the first public building in the city to have electric lights. During its many glorious years as Boston's premier hotel, dozens of notables stayed here, including General Ulysses S. Grant, President Grover Cleveland, P. T. Barnum, Mark Twain, Oscar Wilde, Sarah Bernhardt, and John Singer Sargent.

The white façade of Italian and Tuckahoe marble is ornamented with pediments, bays, and balustrades and topped by a mansard roof with an elaborate three-story peak over the main entrance. The roof was greatly altered, eliminating all its beautiful detail, in the 1970s following a catastrophic fire that killed nine firemen. A memorial to all firefighters is in the Commonwealth Mall. Virtually none of the hotel's interior decor survives.

40 176–178 Commonwealth Avenue

Charles Atwood, 1883

:: What a strange and provocative assemblage! A rusticated stone porch with three entrance arches (serving two houses) joins the buildings, and out of it rise both a bay window and a bowfront tower with conical roof. Rusticated quoins and window trim are set into the brick façade. By the time we reach the top floor, the style has changed from Romanesque to Flemish in the dormer pediments.

176–178 Commonwealth Avenue

Hotel Vendome *King's Handbook*

41 191 Commonwealth Avenue
Weston and Rand, 1872

:: Henry Lee Higginson, a Boston stockbroker and philanthropist best remembered for founding the Boston Symphony Orchestra, built and lived in this building. He called it Hotel Agassiz after his wife, Ida Agassiz, daughter of famed Harvard zoologist Louis Agassiz. Originally there was only one vast apartment of several thousand square feet on each floor, but these were later divided. A rather simple building in the "panel brick" style identified by architectural historian Bainbridge Bunting, it makes its major statement through a series of alternating towerlike bays and gabled projections. Stringcourses demarcate each floor. Ornament is concentrated around the windows and at the top of the fourth and fifth floors.

Higginson detested motorcars and walked from his apartment to his State Street office each day. He had served in the Civil War and made his fortune in the postwar boom. As his motto he took the epitaph of the Duke of Devonshire: "What I gave, I have / What I spent, I had / What I kept, I lost."

42 195 Commonwealth Avenue
J. Pickering Putnam, 1881

:: Elaborate brick and terra-cotta ornament adorn this house, notable both for its octagonal corner tower and its strong and varied pattern of windows defined by stone. A recessed balcony has been tucked in under the roof next to the chimney.

43 St. Botolph Club
199 Commonwealth Avenue
McKim, Mead, and White, 1890

:: The Federal revival style flourished in Boston in the late nineteenth and early twentieth centuries. According to Bainbridge Bunting, forty-nine houses in the Back Bay had been done in the style by 1917. This house, the largest,

195 Commonwealth Avenue

has a symmetrical façade with two bows flanking a central Ionic portico entrance. Small-paned windows would have been more appropriate to the style. The fourth-floor servants' quarters are set back behind a balustrade.

The St. Botolph Club was established in 1881 at 85 Boylston Street for artists, writers, and professional men. The club sponsored the first exhibit of John Singer Sargent paintings in America in January 1888.

44 Mason House
211 Commonwealth Avenue
Rotch and Tilden, 1883
Music room added ca. 1897

:: Surprisingly, behind the simple façade are some of the most elaborate Queen Anne interiors in Boston. The only clue is the entrance set within a curved paneled niche with leaded glass, said by architect Ogden Codman to have been inspired by two Asher Benjamin doorways. The arch has a decorative band of large and small voussoirs.

Each room in the house is treated differently. The library has a cove ceiling with woodwork of quartered oak and a tapestry wall covering, the stair hall is dark mahogany, and the oval dining room has an ornate coffered plaster ceiling and silver chandelier. Arthur Rotch designed the woodwork and much of the furniture for the house, which was built for William Powell Mason and later occupied by his daughter, Miss Fanny Mason.

About 1897 a large 30-by-45-foot music room in the Italian Renaissance revival style was added at the rear of the house, and it may be the finest music room in all of Boston. It has a coffered ceiling with shallow recess dome. Illuminated by indirect electric lighting, it is probably the first architectural element designed expressly for electric light in the Back Bay. Coffered round arches surround three sides of the room, while the fourth side at the room's entrance is a coffered apse-like space. Much of the furniture for the room was purchased in Venice by Miss Mason, who traveled there with her friend Mrs. Jack Gardner. The extensive use of Carrara marble in the room cre-

Mason House

ated a very bright sound.

Miss Mason was noted for her musical interests and knowledge. She had frequent concerts, not only in her Boston home, but also at her estate in Walpole, New Hampshire, and her homes in Beverly Cove and Paris. The list of internationally renowned musicians who performed in her music room would be the envy of any concert hall. Ferruccio Busoni played the inaugural concert and was followed over the decades by many other eminent pianists, including Ignace Paderewski, Alfred Cortot, Arthur Rubinstein, Alexander Brailowsky, Egon Petri,

Music room, Mason House Courtesy Paul Doguereau

Programs for concerts held in Miss Fanny Mason's music room Courtesy Paul Doguereau

George Copeland, Paul Doguereau, and Earl Wild. Vocal recitals were given by Mary Garden, Maggie Teyte, Emma Calvé, and tenor René Clément; and Nadia Boulanger performed with her choral group. Cellist Pablo Casals and violinist Jacques Thibaud also played here in individual recitals and performed as a trio with pianist Alfred Cortot in Miss Mason's Paris apartment. Her musical interests brought her the acquaintance of composers as well. She commissioned a quintet by Bohuslav Martinu (1890–1959) that had its premiere in her music room. The musical traditions begun by Miss Mason were carried on by the authors' good friend, Paul Doguereau, in his music salon, his coaching of concert pianists and through the Peabody Mason Music Foundation he established in her memory.

45 Algonquin Club
217 Commonwealth Avenue
McKim, Mead, and White, 1887

:: Like the Boston Public Library begun the same year, the Back Bay's most palatial club has a limestone façade in the Italian Renaissance revival style favored by Stanford White, the architect. Projecting bays anchor each end of the

façade, which is framed by a heavy cornice and overscale frieze on top and a rusticated ground floor. A two-level Ionic porch rises above the center entrance and is further elaborated by the Palladian window above it on the fourth floor. The ground floor originally projected beyond the face of the building for the entire length, forming a terrace for the second floor. In 1889, however, the club was ordered by the Commonwealth to alter the building to conform to the Back Bay's precise setback requirements.

Algonquin Club

46 Commonwealth Avenue at
21 Fairfield Street
W. Whitney Lewis, 1881

:: W. Whitney Lewis was much influenced by Richardson's Trinity Church Rectory in this house with a projecting chimney–bay window combination on the end, arched side entrance, and gabled peak. The fenestration is disorderly, however, and the ornamentation has gotten out of hand. The addition of paint to the sandstone trim gives the building a Flemish feeling out of character with the original intent.

47 247 Commonwealth Avenue
William Rantoul, 1905

:: Almost Georgian in feeling, this granite bowfront is reminiscent of McKim, Mead, and White's 303 Commonwealth Avenue (1895) and Little and Browne's 118 Beacon Street (1907). This house, however, is less monumen-

Queen Anne oriel window detail,
239 Commonwealth Avenue

tal and more domestic, with its small-scale entry portico, second-floor balconies, center windows with slender sidelights, and stepped-back fourth floor with dormers.

21 Fairfield Street

247 Commonwealth Avenue

48 270 Commonwealth Avenue

Dunham and McKay, 1896

:: Originally the Hotel Tuileries, a residential hotel, the building was designed in the classical vocabulary popularized by McKim, Mead, and White. The rusticated base rises two stories, as does the triumphal arch entry portico with two levels of columns. Windows above are spaced rhythmically—three-two-three—and surmounted by three orders of lintels: flat, segmental, and triangular pediments. A cornice with frieze based on the Greek anthemion rises almost a full floor above the top windows.

Hotel Tuileries, 270 Commonwealth Avenue

49 Charles Francis Adams House

Commonwealth Avenue at 20 Gloucester Street
Peabody and Stearns, 1886

:: Peabody and Stearns were content to leave the strong forms of two gables and a round corner tower with conical slate roof quite unadorned in their design for the home of Charles Francis Adams. What ornament there is, counts. The handsome chimney stack has a single spine running from a carved bracket on the third floor all the way to the top, which has simple bands of moldings. The year 1886 is mounted on the chimney in large numerals. Around the entrance is a broad Richardsonian border of carved filigree.

Charles Francis Adams house

50 287 Commonwealth Avenue

Rotch and Tilden, 1892

:: Greek decorative motifs abound in this extra-wide classical revival house of limestone built for Herbert M. Sears. Anthemion cresting tops the Corinthian entry portico, and another anthemion border runs along the top of the cornice. An egg-and-dart molding follows under the stringcourse at the top of the first floor. First-floor windows are framed with lintels resting upon brackets and a rosette border.

287 Commonweath Avenue

51 Pickman House

303 Commonwealth Avenue
McKim, Mead, and White, 1895

:: The most monumental and austere residence in the Back Bay is perhaps the Pickman house—McKim, Mead, and White's last Back Bay residence. The simple 33-foot-wide bowed façade has a mausoleum-like center entrance. Ornament is confined to the cornice, a garland stringcourse above the third floor, a Greek-key course above the first floor, roundels between the fourth-floor windows, and a relief panel above the center window of the second floor. Inside, a grand staircase with bronze balustrade rises gently to the second floor behind a row of Ionic columns. Mrs. Pickman held coming-out balls for her two daughters here, transforming the house into a Paris street scene for Nancy and into a garden scene for Lucy.

52 John F. Andrew Mansion ▥

Commonwealth Avenue at 32 Hereford Street
McKim, Mead, and White, 1884–1888

:: McKim, Mead, and White introduced the Italian Renaissance revival style to the Back Bay in their mansion for John F. Andrew, one year before their noted Villard mansions were built in New York City. The elliptical projecting corner adds much to the interest of the building and to the street intersection. A simple round tower such as the one two blocks away at 448 Beacon Street is static by comparison. The undulating façade is further enhanced by

Pickman house

304 Commonwealth Avenue (Julius Schweinfurth, 1895)

John F. Andrew Mansion

the continuous balustrade and cornice wrapping around the hip roofline and by the stringcourses beneath the windows of the third and fourth floors.

The low-ceilinged ground floor contains a billiard room and other minor rooms and is faced in stone, in contrast to the brick above. Heavy wrought-iron grilles project from the windows. The tall windows above are given lacy iron balconies. The wrought-iron balcony on the third floor above the Palladian window is from the Tuileries Palace in Paris, which was burned in the revolt of 1874. Windows are trimmed in limestone and reduce in size above the second floor. The house has the first street-level entrance in the Back Bay, which, because of the area's high water table, resulted in a basement barely 6 feet high. Many of the interiors have been preserved and maintained by the MIT fraternity that occupies the house.

53 **Miss Farmer's School of Cookery**
Commonwealth Avenue at 40 Hereford Street
Shaw and Hunnewell, 1886

:: Fannie Merrit Farmer founded her school of cookery in 1902. For many years it was located here, until the building was converted to condominiums. Compare this house with the Andrew house across the avenue, built about the same time. Both are topped

by balustrades that conceal top-floor servants' quarters, and both have stone-faced ground floors with entrances in the center of the long façade. Instead of the elliptical bay and tower of 32 Hereford, here we see two square projecting bays. Curved elements are restricted to the odd entry portico and a bowfront on Commonwealth Avenue. The stone window trim is evocative of the Georgian style rather than the Renaissance style of the Andrew house.

54 **Burrage Mansion** 🏛
314 Commonwealth Avenue
Charles Brigham, 1889
Boston Landmark

:: Here is one exception to Boston's avoidance of flamboyant architecture. Like the New York Vanderbilt mansion by Richard Morris Hunt, this grand house was inspired by the Château

Burrage Mansion

Burrage Mansion, Hereford Street façade

Chenonceaux in France. Both inside and outside, the lush French Gothic and Early Renaissance ornament are quite overwhelming. The roofline along Hereford Street is particularly evocative, with two turret towers, several decorated chimneys, and dormers. A charming greenhouse with curved glass roof and dome is attached to the back of the house.

55 Hotel Lafayette
333 Commonwealth Avenue
Dunham and McKay, 1895

:: This is by the architect-contractors who designed and built the former Hotel Tuileries in the same neoclassical vein. The entrance here is less monumental, but the window spacing and treatment are identical except for the Hotel Lafayette's two bay windows.

56 Ames Mansion
355 Commonwealth Avenue
Carl Fehmer, 1882

:: H. H. Richardson prepared a sketch design for the Oliver Ames mansion, but for some reason Carl Fehmer became the architect. Ames made a fortune in manufacturing and railroads and was governor from 1887 until 1890. The mansion is the largest in the Back Bay and has some of the most opulent interiors. It was the first Back Bay house to draw on the style of the French chateaus of the Loire Valley. A solid brownstone block without the three-dimensional modeling of the Burrage mansion one block away at 314 Commonwealth, it has a deep mansard roof penetrated by dormers and chimneys. The end bays of the Massachusetts Avenue façade project slightly and are expressed in the roof. Running around the house between the first- and second-floor windows is a frieze of putti and floral ornament depicting household activities such as dining, reading, and musicmaking. For many years the

Chimney, Ames Mansion

Wrought-iron window guard, Ames Mansion

Harvard Club (Parker, Thomas, and Rice, 1912), 374 Commonwealth Avenue

headquarters of the National Casket Company, the mansion was converted to an office building.

57 10 Marlborough Street
Little and Browne, 1905

:: This early twentieth-century Georgian revival house was once the home of Edwin O'Connor. His novel *The Last Hurrah* depicts the conflicts between Boston Brahmins and the Irish during the years of James Michael Curley.

58 17 Marlborough Street
1863

:: In an unusual solution to the challenge posed by the narrow bay-fronted house, the entrance is placed in the center of the bay rather than to one side. An entry portico with columns projects beyond the bay, flanked by narrow arched windows. Henry Lee Higginson conceived the founding of the Boston Symphony Orchestra here, when it was the home of his friend George Howe.

59 First Lutheran Church
Marlborough Street at 299 Berkeley Street
Pietro Belluschi, 1959

:: An intimate landscaped courtyard provides access to the simple church interior, illuminated by a narrow band of clerestory windows beneath the shallow vaulted ceiling. Natural wood and tan brick are the primary materials. The exterior form ignores its Victorian neighbors.

60 French Library in Boston
53 Marlborough Street
1867

:: The house used as the French Library was built for Edward and Charles Codman and given to the library by a later owner, Francophile Katherine Lane Weems. The large house has a sym-metrical façade with mansard roof, three-story bays on each side of the center entrance, and a rusticated ground floor. A library extension was added to the side. The salon is said to be based on the Empress Josephine's private parlor at Malmaison. A fine tall iron fence surrounds the property.

61 First and Second Church 🏛
Marlborough Street at Berkeley Street
Ware and Van Brunt, 1867
Paul Rudolph, 1971

:: William Robert Ware and Henry Van Brunt, both Harvard graduates in the early 1850s, studied architecture in the New York atelier of Richard Morris Hunt. In 1863 they formed their Boston partnership where, like Hunt, they also taught students. Ware established the School of Architecture at MIT in 1865, based on the École des Beaux-Arts in Paris.

For First and Second Church, founded in 1630 and one of the nation's oldest congregations, the architects

First and Second Church

looked to the English country churches of the Middle Ages for inspiration. The square stone tower is particularly appealing. Its slender octagonal stone spire, a broach spire, becomes four-sided at its base, the juncture pointed up by four small Gothic windows called "lucarnes." The base of the tower widens as it approaches the ground and has diagonal buttresses at the corners.

Most of the church burned in 1968. Paul Rudolph's replacement preserved the tower, porch, and end wall—except for the unfortunate removal of the peak—and created an amphitheater-like entry. The odd-angled geometry was not fully resolved, but it allowed the addition of a small underground parking garage. The main structural material inside and out is Rudolph's favorite rough striated concrete, as in the Hurley Building and his School of Arts and Architecture at Yale.

62 Marlborough Street at 271–279 Clarendon Street
1869

:: Five houses are grouped together in a single mass with an apparently common mansard roof, and enormous gains are made aesthetically. Imagine the jumble if each house had tried to differ from its neighbor! The projecting oriel windows provide three-dimensional interest, as do the two bows on the corner house. The entrance of the corner house was originally on Marlborough Street, where there is now a bay window, but was moved to Clarendon Street when the house was joined to its neighbor at 273.

63 Hollis Hunnewell Mansion
Marlborough Street at 315 Dartmouth Street
1870

:: Mansard-roofed towers are the theme of several nearby houses. In this mansion built for Hollis Hunnewell, square towers of different heights flank the entrance. Similar towers appeared six years later in the adjacent house at 151 Commonwealth Avenue, then in 1881 in the Vendome addition and in

Entrance, 81 Marlborough Street

Hollis Hunnewell Mansion

1882 in the addition to the Ames-Webster mansion across the street.

64 Crowninshield House
164 Marlborough Street
Henry Hobson Richardson, 1870
National Register of Historic Places

:: One of the least interesting of Richardson's works, this early house built for Katherine Crowninshield does exhibit some imaginative decorative work, including a wrought-iron entry canopy and ornamental tiles set into the brick, as well as decorative brick-work and odd hooded dormers. The wrought-iron fence by an unknown de-signer is seen at several locations in the Back Bay and features balls atop all the verticals and hearts penetrated by forged diamond pendants.

65 Cushing-Endicott House ⅲ
165 Marlborough Street
Snell and Gregerson, 1871

66 326–328 Dartmouth Street
Snell and Gregerson, 1872

:: The Marlborough Street house and the two next door on Dartmouth Street were designed as an ensemble. The two taller matched end houses bal-anced the lower but wider symmetrical façade of the center house with its two projecting bays flanking the entrance. Unfortunately, the three houses have not been maintained as a group and no longer match.

Although the center house looks wide on the façade, its plan is T-shaped and reduces to a 15-foot width in the rear, while the end house becomes wider at the back. The façade of num-ber 165, executed in the French Aca-demic style, is particularly handsome. Symmetrical bays with double dormers balance the center entrance portico of four columns topped by an ornamental iron railing. Windows are outlined in in-ventive stone trim, not strictly in the

Chimney detail, Crowninshield House

271–279 Clarendon Street

Cushing-Endicott House

classical tradition. The main rooms of the house are on the second floor, which has 14-foot ceilings. The kitchen was placed on the entry level, unusual for a Back Bay house of the period.

Until 1958 the house had many of its fine original furnishings and decor and had been continuously occupied by only two families, the Cushings and the Endicotts. In 1903 Mrs. Endicott lent John Singer Sargent one of the bedrooms to use as a studio.

191 Marlborough Street

67 191 Marlborough Street
Carl Fehmer, 1881

:: The 32-foot-wide site made possible a generous Romanesque recessed portico with columns and wrought-iron infill in the arch and broad porch, both of Nova Scotia sandstone. The house is considered to be one of the best examples of Ruskin Gothic in the area.

68 225–231 Marlborough Street
Louis Weissbein, 1873
233–239 Marlborough Street, 1874

:: An exceptionally pleasing and harmonious row of narrow houses, mainly four stories, has been created within a limited vocabulary. Each has a mansard roof with pedimented dormers and an oriel window on the second floor. Small front gardens are defined by wrought-iron fences. On the first floor there are two arched openings: one the door, the other a window in a small reception room.

69 Marlborough Street at
12 Fairfield Street
Cabot and Chandler, 1879

70 8 and 10 Fairfield Street
Sturgis and Brigham, 1879

:: Often in the Back Bay a particular style took root on one street and spread to neighboring houses. On Fairfield Street the Queen Anne style, with its picturesque massing and variety of sur-

Wrought-iron fence, 12 Fairfield Street

face ornament, is seen at numbers 8, 10, and 12. A variety of brick types—Bainbridge Bunting counted twenty at 12 Fairfield—creates wonderful decoration, from rolled window jambs or cornices, to a fantastic base for the oriel window. A delightful wrought-iron fence of S scrolls and tridents defines the side yard.

71 Marlborough Street at
18 Fairfield Street
Peabody and Stearns, 1878

Oriel windows, 286–290 Marlborough Street

72 20 Fairfield Street

W. Whitney Lewis, 1875

:: Here are two more charming Fairfield Street houses, one almost minia-
turized by its larger, more aggressive
neighbor. W. Whitney Lewis, architect
of number 20, was born in England. In
1871 he arrived in Boston and began
designing houses in the Ruskin Gothic
style under the influence of H. H.
Richardson. Lewis also designed the
house across the street at 21 Fairfield.

73 The Marlborough

416 Marlborough Street
Willard T. Sears, 1895

:: Apartment hotels were said to shelter "the newly wed and the nearly
dead." Many had restaurants as well
as maid service. Elevators, private
bathrooms, and central heating were,
by the late nineteenth century, standard
luxuries in such buildings. While this
building has some interesting brownstone trim and ironwork and an appealing round corner, its overall massing
and façade organization lack the imagination of Sears's later Hotel Cambridge.

74 Emmanuel Church

15 Newbury Street
Alexander R. Estey, 1862
Enlarged: Frederick R. Allen, 1899
Leslie Lindsey Memorial Chapel:
Allen and Collens, 1920–1924

:: This towerless church was actually
built in three parts designed by three
different architects. The original was a
small Gothic country church by Alexander R. Estey, who also designed the
fine, well-preserved Church of Our Saviour at 23 Monmouth Street, Brookline.
Emanuel Church was the first church in
the Gothic revival style in the Back Bay
and also one of the first to use Roxbury
puddingstone. In 1899 the church was
enlarged by the addition of a new
east–west nave, usurping the former

18–20 Fairfield Street

Stonework, The Marlborough

Door hardware, Leslie Lindsey Memorial
Chapel

church lawn. The original nave then
became a transept.

Leslie Lindsey Memorial Chapel
was designed in the 1920s by Allen and

Collens, the architects of New York's Riverside Church. Mr. and Mrs. William Lindsey commissioned the chapel in memory of their daughter, Leslie, who perished in the sinking of the *Lusitania*. The ornamental work here is of high quality, with ironwork by F. Koralewski and the high altar and stained glass by Sir Ninian Comper.

75 37 Newbury Street
Gwathmey, Siegel, 1980

:: Built as the showroom and office building of Knoll International, manufacturers of contemporary designer furniture and textiles, this building proclaims its modernism in concrete, glass block, and plate glass. Replacing a brownstone gutted by fire, it avoids the forms, materials, and general character of its context. A glass-block stairwell, reminiscent of Le Corbusier's Carpenter Center, rises the full height of the building. A glass entrance is tucked between this and a projecting curved plate-glass show window. Three floors of showrooms are transparent and set back below three floors of office space.

76 Church of the Covenant
67 Newbury Street
R. M. Upjohn, 1865–1867

:: R. M. Upjohn was the son of Richard Upjohn, a leader in the English Gothic revival and architect of Trinity Church in New York City. Upjohn senior had moved to Boston in 1834 and worked for Alexander Parris for several years. Young Upjohn followed his father's lead in this Gothic revival structure of

Church of the Covenant

37 Newbury Street © Steve Rosenthal

Roxbury puddingstone with its impressive 236-foot spire, accentuated with two levels of pinnacles and lucarnes.

Three-stepped setback buttresses give the tower its solid monumental feeling of growing from the ground to lofty heights. The Gothic forms of the church's nave, transept, and buttresses are further heightened by their pinnacles and pointed gablets at the rooflines. Its main entrance is through a tripartite porch of Gothic trefoil arches. Interior decoration includes a Favrile glass lantern by one of Tiffany's designers, from the Tiffany Chapel at the 1893 Chicago World's Fair. The church was originally the Central Congregational Church, formed in 1835 on Winter Street.

77 Trinity Church Rectory
Newbury Street at 233 Clarendon Street
Henry Hobson Richardson, 1879
Third-story addition: 1893
National Register of Historic Places

:: Richardson designed the rectory for his friend Phillips Brooks, rector of Trinity Church. The entrance façade, balanced but asymmetrical, is organized in thirds. A large Romanesque arch with light and dark stone voussoirs and recessed entrance dominates the center third, and the end thirds are defined by the pointed gables. On the end wall on Newbury Street the chimney is imaginatively combined with projecting windows, making a sort of bay.

The house was designed about the same time as Sever Hall at Harvard and exhibits some of the same features, among them the rhythmic placement of window openings and the fine brickwork, including edge roll moldings of brick around windows, ornamental carved brick panels, and marquetry. The brick for both buildings came from the North Cambridge brickworks of M. W. Sands.

Trinity Church Rectory

109 Newbury Street

A floor was added to the house in 1893 to accommodate the new rector and his family (Brooks was a bachelor). The original roof design with dormers was retained, and the new floor was in effect slipped between the second floor and the roof, with remarkably little aesthetic damage.

78 109 Newbury Street
Charles A. Cummings, 1871

:: This and the house down the block at 277 Dartmouth Street were designed by architects as their own houses, and both express a penchant for the medieval. Two donjon towers with conical slate roofs flank the center entrance bay. A variety of decorative brickwork is used. The architect, Charles Cummings, was selected to design New Old South Church shortly after the completion of his house.

79 Hotel Victoria
Newbury Street at 275 Dartmouth Street
J. L. Faxon, 1886

:: J. L. Faxon indulged in a variety of fantasies in his design for the Hotel Victoria. Its castellated form with crenellated parapet and corner battlement ripples with bays of every type. Window treatments vary from floor to floor, with emphasis on the Moorish in the lower levels.

80 Newbury Street at 277 Dartmouth Street
J. Pickering Putnam, 1878

:: J. Pickering Putnam, architect, built this as his own house. Like the house at 109 Newbury, it draws its inspiration from the medieval period. This is most evident in the complex, picturesque roof with its projecting gabled bay, two bay towers, and a charming bartizan visually supported on a column in the rear corner. For many years the building was a restaurant founded by Josef, society restaurateur, who served for more than twenty years at the Ritz and the Copley Plaza before starting his own restaurant.

81 Boston Art Club 🏛
Newbury Street at 270 Dartmouth Street
William Ralph Emerson, 1881

82 Boston Bicycle Club
152 Newbury Street
George Meacham, 1884

:: What a fanciful building! At first glance the Boston Art Club may appear awkward, even ugly in its odd assem-

277 Dartmouth Street

blage of dissimilar forms. An example of the Queen Anne style, it was inspired by a variety of picturesque medieval elements. A hexagonal tower with a double curved roof rises out of the square corner, the transition effected by means of another peculiar detail, a stone balcony visually supported on a single Byzantine column. Related to the tower roof is the charming small dormer on the Dartmouth Street façade over the handsome carved archway. Enormous carved terra-cotta scroll brackets visually reinforce the gable-roofed portions of both façades. Rusticated quoins, voussoirs, and lintels dramatize the form. The interiors were as highly decorated as its façades would suggest.

William Emerson, nephew of Ralph Waldo Emerson, also designed the

Boston Art Club *King's Handbook*

"house of odd windows" on Beacon Hill, the Massachusetts Homeopathic Hospital on East Concord Street between Harrison and Albany, and the peculiar One Winthrop Square. Emerson always toyed with the traditional architectural vocabulary, testing its limits. Even today, more than a century after its construction, this building is a surprise and an enigma.

In 1889 the Art Club acquired the neighboring Bicycle Club by George Meacham, the architect who planned the public garden. That exuberant little building simply added another layer of complexity to Emerson's composition.

83 Newbury Street at 26 Exeter Street ⅲ

Hartwell and Richardson, 1884
Restaurant renovation: Childs, Bertman, Tseckares, Casendino, 1974–1975
School conversion: Symmes Maini & McKee Associates, 2005

:: A distinctive form of worship led the Working Union of Progressive Spiritualists to build this Richardsonian Romanesque building a decade after Trinity Church. Though initially well endowed, as their numbers declined the First Spiritualist Temple moved downstairs in 1914 and rented out their assembly hall as a theater. For decades it was the only place a proper Boston woman would go to see moving pictures in the afternoon. Its dignified architecture was uniquely Boston, with

none of the kitsch that typified large movie palaces. Often filling in at the box office, longtime manager Viola Berlin booked European and British imports. Despite midnight *Rocky Horror* showings that subsidized the more esoteric fare in its last decade, the arrival of a nearby multiplex spelled doom for the Exeter Street Theater.

In 1985, despite intense neighborhood opposition, the original interior was demolished to accommodate a home furnishings shop. The ground floor was renovated as a restaurant with a greenhouse extension. A disruptive decade followed as the Spiritualist Temple became a bookstore, a dot-com office, and then vacant in quick succession after fire damage.

Though the School Department abandoned Prince School across the street, there were still plenty of young neighborhood children. Adapted once more, Richardson's building became a private elementary school, expanding from the Saltonstall house at 30 Fairfield.

84 Prince School

Newbury Street at Exeter Street
George A. Clough, 1875
Renovation: Grassi Sharkey Design Group, 1985–1987

:: This school was closed and converted to a residential/commercial complex, sacrificing much of its architectural merit in the process. Its original tall mansard and hipped roofs topped by iron cresting and cupolas were a French composition of center pavilion and two end pavilions.

85 Boston Architectural College

320 Newbury Street
Ashley, Myer and Associates, 1963–1966

:: This contemporary school fits quite well into its nineteenth-century context, partly because of the deconstruction of its mass. The long-span

26 Exeter Street

concrete frame permits maximum flexibility in interior arrangements and a variety of façade treatments, from the open ground floor to partially screened studios to the almost completely enclosed meeting room and library. The ground-floor exhibition hall features frequently changing public exhibits on architecture, urban design, and related arts. The stark concrete rear elevation has been decorated with a trompe l'oeil Renaissance sectional view by Richard Haas (1977), visible from Boylston and Newbury Streets.

Boston Architectural College

86 Newbury Street Stables
Newbury Street between Hereford Street and Massachusetts Avenue
1875 and later

:: Back Bay residents who did not have their own stables kept their horses and carriages in the stables in this block or in the area of Beacon Hill between Charles Street and the river. Stables still survive in both areas, converted to commercial and residential space, while large garages have been built to store automobiles. An area of unique charm for the Back Bay, the low carriage houses retained their individualistic character when businesses moved in.

Richard Haas mural and converted Newbury Street Stables

Prince School in the late 1800s

87 360 Newbury Street

Arthur Bowditch, 1918
Renovation: Frank O. Gehry with
Schwartz/Silver Architects, 1989

:: The collaboration between Schwartz/
Silver and Frank Gehry, at that time
only known for his use of chain-link
fence as a decorative element, produced an eye-catching improvement of
an eyesore. The blank back wall of the
former warehouse was clad in sheets
of slate-colored lead-coated copper to
protect the deteriorating concrete.
Slate-gray metal-sheathed struts define
the two-story penthouse addition and
also climb the façade on several lower
floors over the main entrance on Newbury Street, creating an aggressive profile. The lobby is backlit yellow onyx
and dark birch panels framed in brass.

360 Newbury Street

Bay State Road and Boston University

Boston Architectural Conservation District

Bay State Road is a lovely avenue of
dignified homes in a variety of turn-of-
the-twentieth-century revival styles
with many fine examples of historic
ironwork on garden fences, balconies,
and even one elaborate two-story
wrought-iron verandah at number 83
that suggests New Orleans's French
Quarter. The front garden of number 121
has a sculpture by George Greenmayer.

The street was laid out in 1889 as
an extension of the Back Bay. Filling
this land wasn't likely until Frederick
Law Olmsted's design for the Fens
solved the problem of Roxbury sewage
in the Muddy River. The waterside was
preferred and quickly filled with large
homes and distinguished residents. Dr.
Eliot P. Joslin, the diabetes specialist,
moved into the classical revival house
at number 81.

Pie-Shaped House

Bay State Road residents felt cut off
from the Back Bay after 1891 when the
Harvard Bridge connected Cambridge's
Massachusetts Avenue with the quiet
Boston street West Chester Park (now
Massachusetts Avenue). Traffic flowed
from Dorchester to Arlington along
what became a heavily trafficked thoroughfare. Most of the Bay State Road
houses were acquired by Boston University and now serve as offices, clubs,
and residence halls.

88 52 Bay State Road
1910

:: The impressive double-wide brick façade belies the pie-shaped house behind it. Georgian details abound— keystones over windows, white bracketed dentil cornice surmounted by balustrade—but there wasn't enough land to put up a full house. At the corner the house narrows down to nothing, becoming an Edwardian folly.

89 57 Bay State Road
Arthur Little, 1890

:: Architect Arthur Little of Little and Browne built his own home here as soon as the lots were offered, but across the street from him, the difficult triangular lot stood vacant for more than a decade. His Federal revival house has a two-story ballroom with large Palladian windows.

90 112 Bay State Road
1910

:: Though built by speculators, this house has an unusual multicolor Flemish and gauged brick façade stylishly topped by a red tile roof. Regrettably, the brickwork is marred by repairs that ignore the style and pattern. Brick ornament was popular in the eighteenth century because brick masons were cheaper than stone carvers. It was no longer cheap when this house was built, but the attractions of this decorative technique make this narrow house stand out among its larger neighbors.

91 149 Bay State Road
Peters and Rice, 1900

:: Dr. Charles Goddard Weld's house at the corner of Sherborn Street is one of three neighboring houses designed by W. Y. Peters of Peters and Rice. It is an exuberant High Georgian revival style with heavy-handed quoins, Gibbs surrounds, and a cartouche window ornament.

Arthur Little House, 57 Bay State Road

Entrance, Dr. Charles Goddard Weld House, 149 Bay State Road

92 225 Bay State Road
Chapman and Frazier, 1905

:: This was the Tudor revival mansion of the William Lindseys who built the Lindsey Memorial Chapel at Emmanuel Church. Sitting closest to Boston University, it has served as a faculty club and pub since Boston University acquired it.

William Lindsey House, 225 Bay State Road

Boston University

Boston University managed the special problems of the long, narrow urban campus squeezed between a major artery, Commonwealth Avenue, and the Charles River by acquiring most of Bay State Road and expanding vertically. Under Josep Lluis Sert's guidance, the campus reoriented toward the river. His 1960s buildings illustrate many of his techniques for enriching huge concrete structures: sunscreens, decorative window divisions, scoop clerestories, asymmetrical massing,

expressed structure, projecting bays, and balconies. Spaces between buildings were carefully designed for student circulation and enjoyment. The terracing of the library reduces its apparent bulk and, together with the central quadrangle, provides a broad, low setting for the Law and Education Tower.

In the 1990s, having exhausted the riverside opportunities, Boston University reversed course, building the Photonics Center on a sliver of land hugging the Massachusetts Turnpike.

93 Photonics Research Center
Boston University
8 St. Mary's Street
Cannon Design, 1996

:: Here is a deft contemporary use of moderne details, a surprising architectural statement in a setting between highway and banal buildings. Though it runs a full block toward Kenmore Square, the mass is broken up in a number of different ways, with projecting bays and indented corners making it appear svelte. The projecting light mast is a symbol for its joint ventures with industry to develop and commercialize new products.

Boston University, Gothic revival chapel (Ralph Adams Cram) and courtyard with Law and Education Tower (Sert, Jackson and Gourley) © Lois M. Bowen

Boston University buildings by Sert, Jackson and Gourley © Steve Rosenthal

Photonics Center

94 **DeWolfe Boathouse**
Boston University
619 Memorial Drive, Cambridge (across
the Charles River from George Sherman
Union and Mugar Memorial Library)
Architectural Resources Cambridge,
1999

:: Although located on the Cambridge
side of the river, the boathouse is most
visible from the main campus. It combines a traditional vocabulary of eyelid
windows on each end and a large
arched window centered above five
boat bays. Its color palette of cream
and yellow is punched up with bright
red doors. Inside, the color scheme

DeWolfe Boathouse, Boston University © Nick Wheeler, courtesy of the Frances Loeb Library,
Harvard Design School

continues, and oars are used everywhere as stair rails and even lighting fixtures. The boathouse is the starting point for the annual Head of the Charles Regatta.

Copley Square

The filling of the Back Bay attracted Boston's major institutions as the social leaders built grand homes on the neighborhood's residential streets. Most clustered around a large square named in honor of the great Boston painter John Singleton Copley. The Boston Public Library, New Old South Church and Trinity Church still attract throngs of architectural enthusiasts. Other important buildings were demolished—the Ruskinian Gothic style Museum of Fine Arts, S. S. Pierce and Hotel Westminster. In their day, the square was two triangles as Huntington Avenue cut through to Boylston Street. Eliminating the diagonal in the 1870's never resulted in a square as impressive as the surrounding architecture.

Copley Square and Trinity Church

95 Copley Square Plaza
Clarke & Rapuano with Dean Abbott, 1984–1990

:: Though Sasaki Dawson and DeMay's 1969 formalist scheme related to Trinity Church with a diagonal entrance from Clarendon Street through precise rows of trees, a neighborhood organization was unhappy. A subsequent redesign was plagued with maintenance problems. Trees died and grass flooded, and when it became a farmers' market, their trucks weren't accommodated. The grandeur had been lost where once the Anvil Chorus from *Il Trovatore* was performed by an orchestra of 1,000 players, a chorus of 10,000, an organ, drum corps, ringing church bells, cannons, and 100 firemen striking anvils with sledge hammers.

The end of the annual marathon race is commemorated with the 1993 Nancy Schön sculpture of the tortoise outdistancing the hare in front of the fountain.

96 Trinity Church 🏛
Copley Square
Henry Hobson Richardson, 1872–1877
Portico and front tower peaks, 1890s
National Historic Landmark
Undercroft renovation: Goody Clancy, 2005

:: With Trinity Church, H. H. Richardson reached the peak of his career and created one of the great monuments of American architecture. The parish, founded in 1734, decided to leave its second church on Summer Street and Bishop's Alley. Six architecture firms were invited to submit designs for a new church on the triangular Copley Square site, $300 to be paid to each of the designers. Richardson was one of the invited competitors, partly because of the impressive tower of his First Baptist Church (then Brattle Church), nearly completed on Clarendon Street. He was living in New York City at the

Trinity Church

time, but he knew several members of the building committee who had been Harvard classmates or clubmates at the Porcellian, a definite asset to him. The other competitors were Sturgis and Brigham, Richard Morris Hunt, Ware and Van Brunt, and Peabody and Stearns, all of Boston, and William A. Potter of New York City.

Richardson was awarded the commission in June 1872 for a Romanesque design that was a sharp contrast to the prevailing Victorian Gothic style favored by other competitors. Upon receiving this commission, he moved his practice to Brookline. There he surrounded himself with his work, his library, his family, and many apprentices to whom he was a great teacher and friend, treating them almost as members of his own family.

Richardson's design for Trinity Church solved many problems of a site that was small, triangular, isolated by streets, and a visual focus for the surrounding area. Instead of a long Gothic nave with front or side tower, Richardson felt a more compact Greek cross plan with a large central tower was better suited to the site and would give

Portrait of H. H. Richardson by Hubert Herkomer

the tower prominence from the surrounding streets. In his words: "The struggle for precedence, which often takes place between a church and its spire, was disposed of by at once and completely subordinating nave, transepts, and apse, and grouping them about the tower as the central mass." The "lowness" of the Trinity service gave him design freedom he would not have had with a "higher" church. The rector, Phillips Brooks, preferred the Romanesque style to the Gothic, because the Gothic was associated with late medieval Catholicism. It is important to note, however, that Richardson was not a true revivalist but had his own style freely drawn and adapted from many

Richardson's conceptual sketch for Trinity Church

periods, from early Syrian Christian to American colonial.

In the course of construction, Richardson greatly improved and simplified his original design by replacing the tall, octagonal, rather slender lantern with a massive square tower inspired by that of the Cathedral of Salamanca. Richardson had the rare ability to see faults in his own work and to improve it, as illustrated by his final design for Trinity, which far surpasses his original winning conception. Richardson himself said, "I really don't see why the Trinity people liked them, or, if they liked them, why they let me do what I afterwards did." Stanford White, later of McKim, Mead, and White, apprenticed under Richardson for several years (1872–1878) and worked on the tower. The more detailed, intricate design of the tower is thought to be the

influence of White, for the lower part of the church is more simple and massive in the Richardson tradition.

Richardson had been under pressure from the engineer and building committee to reduce the weight of the tower as originally planned, since the church was to be built on the wet filled land of Back Bay. The final tower weighs 90 million pounds and rests on 2,000 wooden piles arranged in a 90-foot square. On top of the piles stand four granite pyramids 35 feet square and 17 feet high; they support the corner piers of the tower. Because the pilings are of wood, they must be kept submerged in water. The level of the water table beneath the church is constantly monitored.

The auditorium is actually three squares in plan, one square being the apse, one the crossing, and one the nave. The total length from the apse to the façade is 160 feet; the width of the transepts, 121 feet. The ceilings are 63 feet at the highest point, and the tower ceiling is 103 feet. The tower roof rises 211 feet from the ground to the top of the finial.

Granite was chosen for the major building material because of its strength, and was quarried in Dedham; Quincy; Westerly, Rhode Island; and the Maine coast. Color was an important part of Richardson's concept for the building, both inside and outside. He

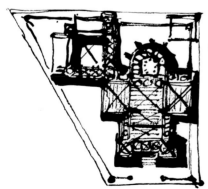

Richardson's early sketch for the plan of Trinity Church

chose red Longmeadow sandstone for the trim. For the roof and louver boards he used semi-glazed red tiles made in Akron, Ohio, while the rolls and crockets—the knobby projections on the tower ridges—were made in Chicago. The influence of the Romanesque of the Auvergne region of southern France is evident in the marquetry. When the exterior was cleaned, Bostonians were shocked to see its original lively colors.

Richardson persuaded the painter John La Farge, assisted by the young Augustus Saint-Gaudens, to execute the rich and colorful interiors he envisioned. The color of the granite was too cold and harsh for Richardson's concept. Plastered walls were painted and stenciled in dull terra-cotta, gold, and blue-green. Furring and plaster-encased granite piers appear to be clusters of delicate columns. Stained-glass windows were crafted by John La Farge, Edward Burne-Jones, William Morris, and others. Black walnut woodwork was used in the church and chapel, ash and oak in the vestibule. Wooden truss-like members at the arches of the crossing are actually decorative casings for iron tie rods that were installed as a precaution, not a necessity. None of the stonework in the building requires any metal reinforcement.

The parish, desperate for a meeting place after the great fire of November 1872 destroyed its Summer Street church, had been meeting in temporary quarters in the MIT lecture hall. At last, on February 8, 1877, the subscribers could sit in their handsomely carved Richardson-designed pews. Upstairs the balcony seats were free to all.

Though the church was finished, the façade did not appear as it does today. Instead of the projecting sculpted portico, it had an imposing tall flat façade. The two front towers were also much simpler—and much disliked by Richardson, who urged the church to have them rebuilt. In 1882 Richardson

Sanctuary, Trinity Church © Trinity Church

Cloister, Trinity Church

visited St. Trophime in Arles, France, and sketched a design for a portico addition to Trinity based on it. The porch and front towers were finished after Richardson's death by his successor, Hugh Shepley, between 1894 and 1897 and are probably more elaborate than Richardson intended.

The Parish House, begun March 1874, was in use that November. The design of its roof resembles the Sherman house in Newport, designed by Richardson in 1874. The pyramidal roof forms build up to the larger mass of the church. The cascading cloistered exterior staircase leading to the second-floor chapel links the cloister and the church. The two dormers relate to the four tower dormers.

A statue of Phillips Brooks—first rector of the Copley Square church, Episcopal Bishop of Massachusetts, and author of "O, Little Town of Bethlehem"—was finished by Augustus Saint-Gaudens in 1910 and stands on the north side of the church.

In the first decade of the twenty-first century, the La Farge–painted decoration was "brightened" to "saturated Pompeian red" and geothermal wells were drilled to provide sustainable heating and cooling. Digging a deeper basement created an informal assembly room below the church. Etched-glass partitions by Alexander Beleschenko diffuse the gloom.

New Old South Church

97 New Old South Church 🏛

Copley Square at 645 Boylston Street
Cummings and Sears, 1874–1875
Tower rebuilt 1941
Restoration: Shepley Bulfinch
Richardson and Abbott, 1985
National Historic Landmark

:: The Old South Church moved to Copley Square from its eighteenth-century meetinghouse on Washington Street. The northern Italian Gothic design creates wonderful skyline views from many directions with its tall campanile and Venetian lantern. It is the perfect focus for the pivotal corner of Copley Square, counterpoint to the horizontal mass of the Boston Public Library and the monolithic Trinity Church.

Exterior ornament is abundant and well executed, including multicolored stone inlays, zebra-striped arches, tracery, and ironwork. A stone set into the portico wall records the death of one of the original members of Old South Church, John Alden, eldest son of John and Priscilla Alden of Plymouth Colony. A Paul Revere chalice is in the church's

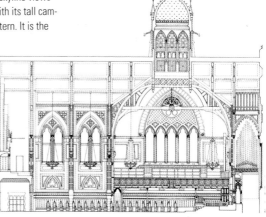

**Interior, New Old
South Church**
© Shelpey Bulfinch
Richardson and Abbott

silver collection. After the original 246-foot tower was built, it began to lean until it was 36 inches out of plumb. It was finally taken down in 1931 and rebuilt lower in 1941.

98 Boston Public Library 🏛
Copley Square
McKim, Mead, and White, 1887–1895
700 Boylston Street addition: Philip Johnson, 1971
National Historic Landmark

:: The Boston Public Library was founded in 1848 by an act of the Massachusetts Legislature. Opened in 1854, it was the first large city library for the general public in the United States. It left its building on Boylston Street opposite the Common for this imposing Copley Square landmark.

Charles Follen McKim had attended Harvard and apprenticed under H. H. Richardson in Boston. Later he married into the Boston Appleton family. These Boston connections certainly helped him secure the commission, but the crucial factor was that a library trustee much admired the Villard houses he had designed in New York. His Renaissance revival design for the library was a sharp change of direction for American architecture and remained influential for the next forty years. It stirred

Wrought-iron lanterns, Boston Public Library

considerable comment, not all of it positive. The *Boston Globe* compared it to the city morgue, while another critic termed it a warehouse.

In fact, it is an Italian Renaissance palazzo, influenced strongly by both Alberti's San Francesco at Rimini and Labrouste's Bibliotheque Saint Genevieve (1843–1850) in Paris. A row of equally spaced arched windows rise above the rusticated ground floor with three entry arches graced by fine iron gates and swooping lanterns. The handsome bronze doors are by sculptor Daniel Chester French and represent

Library courtyard

Bates Hall, Boston Public Library Courtesy of the Boston Public Library

Music and Poetry, Knowledge and Wisdom, and Truth and Romance. The building effectively integrates sculpture, painting, architecture, and engineering.

Interior space is organized about the grand staircase and entrance hall of beautiful Monte Riete, or Convent Siena, marble, a material difficult to obtain. Murals around the staircase and the second-floor corridor are by Puvis de Chavannes of Paris. The tile vaults on the ground floor, the first extensive use of tile vaulting in the country, are by the Guastavino firm of New York and Boston.

Bates Hall, the grand reading room—217 feet long, 42 feet wide, and 50 feet high—runs along the entire front of the second floor and has a barrel-vaulted ceiling terminating in

coffered apses. The hall is named after Joshua Bates, the library's first great benefactor. In the book delivery room is Edwin Austin Abbey's 1895 Pre-Raphaelite mural, *The Quest and Achievement of the Holy Grail*. At the opposite end of the corridor is the Elliott Room, with the ceiling painting *The Triumph of Time* by Boston artist John Elliott, who was the husband of Maud Howe Elliott, daughter of Julia Ward Howe. At each end of the Chavannes Gallery are the Venetian and Pompeian lobbies, which lead to the delivery room and Elliott Room.

Ascending the staircase to the third floor one reaches the Sargent Gallery, named for John Singer Sargent, who decorated it with his murals *Judaism and Christianity*. One of the most dazzling features of the library is the inner Italian courtyard, based on the Cancelleria Palace in Rome.

Making an addition to such an extraordinary piece of architecture was a challenge of the highest order. Philip Johnson composed a striking but unrelated façade. The rare book room on the third floor is his most successful addition. The interior connection between the two buildings is tenuous and circuitous.

99 Copley Plaza Hotel
Copley Square at 138 St. James Avenue
Blackall and Hardenberg, 1910–1912

Copley Plaza Hotel

:: Henry Hardenberg, architect of the Plaza Hotel and the Dakota apartment building in New York City, designed the hotel in association with Clarence Blackall, a local architect. The Italian Renaissance revival façade is of rusticated limestone, with a large central bowfront flanked by two entry porticoes. The lavish theatrical interiors of its ballroom, restaurants, bar, function rooms, and lobby are well preserved and deserve a look. John Singer Sargent had a suite of rooms in the hotel from 1919 until his death in 1925.

100 John Hancock Towers 🏛
Copley Square at 200 Clarendon Street
I. M. Pei, 1972–1975

101 200 Berkeley Street
(The Berkeley Building)
Cram and Ferguson, 1947

:: The old John Hancock tower has a uniquely identifiable form on the skyline, with its truncated stepped pyramid and weather beacon:

Steady blue, clear view;
Flashing blue, clouds due;
Steady red, rain ahead;
Flashing red, snow instead.

Copley Square and John Hancock Towers
© Peter Vanderwarker

The stylized, rather heavy decoration visible at the ground-floor entrance to the auditorium on Berkeley is not unlike some postmodernist work done in the 1980s. The building has exhibits of old Boston.

In contrast to the mass and solidity of the old tower, the 1970s tower pretends not to be there at all. Its finely detailed reflective skin makes it more sky and light than building. In fact, there was considerable debate as to whether a tower should be placed on this important and difficult site, with two nineteenth-century monuments—Trinity Church and the Public Library—so near. The way the narrow slab is twisted with its knife edge thrusting into Copley Square makes it appear ever so slender from some vantage points; from all angles the reflections of clouds and Trinity's tower are striking. Some have called it a good solution to an impossible design problem.

Even more remarkable than its visual form is its engineering—or should one call it "after-the-fact engineering"?—which required complete replacement of its large plate-glass curtain-wall panels, reinforcement of the steel frame of the structure, installation of a complex monitoring system to detect deflections in the glass to warn of possible breakage, and a "tuned mass damper," a rolling weight on a film of oil on the fifty-eighth floor to counter high wind stresses.

102 Back Bay Station
between Clarendon and Dartmouth Streets near Stuart Street
Kallmann, McKinnell, and Wood, 1987

:: Giant arches of laminated wood span the great concourse space of glass block and concrete. The Clarendon Street entrance is reminiscent of an Italian piazza, with a pair of campanile-like ventilation towers. The piazza is defined by an elaborate brick and concrete wall with arched relief motifs related to the barrel vault of the main hall. Tina Allen's statue of civil and labor rights leader A. Philip Randolph honors his many accomplishments, including leadership of the Brotherhood of Sleeping Car Porters in 1925. One of a series of transit stations built as part of the Southwest Corridor, it serves Amtrak, the MBTA Orange Line, and commuter trains.

103 Copley Place
Copley Square at Huntington Avenue
The Architects Collaborative with Hugh Stubbins and Associates and Zaldastani Associates, 1980–1984

:: This corner of Copley Square was once effectively anchored by the extravagant neo-Romanesque S. S. Pierce building. Dallas or Houston seems to have been the inspiration for the marble atrium shopping mall and mixed-use project that replaced it. Located next to some of Boston's most cherished landmarks, the nine-and-a-half-acre site is at the intersection of several major streets and over the Massachusetts Turnpike and railroad tracks.

Pedestrian access is tenuous, depending too much on upper-level bridges, and the entire project is too introverted and claustrophobic.

Prudential Center Area

A new scale was introduced into the Back Bay with the construction of the Prudential Center, built over the expansive old railroad yards as one of Boston's early and controversial urban renewal projects. It was one of the first expressions of urban designer David Crane's later "capital web" concept, which focused new high-density development along a spine while retaining the historic infill. The scheme has now filled out, with a spine of high-rise construction stretching from Prudential Center to Government Center.

104 Prudential Center Complex
800 Boylston Street
Charles Luckman and Associates and Hoyle, Doran, and Berry, begun 1959
Renovation: CBT/Childs Bertman Tseckares; Carr, Lynch and Sandell; Halvorson Design Partnership, 2003
Hynes Convention Center addition/

Hynes Convention Center

renovation: Kallmann, McKinnell, and Wood, 1988

∷ In the original project, large freestanding masses—offices, hotel, and apartments—hovered over vast elevated plazas, concealing underground parking garages. Design of the plazas and the uses to which they might be put were never well considered, and they presented an oddly sinister and surrealist landscape. The shopping mall had to struggle for survival because of basic flaws in its conception. Raising it one level above the street, where it could be neither seen nor easily reached, was the first mistake. Heavy winds funneled through the shopping arcades despite the addition of protective walls. The tower, whether loved or despised, became a regional as well as a local landmark, too rarely out of sight.

In the late 1980s the ungainly Hynes Convention Center was expanded out to Boylston Street and into the right side of the empty Prudential forecourt. Adding a colonnade along the sidewalk gave definition to Boylston Street. It attempted to relate in scale and materials to its Back Bay setting, adopting the granite and setbacks of the Boston Public Library nearby. The

severe gray interior is reminiscent of an early twentieth-century German railroad station, as is the striking entrance canopy not quite on axis with Gloucester Street.

Many of the flaws of the Prudential plaza level were remedied in a later redevelopment by strengthening connections with the street level and creating active street edges. Commercial activity was greatly intensified in a glassenclosed shopping galleria focusing on the 480-foot-long Winter Garden.

105 Tennis and Racquet Club
939 Boylston Street
Parker, Thomas and Rice, 1904

∷ The handsome Tennis and Racquet Club started out as one of the Back Bay's exclusive clubs for men. This one focused on the arcane sports of court tennis and rackets (not racquetball). It is one of only nine facilities in the United States for court tennis, a game whose complex rules and strange court originated in the medieval castles and monasteries of Europe. Masterful players score effective bounces off asymmetrical protuberances meant to represent royal boxes, tented seating, or other remnants of the original settings.

Tennis and Racquet Club

116 Huntington Avenue

Courts are housed behind the solid upper walls of patterned brick, circled by a clerestory of square windows just beneath the generous eaves of the hip roof. A monumental entrance with over-scale brackets, voussoirs, and laurel garland is set into the ground-floor brickwork, which has been treated like rusticated stone.

106 Engine and Hose House Number 33
941 Boylston Street
Arthur H. Vinal, 1885
Renovation: Arrowstreet, 1971

107 955 Boylston Street
Arthur H. Vinal, 1886
Renovation: Graham Gund Associates, 1975

:: These buildings were originally de-signed to serve as fire station, police station, and stables. Romanesque in-spired, they feature round-arched win-dows and doorways with wide trim in both rough and smooth stone. The pic-turesque turret tower served as a hose drying tower. Renovation of the fire station provided a home for the Insti-tute of Contemporary Art until it relo-

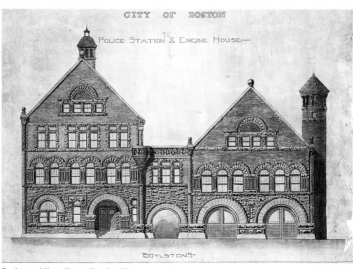

Engine and Hose House Number 33 Arrowstreet, Inc.

cated to the South Boston waterfront in December 2006.

108 116 Huntington Avenue
Childs, Bertman, Tseckares, 1990

:: This round-cornered building helps define the street space of Huntington Avenue. Conceived to fit into its Prudential Center context, 116 Huntington is built of brick and limestone-colored precast concrete. The restrained design recalls buildings of the 1920s and 1930s, especially in the façade organization. One example of the effects of the overbuilding encouraged in the late 1980s, this building stood locked and empty for several years after construction was completed.

109 Christian Science World Headquarters
Massachusetts Avenue at Huntington Avenue
Church: Franklin J. Welch, 1893–1894
Church enlargement: Charles E. Brigham and Solon S. Beman; Brigham, Coveney and Bisbee, 1903–1906
Administration Building, Colonnade Building, and Sunday School: I. M. Pei and Partners and Cossutta Associated Architects, 1968–1973
Landscape: Sasaki, Dawson, DeMay
Publishing house: Chester Lindsay Churchill, 1932
Publishing house renovation: Ann Beha Architects, 2002

:: Though it became the most monumental public space in Boston, the Christian Science World Headquarters began modestly with the small square-towered Romanesque church by Welch. The mammoth "addition" by Brigham and Beman, basically a classical revival basilica, seats 5,000 people and has the largest pipe organ in the Western Hemisphere, an Aeolian Skinner manufactured in Boston.

It was not until the Pei-Cossutta involvement, however, that it assumed its present scale. Until the late 1960s a

Berklee Performance Center (Kubitz and Pepi), 136 Massachusetts Avenue

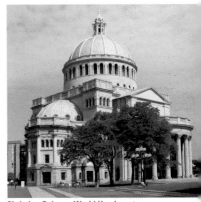

Christian Science World Headquarters

row of residential and commercial buildings along Massachusetts and Huntington Avenues obscured all but the dome of the church. Their plan demolished these obstacles and made geometric sense of what had been built, much in the way Bernini's piazza for St. Peter's in Rome monumentalized an already existing building. A large semicircular portico was constructed of limestone to form a main entrance on the Massachusetts Avenue façade. The concerns were formal, in the Renaissance and Baroque traditions.

The Colonnade Building, seemingly inspired by Le Corbusier's highly sculptural Chandigarh with its deep recesses and trough roof, screens the chaotic urban fill behind it. It also creates a backdrop for the plaza and its nearly

700-foot-long reflecting pool. The tower is a vertical focus balancing the dome and terminating the plaza. Access to the underground parking garage is inconspicuous. At the southwest corner of the plaza, the quarter-circle Sunday School screens Horticultural Hall and connects the Huntington and Massachusetts Avenue faces.

In 2002 the Mary Baker Eddy Library for the Betterment of Humanity was inserted into the eleven-story former publishing house of the Christian Science Society. The Mapparium was retained while interactive displays of world events were added, featuring the *Christian Science Monitor*. Removing most of the high stone wall that had lined the Massachusetts Avenue sidewalk and adding a glass-curtain wall entrance opened the building to passersby.

110 Church Park Apartments and Garage
221 Massachusetts Avenue
The Architects Collaborative, 1973

:: The long, repetitive concrete grid of the Church Park façade was designed to serve as a low-profile background for the foreground architecture of the Christian Science complex.

111 Horticultural Hall 🏛
300 Massachusetts Avenue
Wheelwright and Haven, 1901
National Register of Historic Places

:: The Massachusetts Horticultural Society was founded in 1829 to advance the knowledge and practice of horticulture. After leaving its exuberant French Second Empire building on Tremont Street at Montgomery Place, it occupied its new headquarters for a century. The grandiose English Baroque façades boast overscale pilasters, garlands, and wreaths. The brick of the giant corner pilasters has been set in the manner of large rusticated stones. It is an appro-

priate partner to the more sedate Symphony Hall across the street.

Edmund March Wheelwright, Boston's city architect, also designed the New England Conservatory, the Massachusetts Historical Society, and the Longfellow Bridge.

112 Symphony Hall 🏛
Massachusetts Avenue at Huntington Avenue
McKim, Mead, and White, 1900
National Register of Historic Places

:: Henry Lee Higginson did more than build Boston Symphony Hall; he founded the orchestra and hired and paid all the musicians and conductors. In his youth he had studied music in Vienna, attending many concerts in the great halls of Europe. The Grosse Musikvereinssaal in Vienna and Leipzig's Gewandhaus became the models for Boston's hall. Higginson also insisted that a young assistant professor of physics at Harvard, Wallace Clement Sabine, be consulted on the acoustics. Sabine was one of the first to study acoustics in a quantitative way and was so sure of his scientific basis that he guaranteed the hall would be acoustically perfect. Fortunately, he was correct, and the result is a Stradivarius among concert halls.

Like the Gewandhaus, the interior concert hall space is basically a double cube. Plentiful high-relief ceiling ornament, elaborate grills fronting the balconies, wall niches with statuary, and 2,631 hard seats resting on resilient wood flooring provide the resonance and reflectivity needed for a rich, sonorous hall. The green leather surface on the seats turned black after decades of use, and many were replaced with synthetic leather. The fan windows, which originally gave natural light, were blocked up during World War II and remain covered. The shallow balconies prevent any acoustically dead spots. Centered above the proscenium

Horticultural Hall

of the orchestra stage, a cartouche bears the name of Beethoven, whose Missa Solemnis inaugurated the hall. Monograms on the staircases represent the intended name, Boston Music Hall, a tribute to the performance site for most concerts in the nineteenth century.

McKim's design in the Italian Renaissance style is restrained. All flourishes are within the concert space. The statuary adorning the interior of the hall was intended to be repeated on the roofline, but McKim's elaborate façade flourishes were cut for budgetary reasons.

Bostonians cherish their symphony. Friday afternoon subscriptions have been handed down from generation to generation, so many of the best seats have been in the same families for fifty years or more. But Higginson set aside the excellent second balcony seats for those who could not afford subscriptions, selling them at 25 cents just before the concert. Thus was born the concept of "rush seats."

The Massachusetts Historical Society and Symphony Hall led the move to Boston's new Fenway cultural center at the close of the nineteenth century. The Horticultural Society, New England Conservatory, and Jordan Hall immediately followed. Isabella Stuart Gardner built her palace there and, last of all, came the Museum of Fine Arts from Copley Square.

113 Massachusetts Avenue MBTA Station
Massachusetts Avenue near St. Botolph Street
Ellenzweig Associates, Inc., 1986

:: This streamlined transit station of aluminum and glass is one in a series built as part of the Southwest Corridor Transportation Project. It serves the

Symphony Hall © Courtesy Boston Symphony Orchestra

Orange Line, relocated here when the elevated tracks on Washington Street were demolished.

St. Botolph District

Boston Architectural Conservation District

In England, *Boston* was a contraction of "St. Botolph's town." This street recalls the origin of the city's name. During the filling of the Back Bay from 1857 until 1882, the triangular area surrounded by the Boston–Albany railroad tracks on the north, the Boston–Providence tracks on the south, and Massachusetts Avenue on the west remained unfilled. In 1871 the land was sold to the Huntington Avenue Land Trustees, who subdivided it into lots and sold them at auction. Speculative builders began building houses there in the 1880s, near the Massachusetts Avenue end of the triangle. The early brick row houses were single-family dwellings, but by the 1890s they were mainly four-family flats.

From the beginning the area attracted artists, writers, and musicians, including sculptor Bela L. Pratt, poet Edwin Arlington Robinson, and writer Philip Henry Savage. A painting of the street, *Noontime, St. Botolph,* by the New York painter George Benjamin Luks (known as "Lusty Luks" for his earthy subjects) hangs in the Museum of Fine Arts. As described in the museum's slide catalogue, "Ochre-brown and red-brick houses with their purple and white striped blinds are streaked with purple shadows. An ice man, in yellow, walks in the pink and yellow street beside green grass."

Harcourt Street was the original location of the Harcourt Bindery, which later moved to Melcher Street in the leather district. The stained-glass studio of master craftsman Charles Connick was founded on Harcourt Street in 1912. The studio made windows for St. Patrick's and St. John the Divine in New York City. Following Connick's lead, another stained-glass shop, the John Terrance O'Duggan Studio, opened in 1935 in a house at 116 St. Botolph Street.

Throughout its history the area has had an interesting mixed-use character combining residences, businesses, a series of schools, and light industry. The railroad-track barriers kept it separated from the Back Bay until the development of the Prudential Center. Thus its orientation was toward Massachusetts Avenue and, over several bridges, to the South End. The redeveloped Southwest Corridor has reduced the barriers between the South End and the St. Botolph Street neighborhood.

114 Musicians' Mutual Relief Society Building
52–56 St. Botolph Street
Cabot and Chandler, 1886
Renovations: Maher and Winchester, 1913; Eisenberg Haven Associates, 1982

:: This neoclassical brick hall is a simplified version of Horticultural Hall. Above the large arched windows with keystones, the names of composers are carved in stone beneath the cornice. Separating each pair of composers is a decorative stone lyre at the top of a pilaster. The building was originally the Allen Gymnasium Company, but was converted and newly ornamented for

Musicians' Mutual Relief Society Building

use by the Musicians' Mutual Relief Society in 1913. It housed a large meeting hall, offices, and later a restaurant, barbershop, and billiard alcoves.

115 The School-House Condominiums
145 St. Botolph Street
Edmund March Wheelwright, 1891
Renovation: Graham Gund Associates, 1980

:: Originally the Charles E. Perkins Elementary School, the building was recycled in 1980 as twenty-one condominiums. Each of the original ten classrooms became a one- or two-bedroom unit, with living rooms located at the corners to obtain a double exposure through the large windows. Six units—three flats and three duplexes—are located in the trussed flat hip roof, where recessed outdoor decks and windows were added. The building was the first in the area to use buff-colored brick.

116 Albemarle Chambers
off St. Botolph Street on Albemarle Street
Israel Nesson, 1899

:: Although this group of twelve "three-decker" apartments was designed as modest tenements, the court-

Lobby, The School-House Condominiums
© Steve Rosenthal

yard provides an unexpected amenity. A purely ornamental Dutch gable projects above the central section, while swags, wreaths, and pilasters in a classical vein ornament the simple façade.

117 Southwest Corridor Park
Landscape architects: Rôy Mann Associates (master plan); Moreice and Gary (Back Bay), Carol R. Johnson Associates (Ruggles), Mason and Frey (Forest Hills), Huygens and DiMella, Inc. (Jackson Square); community coordinator: Harry Ellenzweig Associates, 1989

Albemarle Chambers

Southwest Corridor Park

:: From the nineteenth century until the late 1980s, a railroad corridor separated Roxbury from Jamaica Plain and the Fenway, and the Back Bay from the South End. This gap was bridged by the Southwest Corridor Park, part of a massive $780 million rail, transit, and park project developed by the Massachusetts Bay Transit Authority. Boston has never been timid about large-scale projects, but this nearly 5-mile, fifty-five-acre linear park was the largest of its type since Frederick Law Olmsted conceived the Emerald Necklace.

The Orange Line elevated transit line was rerouted from Washington Street in the South End and Roxbury to run alongside the existing depressed commuter and intercity railroad tracks. The entire South End section beginning

at Back Bay Station was then decked over to create open space. The park, varying in width from 60 feet to 0.25 mile, continues into Roxbury and Jamaica Plain on a swath of land cleared for the notorious, unbuilt Inner Belt Highway.

The open-space corridor varies from basketball courts and land for urban gardeners to traditional landscaping with bicycle and walking paths. Community groups participated in programming sections adjacent to their neighborhoods. Near Dartmouth Street, granite stelae are literary sculptures incised with quotations from contemporary Boston writers. In 2003 Titus Sparrow Park was designed by Halvorson Design Partnership on West Newton Street at Southwest Corridor Park.

FENWAY

The Fenway was the first Boston neighborhood developed with a large park at its center. Construction began to surround the Back Bay Fens in the 1890s amid great enthusiasm. The huge New Riding Club brought prominent Bostonians to the bucolic area. Within a decade of the opening of the club, a wave of construction was under way for Boston's major cultural institutions, initially on Boylston Street and Huntington Avenue, newly extended beyond Massachusetts Avenue. Land was cheap and available in large lots for the many institutions that relocated here. The Historical Society, Symphony Hall, and the Opera House were soon joined by the Museum of Fine Arts. Boston Latin School, Harvard Medical School, music conservatories, and the Wentworth Institute arrived along with colleges including Simmons, Emmanuel, and Boston State.

While Mrs. Jack Gardner built her sumptuous palace on the southwest side of the park, others did not join her. Because Bay State Road was developing at the same time and filling up with gracious Back Bay–style homes, residential construction lagged in the Fens and provided a different housing type. Rather than individually designed showy homes, rows of identical practical houses and four-story walk-up flats were built on the short side streets. Though largely red brick, a group of yellow brick houses was built on Edgerly Road. Innovation is evident also in the tile façades on affordable apartment buildings that introduced a new style to the city. It was picked up as trim even on brick row houses. When Northeastern University arrived, it built its entire campus in light gray brick, echoing the neighborhood's white tile and distinguishing it from the many local red brick colleges.

1 Research Building, Harvard Medical School
77 Avenue Louis Pasteur
Architectural Resources Cambridge, 2003

:: The largest research facility built for Harvard Medical School serves 800 researchers and staff in genetics and pathology, as well as the faculties of the school's teaching hospitals. Eschewing the classical revival style of the Louis Pasteur quadrangle built a century earlier, the architects chose medical scrubs green metal and glass applied in a slick skin over a frameless box. A green granite wall shields the driveway to the underground garage. An auditorium has visible ramps encircling it. The ten-story tower was set back behind the linear four-story conference center and service facilities on the street frontage.

Research Building, Harvard Medical School © Jeff Goldberg/Esto

2 St. Clement's Archdiocesan Eucharistic Shrine
1101 Boylston Street
Allen and Collens, ca. 1920

:: Although its tower has been demolished, the strong form of St. Clement's nave with set-back stepped buttresses and fine Gothic revival interior demonstrates the architects' prowess in this style. Their other notable buildings include the Lindsey Memorial Chapel at Emmanuel Church and Riverside Church and the high altar of St. Patrick's Cathedral, both in New York City.

Merck Research Laboratories, 33 Avenue Louis Pasteur (Kling, 2005)

3 Berklee College of Music
1140 Boylston Street
Arthur Bowditch, 1901

:: The animated façade of the Berklee College of Music might be termed "cartoon Georgian." Gibbs surrounds run wild, and on the second-story windows they are extended to form three stone stringcourses. Several of the windows have elaborately carved brackets added to their keystones. The third-story windows have heavy bracketed projecting lintels and delicate cast-iron balconies, while the small windows have the Gibbs surround. All the fourth-floor windows are ornamented with Gibbs surrounds, and each large window has a carved swag beneath the sill. The fantasy continues in the entrance portico of banded Ionic columns with alternating stripes of fluting and vermiculated stone.

4 Massachusetts Historical Society
1154 Boylston Street
Edmund March Wheelwright, 1899
National Historic Landmark

:: The dignified Georgian revival brick and stone double bowfront Historical Society building employs many classical motifs. Doric columns support a narrow architrave and frieze ornamented with triglyphs to form the entrance portico in the chamfered rusticated stone of the street-level façade. On the upper levels Ionic pilasters frame the central windows, which have partial Gibbs surrounds and a fanlight over the third-story center window. Windows of the bows are simpler, with keystoned lintels and no surrounds. Four bas-relief swags complete the ornamentation beneath the cornice and balustrade.

The Massachusetts Historical Society was founded in 1791 and was located in a room donated by Charles Bulfinch above the arch of his crescent on Franklin Place. America's oldest historical society remained there until 1833, when it moved next to King's Chapel Burying Ground. After it relocated into its building at this address, the Boston Medical Library decided to build on the lots next door, dedicating its building in 1901. Its architect, Robert S. Peabody, built his large house beside it. These buildings still stand but have been put to new uses.

Berklee College of Music

Massachusetts Historical Society

5 Harvard Community Health Plan
Brookline Avenue at 2 Fenway Plaza
1925–1939
Renovation: Steffian Bradley Associates, 1979

:: These buildings, built as warehouses and offices for the S. S. Pierce and Firestone Tire and Rubber Companies, were recycled as an ambulatory health-care center and management offices for the Harvard Community Health Plan. The glass-enclosed atrium and automobile ramp are additions to the original structures. Each medical department has been treated as a separate unit to reinforce the sense of individualized medical care for both staff and patients. The same firm designed the original HCHP building, completed in 1972, at nearby Kenmore Square.

6 Fenway Park
Brookline Avenue at Jersey Street
1912; rebuilt 1934

:: The oldest and smallest facility in Major League Baseball is tucked tightly into an urban corner of Kenmore Square. Its "Green Monster," the 37-foot-tall green left field wall, compensates for the short 315-foot depth of left field. Constructed for the 1912 season and rebuilt in 1934, with numerous additions and alterations since, Fenway Park has a "depression-style" brick façade that lacks architectural presence. Inside, where the legendary intimacy keeps the audience in the center of the action, is another matter.

Campaigning here in 1940, Franklin Delano Roosevelt promised not to send Americans to the war in Europe.

7 Kerr Hall
96 The Fenway
Kilham & Hopkins, 1914

:: At the turn of the twentieth century, the ladies of Emmanuel Church wanted to increase female enrollment in local colleges. They raised funds and built Students' House for eighty-five women. It was near Simmons Female College but open to women attending any Boston-area college. In 1972 it was purchased by Northeastern University.

8 Forsyth Dental Infirmary for Children
140 The Fenway
Edward T. P. Graham, 1915

:: The Forsyth family of Roxbury established a children's dental infirmary in 1910. The classical style was considered appropriate for any institution of this period, from post office or police station to school or morgue. Early nineteenth-century Boston architects such as Alexander Parris also turned to classical sources for a variety of public buildings (including Faneuil Hall Marketplace, U.S. Custom House, and St.

Fenway Park © *The Boston Globe* (Bill Brett, photographer)

Paul's Cathedral). Here an arcade of engaged Doric columns with Ionic capitals wraps around the building, resting on a first story of chamfered rustication.

9 Isabella Stewart Gardner Museum ⅲ
280 The Fenway
Willard T. Sears, 1902
National Register of Historic Places

∷ Here is the personal "palace" of Mrs. John Lowell Gardner Jr. It was built to house an extraordinary Boston woman and her unique collection of art and furnishings, much of it acquired with the advice and assistance of Bernard Berenson, the noted art historian. Fabulous stories circulated about

"Mrs. Jack" walking down Tremont Street with a lion on a leash, taking up Buddhism, and spending lavish sums on her wardrobe and jewels when neither was an appropriate concern for a proper Boston lady (which she was not). The stories may seem suspect until one considers the tangible evidence that survives. The force of her personality and her extravagance are undeniable in the art she collected. This museum was indeed her personal home, and that is the most outlandish story of all. Everything is still in exactly the place where she left it and can never be relocated, according to the strict terms of her will.

The plain exterior encloses a fantastic Venetian interior. An arcade of

Isabella Stewart Gardner Museum © Isabella Stewart Gardner Museum

colonettes supporting semicircular arches surrounds the garden level of the landscaped courtyard. At the upper level the pink-and-white mottled walls are punctuated with tripartite windows with balustrades or balconies. The four-story courtyard is a delightful space by day, but by night it becomes magical, with candelabras and sconces glowing in the richly decorated rooms overlooking it.

Mrs. Gardner's private quarters on the fourth floor opened to the public for the first time on the building's hundredth anniversary.

New Riding Club

10 New Riding Club
52 Hemenway Street
Willard T. Sears, 1892
National Register of Historic Places

:: The New Riding Club was organized in 1891 as a private club for prominent Bostonians, with stables convenient to the new bridle paths through the Fenway. The riding instructor, Henri de Bussigny, was as famous and socially indispensable as the dance master Lorenzo Papanti. The former French cavalry officer was a rigid product of St. Cyr and a first-rate horseman of the French classical style.

Despite too many materials and motifs, this very long stable in the Tudor revival style resonates with appealing bits and pieces. Stucco with faux half-timbering dominates the upper floors, while tan brick with red brick round arches on the first floor produce a bizarre juxtaposition of northern European and Mediterranean styles. The building contained clubhouse facilities, a stable, a riding room, and space for grooming, shoeing, feeding, exercising, and veterinary care of members' horses. Well into the twentieth century, the riding ring was converted to tennis courts and other parts of the building became residential.

11 Boston University Theatre
264 Huntington Avenue
J. Williams Beal's Sons, 1925

:: A charming small theater is behind this Georgian revival façade of brick and stone. Originally called the Repertory Theater, it is reminiscent of the Wilbur Theatre, built eleven years earlier. Ornamentation is concentrated at the two ends of the façade, where symmetrical porticoes on slender columns are at the entry level and matched pairs of fluted Corinthian pilasters frame pedimented windows and festooned oculi above.

12 New England Conservatory of Music and Jordan Hall
290–294 Huntington Avenue
Wheelwright and Haven, 1901, 1904
National Register of Historic Places

:: The New England Conservatory, the first music college in the country, was established in 1867 after many years of effort by Dr. Eben Tourjee. Its early classes were held in rooms in the old Music Hall building, now the Orpheum Theater, until 1882 when it took over the St. James Hotel, now the Franklin

Square House, in the South End. Twenty years later the conservatory moved into a new structure built specifically for it in the new Boston cultural center developing on Huntington Avenue.

The conservative classical revival façade offers no surprises or innovations. The brickwork is modeled to suggest coursed rustication on the ground floor, and quoins define corner pavilions and the entrance bay on the upper floors.

The most interesting part of the complex is the interior of Jordan Hall, an auditorium built in 1904 by Eben Jordan. The founder of the Jordan Marsh department store had also provided funds for two other Boston theaters: the Majestic and the old Huntington Avenue Opera House that was demolished in 1958. This fine concert hall has a peculiar seating and floor design that gives patrons the tipsy feeling of being on a boat. Presumably to provide good sight lines, all the rows of the balcony slant downhill, while on the main floor odd sections of seats create aisles that dead-end in the middle of the auditorium.

13 Northeastern University
360 Huntington Avenue
Shepley Bulfinch Richardson and Abbott, 1934 and later

:: In their original master plan and architecture for Northeastern University in 1934, the architects sought a completely different image from that of their many Harvard buildings, which were rooted in early American and English traditions. Stripped of all specific historical references, the austere light gray brick buildings nevertheless have a neoclassical feeling in their symmetry and proportions.

The 1965 Carl S. Ell Student Center featured a 60-foot-high Great Hall, the focus for student extracurricular activities. Its modular structure of sandblasted concrete columns, beams, and

Boston University Theatre

New England Conservatory of Music and YMCA

exposed coffered ceilings accommodates a variety of spaces, including a cafeteria, ballroom, experimental theater, banquet hall, meeting rooms, practice rooms, and offices.

14 Multi-Faith Spiritual Center
346 Ell Center, Northeastern University
Huntington Avenue
Office dA, 1994

:: Avoiding any symbols of specific religions while providing a space that suggested worship was the goal. To cap the neutral space, the designers relied on a dome as the universal architectural form for houses of worship.

15 Kariotis and Cargill Halls
Northeastern University
55 Huntington Avenue
Herbert S. Newman, 1982

:: The architect broke out of the rigid context established in previous decades, inaugurating the dramatic shift in Northeastern University's architecture that came over the next decades as it doubled and tripled in size. Elements of neighboring buildings are drawn in, such as the quoins and the combination of brick with light concrete trim in Kariotis Hall, but the Baroque curves and bulges seem to come only from the architect's imagination. The end result improves the older buildings by juxtaposition.

Kariotis Hall

16 Badger-Rosen SquashBusters
Northeastern University
795 Columbus Avenue
Childs, Bertman, Tseckares, 2003

:: The biggest deviation from Northeastern University's architectural tradition is this silver curving structure on pilotis. One of the innovative athletic programs for "at-risk" youths, SquashBusters was organized in 1996. Since moving into this facility, the capacity has expanded and the age range has increased to sixth-through-twelfth grade.

17 Ruggles Street Transit Station
near Columbus Avenue
Stull and Lee, Inc., 1988

:: The Ruggles Street Transit Station is a multimodal transportation node servicing the Orange Line, buses, commuter rail, and Amtrak lines. A long barrel vault framed within a concrete arch serves as an entry portal to Northeastern University, which has grown to encircle it. For four decades beginning in 1871, this was a baseball field. In 1888 a double-decked stadium for spectators was built with distinctive end towers. It became the home of the Boston Braves.

West Campus Residence Halls

Badger-Rosen SquashBusters

College of Computer and Information Science and Residence Hall

18 Museum of Fine Arts

465 Huntington Avenue
Guy Lowell, 1907–1909
Additions: Hugh Stubbins and
Associates, 1966–1970; The Architects
Collaborative, 1976; I. M. Pei, 1981;
Foster & Partners with Childs Bertman
Tserkares, 2008
Tenshin-En Japanese Garden: Kinsaku
Nakane with Halvorson Design
Partnership, 1988

Ruggles Street Station

:: The Museum of Fine Arts, incorporated in 1870, held exhibits on the top floor of the Boston Athenaeum until 1876, when it acquired an ornate Victorian Gothic building on Copley Square. In 1909 it followed other Boston institutions to the Fenway cultural center, building this massive granite classical revival building on twelve acres.

Its two original façades on Huntington Avenue and the Fenway offer a contrast. An Ionic temple portico announces the Huntington entrance, and the two flanking wings, each with smaller temple porches, embrace the entrance courtyard and its incongruous equestrian statue of the American Indian. On the Fenway side, the scale is more monumental. A long Ionic colonnade rises two stories across the flat façade.

While the exterior form conveyed a sense of simplicity and organization, interior circulation became more complex with each addition, a problem Norman Foster tried to resolve in his American Wing. In contrast to I. M. Pei's West Wing addition, with its understated façade of gray granite matching the original building, Foster relied heavily on glass, as he did in renovating Berlin's Reichstag. By enclosing the two large courtyards, he sought to reestablish their role as organizing points for the series of enfilade galleries that encircle them.

Tenshin-En, the Garden of the Heart of Heaven, is a walled Japanese garden located on the Fenway side of the

Museum of Fine Arts

museum. It was designed to suggest mountains, ocean, and islands in the New England landscape.

19 Fenway Studios
30 Ipswich Street
Parker, Thomas, and Rice, 1905
Renovation: Lajas Heder & Associates, 1982
National Register of Historic Places

:: Happily, the Fenway Studios building is still populated by artists, and hopefully it always will be under the limited equity cooperative by-laws implemented in 1982. The cleverly organized two-story units have abundant light from the large windows. A skip-floor corridor system allows cross ventilation as well. The interiors are redolent of the turn-of-the-twentieth-century artistic life usually found only in novels.

Harvard Medical School

20 Joslin Diabetes Center
near Longwood Avenue at 1 Joslin Place
Payette Associates, 1974–1976
Renovation and addition: Ellenzweig Associates, 1994

:: The center accommodates the study and training of ambulatory diabetic patients, a field pioneered by Dr. Eliot P. Joslin. Due to site constraints, the expansion was vertical. The three-story addition and penthouse are metal clad to contrast with the concrete base. All construction work took place in the context of an existing functioning nursing unit that could not be disrupted.

21 Harvard Medical School
200–260 Longwood Avenue
Shepley, Rutan, and Coolidge, 1907

:: A grand composition in white marble on axis with Avenue Louis Pasteur, the Harvard Medical School is one of the high points of Boston's turn-of-the-twentieth-century classical revival style.

22 Francis A. Countway Library of Medicine
Harvard Medical Center
off Longwood Avenue at 10 Shattuck Street
Hugh Stubbins and Associates, 1965

:: This is the oldest and one of the largest medical books collections in

Fenway Studios

the country. Open stacks overlook the seven-story court. Reading alcoves ring the perimeter and are articulated on the exterior as projections on the upper levels, while individual study carrels project over the central space.

Park Drive

Park Drive and Boylston Street enclose a small neighborhood sited among many outstanding institutions. The developers of the Fenway expected this area to become one of the most fashionable and sought-after in the city, but as it turned out, Bay State Road and the streetcar suburbs of Newton and Brookline took precedence. Although much of the architecture was purely speculative development, there is some outstanding terra-cotta ornament. Along the west side of the Back Bay Fens, the curving roadway is lined with harmonious façades. The simple blocks of apartments enjoy an enviable view of what remains of Frederick Law Olmsted's landscape design for the Fens.

23 Holy Trinity Orthodox Church
165 Park Drive
Constantine Pertzoff, 1960

:: The Holy Trinity Russian Orthodox congregation was organized in 1910. After half a century in rented spaces, they were able to build this modern Russian revival–style church. Intersecting elliptical barrel vaults were decorated with traditional Russian motifs, including onion finials and an onion dome.

Following the 1999 Kosovo war, Serbian medieval churches, monasteries, nunneries, and cemeteries were destroyed as Orthodox Christians were ethnically cleansed from most of the Serbian province. Not all the refugees were Serbs. Albanian Orthodox Christian refugees came to Boston, expanding the important local Albanian community.

Glazed terra-cotta façade, Fenway

Holy Trinity Orthodox Cathedral

Nikon Liolin, already archbishop of the Boston Albanian Orthodox Archdiocese, was installed as Bishop of Boston for the Orthodox Church of America at the renamed Holy Trinity Orthodox Cathedral in 2005.

24 Annunciation Greek Orthodox Cathedral
514 Parker Street
1924

:: Classical pedimented pavilions project from the church. The real attraction, architecturally, is inside. The richly decorated interiors are executed in the Byzantine manner with gold mosaics and a profusion of color. The congregation held services in a rented hall on Tyler Street from 1899 until 1907, when they moved into Church of the Annunciation on Winchester Street.

Longwood and Cottage Farm

Griffins reminiscent of medieval Venetian ironwork, 121 St. Stephens Street

Longwood and Cottage Farm 𝕚𝕚
Chapel, Colchester, Hawes, Kent, Monmouth, and Ivy streets
National Register of Historic Places

:: The Back Bay Fens empties into the Riverway, which separates the Fenway district from Longwood and Cottage Farm. These quiet, old Brookline residential quarters are closely connected with the medical institutions along

Queensberry Street

Red brick four-story apartment buildings line the street in a harmonious row. Each building has a columned portico center entrance with bay windows at each end. White-glazed terra-cotta tile provided ornamentation for windows, stringcourses, and entrances, although much has been removed. Balconies project from occasional second- and third-floor windows. Cafés and restaurants arrived en masse on both Queensberry and Peterborough Streets late in the twentieth century, but the first mixed use was much earlier: A baker lived above his shop at 37 Queensberry Street.

Amos Lawrence House (1851), 135 Ivy Street

George Minot Dexter House (1851), 156 Ivy Street

Longwood. Crossing the bridge opposite Louise Nevelson's sculpture *Sky Covenant* in front of Temple Israel, the scene changes abruptly.

David Sears, a wealthy Bostonian whose home became the Somerset Club, developed the Longwood area in the 1860s as an exclusive inner suburb for himself, his family, and his friends. For his model he took the English country village of Colchester, his family's ancestral home. Streets with English names—Colchester, Monmouth, Kent—focus on Longwood Mall. The name Longwood is from Napoleon's St. Helena country estate.

Although Sears's own estate is gone, several churches and "cottages" of Roxbury puddingstone in the romantic English country style remain and give the area its distinct flavor. Christ Church, built in 1860–1862 by Sears as his family chapel, was designed by Arthur Gilman, also architect of the Arlington Street Church, and was based on St. Peter's Church in Colchester. It stands on a slope next to the Tudor revival Longwood Towers and overlooks Olmsted's green Riverway Park. St. Paul's (on St. Paul Street), designed by

Richard Upjohn and built in 1848–1851, is another of the picturesque churches and perhaps the first to use puddingstone. Unfortunately, it suffered extensive fire damage, but the shell survived and has been rebuilt as one of Boston's first solar-heated churches.

Until the turn of the twentieth century, the area remained rural in feeling, with only a few houses scattered among the fields. Although now surrounded by development, the 1851 stone houses George Minot Dexter designed for himself and Amos Lawrence can be seen at 135 and 156 Ivy Street and still possess their original charm.

25 Church of Our Saviour
23 Monmouth Street
Alexander R. Estey, 1868
Tower rebuilt: Allen and Collens, 1932
Parish hall
Cabot and Chandler, 1880, and Sturgis and Cabot, 1913 and 1921
Rectory
Arthur Rotch, 1885

:: Although the work of several architects over many years, the Church of Our Saviour complex skillfully joins church, parish hall and rectory with a charming cloister. The stained-glass windows are by Edward Burne-Jones, Tiffany, Charles Connick, and others. The church was built in 1868 by brothers William and Amos Lawrence for their family and friends who had built homes in the Cottage Farm area across Beacon Street from David Sears's Longwood estates. "It was a sight seen oftener in old England than in this country—the two venerable brothers with their families joining the group of neighbors as they walked to the door of the memorial church, then worshipping together like one large family" (Victorian Society, *Victorian Boston*). Remarkably, this remains even now a picturesque Victorian parish church with English village atmosphere.

Church of Our Saviour

26 Longwood Towers

(formerly Alden Park Manor)
20 Chapel Street, Brookline
K. M. DeVos and Company with George R. Wiren and Harold Field Kellogg, 1922–1925

:: An early twentieth-century concept perfectly suited to the twenty-first century incorporates a vast three-story structure beneath a pastoral green. Garages, meeting rooms, service facilities, and a restaurant are united under one roof with access to all three Tudor-style residential towers—which appear from outdoors to sit neatly and separately on English lawns. Underground areas are entered at grade level on a lower street. Crenellated brick towers and parapets are details at the service of an ingenious site plan.

27 Ruggles Street Church

Audubon Circle at 874 Beacon Street
Ralph Adams Cram, 1913–1917

:: This handsome Georgian revival church was built by the congregation of the Second Unitarian Church of Boston. An elaborate tower stands at the intersection of the low gambrel-roof colonial wing and the taller classical gable of the nave, certainly a strange juxtaposition of styles. A Palladian window tops the gambrel end, while the sanctuary entrance is highlighted with banded rustication and quoins.

Ruggles Street Church

Longwood Towers

Lawn entrance, Longwood Towers

CHARLESTOWN

Surrounded by rivers and bay, Charlestown was all about water from its earliest days. The 1629 settlers blamed brackish water and the general aspect of Charlestown for the sickness and death that beset their population. When the Rev. William Blackstone invited them to move to the Shawmut peninsula, promising abundant fresh springs, many readily agreed. To the distress of those who didn't go, they took a fine house frame with them across the bay.

The small group that stayed in Charlestown prospered, perhaps benefiting from the reduced demand on water. By 1650 Captain Edward Johnson described a thriving town: "It hath a large market-place near the water side built round with houses, comely and fair, forth of which there issues two streets orderly built with some very fair houses, beautified with pleasant gardens and orchards."

None of the seventeenth-century buildings survive, but Town Hill, Main Street, and Winthrop Square have prodigious concentrations of late Georgian and Federal dwellings. Monument Square is a showplace of Victorian architecture. The Navy Yard preserves more than two centuries of the nation's naval history. Lynde's Point became Prison Point, site of the (demolished) prison designed by Charles Bulfinch. Sacco, Vanzetti, and Malcolm

X were among its famous inmates. Nearby, ropewalks were built at the corner of Lynde and Arrow Streets in 1794.

Charlestown has been noted for political leadership since its beginning and played a large role in the Revolution. In 1775 the British burned most of the town, a loss of more than 500 pre-Revolutionary houses, barns, mills, and shops, but important Revolutionary War sites remain. Its citizens returned and began rebuilding their town in the late eighteenth century. As a result of its long and glorious history, Charlestown is a must-see for American history buffs and an integral part of any architectural tour of Boston.

---

1 Leonard P. Zakim Bunker Hill Bridge
Charles River
Christian Menn, 2003

∷ The first bridge to Charlestown was built in 1786. Before that, traffic between Boston and Charlestown was via the Great Ferry established by Edward Converse in 1601. In the mid-eighteenth century the profits from the ferry were donated to Harvard College, until it went out of business after completion of the first bridge. The eighteenth-century bridge was replaced in 1899.

A century later the widest cable-stayed bridge in the world provides a striking entrance to Boston from the north. Inverted 270-foot slingshot towers employ replicas of the Bunker Hill obelisk to support ten traffic lanes. At night it shimmers in the theatrical lighting of its fanned cables. The bridge is more complex than its pure profile suggests. Barely noticed are the outrigger lanes hanging off its west shoulder or the tangle of tracks and tunnels it strides over. Its double name indicates its dual commemoration of Revolutionary War Charlestown patriots and a twentieth-century civil rights activist.

Leonard P. Zakim Bunker Hill Bridge © Peter Vanderwarker

2 Paul Revere Park
1978
Redesign: Carr, Lynch, 1999

:: Did Paul Revere watch Old North from here on the night of his famous ride? The redesign of the park changed the undefined grassy lawn into a complex combination of tile, stone walls, columns, a spiral ramp, tot lot, boardwalk, Robert Frost poem quote, map of Revere's ride, and performance space. This was the first of six parks reclaiming Charles River edges that had been lost to public access.

Paul Matisse's sculpture *Charlestown Bells* is on the Charlestown end of the footbridge crossing the river at the Colonel Richard Gridley locks. Like the interactive sound sculptures by Matisse in the Kendall Square MBTA Station, the bells were designed to let pedestrians play them as they pass.

3 William Kent Elementary School
50 Bunker Hill Street
Earl R. Flansburgh and Associates,
1970–1972

:: Located on a steeply sloping site in a neighborhood of nineteenth-century row houses, the school uses the classroom module to reflect the scale of the neighborhood architecture. The large masses of the auditorium and gymnasium are tucked into the hill, serving as a backdrop for the tiered classrooms.

4 Bunker Hill Burying Ground
197A Bunker Hill Street
1801

:: As morning dawned on June 17, 1775, the circumstances of the defense of the Revolutionary forces against the British revealed a need for protection from the north. There was an old rail fence offering none, but they quickly covered that with hay so at least there would be visual screening of their movements. Beyond the end of the fence a stone wall was reinforced

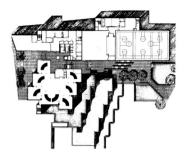

Plan, Kent Elementary School © Flansburgh and Associates

down to the river's edge. The shots fired from behind this wall foiled the British attack from along the beach. Within the Bunker Hill Burying Ground is a granite marker showing the location of the old rail fence from the Battle of Bunker Hill. Also on the grounds are two old street signs relating to Charlestown's early nineteenth-century past.

5 308 Bunker Hill Street
late nineteenth century

:: This large, handsome Victorian house has a mansard roof and projecting central pavilion above the entrance. The two brick stories are capped by a cornice at the base of the mansard-roofed third story. Stone window lintels are connected by a horizontal stringcourse.

6 St. Francis de Sales Church
303 Bunker Hill Street
Patrick C. Keeley, 1859

:: While English descendants had dominated Charlestown in the first century of the town's history, by 1860 40 percent of the population was Irish. Thus there was a sudden surge in the building of Roman Catholic churches in the second half of the nineteenth century. St. Francis de Sales was an important parish church constructed in the

Romanesque-Celtic revival style of the Victorian period. The stone exterior is decorated freely with quoins and has both Romanesque and Gothic windows. The stubby spire is ornamented with diagonal ribs.

Cordis Street

Cordis Street was named for Captain Joseph Cordis, who lived nearby on Main Street and laid this street out in 1799. It is a short street with many early houses, including the 1802 Getchell and Hyde houses at 21 and 32 Cordis. The Swallow mansion at number 33 is a large white Greek revival house with four Ionic columns across the Greek temple façade.

Devens Street

Once named Bow Street, it was called Crooked Lane in 1640 and was the site of the first huts and tents of early settlers Ralph, Richard, and William Sprague about 1630. At the point where the street met the waterline on Tyler's Wharf, there was an establishment in the nineteenth century with "bathing machines" where ladies and gentlemen could enjoy private saltwater bathing in the summer.

7 St. John's Episcopal Church and Parish House 🏛
27 Devens Street
Richard Bond, 1841

:: At the corner of Devens Street and old Rutherford Avenue, the heavy granite square tower with crenellated roofline suggests a fortress. This restrained Gothic revival church is softened by its quatrefoil and arched windows. The timber Gothic rectory next to it was built three decades later and is surely one of the most intriguing architectural designs in Charlestown.

This church compares favorably with the Gothic revival Mission Church of St. John the Evangelist by Solomon Willard on Beacon Hill.

St. Francis de Sales Church

Getchell House, 21 Cordis Street

Swallow Mansion, 33 Cordis Street

St. John's Episcopal Church

8 Dexter Mansion
14 Green Street
1791

:: Samuel Dexter was a congressman, senator, and secretary of the treasury and of war under President John Adams. When built, his house was as grand as his prominence in the new nation would suggest. The wooden house still has its original cupola, although the roof was raised to accommodate a third floor and a wing was added. It became a VFW Memorial Hall in the twentieth century.

9 John Harvard Mall and Town Hill 𝔦𝔦𝔦
National Register of Historic Places

:: Town Hill was the first community settlement in Charlestown. It was laid out by an engineer, Thomas Graves, who assigned each settler a plot of two acres. The first settlers came from Salem in 1629, and by 1630 they had built a small palisaded fort atop the hill (then much higher than now) as protection against the Indians. The name Town Hill has been used since 1629, except for the decade 1635–1645, when it was briefly called Windmill Hill because of the windmill Robert Hawkins built there to grind settlers' corn. No houses survive from the seventeenth century, but fine old cobblestones still pave Harvard Place. The narrow street is nicely framed by dormered brick row houses from the mid-nineteenth century.

The John Harvard Mall is the site of the hill fort built by the settlers. John Harvard was the son of a wealthy tradesman in England and the first

John Harvard Mall

member of his family to go to college. He graduated from Emmanuel College of Cambridge University at the age of twenty-five and three years later received a master's degree. Ordained as a minister, he inherited the remainder of the family fortune, married, and sailed to America with cattle he planned to raise. On the ship with the newlyweds was another recent graduate of Cambridge University, Nathaniel Eaton, and his wife. Both couples settled in Charlestown, where John Harvard began performing the service in the First Parish on a temporary basis.

Less than fourteen months after his arrival in Massachusetts, on September 24, 1638, Harvard died of consumption. Only thirty-one years old, he left half the family fortune he had inherited and his entire library to a college that was to be founded. Nathaniel Eaton was appointed to establish and administer it. The General Court of Massachusetts had voted 400 pounds to start the new institution, which was originally to be called Emmanuel College, but after receiving the library and an 800-pound bequest from John Harvard, the General Court voted in 1639 that the name should be Harvard College.

In 1943 a Harvard alumnus donated the mall to Charlestown in memory of John Harvard. The plaques lining the brick mall describe the history of Town Hill.

Harvard Square

At the edge of Harvard Mall is a charming place named Harvard Square, with a small row of dwellings typical of the early nineteenth century in Charlestown. Each two-storied house with dormered attic has one fireplace on each of the two main floors—the only heat source for much of the nineteenth century. The attics, although inhabited, had no heat unless a small coal stove was added.

10 27 Harvard Square
ca. 1800

:: This house is one of the few stone buildings built in Charlestown. For many years it was the Charlestown Free Dispensary, established in 1814, a combination clinic and pharmacy where drugs and bandages were made and administered. The house was built by General Nathaniel Austin of split stone quarried on Outer Brewster Island, which Austin owned.

Harvard Square

Harvard Street

Harvard Street is the unifying element of Town Hill and is thought to be the site of the first schoolhouse in America. A dignified and lovely curving street today, it has long been the residence of New England notables. On the corner fronting on City Square stood Robbins Tavern until 1818, when it was replaced by the old Town Hall, which was torn down in 1868. The row houses now lining the street were primarily built in the 1850s and 1860s on land then owned by Moses Dow, publisher and educator, who built his own house at number 28.

While the brick row houses provide continuity of enclosure for the street, there is a surprising variety of mid-nineteenth-century styles. Numbers 7–23 are flat-façade houses with restrained decoration, an intentional emphasis on simplicity. Opposite them are richly ornamented larger houses at numbers 22 and 24 and the Dow house

Harvard Street

at 28, with brownstone arched entrances, oriel windows projecting from the second floors, and elaborate lintels, cornices, and French-inspired mansard roofs. Farther up the hill are bowfront houses, making almost a survey of mid-nineteenth-century row house styles between City Square and Washington Street.

11 Edward Everett House
16 Harvard Street
1812
Boston Landmark

:: This fine Federal house was built in 1812 by Matthew Bridge, a shipping merchant and state legislator, for his daughter. Edward Everett purchased it in 1830 but lived there only six years, moving when he was elected governor of Massachusetts. Later he was to serve as secretary of state, U.S. senator, and president of Harvard College. When he left Charlestown in 1836, Everett sold the house to William Carleton, who lived there for almost three decades before founding Carleton College in Northfield, Minnesota.

The large but unostentatious free-standing house of three stories has a hip roof and central entrance door highlighted by a portico with Ionic columns and pilasters. Square granite posts and curb support a cast-iron fence.

12 29–41 High Street
mid-nineteenth century

:: This distinguished row of Victorian houses has flat façades, mansard roofs, and handsome granite front steps leading to the raised entrances. Each of the row houses has an arched window pair on the front parlor overlooking High Street.

13 Steck House
100 High Street
ca. 1790

:: Originally built as a double house, the Steck House now stands as a single house facing its yard rather than the street. It has double chimneys and a basement kitchen opening onto the garden. The third story has the small square windows typical of its period.

Edward Everett House

Steck House

Main Street

Main Street is the long spine running from City Square to the ancient town limits. Since 1640 it has had many names, beginning with the descriptive Country Road, which it truly was when Town Hill was the center of the settlement. After 1670 the town developed further, and it became Town Street. It was paved in 1730 and became Broad Street, where one often heard the horns of foxhunters in October. As stores multiplied near the Charlestown Bridge to sell the many leather products of the morocco factories on Cook's and Henley's Lanes, the name became Market Street. When growth spread farther west, it became Main Street, which it has been for more than a hundred years.

It is rich in old buildings. Many of the brick structures built adjacent to Town Hill along Main Street originally had a combination of uses, with shops on the first floor and residences above, as seen today at 18–34. Across Main Street, taller wood and brick commercial buildings such as number 51 were built in the late nineteenth century.

Main Street

City Square and Roughan Hall

City Square sculpture

14 City Square 𝍢

Landscape design: Halvorson Design Partnership, 1996

:: From the seventeenth century until well into the twentieth century, City Square was the center of Charlestown commerce and government. None of the early structures survive, but the digging of the harbor tunnel in 1991 uncovered remains of the 1630 Great House. It was the settlers' meeting hall and the temporary residence of more than a dozen of them.

Centered on a fountain, the graceful City Square restores the historic heart of Charlestown that was too long a traffic nightmare. Historic and iconic elements are deftly integrated into a peaceful composition that works beautifully from every perspective. Sculptural motifs by David Phillips include: rope, evoking the naval history; maize, the native American staple; a cod, the iconic local fish; and the crane recalling the pre-Revolutionary Three Cranes Tavern. Each gateway to the square has portraits of famous Charlestown citizens.

15 Roughan Hall
Main Street at 15–18 City Square
Arthur H. Vinal, 1892; addition, 1896
National Register of Historic Places

:: Unusual for Charlestown, Roughan Hall is tan brick punctuated with over-size windows and decorated with basket-weave panels. A large hall is located in the double-height fourth floor spanned by Howe trusses. The elaborately decorated hall was first used for dances and lectures and in later years for movies and roller-skating. The building also held offices and shops, and in the basement were three bowling alleys along with billiard and pool tables.

16 John Larkin House
55–61 Main Street
ca. 1795

:: Deacon John Larkin is best remembered as the man who lent Paul Revere a horse for his midnight ride. Larkin's horse, incidentally, was never returned. He built this house to replace his City Square home, which was burned down by the British during the Battle of Bunker Hill. The three-story square wooden house with hip roof, small third-story windows, quoins, and capped and pegged window frames was a prominent Main Street residence.

John Hurd and John Larkin Houses

17 John Hurd House
65–71 Main Street
ca. 1795

:: Next door to Deacon Larkin's house is another late eighteenth-century mansion, this one built for John Hurd, a wealthy Charlestown citizen of the time. Like the Larkin house, it has three stories and a hip roof. Decorative quoins of wood at the corners mimic the shapes of stone blocks used in earlier European architecture.

18 General Austin's Stone House
92 Main Street
1822
Boston Landmark

:: In 1822 General Nathaniel Austin, Middlesex County sheriff and major general of the Massachusetts militia, built this house with commercial space

General Austin's Stone House

on the ground floor. It was here that the first successful Charlestown newspaper, *The Bunker Hill Aurora and Farmers and Mechanics Journal,* was published from 1827 to 1871. Like the small house Austin built at 27 Harvard Square, this building is faced with split stone from his quarry on Outer Brewster Island.

19 Warren Tavern
105 Main Street at 2 Pleasant Street
ca. 1780; renovated 1972

:: This tavern was one of the first buildings erected after the burning of Charlestown by the British. It was named in honor of General Joseph Warren, who died in the Battle of Bunker Hill. General Warren was a member of the Committee of Safety and president of the Provincial Congress in 1774. He arrived on Breed's Hill (known and memorialized erroneously as Bunker Hill) and refused Colonel Prescott's offer to relinquish command, Warren being a higher-ranking officer. Instead the thirty-four-year-old fought as an ordinary soldier under Prescott and was promptly killed. The original tavern sign carried a painting of Prescott's head as its decoration over the door.

The first Masonic lodge in the area, King Solomon's Lodge, was founded here in 1784. It was this lodge that first commemorated the Battle of Bunker Hill with a wooden column in what is now Monument Square. This three-story wooden building and the hall added by the Masonic lodge in 1786 are typical of the utilitarian structures built following the Revolution.

20 Timothy Thompson Sr. House
119 Main Street
ca. 1794; restored 1970s

:: Timothy Thompson and his wife, Mary Frothingham, lost their earlier Charlestown house when it was burned by the British in 1775. Like many other

Warren Tavern

Timothy Thompson Sr. House

inhabitants, they returned and ultimately built a new home. After the death of Mr. Thompson, the first floor was converted to a store and an additional one-story store was attached to the Main Street side of the house.

21 Thompson-Sawyer House
Main Street at 9 Thompson Street
1805

:: Timothy Thompson Sr., who built 119 Main Street, also lived in this house, and it became his daughter's home when she married a Sawyer. Their son, Timothy Thompson Sawyer, was the author of *Old Charlestown* and served as mayor of Charlestown. He was born and raised in this house, which at that time was attached to another house. A two-story addition elongates the front façade of the house, creating a very imposing presence. The main house is actually one room deep, part of a double house divided by a brick party wall.

22 Round-Corner House
121–123 Main Street
ca. 1814

:: The dwelling of Captain Joseph Cordis, who laid out Cordis Street, was on the upper two floors of this brick building. Commercial space was on the first floor. The shop windows are framed by long granite lintels and posts. The most distinctive feature of the building is its inset round corner on Main Street.

23 Armstrong Press and Edmands Hall
125–127 Main Street
1808

:: The mixed-use building was built by John T. Edmands but acquired the name of the publisher and printer whose business was located on the first floor. Samuel T. Armstrong was a prominent politician, serving as mayor of Boston and lieutenant governor of the state. The very controversial First Universalist Society had its first meetings in the hall upstairs before their church was built. There was stern disapproval at the time of anyone who would attend such meetings.

24 Savings Bank Building
Main Street at 1 Thompson Square
Moffette and Tolman, 1876
Boston Landmark

:: Built in the Victorian Gothic style of Pugin, the building has a tall mansard roof penetrated with ornamented peaked dormers. The center bay projects slightly and contains two Gothic arch entrances. Windows of the second floor are topped with pointed arches, while those of the next floor are round. Several stringcourse bands wrap around the façade, connecting the window arches and sills.

Thompson-Sawyer House

Round-Corner House and Edmands Hall

Savings Bank Building

25 Charlestown Branch Library
Boston Public Library
169–179 Main Street
Eduardo Catalano, 1970

:: The eighteenth-century Indian Chief Hotel occupied this site until about 1820, when the Second Congregational Unitarian Church built their brick church here. The original Charlestown Public Library first opened in the Bunker Hill Bank building (Main Street at Henley Street) in 1862 with a collection that included a number of subscriptions to foreign newspapers. Educated Americans at that time read several languages and expected to keep abreast of international affairs. A catalogue of the collection was printed and sold to card holders, who numbered more than 3,000 by the end of the first year.

In 1869 the library relocated to rooms in the City Hall and then moved again to its own building on Monument Square. The library on Main Street is dramatically cantilevered from two points, one on each side of the entrance. The floating effect of the massive inverted U-form of poured concrete is dramatized by its juxtaposition with glass.

26 Mishawum Park Housing
338 Main Street
Freeman and Hardenburgh, 1974

:: The clapboard style of much of Charlestown's old architecture was used in this housing. The pedestrian walkways on the third floor were an innovation in Charlestown.

27 Phipps Street Burying Ground
off Main Street
1630
National Register of Historic Places

:: One of the oldest burial grounds in the country, "Burying Hill," as it was first called, has 300 pre-1700 and Revolutionary heroes among its 1,000 pre-1800 burials. It escaped the British fire

Mishawum Park Housing

in 1775 because it was not associated with any church. Many fascinating examples of early American tombstones can be seen. Originally its setting was prettier, with water on three sides, before extensive filling was undertaken. In 1828 a monument to John Harvard was erected here by Harvard graduates in memory of the young Charlestown resident whose contribution made possible Harvard College. He is not buried here, however; his grave site is presumed lost in the fire of 1775.

Monument Avenue and Monument Square
The obelisk-shaped monument at the end of the vista formally completes the attractive avenue leading uphill to Monument Square. Bordering the avenue is a diverse but harmonious mixture of brick row houses. Some feature bowfronts, some flat façades with oriel windows projecting from the second floors, some elaborate cornices edging flat roofs, or mansard roofs with dormers. There are even clapboard and shingle row houses with bow or stepped façades. Notice the detailing in granite, wood, or cast iron.

The avenue and square were laid out on former orchards and gardens in 1839. G. Washington Warren and Peter Hubbell built the first houses on the square in 1848. It quickly became a most desirable location for prominent Charlestown citizens. Grand houses filled in the four sides of the square, producing the handsome ensemble that remains today. The bowfronts, projecting oriel windows, and dormers or cupolas took advantage of the long views from the hilltop over Boston Harbor, the Mystic River, or the Charles River from their favorable location.

28 Bunker Hill Monument
Monument Square
Solomon Willard, 1825–1843
National Historic Landmark

:: The hill on which Bunker Hill Monument stands is commonly, and mistakenly, referred to as Bunker Hill. This error began about midnight on June 16, 1775, when 1,000 Revolutionary troops under Colonel Prescott's command arrived at what they thought to be Bunker Hill and began digging fortifications. Not until dawn could they see their position clearly. Thus, the Battle of Bunker Hill was actually fought on Breed's Hill, named for the homestead of Ebenezer

Monument Avenue

Cast-iron fence, Bunker Hill Monument

Phipps Street Burying Ground

Breed, who kept a pair of antelope in his yard.

The initial monument was erected by the King Solomon's Lodge of Charlestown in 1794 in the form of a Tuscan pillar in James Russell's pasture. A desire to protect and memorialize the site further led to the formation in 1823 of the Bunker Hill Monument Association, which raised money and purchased the land for the monument. The Marquis de Lafayette journeyed from France to lay the cornerstone in 1825, and in 1843 the dedication ceremony took place with Daniel Webster as orator. A model of the original 1794 monument is displayed inside the obelisk.

Solomon Willard, the monument's designer, was a diversely talented man highly regarded by his contemporaries. He began as a carpenter, then carved figureheads for ships. From there he went into sculpture, then architecture, followed by work as a scientist, quarry master, and scientific agriculturist. In Washington, D.C., he assisted Charles Bulfinch in his work on the Capitol. Besides designing the Bunker Hill Monument, Willard bought a quarry in Quincy to supply the granite. A special tramway was built to move the slabs from Quincy to Charlestown, a significant engineering achievement for the time. The monument was built by Grid-

ley Bryant, father of architect Gridley J. Fox Bryant.

Today the 220-foot obelisk and the nearby 1881 statue of Colonel William Prescott by William Story are the central focus of the square laid out in 1839. Beginning in the 1840s, fine brick row houses for prominent Charlestown citizens were constructed on the four sides of the square park.

29 Phineas Stone House
2–4 Monument Square at Concord Street
ca. 1860

:: This pair of houses opposite the northwest corner of Monument Square was once the handsome Greek revival Phineas Stone house, which explains the central placement of the cupola. The entrance was originally on the uphill end facing the square and had a handsome large white wooden two-story porch with pediment supported by four tall Ionic columns. In front of the porch was a garden enclosed by an ornamental iron fence.

Phineas Jones Stone came to Charlestown as a boy when his father opened a grocery store in 1824. He was a retailer of West Indian goods for many years, selectman of Charlestown, representative to the state legislature, the first president of the Five Cents Savings Bank in Charlestown, and mayor of the town in 1862–1864.

30 6–7 Monument Square
ca. 1858

:: This pair of Greek revival brick bowfront houses is distinctive in having three bows for the two houses. Building the pair in this way, rather than giving one bow to each house in the conventional manner, created a balanced and symmetrical façade with the front entrances equally spaced between the bows for individual identity. The unusual façade produces very different interiors

Phineas Stone House

6–7 Monument Square

21–22 Monument Square

for the two houses. The location of the cupola and the chimneys reveals the double-width house on the left. The cast-iron porches are late nineteenth-century additions.

31 21–22 Monument Square
mid-nineteenth century

:: Two sisters, Helen Sherkanowski Rush and Mary Sherkanowski, operated rooming houses here, describing their adventures and their fascinating guests in a book, *Rooms to Let*. Both houses are of French-inspired design with mansard roofs, but the one on the left is more elaborately decorated, with both front and side oriels, stringcourses between floors, and prominent quoins on the corners.

32 The Schoolhouse on Monument Square Residences
25 Monument square
1907
Renovation: Graham Gund Architects, 1987

:: The former Charlestown High School has been recycled into forty-four apartments, each with a different floor plan. The major interior space is a two-story skylit circulation core with a

screen wall with "windows" separating the corridors from the atrium.

33 23 Pleasant Street
late eighteenth century

:: One of the fascinations of Charlestown is its rich treasure of history. On any street one may encounter architectural remnants of America's early years. This simple wooden house is typical of the late eighteenth-century gambrel-roofed houses of the area.

The Schoolhouse on Monument Square
© Steve Rosenthal

23 Pleasant Street

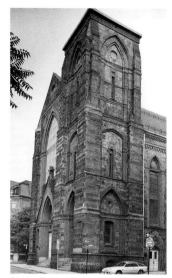

St. Mary's Church

Restored house, Monument Square at
Pleasant Street

34 **St. Mary's Church**
55 Warren Street
Warren, Winthrop, and Soley, 1887

:: This was the site of the thatched
house of Thomas Walford, first settler
of Charlestown in 1625. Walford left in
1631 because of disagreements with
the groups of settlers from Salem on
Town Hill. Since 1892 the site has been
occupied by an imposing stone Gothic
revival church of granite with brick trim.
It has set-back buttresses and a massive tower with lancet windows set in
pointed arches on the upper stories.
Above each door is an ornamental patera rendered in low relief within the
equilateral archway. This structure replaces the small church dedicated in

59 Warren Street

1829 for the first Roman Catholic congregation in Charlestown.

35 **Victorian House**
59 Warren Street

:: This picturesque bowfront house
features a charming bartizan projecting
from one second-story corner. A cor-
beled chimney and second-floor oriel
window adorn the side. The mansard
roof has pointed-arch dormers with iron
cresting above the cornice line.

36 81 Warren Street
1790–1800

∷ This large three-story wood-frame house stands perpendicular to the sidewalk and has the small square third-story windows and corner boards typical of the Federal style. The front door has sidelights of glass. A two-story ell is attached to the far side of the house. This house forms the entrance to Donnell Court, where 81B and 81½ Warren Street are located.

37 81B Warren Street
ca. 1800

∷ Behind the Federal houses on Warren Street is a small late-Georgian wood-frame house with gambrel roof. Two and a half stories high and only one small room deep, the house is a charming example of eighteenth-century Charlestown. It is most easily viewed from Pleasant Street.

38 81½ Warren Street
1875

∷ Within the group of houses in this picturesque court, 81½ is the newest, being a Victorian clapboard house of three stories built in 1875. Note how successfully the various houses cluster together to form a setting in which they enhance each other with very efficient use of a limited land area.

39 83 Warren Street
ca. 1800

∷ This large three-story clapboard house with hip roof is typical of the early nineteenth century. It was restored in 1969 with the corner boards and small square third-story windows retained. Even the corner store was happily integrated into the Federal façade. Its location at the corner of Warren and Pleasant Streets makes it doubly important as a visual anchor for the other early houses clustered about it.

81, 81B, and 81½ Warren Street

40 Row Houses
74–86 Washington Street

∷ This fine row of brick houses has foundations as well as door and window lintels of granite. The gable roofs of the two-and-a-half-story houses are topped with peaked dormers and chimneys. The row is typical of the workers' housing that was often built in nineteenth-century New England industrial towns. It might even have been associated with one of the shipyards, such as Josiah Barker's, not far from here on Washington Street between 1804 and 1835.

Winthrop Square 🏛

Winthrop Street at Adams Street

Like most other squares in Boston, Winthrop never was square. Once called Market Place, when Saturday markets were held here, Training Field was the name given to this area after it was set aside in 1632 for the use of the militia. For two and a half centuries, men trained here and in 1775, 1812, and 1860 departed for battle from this field. It was built up in the late eighteenth and early nineteenth centuries and today is very different from the open meadow surrounded by settlers' farmlands.

41 Old Training Field School
Winthrop Square at 3 Common Street
1828

:: For 140 years this building served as a public grammar school, first in the middle of the training field and, after 1847, in its present position at the side of the square. It then became a private secondary school and later was acquired by the Catholic Church, which used it for St. Mary's School. It was converted to a private residence in the 1980s. The old school building has the simplest of lines. It is embellished only with a roundel centered in the pediment and a semicircular relieving arch in low relief on the front façade.

Old Training Field School

42 Arnold House
Winthrop Square at 14 Common Street
ca. 1805

:: This very large early nineteenth-century clapboard house with corner boards, hip roof, and small square third-story windows forms an attractive edge for the ancient training field. The large two-story ell on its right was converted to a separate residence in the late twentieth century.

Arnold House

43 Salem Turnpike Hotel
Winthrop Square at 16 Common Street
1810

:: The old Salem Turnpike ran close to the edge of the ropewalk building of the Charlestown Navy Yard and behind this house. The two-and-a-half-story hip-roofed building was originally the Salem Turnpike Hotel. Today the original window pattern has been altered on one end. Two small square dormers light the attic at the top of the old hotel.

Salem Turnpike Hotel

Charlestown Navy Yard

National Historic Landmark

The Charlestown Navy Yard was founded in 1800 on forty-three acres at Moulton's Point, where the British landed for the Battle of Bunker Hill. Among the famous ships constructed here were the *Boston* (1799–1800), the *Independence* (1814), and the *Merrimac* (1854–1855), the ship captured by the Confederate forces who ironclad it before its defeat by the Union ironclad *Monitor*. It was here, beginning in 1813, that ships were first built indoors to speed up construction and protect the partially constructed vessels from the weather.

At its peak the Navy Yard employed almost 50,000 workers, and in 1943 a record forty-six destroyer escorts were built. In 1956 the USS *Suffolk County* was the last ship built at the Navy Yard, and in 1971 rope production ceased. In 1974 President Nixon decommissioned the Navy Yard, and it was established as part of the Boston National Historic Park.

Today the Navy Yard has become the largest and one of the most remarkable preservation and reuse projects in the country, with nineteen buildings renovated and more than 2,000,000 square feet of new construction. This water-oriented mixed-use community combines housing for all income groups with recreation opportunities, office and research facilities, and educational and museum sites in a setting of unique historic importance. The streetscape is tree-lined, with paving of brick and granite and historic-style lighting fixtures. Second Avenue, the focus for retail activity in the Navy Yard, became a pedestrian mall. A continuous open and accessible waterfront nearly 3 miles long is part of the 43-mile-long HarborWalk that will eventually encompass the entire Boston waterfront down to the Neponset River in Dorchester. A water shuttle links Dry Dock Number 2 and Long Wharf on the Boston waterfront. The two-time America's Cup winner *Courageous* is now based at the Courageous Sailing Center situated at Pier 4.

44 USS *Constitution* 𝖎𝖎𝖎

("Old Ironsides")
Constitution Wharf
Joshua Humphrey, designer, 1797
National Historic Landmark

:: The USS *Constitution*, built in Boston in 1797 at Hartt's Shipyard, is the oldest commissioned vessel in the

"Old Ironsides" and Officers' Club

U.S. Navy. It fought the Barbary pirates and then was victorious against the British in the War of 1812. It was planned to carry more guns than the typical frigate but also had more sail area on its thirty-six sails, so it could use its speed to sail away from any battle in which it found itself out-gunned. It never lost a battle. After the War of 1812, it served as a training vessel until the twentieth century The frigate's permanent location is now the Charlestown Navy Yard, but each year it makes a tour of the harbor.

45 USS *Cassim Young*
Pier 1
National Historic Landmark

:: This World War II destroyer was built here and served in the Pacific Theater from 1944 to 1946, surviving several kamikaze attacks. It was decommissioned until 1951, when it returned to use for a decade in the Atlantic and Mediterranean.

46 Dry Dock Number 1
Laommi Baldwin Jr., engineer, 1827–1833

:: This and the dry dock built in Nor-folk, Virginia, in 1833 are the first dry docks built in the United States. Both were engineered by Colonel Baldwin. Because the USS *Constitution* was the first ship docked here, it is called the Constitution Dock and was in continuous use until 1974. It remained the only dry

dock at the shipyard until 1905, when the second one was built on the other side of the Shop and Docking Office.

47 Wood and Metal Shop
Building 22, First Avenue near Fifth Street
(now Constitution Museum)
Alexander Parris, 1832

:: In 1828 the Naval Architectural Office developed a master plan for the shipyard that affected the siting and configuration of all subsequent build-ings. The Wood and Metal Shop was the first building planned after the rec-tilinear grid for the site was laid out. It is located adjacent to the previously constructed Dry Dock Number 1. The three-story building is constructed of ashlar granite and features twelve-over-twelve paned window sash. The woodworking shop was responsible for all the carpentry involved in the ships' fittings, and the metal shop forged wrought-iron chains and other metal items for the ships.

48 Shipyard Park
Childs, Bertman, Tseckares, and Casendino, 1980

:: The four-and-a-half-acre park in-cludes a fountain plaza, pavilion, chil-dren's play area, and nautical artifacts. The Massachusetts Korean War Veter-ans Memorial pavilion and sculpture is augmented by audio playback of veterans' stories.

Dry Dock Number 1

Shipyard Park

49 Flagship Wharf
Building 197
adjacent to Shipyard Park
1941
Renovation and addition: The Architects Collaborative, 1990

:: The original brick building was enlarged with two eleven-story wings to accommodate 200 luxury condominiums and commercial space.

50 Anchorage Apartments
Building 103
First Avenue at Ninth Street
1901
Renovation: Bruner/Cott & Associates, 1985

:: This handsome brick building was built in a restrained Greek revival style. It was recycled to provide 112 units of subsidized housing for senior citizens.

51 Charlestown Navy Yard Row Houses
First Avenue at Thirteenth Street
William Rawn Associates, 1988

:: Fifty units of affordable housing, most with water views, were developed by the Bricklayers Union. The larger units are floor-through to provide cross venti-lation by ocean breezes. Upper units have private terraces, while lower units have private yards. The forms are designed to relate to the simple industrial forms of the Navy Yard, yet have a pleasing domestic scale and detailing. On First Avenue its large gabled façade is adorned by three tiers of arches and striped brick facing. A perpendicular arm of brick row houses reaches down to the water and is terminated by a round tower with copper roof. The result is contextually convincing.

52 One Forty Nine at the Navy Yard
Building 149, 1917
Building 199, 1945
Second Avenue between Ninth and Sixteenth Streets
Renovation: Huygens Dimella Shaffer, 1986

:: This adaptive reuse project created 1,300,000 square feet of office and retail space. The industrial character of the warehouses was retained, but two atriums were cut into the center of Building 149 to bring in natural light. A major portion of the building is used for biomedical research by the Medical Research Division of Massachusetts General Hospital.

Charlestown Navy Yard Row Houses © Steve Rosenthal

53 Parris Landing

Eighth Street at First Avenue
Anderson, Notter, Finegold, 1981
Interior renovation: Yoo/Starck, 2006

:: The French designer Philippe Starck is best known in the United States for household objects and hotel interiors in Miami, Los Angeles, and New York. Here he updated five adjoining buildings with his sculptures and white-on-white color palette. The residential project is named for the architect Alexander Parris, who designed a number of granite structures over two decades of work for the Navy Yard.

Other Navy Yard Buildings

The two-story ashlar granite **Shop and Docking Office** (Building 24, 1847) originally had a cupola and a bell that summoned men to the carpenters' shop and rigging loft located here. Sited between Dry Docks 1 and 2, it is one of the few structures built after the 1828 master plan that violates the established grid pattern.

The hexagonal three-story **Telephone Exchange** (Building 21, 1852) is unusually small and ornate in the context of the naval shipyard architecture. Ornamentation includes the projecting stringcourses between each floor and the elaborate modillion block cornice edging the hip roof. A wooden cupola is atop the roof.

Near the Telephone Exchange is the **Bank** (Building 31, 1857). This small one-story building was originally built as an ordnance shell house with no windows. Later it became the commandant's office, and portions of the walls were torn out to make windows; some were bricked up again when it finally became a bank.

The **Ropewalk** was designed by Alexander Parris in 1834–1836. Nearly 0.25 mile long, this is the only remaining ropewalk in the United States. For 135 years all the rope for the U.S. Navy

Ropewalk

Telephone Exchange

was made here, from jute to hemp ropes to modern nylon ropes. Rope makers wrapped the fibers around their waists and fed them into the rope being spun as they moved down the walk on foot. The structure's load-bearing walls are handsome ashlar granite with restrained use of decoration at the corners and entrance. Adjacent to the old Salem Turnpike, it has provided an effective boundary along much of the northwest side of the shipyard property.

The **Tarring House** (Building 60, 1830s), also by Parris, is the long narrow building parallel to the entrance end of the ropewalk. Here all the tar was made and applied to waterproof the rope.

Sails for the ships were cut and assembled in the **Old Sail Loft** (Building 33, 1850) from 1850 until sailing ships were no longer constructed or repaired here. All the work on the sails was done on the floor, which had to be kept absolutely clean, smooth, and free of debris that could damage the cloth. After extensive use the sails would stretch so far out of shape that they no longer provided the original speed and would be returned to the loft for recutting and repairs. Behind the Old Sail Loft is a long, narrow granite storehouse built in 1854. It was here that the canvas and materials for the sails were kept and the completed sails stored until needed.

The earlier of the two **Laboratory Buildings** (Buildings 34 and 62) was originally designed as a storehouse by Alexander Parris in 1837. This three-story building of ashlar granite later became a laboratory where new techniques and products could be tested. The primary ornamental element of the building is the central pavilion with a pedimented gable. Located near one end of the ropewalk is the second laboratory building, also designed by Parris and built in 1842. It was originally used to store hemp for making the ropes.

Old Sail Loft

Old Joiners' Shop

The woodworking that required detailed fitting for cabinetry and combinations of different woods and forms was carried out at the **Old Joiners' Shop** (Building 36, ca. 1850) beginning in the 1850s, when the combination wood and metal shop built in 1832 was no longer large enough for the scale of production. This long structure of granite ashlar is ornamented with smooth granite window lintels and door frames, corner quoins, cornices edging the ridge roof, and the stringcourse of projecting stones running in a horizontal band. The building is sited in accordance with the horizontal grid established by the 1828 master plan for the shipyard.

The **Marine Barracks** were constructed to the right of the Commandant's House in 1823. Used throughout its history as barracks, the original building did not include the porches now attached to the exterior. The parade grounds were directly in front of the barracks.

Commandant's House

The **Commandant's House** (Naval Architectural Office, 1809) is a square brick Georgian-style mansion that was continuously occupied by the shipyard's commanding officer following its construction in 1809. It stands on a small hill with a fine view over Boston Harbor. The house is distinguished by two bows on the front corners that create oval rooms inside, and by its decorative wooden balustrade and porches. The kitchen and formal rooms are all located on the second floor of the mansion, with bedrooms on the third and fourth floors and service functions on the ground floor.

Begun in 1833, the **Officers' Housing** was located in five brick row houses. The row is located between the gate, the Officers' Club, and the Commandant's House and faces the grass lawn that served as the approach to the Commandant's House. The houses are dignified examples of the prevailing residential architectural style of the period in Charlestown and Beacon Hill.

The **Officers' Club** (Building 5, 1799–1803) was the first building constructed at the Navy Yard. It is a simple three-story hip-roof brick building twenty bays long. With this structure a collection of significant architecture built over three centuries began.

54 The Nautica
Constitution Road, adjacent to the Charlestown Navy Yard
Neshamkin French Architects, Inc., 2001

:: Through a participatory process involving the state, the city, and neighborhood residents over a period of twelve years, 117 condominium units were planned and built in stone and brick styles reflecting several centuries of Charlestown history. Underground parking for 306 cars maintained the neighborhood's historic character.

Constitution Quarters (Anderson, Notter, Finegold, 1978–1981) and Shipyard Park
© Peter Vanderwarker

THE EMERALD NECKLACE

Nature was idealized in the nineteenth century. The Romanticists communed with nature to experience God, and the New England Transcendentalists went even further in venerating nature. In an era when nature was valued in an almost religious sense, public parks multiplied.

The landscape design genius Frederick Law Olmsted carried out these popular ideals on the grandest possible scale. After designing Central Park, he was frustrated in his desire to build a regional open-space network throughout New York City. Boston welcomed him. In 1869 he began advising the city on a comprehensive park system. During the next decade he focused on the Arnold Arboretum, Back Bay's Charlesgate, and the Fens. In 1887 he created his plan for an interconnected park system for Boston that would stretch from the Common to Franklin Park, passing through many Boston neighborhoods. Beyond this, he designed a number of other parks and initiated a metropolitan open-space plan.

Albert Fein observed, "Olmsted's record of achievement in Boston after his defeat in New York City was owing to the social and political support he found there. Boston, unlike New York, still retained an effective intellectual and social elite committed to large-scale environmental planning." Olmsted's network of Boston parks remains the largest continuous green space through an urban center in the United States.

1 The Boston Common 🏛

1634

National Historic Landmark
Boston Landmark

∷ The Boston Common has more history than any other park. It was mentioned in town records as early as 1634. After two centuries as a communal pasture, Bostonians were restricted to grazing only one cow on the Common in 1823, and in 1830 cows were forbidden. Though its demise as a bucolic landscape may seem to date from then, it had always served many purposes—capital punishment, military recruitments, troop encampments, landings, and protests. MacArthur Mall, the paved walk paralleling Charles Street, was required to be the width of a regiment.

Public amusement and recreation was a primary attraction of the Common. When British troops destroyed the snow slides of Beacon Hill boys, the boys complained directly to General Gage, who ordered his troops not to disturb their sledding in the future. Before and after the Revolution there were traveling entertainments, puppet shows, telescopes, scales, blowing machines, and booths selling gingerbread, sugar plums, spruce beer, lemonade, oysters, and fireworks called "India crackers." In the mid-nineteenth century a Smoker's Circle was established that became the haunt of fashionable young dandies from Beacon Hill. A fenced deer park was opposite the former public library on Boylston Street. Throughout the eighteenth and nineteenth centuries, a curious custom was the semiannual Feast of Squantum, for which upper-class Bostonians performed Indian rites while mounted cavaliers rode back and forth dressed in white boots and spurs.

But Bostonians did limit the pleasures of the Common. Blacks were not allowed free access to the Common until July 4, 1836. Bathing on the Sabbath was prohibited at the Charles River edge (now Charles Street). Sinners were harangued and doom predicted, a tradition of soapbox oratory still practiced at the corner of Park and Tremont Streets, known as "brimstone corner." Constables drove liquor and gambling stands off the Common on July 4, 1827. There were many hangings and whippings until the gallows were removed in 1817. One of the most infamous injustices was the hanging of Rachell Whall in the late 1700s for the crime of highway robbery—she had stolen a bonnet worth 75 cents.

The Public Garden and Boston Common mid-nineteenth century

Parkman Bandstand, Boston Common

Fountain, Shaw Monument

Fence, Boston Common

Boston Common

Four centuries have seen many changes. The Frog Pond replaces a marshy puddle from the seventeenth century. The handsome neoclassical Parkman Bandstand added symmetrical walkways to the major diagonal paths of convenience. The Common's splendid fence was dismantled for scrap metal during World War II, but because it was cast rather than wrought iron, it couldn't be used for armaments. A legend suggests it was thrown into the Boston Harbor. In 1976 Richard Upjohn's fence design was reproduced and reinstalled. Landscape architect Arthur Shurtleff criticized the addition of parking-garage entrances, subway stations, and an information building. The temptation to fill every open space with plaques, planters, fountains, statues, paved areas, playing fields, equipment, and structures had proved irresistible.

2 Public Garden 🏛
1839
George Meachum, 1859
National Historic Landmark
Boston Landmark

:: The informality of the Boston Common contrasts with the formal flower beds and artificial pond of the Public Garden. Until the early nineteenth century, the land was salt marshes like the rest of the Back Bay. In the winter of 1775, British troops skated on the ice

Public Garden and Swan Boats

George Washington

Make Way for Ducklings, 1987

manner, and in 1861 an idyllic English pond was added with a delightful faux suspension bridge crossing in the center. In the same year a municipal competition was held for the design of the iron fence around the garden. Sixteen years later the Swan Boats began plying the waters and have become a Boston tradition, operated by the Paget family since 1877.

Weeping willows edge the pond while many fine trees grace the twenty-four-acre garden, including large dark beeches, pagoda trees, dawn redwood, American elms, and other ornamental species. As would be expected in a Victorian flower garden, it has numerous ornamental elements: statues, memorials, five granite fountains, a martin house, a wooden pagoda, and a cast-iron Japanese lantern. Near the Charles and Beacon Street entrance, see the *Make Way for Ducklings* sculpture by Nancy Schön, installed in 1987 as a tribute to Robert McCloskey for the book that "made the Public Garden familiar to children throughout the world." Old cobblestones reclaimed from street repairs

Detail, Ether Monument

there, and as a boy, Benjamin Franklin fished on the bank along Charles Street at the foot of the Common.

A botanical garden was begun on the newly filled site in 1839 by Horace Gray and Charles Francis Barnard, a Unitarian minister. In 1859 flower beds and paths were laid out in the French

Cast-iron fence and Edward Everett Hale monument, Public Garden

are the stage for the eight ducklings trailing after Mrs. Mallard.

The Public Garden has survived and much more successfully avoided the predations that have beset other Emerald Necklace parks. Perhaps its rigid and highly structured form has protected it. The Garden accommodates large crowds of people, but their activities are far more restricted than in the Common. One walks or sits and admires the formal beauty, certainly an important function of a garden, and to judge from the huge numbers flocking to it, a function much needed.

3 The Esplanade
1931
National Register of Historic Places

:: It is curious to many visitors that Back Bay houses turn their backs on the Charles River and Esplanade. When Beacon Street houses were built, the smelly mudflats were undesirable. Though the Alster Basin in Hamburg was the prototype for the improvement of the Charles River, the architecture never conformed to that vision even after 1910 when the dam had created a freshwater basin. The road next to the

river retained its name—Back Street.

The Esplanade began as a simple walk along the water, but in 1931 James J. Storrow donated funds to landscape a spacious park with areas for outdoor music and a basin for more protected water activities. The Esplanade offers settings for picnicking, strolling, sailing, sitting, and bicycling. During the summer, outdoor concerts and ballet attract thousands to the Hatch Shell. It was certainly an insult to name Storrow Drive—the 1951 highway that usurped much of the park—for the benefactor who made such an effort to create a quiet place of natural beauty.

The Esplanade

4 Nashua Street Park
Halvorson Design Partnership, 2004

:: Olmsted's Charlesbank was modified into nonexistence, but at Nashua Street Park it is reborn in modern dress. The greening of Boston's water edges reached the lower Charles River with this extension of the Esplanade to the HarborWalk. A 70-foot-wide stairway brings people to the water and functions as an amphitheater to watch sports and fireworks. To avoid collisions between movement modes, a meandering pedestrian path beside the river is rough-surfaced while the lane for inline skaters and bicyclists next to the road

Fog mist on the spiral sculpture, Nashua Street Park © Halvorson Design Partnership, Ben A. Watkins

is smooth-surfaced asphalt. The park is a very welcome return of public access to this stretch of riverbank.

5 Commonwealth Avenue Mall 🏛
begun 1858
Boston Landmark

:: Boston's version of a Parisian boulevard forms the spine of the Back Bay. Protecting the four parallel rows of stately American and English elms from disease involved a major effort that sometimes failed. A hardier, smaller variety of elm has been planted to replace lost trees.

In the nineteenth century handsome iron fences enclosed all Boston's urban greens. The fence separating Commonwealth Mall from the streets was dismantled for scrap iron in the early twentieth century. Down the center of the promenade, a series of statues provide rhythmical vertical foci on each block. The first was the granite figure of Alexander Hamilton installed in 1865 facing the Public Garden at Arlington Street. Many statues followed, including General John Glover, Patrick Andrew Collins, William Lloyd Garrison, Samuel Eliot Morison, and Dominic Sarmiento. The procession concludes

70-foot-wide granite steps down to Charles River, Nashua Street Park © Halvorson Design Partnership, Ben A. Watkins

William Lloyd Garrison monument, Commonwealth Avenue Mall

Boston Women's Memorial, Commonwealth Avenue Mall

Leif Eriksson at the Charlesgate

with Leif Eriksson gazing over Charlesgate toward Kenmore Square.

At Dartmouth a black granite horizontal memorial honors firefighters who died in the Hotel Vendome fire. A vertical figure or ladder with empty coat would have been consistent with the visual rhythm of statuary in the mall. Near Fairfield the 2003 Boston Women's Memorial by sculptor Meredith Bergmann admirably fulfills that pattern while commemorating three outstanding women: Phyllis Wheatley, a West African slave who became a literary prodigy in Boston; the abolitionist and women's suffrage publisher Lucy Stone; and Abigail Adams, intellectual wife and mother of presidents.

6 Charlesgate
Frederick Law Olmsted, 1870s

∷ Charlesgate is the tragedy of the Emerald Necklace. Olmsted's charming naturalistic landscape was decimated by the Bowker overpass. Picturesque paths under overhanging trees framed Stony Brook and connected the Charles River Esplanade, Commonwealth Mall, and the Back Bay Fens. Two stone bridges can still be seen, but landscape restoration is desperately needed.

7 Back Bay Fens ⅲ
Frederick Law Olmsted, 1879
National Register of Historic Places
Boston Landmark

∷ The Back Bay Fens and their adjoining parks formed the first linear park system in the country. It is a good example of the nineteenth-century English landscape movement. Idyllic views, romantic bridges, floating mists, and tall reeds gave the Back Bay Fens a distinct personality. Reeking salt marshes were brilliantly transformed into freshwater fens through artful damming and landscape design.

The wild English garden quality that is part of the attraction of the park is an

H.H. Richardson's puddingstone bridge, Back Bay Fens

example of the beneficial results neglect can have. As Olmsted said, one of the nicest things an insensitive parks commission can do for its properties is simply to neglect them, since landscaping is rarely damaged and is often enhanced by neglect, whereas the construction of facilities within park properties can cause damage that requires generations to correct.

Norman Thomas Newton wrote in *Design on the Land* that "the 'blooming islets' that Olmsted planned are gone. An athletic field of indifferent quality, a geometric rose garden, and a war memorial occupy what were once quiet marsh-meadows. East of Agassiz Road the former marsh-meadow has been given over for many years to 'victory

Riverway

gardens,' flower and vegetable plots planted and maintained by individual citizens on application and permit. All of these varied elements are of course laudable in themselves, but they hardly represent appropriate uses for the Fens, if only because they are wholly disruptive of what would otherwise be a placid scene. Moreover, for their own good these activities deserve locations better adapted to their several purposes."

Subsequent improvements to the park bridges and pathways have been utilitarian rather than following the picturesque tradition. All of Olmsted's original swamp plantings should be restored for the park to return to its full glory. Happily, H. H. Richardson's fine puddingstone bridge of 1880 survives as he designed it. In cities throughout the country, green parks are often seen as an opportunity for development. Despite unsympathetic alterations, the Fens is still an outdoor room for the city where anyone can lean on the railing of a bridge gazing into sleepy water or lie in the grass with a good book.

8 Riverway and Olmsted (Leverett) Park ⅲ

Frederick Law Olmsted, 1881
*National Register of Historic Places
Boston Landmark*

:: The sinuous curves of this linear park are dictated by the natural contours of the Muddy River. Along the banks woodsy paths invite pedestrians, bicyclists, and even horseback riders. Originally the Riverway linked the Back Bay Fens with Olmsted Park and Jamaica Pond. Unfortunately, the Park Drive section has been destroyed. An entire block-long segment was sold for commercial purposes, a serious relinquishing of the public trust by city officials. The opportunity to restore it occurred when the building was abandoned. Most of the Riverway remains nearly as Olmsted intended, with fine masonry bridges linking the two banks at several points.

9 Jamaica Park ▥

Frederick Law Olmsted, 1892
National Register of Historic Places
National Historic Landmark (Jamaica
Pond Boathouse)
Boston Landmark

:: Three adjacent ponds—Jamaica, Ward's, and Leverett—form the focus for Jamaica and Olmsted Parks, with Jamaica Pond the largest body of water in the green space network. Jamaica Park was designed as a water activity park, with a boathouse and dock in a Tudor revival, half-timbered style. The continuous path surrounding the pond remains popular with walkers, joggers, inline skaters, and tots on tricycles.

The white pine trees inspired the name Pine Bank for the site of the former Perkins mansion at the northern side of the pond. Opposite Pine Bank was the summer home of historian Francis Parkman, where a monument by Daniel Chester French was erected in 1906.

10 Arnold Arboretum ▥

Charles Sprague Sargent and Frederick Law Olmsted, 1872
National Historic Landmark

:: The Arborway, a vehicular parkway, links Jamaica Park to the Arnold Arboretum and the arboretum to Franklin Park. When built, it contained a carriage road, a saddle path, and a pedestrian walk down the central green space between two traffic ways. The arboretum was laid out by Charles Sprague Sargent with the advice of Olmsted. The intention was to make a living museum of trees for both study and pleasure. The planting areas are arranged in a species-by-species progression that is scientifically formal, but the original design was intended to

look like a typical New England rural landscape with no sense of formal landscaping and no open lawns or meadows. At one time more than 5,000 species and varieties of trees and shrubs grew in the arboretum. The city provides policing and road maintenance, but the plants and park areas are all under the care of Harvard University, which has a 999-year lease on everything but the roads.

11 Franklin Park

Frederick Law Olmsted, 1885
National Register of Historic Places
Boston Landmark

:: Olmsted's 520-acre masterpiece combined vast rustic scenery with H. H. Richardson architecture, Daniel Chester French sculpture, sheep to trim the grass, and a dairy for healthful refreshments. In his "Notes on the Plan of Franklin Park," Olmsted described his vision: "The plan looks to its being maintained in quietness: quietness both to the eye and the ear. A grateful serenity may be enjoyed in it by many thousand people at a time if they are not drawn into throngs by spectacular attractions, but allowed to distribute themselves as they are otherwise like to do." Only Franklin Park was large enough to accomplish this rural ideal within a band of transition and service areas separating it from the city.

The design was influenced by Joseph Paxton's "People's Park" at Birkenhead, England. In the nineteenth century a park carriage service was operated by Bacon and Tarbell, providing up to eleven passengers with the pleasures of a carriage drive through the grounds and allowing them to dismount for a picnic or stroll and return in a later carriage. The park was enormously popular and intensely used into the early twentieth century.

The character of the park has changed greatly since Olmsted's time.

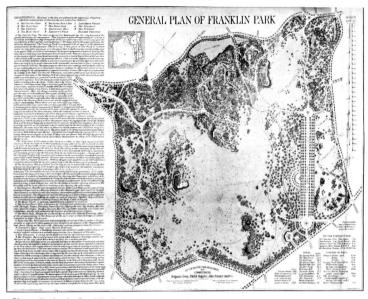

Olmsted's plan for Franklin Park, 1885   Olmsted Office Portfolio

In *Design on the Land,* Norman Thomas Newton wrote, "Franklin Park today would not be likely to elicit from John Charles Olmsted a repetition of the words of praise he voiced in 1905, save as they reflected his justifiable admiration for the sensitivity and skill with which his elder had realized the fine potential of the area." The "attractions" he barred have been constructed in abundance: a golf course with clubhouse, tennis courts, baseball fields, and a large zoo replaced the sylvan landscape. The imposing 1896 Refectory that served as the transition point from streetcar service to carriage rides within the park was demolished in the late twentieth century. Nevertheless, some elements of the original design may be discovered by the determined visitor: Scarborough Pond, some origi-nal tree species, and natural stone stairways and bridges, as well as out-croppings of the famous Roxbury pud-dingstone that Olmsted incorporated in his design.

12   Franklin Park Zoo
Huygens and Tappé, 1972–1979
Weidlinger Associates; Huygens and Dimella, 1989

:: The zoo replaced Olmsted's Greeting in the early twentieth century. A rem-nant from that era is the 1913 Chinese Pagoda Bird House, renovated by Geo-metrics in the 1970s. Later the empha-sis changed to African wildlife in four major ecologies representing desert, tropical forest, veldt, and bush forest with appropriate botanical exhibits. The Outback Trail added Australian exhibits.

HARVARD
AND MIT

Harvard University and the Massachusetts Institute of Technology (MIT) have together amassed a collection of architecture of international importance. Harvard, the oldest and until the end of the seventeenth century the only college in the Americas, built significant architecture long before MIT arrived in Cambridge. Harvard possesses the only Le Corbusier building in America, but MIT has scored a number of architectural coups and turned its campus into a contemporary sculpture garden. Smaller and far newer, MIT is racing ahead in the twenty-first century.

Old Cambridge, as Harvard's neighborhood is called, is a cosmopolitan place with leading intellectuals and students from around the world. Its mythic college hangout, Harvard Square, is actually a bustling modern shopping center. Though Cambridge is as old as Boston, you'd hardly know it. You won't find seventeenth-century buildings on their original sites. While Boston abounds in urban seventeenth-century lanes that retain their width, tight building enclosure, and scale, Cambridge streets are nineteenth-century size or larger. There has been surprisingly little reverence for the historic environment here outside the venerable halls in Harvard Yard.

Boston had well-organized preservation activists beginning in 1886, and much was admirably preserved long before that, especially under Charles Bulfinch, heading the Board of Selectmen for three decades. Cambridge waited until the late twentieth century to save what little history remained in Harvard Square. Historic façades were sliced off and glued on neomodernist boxes. Old houses were ripped from their foundations and relocated in make-believe settings. Preservation was misunderstood and gained a bad name by ignoring context. Only Benjamin Thompson in the 1960s introduced a more intimate scale by carving out a passage through a Brattle Street block, a scale inadequately appreciated by the community at the time.

Creating the Harvard Square Defense Fund brought out a surprising assertiveness in the community, particularly against contemporary architecture. Decades after I. M. Pei's Kennedy Presidential Library was rebuffed, Hans Hollein's book conservation center at 90 Mount Auburn was defeated. The all-powerful Harvard University was tamed into submission, no longer prepared to commission giants as it had in prior eras when it hired Bulfinch, Richardson, Gropius, and Le Corbusier. Its ambitious building projects continued across the river in Allston and Brighton, just not in Cambridge.

While battles raged around Harvard Square, downriver MIT and Kendall Square built green and flashy with abandon, grabbing all the attention. The contrast between the two campuses offers a splendid tutorial on architectural theory and practice over three centuries. Choose high-tech cutting edge or dignified red brick tradition. Both campuses offer wonderful opportunities to observe, appreciate, and learn on a stroll.

Harvard University

In the early seventeenth century, when it was only a house on nine acres, students paid tuition in farm produce, livestock, and useful items: cutlery, an ax for chopping firewood, even a pair of used boots if they fit. It was almost a theological school, since its purpose was to educate ministers. Half of the seventeenth-century graduates filled positions in New England churches. Attendance at morning prayer and evensong remained compulsory into the nineteenth century.

Henry James described the campus as an "irregular group of heterogeneous buildings," a description as fitting today as in 1886. Although it includes a number of significant pieces of architecture by alumni, insensitive alterations, siting, and mediocre neighboring buildings detract from their appreciation. Carpenter Center, the only North American building by Le Corbusier, could not be more inappropriately located and landscaped. Other architectural treasures pop up here and there about the Harvard campus, tolerated perhaps, but never given much consideration.

1 Harvard Yard 🏛
National Register of Historic Places (Old Harvard Yard)

:: For most visitors, Harvard Yard is the essence of Harvard. Today the university has spread far and wide, crossing the Charles River and reaching deep into Allston. Although inspired by Cambridge University, where the first leaders of the college had been educated, the campus avoided emulating its cloisters and enclosed courtyards. Instead it expresses the New England tradition of Georgian buildings placed in fields of green. It set a pattern replicated by countless colleges across the United States. The Harvard campus stood wide open until the twentieth century, when

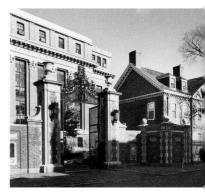
Gate, Harvard Yard

the yard was enclosed and gated by McKim, Mead, and White's brick and iron fence design.

Several campus plans were prepared over the years, including one by Bulfinch and another by Cass Gilbert, but these were ignored. One area planned by Harvard, Tercentenary Quadrangle, is heavy-handed, with the overscale Widener Library and the overcute Memorial Church playing off each other to achieve a very effective high kitsch. Nevertheless, the Yard holds most of the best within sight of Daniel Chester French's 1884 seated John Harvard.

2 Benjamin Wadsworth House
1341 Massachusetts Avenue
1726

:: The Wadsworth house was built as the residence for the college's fourth president on the site of the earliest

Benjamin Wadsworth House

Harvard building, the Peyntree House, used by Harvard College in the mid-seventeenth century. It was the residence of nine Harvard presidents. When Massachusetts Avenue was widened, the house lost its front yard.

3 Massachusetts Hall 🏛
Harvard Yard
1718
National Historic Landmark

:: Three halls—Massachusetts, Hollis, and Stoughton—surround two early quadrangles of the Yard. All were built as dormitories. The stacked suites are organized around entries with individual stairways that minimize corridors. The social orientation is thus vertical rather than horizontal, and the basic social unit is limited to the number of suites with direct access to each stair. Most of the later Harvard dormitories, called houses, followed this layout. While the suite concept was retained, their composition was altered to include a shared sitting room and separate bedroom-studies. The interiors of Massachusetts Hall have been extensively altered.

Massachusetts Hall

4 Harvard Hall 🏛
Harvard Yard
Sir Francis Bernard, 1766
Altered: Richard Bond, 1842; Ware and Van Brunt, 1870; Ashley, Myer, 1968

:: The present Harvard Hall is the third building of the same name and the second to occupy this site. The 1642 hall collapsed. Since its condition was considered too poor to repair, the second Harvard Hall was constructed between 1672 and 1682. But the second hall burned, and the present structure was its replacement.

Harvard Hall

Harvard Hall was the center of the early college, with the library and rooms for tutors and students on the upper floors. Like their English university models, the accommodations were organized as suites with a bedroom for two students attached to a tiny study for each. The great hall that served as chapel, lecture hall, dining hall, and ceremonial center for the college dominated the ground floor. Built perpendicular to the street, the third Harvard Hall began the definition of two quadrangles. Major alterations since its construction include the 1842 central pavilion and the wings of 1870.

5 Stoughton Hall 📷
Harvard Yard
Charles Bulfinch, 1804–1805

6 Hollis Hall
Harvard Yard
Thomas Dawes, 1762–1763
National Register of Historic Places

:: The first Stoughton Hall, built in 1763, was demolished. Charles Bulfinch, a 1781 Harvard graduate, was asked to replace it with a design based on Hollis Hall, where he had occupied room 11 during his final year. The brick mass is the essence of the "Harvard look," standing solidly and simply on its low granite foundation and penetrated by dozens of twelve-over-twelve paned windows. Massive chimneys pierce the hip roof. The central pediment contains

Stoughton Hall

a single window with bull's-eye windows on each side. The building cost $29,048.31, of which $18,400 was raised by lottery. Bulfinch was paid only $300 for his drawings and supervision of construction.

7 Holden Chapel
Harvard Yard
1742 (significantly altered)
National Register of Historic Places

:: This tiny Georgian chapel has barely survived numerous alterations throughout its history. After two decades as a chapel, it was roughly tossed from one use to another: fire wagon stable, storehouse, carpentry workshop, chemistry laboratory. After serving as a barracks in the Revolutionary War, it became the medical college. Excavations for lower-level expansion uncovered bones from cadavers dissected in anatomy class. Renovations continued into the twenty-first century. The doors, windows, entablature, and pediment have all been changed, and the original west entrance was abandoned and a new entrance installed on the rear east façade. While technically an eighteenth-century building, it really is more of a severely wounded refugee after generations of mistreatment.

Holden Chapel

8 University Hall 🏛

Harvard Yard
Charles Bulfinch, 1813–1814
Altered: 1842; Bruner/Cott, 2001
National Historic Landmark

:: Bulfinch prepared three alternative designs for University Hall, of which the two rejected designs were the most monumental, having pediments, columns, and domes. This building is a straightforward hip-roofed mass of Chelmsford granite ashlar with a rusticated basement. The two entrances are defined by a favorite Bulfinch device of paired two-story Ionic pilasters, joined by a central entablature topped by a balustrade. A portico was added during construction and then removed in 1842, to the benefit of the building.

The first floor was organized into four dining halls, one for each class, separated to minimize friction between classes. However, the walls separating the rooms contained large round openings high on the walls through which food and harsh words were tossed! Kitchens were in the basement, and the second floor had a chapel in the center and recitation rooms in the wings. The third floor held more recitation rooms and the galleries for the chapel. The chapel is expressed on the exterior by the tall arched windows. The interiors have been altered.

9 Memorial Church

Harvard Yard
Coolidge Shepley Bulfinch and Abbott, 1931

:: Under president Abbott Lawrence Lowell, Harvard's Widener Library and Memorial Church were built to define an entirely new kind of space in the Yard, Tercentenary Quadrangle. Designing a church to face the enormous, static colonnade of Doric columns on Widener's façade was not easy. Yet Memorial Church, small as it is in comparison to its gigantic neighbor, man-

University Hall

Memorial Church © William M. Rittase

ages to be equally emphatic in its Georgian revival style. The small and precise Doric colonnade exaggerates the apparent size of the spire above. Memorial Church seems older and more significant than it actually is but is a visual focus for the university.

10 Widener Library

Harvard Yard
Horace Trumbauer, 1913

:: Harvard's library outgrew the elegant Gore Hall pictured on the City of Cambridge seal, and it was demolished in 1913. Widener Library was designed by a Philadelphia architect selected by the family of Harry Elkins Widener, whose memory they wished to honor. Widener had died on the *Titanic*.

Much of Trumbauer's work was designed by Julian Francis Abele (1881–1950), a black architect who was Trumbauer's chief designer from 1908 to 1938, when Trumbauer died. Abele studied architecture at the University of Pennsylvania and at the École des Beaux-Arts in Paris, where he was the first black graduate. In addition to Widener Library, Abele's notable designs include the Duke University campus, the Philadelphia Museum of Art, and numerous grand homes. He designed Newport mansions such as the Elms and Miramar, the summer home of the Wideners.

11 Sever Hall 🏛

Harvard Yard
Henry Hobson Richardson, 1878–1880
National Historic Landmark

∷ One of Richardson's finest works, Sever Hall succeeds on several levels. It relates well to the eighteenth-century buildings of the Yard by adopting similar massing, proportions, and materials. The large pediment on the front entrance and the small one on the rear relate to the colonial era of the neighboring buildings.

Widener Library

As in the Trinity Church Rectory in the Back Bay, built about the same time, the brickwork is extraordinary, with roll moldings around doors and windows and fluted brick chimneys. For every six courses of stretchers, there is one of headers. Red mortar was used in the original building, but this has not been maintained. In addition to the red brick, the façade has Longmeadow sandstone. The roof is of red tile. Note the bowed section of the rear façade, an original Richardson device for animating the solid flat plane. The size and rhythmic spacing of the many window openings are a key part of the design, and rather than being regular and static, are richly varied. The ideal time to appreciate this is at night with the building lit from within.

Children enjoy the "whispering

Sever Hall

gallery" effect of the arch at the main entrance. Speak quietly toward one side of the arch, and the sound will be reflected around to someone listening at the other side.

12 Warren House
12 Quincy Street
early nineteenth century

:: This wood-frame house has a trap-door installed by Latin professor Charles Beck, a former owner. It leads to a secret room used to shelter slaves escaping on the Underground Railroad. The English Department has been located here since 1899, when it was donated to Harvard by Henry Clarke Warren.

13 Carpenter Center for the Visual Arts ⅲ
21 Quincy Street
Le Corbusier with Sert, Jackson, and Gourley, 1961–1963

:: The only building in North America by the French architect Le Corbusier, the Carpenter Center for the Visual Arts is a piece of sculpture designed for human use. The form expresses the architect's desire to expose students to the arts. A diagonal ramp gradually ascends from

Quincy Street to the second level, a glass-enclosed exhibition hall, and then passes through to the other side and down to street level. Along the way it offers views into the Sert Gallery and café, later alterations that give credit to Le Corbusier's protégé, Josep Lluis Sert, who championed the project. Another pathway cuts through underneath the ramp to the lower level that houses the Harvard Film Archives.

The spatial drama and bold concrete forms are achieved with the architect's trademarks: round concrete columns, sunscreens, and glass block. The building has rarely been used in the way Le Corbusier envisioned it and sits rather crowded and uncomfortable amid its tradition-bound neighbors. It is the work of a master and deserves better treatment in its use and site development.

14 Fogg Art Museum
32 Quincy Street
Coolidge Shepley Bulfinch and Abbott, 1925–1927

:: Behind the dignified neo-Georgian façade of the Fogg Museum is a replica of the San Gallo loggia at Montepulciano, Italy, the most striking aspect of the building.

Carpenter Center for the Visual Arts © Shaw Studios

Fogg Art Museum Sigurd Fischer © Shepley Bulfinch Richardson and Abbott

Courtyard, Fogg Art Museum Sigurd Fischer © Shepley Bulfinch Richardson and Abbott

15 Werner Otto Hall
Prescott Street, behind Fogg Art Museum
Gwathmey Siegel and Associates, 1991

:: The Busch-Reisinger collection moved here from the picturesque German romantic revival building at the head of Quincy Street. This structure was added to the back of the Fogg Museum next to the Carpenter Center and provides a destination for Le Corbusier's ramp. The former Busch-Reisinger Museum building is now Adolphus Busch Hall, home of the Center for European Studies.

16 Sackler Museum
485 Broadway
James Stirling, Michael Wilford Associates with Perry, Dean, Rogers and Partners, 1984

:: Across Broadway, the Sackler Museum occupies a difficult, though important, site and should be viewed in the context of its neighbors: Gund Hall by John Andrews, the Victorian fantasy of Memorial Hall, the Germanic nostalgia

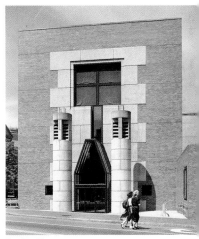

Sackler Museum

of Adolphus Busch Hall, and Le Corbusier's Carpenter Center. Except for the Fogg Museum of Coolidge et al., none of these relate to each other or to the Harvard campus in an obvious way. In fact, in presenting his design, British architect James Stirling described the surrounding Harvard campus as an "archi- tectural zoo." The Sackler Museum adds another strange beast to the lineup.

Working in the postmodernist idiom, Stirling seems to have borrowed one theme from each of the neighbors. The building is faced in polychrome brick in response to the colorful Memorial Hall. At the narrow end facing the Fogg Museum is a monumental entrance flanked by pylons reminiscent of the Gund Hall columns and framed by a Herculean Gibbs surround, mimicking Harvard's Georgian style.

The Sackler houses ancient Oriental and Near Eastern art and includes space for special exhibitions, classrooms, offices, curatorial and service departments, library collections, and a large lecture hall.

17 Gund Hall
48 Quincy Street
John Andrews, Anderson and Baldwin, 1969

:: Gund Hall, the Graduate School of Design, takes the form of a giant stairway with design studios on the steps and the entry area, library, and lecture hall sheltered beneath the steps. Having all the design studios in one vast stepped space is an appealing notion intended to promote communication between students and classes in a curriculum in which so much is learned from one's peers.

18 Adolphus Busch Hall
Kirkland Street at Divinity Avenue
German Bestelmeyer, 1916–1917
Renovation: Goody, Clancy & Associates, 1989

:: Designed by Dresden architect German Bestelmeyer to house a Germanic museum, this building was a gift to Harvard from beer magnate Adolphus Busch and his wife, Lilly Anheuser Busch. Their son-in-law, Hugo Reisinger, and his wife continued to contribute to the museum, and thus the name was later changed to the Busch-Reisinger Museum. Although the structure was

Gund Hall

completed in 1917, the museum did not open until 1921 because of anti-German sentiments after World War I. Before its opening twelve stained-glass windows were destroyed by vandals. During World War II German art banned by the Nazis was exhibited here and much of the building was used by the U.S. Army.

In 1989 the interiors were totally renovated with a new stairway constructed in the main hall. The original porphyry marble columns, quarry tile floor, wooden ceiling, chandelier with Hapsburg double-headed eagle, and the courtyard suggest the extravagance of the original building. The Germanic romantic revival exterior retains its decorative urns, balustrades, and the figures of Wotan, Brunnhilde, Siegfried, and Alberich from Wagner's Ring cycle. When the Busch-Reisinger art collection moved to Werner Otto Hall, the Minda de Gunzberg Center for European Studies replaced it.

19 Memorial Hall 🏛
just north of Harvard Yard
Ware and Van Brunt, 1870–1874
Basement commons: Bruner/Cott with Venturi Scott Brown, 1995
Clock tower restoration: Childs, Bertman, Tseckares, 2001
National Historic Landmark

:: Exuberant "Mem Hall" is a sentimental favorite and a wonderful Victorian medieval pile in the colorful Ruskin Gothic style. Henry James thought the architecture hysterical. Two Harvard graduates won the architectural competition to design a memorial to the students and graduates who had served on the Union side in the Civil War. William Robert Ware, class of 1852, and Henry Van Brunt, class of 1854, had been students of Richard Morris Hunt in New York and set up a practice in Boston in 1863. Their solution was a building on an entirely different scale from the established seventeenth- and eighteenth-century campus.

In plan it is a Gothic cathedral with the transept serving as entrance. The apse is Sanders Theater and the nave is a large hall, originally a dining hall. Sanders Theater is said to be modeled on London's Fortune Theater. The interiors feature fine trusses, woodwork, and decorated walls. The hall has not only housed large lecture classes, registration, and ceremonial functions, but has been the location of many important lectures and concerts since its dedication.

The clock tower—destroyed in a 1956 fire—was rebuilt nearly half a century later, returning its original crown.

Memorial Hall Tower spire

20 Sherman Fairchild Biochemistry Laboratory
9 Divinity Avenue
Payette Associates, 1979–1981

:: This DNA research facility houses laboratories, offices, and classrooms. Since the research requires sophisticated technology and is potentially hazardous, it was necessary to protect the researchers and the surrounding community. Barriers prevent researchers from inadvertently contaminating themselves or the environs. Other safety features include breakout panels between adjoining labs and balconies outside each module for refuge.

Entrance, Memorial Hall

21 Divinity Hall
14 Divinity Avenue
Solomon Willard and Thomas W. Sumner, 1825

:: One of the early and most important buildings constructed outside the Yard is still a prominent Harvard landmark. The chapel was extensively modified in 1904 by A. W. Longfellow.

Divinity Hall

based on shellfish, another on insects, and the third on plants.

23 Rockefeller Hall
47 Francis Avenue
Edward Larrabee Barnes, 1971

:: The irregular form of this small dormitory for the Divinity School confronts varied boundary conditions, including a Gothic classroom building, an older residential neighborhood, a parking lot, and a large cyclotron. The design responded with stepped-back massing and butt-joint corner windows.

22 Harvard Biological Laboratories
16 Divinity Avenue
Coolidge Shepley Bulfinch and Abbott, 1930

:: This was the first "modern" building at Harvard and possibly the first significant "modern" one in Boston. The simple masses punctured with factory sash windows are humanized with delightful and well-integrated ornamentation based on biological themes. A pair of large but friendly rhinos stands guard outside the entrance, while above them a herd of elephants cavorts in the carved brick frieze executed by Katherine Ward Lane. Each of the three pairs of doors has different grillwork: one is

24 Josep Lluis Sert House
64 Francis Street
Josep Lluis Sert, 1958

:: Behind the one-story natural brick perimeter wall is a very successful house organized around three courtyards, Sert's experiment with a Mediterranean-style house in a northern climate. All rooms are oriented to the courts, each of which has a subtly different, restrained paving and landscape plan. The house combines unusual privacy and a spacious sense of openness, with wall and floor planes carried outdoors along the white-painted brick walls of the courtyards.

The Catalan native was a friend of important artists including Miró, Calder, and Picasso, whose work was in most

Carved brick bas-relief, Biological Laboratories Paul J. Weber © Shepley Bulfinch Richardson and Abbott

Rockefeller Hall

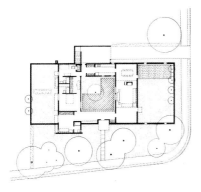

Plan, Josep Lluis Sert house

of the rooms of the house. In 1937, as the Spanish Civil War was flaming, Picasso's *Guernica* debuted in Sert's Spanish pavilion at the Paris Exposition.

25 Science Center
north of Cambridge Street Underpass
Sert, Jackson and Associates,
1970–1973
Addition: Leers Weinzapfel Associates,
2004

:: The largest building on the Harvard campus is best experienced from the sunny glass-roofed arcade that provides access to the major public spaces of the building. The complex exterior form expresses the five components of the center: the long laboratory mass paralleling the arcade, the terraced classroom wing for the mathematics department, the low science library and administrative wings, and the spider-roofed building containing four demonstration theaters. Use of precast concrete components— "ladder" columns and girders—allowed rapid construction.

26 Tanner Fountain
front of Science Center
Joan Brigham, Peter Walker and the
SWA Group, 1984

:: This unusual fountain is made of a casual circular grouping of 159 New England field boulders set in grass and

Tanner Fountain

asphalt. It is intended to evoke the mystery of primeval places and to express the rocky landscape of New England. The fountain alters with the seasons and time of day; in summer dozens of nozzles emit a fine mist, and in winter the rocks are shrouded in clouds of steam. People are attracted to the rocks as sitting places; the fountain sprays begin slowly so that they have time to escape without getting very wet.

27 Austin Hall 🏛
Harvard Law School
across from the Common
Henry Hobson Richardson, 1881–1883
National Register of Historic Places

:: Richardson's concern with color in architecture is evident here, as it is in his earlier Trinity Church and Sever Hall. The dark Longmeadow sandstone ashlar is trimmed with pale yellow Ohio stone and decorated with bluestone marquetry inspired by the southern Romanesque decoration that Richardson had studied in the Auvergne region of France. The stone arches and columns are decorated with delightful carving, including Richardson's monogram interwoven with tools of the architect. Origi-

Austin Hall

nally the exterior appeared gaudy to many observers, but with the passage of time, either it has mellowed or we have become accustomed to it.

Inside, the fireplace in the James Barr Ames Courtroom (originally the library) is a National Historic Landmark in itself, an outstanding example of Richardson's ornament with rich stone corbels supporting the mantel. The interior spatial organization is communicated on the exterior both by the massing and by the window treatment. The large central mass is flanked by lower wings. Three massive Romanesque arches with a deeply recessed porch define the entrance, while the off-center stair tower provides counterpoint in the generally balanced design. The building was constructed for the now unbelievably small sum of $145,000.

28 Harkness Commons and the Graduate Center 🏛
near Oxford and Everett Streets
Walter Gropius and The Architects Collaborative, 1950

:: The first Harvard building in the international style was the work of Walter Gropius, founder in 1919 of the influential Bauhaus, a school of architecture and design in Dessau, Germany. After the Nazis closed the Bauhaus, Gropius was invited to head the Harvard Graduate School of Design, a position that he held for many years. A number of his students and associates followed him to America, including Marcel Breuer, Gyorgy Kepes, Laszlo Moholy-Nagy, and Mies van der Rohe. In 1945 he founded The Architects Collaborative in Cambridge.

Gropius's principles of functional design, using technology to serve social needs and making a sharp break with sentimental tradition, are evident in this austere factory-like complex. Seven buff-colored brick dormitories

Harkness Commons and the Graduate Center © Robert Damora

are linked by covered walkways, forming several courtyards. The focus of the group is Harkness Commons, which contains recreational areas and a second-floor dining hall reached by a long ramp. Gropius felt that art and architecture should be integrated, and this building incorporates several works of art: a brick design by Joseph Albers, a tile wall by Herbert Bayer, a ceramic mural by Joan Miró, a wood bas-relief by Jean Arp, and a metal sculpture by Richard Lippold.

29 **Naito Chemistry and Bauer Laboratory Building and Center for Genomic Research**
12 Oxford Street, next to the Peabody Museum
Ellenzweig Associates, 2003

:: The Naito laboratories were squeezed onto the former parking lot of the Cabot Science Complex. A three-story glass bridge connects to Sherman Fairchild Biochemistry Laboratory. Cabot Courtyard and Frisbie Place are intended to replicate traditional college quadrangles.

Arrow and Mount Auburn Streets
In the second half of the nineteenth-century, the Reversible Collar Company factory occupied 18,000 feet of land between Arrow and Mount Auburn Streets and Massachusetts Avenue. In 1866 they made paper collars and cuffs. Later they developed a highly polished layered starched muslin, which was more durable and could be wiped clean.

30 **Apthorp House**
Bow Street at Adams House behind Randolph Hall
1760

:: The Rev. East Apthorp's eighteenth-century house serves as the master's residence for Adams House.

Naito Chemistry and Bauer Laboratory Building and Center for Genomic Research

31 **Lampoon Castle**
Bow Street at Mount Auburn Street
Wheelwright and Haven, 1909
National Register of Historic Places

:: The whimsical home of Harvard's undergraduate humor magazine was paid for by William Randolph Hearst and Isabella Stewart Gardner. In a triumph of sentiment over sense, the entrance tower at the point of the tiny triangular site suggests a man in a

Lampoon Castle

bowler hat. Beneath the eyes and nose a flagpole seems to be a rudely projecting tongue. The copper ibis on the roof has been a prize sometimes captured by rival clubs. The *Lampoon* was founded in 1876.

32 Quincy Square
Bow Street at Quincy Street and Massachusetts Avenue
Halvorson Design Partnership, 1997

:: The small triangular island gained a stunning iron fence that is contemporary yet eminently respectful of its context.

Harvard's Houses 𝄢
The prospect of Harvard's houses along the Charles River is one of the most impressive faces of Cambridge. Harmonious and traditional, the cluster of neo-Georgian houses suggests a lineage far older than their 1930s origins. Loosely inspired by the courtyard colleges of Cambridge University in England, they were designed by Shepley Bulfinch Richardson and Abbott in the same decade they designed very different campuses, including Northeastern and Stanford in Palo Alto, California. Later Harvard houses were not always as successful, suffering from a lack of continuity in scale, materials, and design.

Prior to the 1930s creation of the

Lowell House Sigurd Fischer © Shepley Bulfinch Richardson and Abbott

house system, most Harvard students lived off-campus due to limited accommodations in the Yard. Between 1891 and 1904 seventeen private dormitory halls were built on the "Gold Coast": Plympton, Holyoke, Linden, Mount Auburn, and Massachusetts from Dunster to Bow. Four halls were purchased and joined together in 1932 to form Adams House.

33 Peabody Terrace 𝄢
Charles River at 900 Memorial Drive
Sert, Jackson and Gourley, 1964
Renovation: Bruner/Cott, 1993–1995

:: This married student housing was innovative in its era. Low-rise structures of three, five, and seven stories relate to the scale of the neighborhood and form courtyards, recalling the designs of other Harvard housing along the river. The three twenty-two-story towers employ an ingenious skip-floor system in which elevators stop every third floor, allowing several floor-through apartments. A three-dimensional grid of balconies, sunscreens, and privacy baffles establishes the scale.

Peabody Terrace © Phokion Karas

34 John W. Weeks Footbridge
Charles River
McKim, Mead, and White, 1924

:: The Georgian revival footbridge crosses the Charles River at Leverett House near DeWolfe Street, connecting to the business school designed by the same architectural firm.

35 Weld Boathouse
Charles River at the Larz Anderson Bridge

:: Rowing on the Charles has been popular for several centuries. The Harvard rowing team began sporting crimson scarves in the mid-nineteenth century, and in 1910 crimson became Harvard's official color.

36 Northeastern University Henderson Boathouse
Charles River at 1345 Soldiers Field Road, Brighton
Graham Gund Architects, 1989

:: Boathouses have long been a feature of the Charles River. In the nineteenth century they grew large and elaborate to house dozens of sculls and shells for clubs and university teams. The daily drills and races of rowing crews still delight many fans living on both sides of the river. In the boathouses, crews exercise and shower, and their shoes are nailed or screwed into the shells. All boathouses have repair shops for the delicate shells, and handmade oars and the long slender

Weeks Bridge and Harvard Houses

Henderson Boathouse, Northeastern University © Steve Rosenthal

lightweight shells are still turned out in some.

The Henderson Boathouse was built when Northeastern University attracted the late, legendary Charlie Smith away from Harvard. "He was the kind of guy who could do anything—weld, patch, make structural repairs, even make his own oars from scratch," according to Dan Boyne, Harvard's recreational sculling director. Northeastern decided it was time to stop renting boathouse space and built its own. The towers, dormers, and porches were chosen to mirror the elements of the nearby nineteenth-century boathouses.

37 Winsor and Belmont Hill Schools Boathouse
Charles River at 5 Greenough Boulevard
Renovation: Architectural Resources Cambridge, 2002

:: Due to the fragile nature of the site, neither a septic system nor a sewer con-

John Hicks House

Belfer Center for Public Management
© 1984 Nick Wheeler

nection was permitted. Instead, composting toilet facilities were installed.

38 Winthrop Square
John F. Kennedy Street at Winthrop Street

:: This is the oldest square in Cambridge. It was at the heart of Newtowne, the 1631 settlement established 5 miles up the Charles River from Boston and Charlestown. It served as a market square until it was fenced and planted for common grazing in 1846. Several modern streets are laid over the seventeenth-century roads—Winthrop, South, John F. Kennedy, Dunster, and Eliot Streets follow parts of Spring, Long, Woods, Water, and Creek Lanes.

39 John Hicks House
64 John F. Kennedy Street
1762

:: This pre-Revolutionary house was moved from Dunster and Winthrop Streets to serve as the library of Harvard's Kirkland House.

40 Belfer Center for Public Management
John F. Kennedy School of Government
John F. Kennedy Street at Eliot Street
Architectural Resources Cambridge, 1984, 1986

:: Adjacent to the Littauer Center, the second phase of construction at the Kennedy School of Government offers an engaging and amusing twist on the red brick campus traditions with a vocabulary of exaggerated gables, chimney forms, and pitched slate roofs. The designers took their cues from the animated rooflines of the nearby Harvard houses. The building defines a private grassy retreat.

41 A. Alfred Taubman Building
John F. Kennedy School of Government
off John F. Kennedy Street on Eliot Street
The Architects Collaborative, 1990

:: The Taubman Center for State and Local Government and the Joan Shorenstein Barone Center on the Press, Politics and Public Policy are located in the third phase of the Kennedy complex. The central land-scaped pedestrian spine leads to the Charles Hotel, John F. Kennedy Park, and the Charles River.

42 John F. Kennedy School of Government
79 John F. Kennedy Street
Architectural Resources Cambridge, 1978, 2003

:: The Forum in the Littauer Center of the John F. Kennedy School of Govern-ment is a daytime lounge and café that seats up to 600 for town meetings, election debates, and political panels.

43 John Fitzgerald Kennedy Park
John F. Kennedy Street at Charles River
Carol R. Johnson and Associates, Inc., 1987

:: MBTA's former Bennett Street yard was chosen as the site for the Kennedy Presidential Library in 1965. Community opposition was overwhelming, and the family chose Columbia Point instead. The park was the outcome, which may explain its failure to provide a suitable edge to the Charles greensward.

A. Alfred Taubman Building

Littauer Center Forum © Warren Patterson

Harvard Square and Brattle Street
National Historic District
Until 1638 Cambridge was called New-towne, a grid-pattern fortified settle-ment surrounded by stockades. The primary motivation for the planning of Cambridge had been defensive. The area was closely gathered south of the present Brattle Square, and Brattle Street connected it with the Watertown settlement. Wealthy British sympathiz-ers lived along Brattle Street, and thus it gained the popular name, Tory Row.

Among the half-dozen surviving pre-Revolutionary mansions are some late nineteenth-century houses and the 1890 Brattle Hall, which in 1953 be-came the famed Brattle Theater. One-third of the houses between Brattle Square and Elmwood Avenue are twen-tieth century. The section of the street immediately adjacent to the Brattle Square commercial area was part of the twenty-two-acre Thomas Brattle estate, which ran from Story Street to James Street and to the river. Houses were not built here until the early nine-teenth century, when the estate was broken up after Brattle's death.

44 William Brattle House
42 Brattle Street
ca. 1727
National Register of Historic Places

William Brattle House

:: The Brattle house begins the series of eighteenth- and nineteenth-century clapboard houses along Brattle Street. It is followed by the 1808 Hancock-Dexter-Pratt house at number 54 (the home of Longfellow's village blacksmith), the 1772 Read house, the 1827 Nichols house, and the seventeenth- and eighteenth-century Henry Vassall house at 94 Brattle.

45 "Architects' Corner"
Brattle at Story Street

44 Brattle Street
Sert, Jackson and Associates, 1970–1971

TAC Building
Walter Gropius/The Architects Collaborative, 1967, 1970

14 Story Street
Earl R. Flansburgh and Associates, 1970–1971

:: Three architects built quarters for their own offices in "Architects' Corner," at Brattle and Story Streets, in one year. They coordinated the scale, window treatment, and materials of the buildings and opened an interior pedestrian walkway through the center of the block. The quiet, tree-shaded brick alley lined with shops has been a hit from the start and inspired adjacent property owners to relate to it.

46 Design Research Building
48 Brattle Street
Benjamin Thompson and Associates, 1969

:: The home furnishings and design firm called Design Research, or DR, started a national love affair with modern-design products for the home and body. Imitators are found in every city today. Benjamin Thompson, founder of DR, imagined that Americans could be convinced to buy the best new in-

Courtyard, 44 Brattle Street Office Building © Steve Rosenthal

dustrial design from Scandinavia and Italy and showed everyone else how to do it, choosing the products himself and designing all display fixtures and fittings for the shops.

This building's in-and-out glass façade multiplies the display windows. The butt-joint glass walls are all the rage in the twenty-first century. Inside, alternating levels pull shoppers up and through merchandise areas. The concrete-slab construction uses continuous unframed glass sheets, a style that swept the country and is a feature of the 2006 Institute of Contemporary Art. With the death of DR, the building became a Crate and Barrel store.

Design Research Building

47 Longfellow Chestnut Tree Memorial
54 Brattle Street
Dimitri Gerakaris, 1989

:: A chestnut tree of forged steel by artist-blacksmith Dimitri Gerakaris commemorates that of the village blacksmith in Longfellow's poem. It also marks the fiftieth anniversary of the nearby Cambridge Center for Adult Education. The anvil and tools were made by the artist to fabricate much of this piece and were then incorporated into the sculpture.

48 Gutman Library
Brattle Street and Appian Way
Benjamin Thompson and Associates, 1972
Landscape: Carol R. Johnson and Associates, Inc.

:: To preserve the openness of Brattle and the side streets, the building mass is set back from the corners, creating small landscaped areas. It is symmetrically formed about a diagonal axis running through the corner entrance. By placing one floor below grade with depressed landscaped areas to bring in light and views, the architects reduced the building's apparent height and mass.

Longfellow Chestnut Tree Memorial
© 1989 Dimitri Gerakaris

The disciplined structure of sandblasted concrete exposes its lively interior color and activity to the street, relating to Thompson's Design Research Building across the street and to the general Brattle Street ambience. Two historic buildings, the Read house (1772) and the Nichols house (1827), were preserved by being moved from the site and are now adjacent at Farwell Place.

49 Loeb Drama Center
64 Brattle Street
Hugh Stubbins and Associates, 1959

:: The Loeb Drama Center was the first fully flexible theater in the country. It can be quickly and mechanically converted from a proscenium stage to

Elizabethan thrust or to theater-in-the-round. Sight lines and acoustics are excellent, and the ceiling grid allows great flexibility in lighting arrangements. A serpentine wall encloses the side terrace, where audiences gather during intermissions. Although the theater was built for Harvard and Radcliffe undergraduates, it later became the home of the American Repertory Theater as well.

Read and Nichols Houses

50 Stoughton House 🏛
90 Brattle Street
Henry Hobson Richardson, 1882
Renovation: Architectural Resources
Cambridge, Inc., 1990

:: Mrs. M. F. Stoughton commissioned Richardson to design her house in 1882, only a year after he started to work on Sever Hall. Described by Henry-Russell Hitchcock as "perhaps, the best suburban wooden house in America," it is a horizontal L-shaped mass. As in Sever Hall, the stairway is expressed in a towerlike projection with conical roof on the inside corner. Next to the stair is the front entrance in a recessed two-story porch. Windows are composed of many small panes with heavy muntins. Originally the roof had wood shingles and the wall shingles were smaller, but these have been replaced. Additions and interior alterations have been made to Richardson's design.

Gothic revival Burleigh House (1847), 85 Brattle Street

51 Philip Johnson Courtyard House
off Brattle Street at 9 Ash Street
Philip Johnson, 1941

:: After beginning a career in art history, Philip Johnson returned to Harvard to study architecture. For his student thesis, he built himself this house. Behind the high wall surrounding the property is a comfortable small house oriented inward to the courtyard.

Terrace, Loeb Drama Center

Stoughton House

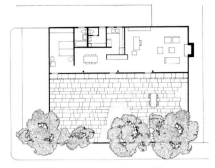

Plan, Philip Johnson Courtyard House

52 Vassall-Craigie-Longfellow House iii
105 Brattle Street
1759
National Historic Landmark

:: The most famous Brattle Street house was the residence of Henry Wadsworth Longfellow for most of his life. The poet came to the house as a boarder in 1837. His father-in-law bought it in 1843 when Longfellow married Fanny Appleton. It is sometimes attributed to Peter Harrison, the admirable architect of King's Chapel, Christ Church, and other New England landmarks. The house is an elaborate and elegant Georgian mansion with two-story pilasters and center pediment on its façade, the whole set on a terrace surrounded by a balustrade.

Toward the Charles River end of Longfellow Park is Daniel Chester French's bust of Longfellow.

53 Hooper-Lee-Nichols House
159 Brattle Street

:: Part of this architectural palimpsest, home of the Cambridge Historical Society, dates from the late seventeenth century.

54 Longy School of Music Concert Hall
1 Follen Street
Huygens and Tappé, 1973

:: The Longy School of Music is located in the Edwin H. Abbot house, an 1889 Richardsonian Romanesque structure of brownstone and brick. The concert-hall addition very successfully combines library and concert functions in one space. Several details of the old house are repeated in the concert hall. The fine acoustics of the intimate hall have made it popular with Boston musicians.

Vassall-Craigie-Longfellow House

55 Christ Church

Zero Garden Street
Peter Harrison, 1760
Altered: 1790 and 1825–1826
National Historical Landmark

:: The oldest church building in Cambridge, Christ Church was designed by the Newport architect Peter Harrison. It is similar to Harrison's King's Chapel with its square tower, but it has no gallery and is constructed of wood. Since it was a Tory church, it suffered bad treatment during the Revolution, and not until the nineteenth century was well under way did it have a rector again.

56 Farwell-Read Block

Harvard Square
1780 to 1820
Renovation: Symmes Maini & McKee Associates, 1999

:: The 1896 façade unites remains of the eighteenth-century Read house and three early nineteenth-century buildings. After a bruising five-year battle, the developer was convinced not to level the site. Instead, the façade and the historic structures up to a depth of 18 feet were restored with a contemporary 40,000-square-foot building behind.

57 Harvard Square Station

Skidmore, Owings & Merrill, 1981–1985

:: Harvard Station was rebuilt as part of the subway extension. Most notable is the stained-glass mural by artist Gyorgy Kepes. On the crowded street level, roads and plazas were redesigned with an emphasis on pedestrian needs. Excavations for the new line kept Harvard archeologists busy retrieving and classifying 150,000 fascinating artifacts, including stone tools from a prehistoric hunting camp dating from 1500 B.C.

Above the station the 1927 Out of Town News kiosk is on the site of the seventeenth-century house occupied by poet Anne Bradstreet in 1631.

Christ Church

Cambridge milestone

Holyoke Center © William Tobey

58 Holyoke Center

1350 Massachusetts Avenue
Sert, Jackson and Gourley, 1961, 1965
Landscape: Sasaki, Dawson, DeMay

:: Harvard demolished a block of buildings—including Holyoke House, Little Hall, Union Railroad Stables, and Dunster Court—to create the site for their first high-rise complex of shops, offices, health center, and parking. While the older buildings had hugged the sidewalk, the H-shaped structure is set back from Mount Auburn Street and Massachusetts Avenue to form small plazas. A two-story pedestrian way through the building provides a mid-block link between the two streets. The façades are organized around a human-scaled module of clear and translucent panels placed according to the needs of individual office occupants. Sunscreens, fins, and varied finishes enrich the concrete form in the manner of Le Corbusier. The interiors and furnishings, also by the architects, are in harmony with the architecture.

Massachusetts Institute of Technology

Founded in 1861 by William Barton Rogers, MIT was first located in the Mercantile Building in downtown Boston. In 1863 it moved to the Back Bay, next door to its near twin, the Museum of Natural History. By 1902 the school had outgrown this building with no possibility of expanding in the built-up Copley Square district. An extensive search was conducted, and the present site on marshlands that had been filled for real estate development in the 1880s was chosen in 1909.

The traditional quadrangle organization of Harvard is nowhere echoed at MIT, whose several formal courts are dramatically highlighted by powerful

Massachusetts Institute of Technology

sculptures. By the turn of the millennium, the 1960s Art on Campus project had grown into the preeminent university collection of twentieth-century artists, among them Bertoia, Burton, Calder, Graham, Lipschitz, Moore, Nevelson, Noland, Pardo, Ritchie, Picasso, Stella, and Witkin.

59 Maclaurin and Rogers Buildings ⅲ

77 Massachusetts Avenue
William Welles Bosworth, 1913–1916
Killian Court addition: Bosworth and
Harry J. Carlson, 1937

:: MIT selected William Welles Bosworth as architect, after having considered Désiré Despradelle, a French-born member of the architecture faculty, and Cass Gilbert, MIT graduate (1879) and designer of the University of Minnesota campus. Besides being an MIT graduate (1889), Bosworth had worked for H. H. Richardson and Frederick Law Olmsted and had studied at the École des Beaux-Arts in Paris. In contrast to Harvard's individual brick buildings set in open green space, Bosworth's design is conceived as a single neoclassic limestone building that reaches out to define space in the manner of Versailles. Bosworth's expertise in French style was later reaffirmed by his work in the 1920s as director of the reconstruction of Versailles, Fontainebleau, and Rheims Cathedral.

Two Pantheon-inspired domes identify the foci of the grand composition. The largest dome on the axis of the Great Court (now Killian Court) rises behind the imposing Ionic portico, while the other dome defines the main entrance portico and four-story hall on Massachusetts Avenue. Ironically, the big coffered dome with oculus can only be experienced from the upper level of Baker Engineering Library. Another mismatch between form and function is found in the Great Court, which wants to be the major entrance and activity space but, in fact, is largely symbolic and little used. The real hub of activity is the Massachusetts Avenue entrance and the spine that links the campus from east to west.

Except for the Pantheon entrance hall on Massachusetts Avenue, the several miles of monotonous interior corridors have no classical pretensions. They are more like a factory and, in fact, are built for industrial live loads. Despite the building's lack of interior charm, it has proved to be remarkably rugged and adaptable to changing needs. Through its interconnected corridors the life of the institute moves at a brisk pace, but it is not picturesque, quiet, or sentimental. Thus MIT achieved for itself a fitting contrast to Harvard, representative of the differences in the education offered.

60 Chapel ▥

Building W 15, west of Massachusetts Avenue
Eero Saarinen, 1955

:: MIT's Chapel is as exquisite and understated as it is small. The brick cylinder with small moat is handsomely paired with Kresge Auditorium and relates to the domes of the main MIT buildings and to the brick curves of Baker House. Low arches at the bottom

Henry Moore's *Three-Piece Reclining Figure, Draped* (1976) in Killian Court

Interior, MIT Chapel © The MIT Museum

allow the light reflected from the water to cast fascinating shifting patterns on the undulating interior brick shell. A luminous Bertoia altarpiece screen shimmers with light from the skylight above.

61 Kresge Auditorium ▥

Building W 16, west of Massachusetts Avenue
Eero Saarinen, 1954–1955

:: Saarinen quite properly argued against the river site that had been chosen for Kresge Auditorium. Fortunately, he was successful in convincing MIT that his building would be much more effective as a focus on the main axis of the campus. Saarinen prepared the site plan as well as the architectural designs for the auditorium and chapel. While Harvard seems almost the unwilling possessor of a Le Corbusier building, MIT proudly displays these two Saarinen gems. Kresge auditorium is an elegant shallow dome, recalling the domes of the MIT main buildings, balanced on three corners with glass-walled public gathering spaces around the periphery. The wood-paneled hall is arguably the finest twentieth-century auditorium space in the Boston region in terms of design.

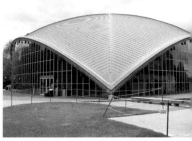

Kresge Auditorium

62 Julius Adams Stratton Building, Student Center

Building W 20, west of Massachusetts Avenue
Eduardo Catalano, 1964
Renovation: Bruner/Cott & Associates, Inc., 1988

:: The bold horizontal form of the Student Center exhibits the structural possibilities of reinforced concrete. The building steps to the side of the main MIT axis, allowing the Pantheon dome entrance of the Rogers Building across Massachusetts Avenue to command the space.

63 Albert and Barrie Zesiger Sports and Fitness Center

Building W 35, west of Massachusetts Avenue
Kevin Roche and John Dinkeloo & Associates, 2003

:: Several levels of exercise rooms overlook the Olympic-scale swimming pool. The mural by Matthew Ritchie is appropriately titled *Games of Chance and Skill.*

64 Athletics Center

Building W 34, near Kresge Auditorium
Davis and Brody, 1980

:: The Athletics Center is on the main east–west axis of the campus amid the other athletic buildings. Earlier facilities

Baker House © The MIT Museum

are primarily the work of Anderson, Beckwith, and Haible and include Briggs Field House (1939), Rockwell Cage (1948), and the Dupont Athletic Center (1959). Seen from the playing fields, the zigzag stairs relate to Alvar Aalto's Baker House to the south.

65 Baker House ▥

Building W 7, Memorial Drive
Alvar Aalto with Perry, Shaw and Hepburn, 1947–1949

:: Baker House reflects the scale, formalism, and linear orientation to the river established in the Maclaurin and Rogers buildings. Inside, it entirely lacks the flexibility of the early buildings and is instead a fascinating arrangement of rooms, which maximizes river views. Where the main MIT buildings turn square corners, Baker House undulates along the riverbank. From the entrance pavilion there is a view through the building to the playing fields beyond. In contrast to the river façade, the rear side has a strong angular expression of the staircases. The building is best viewed from an angle while walking along the sidewalk so the rippling façade can be enjoyed. Baker House appears to be squeezed between its neighbors, too big for its site, much like Le Corbusier's Carpenter Center. All the furniture is by Aalto. His furniture has since become known and coveted in the United States.

West Campus Houses © Steve Rosenthal

66 West Campus Houses
Building W 70, adjacent to 500 Memorial Drive
Sert, Jackson and Associates, 1975

:: This dormitory is organized into six linked but separate houses, each with a river view. The stepped roofs of the south-facing houses form roof decks. The same architects are responsible for the adjacent dormitory, 500 Memorial Drive (1980–1982).

67 Tang Hall
Building W 84, far west end near Audrey Street
Hugh Stubbins and Associates, 1972

:: High-rise development on the MIT campus has been carefully controlled to protect the scale and dominance of the original horizontal buildings. The chamfered-corner layout of Tang Hall provides eight corner living rooms on each floor. Each apartment has a view of the Charles River. Precast 59-foot façade components are structural and consist of a spandrel and two columns. The designers significantly reduced building costs by combining structure and cladding.

68 Simmons Hall ☰
229 Vassar Street
Stephen Holl with Perry Dean Rogers Partners, 2005

:: Unlike Gehry, Catalano, Correa, Aalto, Saarinen, and Pei, whose impor-

Simmons Hall

tant buildings are gathered on the MIT campus, Holl's work does not have an identifiable "look" or palette of materials. While Ronchamp was the reference for earlier buildings, it is Le Corbusier's skyscraper for Algiers, with its ice-cube-tray squares and large multistory cutouts, that appears to be the inspiration this time.

Simmons Hall's three ten-story towers sheathed in sanded aluminum are joined by bridges, leaving giant cutouts. The resulting form negates the tower structures, taking on a horizontal massing. Rigidly repeated 2-by-2-foot perforations suggest early computer punch cards. The effect at night is dramatic, with all the little windows alight. Even in daylight, free of normal clues of scale, it becomes pure sculpture. Viewed at an oblique angle, color within the cutouts represents structural loads: red is high, yellow is medium, and blue is low.

In contrast to the rectilinear grid skin, lounge spaces are organic—suggesting intestines, womb, or other organs—with a sky aperture but no windows. The nine small deep-set windows in dorm rooms seem cagelike because they segment the view.

69 The Warehouse Graduate Residence
224 Albany Street
Renovation: The S/L/A/M Collaborative, 2001

:: Exposed brick, timbers, glass block, and not one atrium, but several, in a former warehouse add up to a popular graduate student housing facility for MIT.

The Warehouse Graduate Residence
© Woodruff/Brown Photography

University Park

The former industrial and warehouse zone of Cambridge between the Boston and Maine Railroad, the Charles River, and Massachusetts Avenue became a prime opportunity for housing conversions when Kennedy Biscuit Company (the Fig Newton bakery), Necco, and other companies left. One section adjacent to MIT's west campus, University Park, was purchased by MIT. It offered long-term leases for development of office and laboratory buildings as well as new and renovated rental apartment buildings. The symbolic heart of the residential units is Halvorson Design Partnership's passive green University Park Common. A huge spool from the Simplex Wire & Cable Company serves as a sculptural artifact of the industrial past.

University Park Commons and Loft 23

70 Library of Art, Architecture, and Planning
Building 7 A, off Massachusetts Avenue
Addition: Schwartz & Silver, 1990

:: Elegantly and precisely slipped into a non-site above a truck turnaround on the cramped back side of 77 Massachusetts Avenue is a six-story library stack. This crisp design creates form with an assurance rarely seen since the demise of modernism. The steel-framed, clear

Cambridgeport history sculpture, University Park Commons

anodized aluminum–clad 30-by-100-foot sliver nestles against the retained exterior of the original building, grazing rather than joining it. The books are protected from ultraviolet radiation by heat mirror glass, a glass and plastic sandwich developed at MIT in the 1970s. The best view is inconveniently from the truck loading zone.

71 Dreyfus Building
Building 18, next to Green Building
I. M. Pei and Partners, 1967–1970
Landscape: Sasaki, Dawson, DeMay

:: The design of the Dreyfus Building incorporates existing pathways by cantilevering the end of the structure on two diagonal columns. The window grid is formed of diagonal columns and spandrels, which frame deeply recessed windows. An elegant three-level bridge of glass and concrete connects the building with Anderson, Beckwith, and Haible's precisely detailed Dorrance and Whitaker Buildings (1952, 1963).

72 Green Building, Center for Earth Sciences
Building 54, east of main building
I. M. Pei and Partners, 1962–1964
Landscape: Sasaki, Dawson, DeMay

:: I. M. Pei, who helped prepare the master plan for this section of the campus, also designed three buildings in the quadrant. The most prominent of these is the Green Building, a highly sculptural tower of twenty-one stories that dominates views of MIT from Boston. It is interesting how frequently Pei has chosen to introduce vertical elements into essentially horizontal contexts, for example his Christian Science tower and the Harbor Towers.

In the case of MIT, he felt the tower would provide a vertical focus and would help organize the disparate surroundings. Constructed of cast-in-place sandblasted architectural concrete, its color is similar to that of the lime-

Library of Art, Architecture, and Planning
© The MIT Department of Facilities

Alexander Calder's *The Big Sail* **and Dreyfus Building**

stone of its neighbors. The load-bearing exterior walls allow column-free 48-by-93-feet floors. Alexander Calder's monumental black steel sculpture, *The Big Sail* (1965), is effectively sited in front of the building at the entrance to the courtyard from Memorial Drive.

73 Landau Chemical Engineering Building
Building 66, Ames Street
I. M. Pei and Partners, 1973–1976

:: With the Landau Building, Pei completed his group of related spaces and buildings for MIT. The thirty-degree angle of Main Street to Memorial Drive is reflected in the form, with its chisel-pointed end that threatens to slice Ames Street. The two-story portico frames views of the Stata Center. Louise Nevelson's dramatic black steel sculpture, *Transparent Horizon* (1975), stands outside the building between Bosworth's East Campus Alumni Houses (1924).

Vassar Street

This unpretentious industrial back street experienced a face-lift at the turn of the millennium as high-profile archi-tecture replaced humble laboratory sheds and the power plant went high style. Laurie Olin's design widened sidewalks with diverse paving materials separating pedestrians from a German-style bike lane. Embedded solar-powered pedestrian alert lights at driveway conflict points, planters, and new street lighting added to the cleaner look.

Landau Chemical Engineering Building

74 Ray and Maria Stata Center for Computer, Information and Intelligence Sciences ⅲ
32 Vassar Street
Gehry Partners LLP with Cannon Design, 2004
Landscape: Olin Partnership, 2004

∷ A splashy megabuilding replaced temporary World War II laboratories demolished in 1999. Building 20 was famously the site of Noam Chomsky's linguistics theory revolution and many scientific discoveries, including radar, atomic clocks, and underwater cameras. The sloppy, freewheeling spaces imposed no restraints on researchers inclined to poke holes through walls or remove windows.

Such casual adaptations are un-thinkable in the status symbol that re-placed it, though the architecture tries hard not to be serious despite its enor-mous price tag. Windows appear not to fit—projecting out or angling awk-wardly in—articulating the mundane to

Louise Nevelson's *Transparent Horizon* (1975)

Vassar Street

give it significance. Three acres of jum-bled, folded, falling planes of stainless steel, multicolor enamel, titanium, and brick form the chaotic façade of two eight-story U-shaped towers.

Stata grey water garden and Compton Laboratory (Skidmore, Owings & Merrill, 1957)

Ray and Maria Stata Center

Behind the showy skin it is not all sheetrock, plywood, and concrete floors. There are tricks here, too. Walls are canted or appear to dangle in midair. Some deviant elements are so convincing that they induce vertigo in students. Excessive transparency provoked goldfish syndrome in researchers engaged in demanding scientific work at the bottom of chimney-shaped laboratories with unknown observers peering down four or five stories above them. Despite these complaints, the Stata Center has created excitement among undergraduates. MIT's detailed architectural program, which stressed accidental cross-pollination and spontaneous collaboration between different disciplines, was realized in the winding internal "student street" with its gigantic blackboards, study nooks, and open seminar areas.

75 Brain and Cognitive Sciences Complex
43 Vassar Street
Charles Correa with Goody, Clancy & Associates, 2005

:: The sober yet graceful architecture of this enormous complex is a reaction to its hyperactive neighbor across the street. At the dedication Charles Correa explained, "We tried a great number of alternate variations, and found it best to run the racetrack parallel to Vassar, so that we could face our rather exuberant neighbor across the road full frontal and thus endeavor to bring back some of the calm, the confidence, the disciplined logic, of Science."

Uniting the McGovern Institute for Brain Research, the Picower Center for Learning and Memory, and the Department of Brain and Cognitive Sciences under one roof was a challenging and complex task. Built over railroad tracks, the 376,000 square feet of labs and offices for teams of neuroscience, biology, cognition, and computer scientists had to be completely isolated from the vibrations. Elaborate calculations were made of the movement in order to stabilize the building. Faculty critiqued the engineers' initial presentation, pointing out significant errors and correcting the

Brain and Cognitive Sciences Complex

of gloomy basements, the usual location for such facilities. Huge vent stacks on the roof provide air circulation for animal subjects. None are primates.

Except for the large cutouts on the Main Street façade and the shock of seeing a freight train burst out of one of the elegantly detailed openings, most of the drama is inside. The large atrium isn't just for drama, though, serving as it does multiple practical purposes, including lightening the load spanning the rail corridor beneath it. The atrium also contributes to the building's energy efficiency, along with its heat recovery systems, gray water recycling, and high-performance walls.

76 Chilled Water Plant Expansion
59 Vassar Street
Ellenzweig Associates, 2001

:: Acoustical glass showcases the pipes and machines as industrial sculpture. The metal end wall is iconic in its bright red.

77 Wiesner Building
20 Ames Street
I. M. Pei & Partners, 1985

:: While I. M. Pei did not regard the Wiesner Building as a major architectural statement, it is an example of collaboration between an architect and three artists, reflecting the purpose of the building. The artists took responsibility for aspects that would normally be in the domain of the architect alone. The Wiesner Building houses the Arts and Media Center, including three art galleries, workshops and laboratories, auditorium, and the Experimental Media Theater, a four-story windowless cube for exploring nontraditional performance media.

University Chilled Water Plant expansion
© Steve Rosenthal

structure before final plans were drawn.

Sensitive experiments conducted here included analyzing hummingbird brain functions. Uncharacteristically, the animal laboratories are located in sunny glass-walled upper floors instead

The building is intentionally unrelated to its context. The white aluminum—sheathed box is rather antiseptic both outside and inside. The shiny panels suggest a laboratory, an

Wiesner Building

impression that is reinforced by the clinical detailing. The multistory atrium space is dominated by Kenneth Noland's relief mural. Scott Burton, a sculptor who specializes in seating, designed the stairwell and balustrades and related seating in the atrium. Richard Fleischner, an environmental artist, designed the plantings and geometrically paved courtyards surrounding the building, as well as the lattice benches in a Wiener Werkstätte or MacIntosh revival style. A sculptural arch of concrete forms a gateway to the east campus.

78 Whitaker College of Health Sciences, Technology, and Management and Health Services
Buildings E 23 and E 25, 25 Carleton Street
Gruzen Partners and Mitchell, Giurgola, 1979–1981

:: The form of this building clearly notes its two components in the two legs of the L, which are joined by a luminous atrium. The geometry of this space is governed both by the skewed grid of the east-campus streets and by the main MIT axis, which penetrates

the atrium at an odd angle. The architects prepared the master plan for this sector with the aim of integrating the Sloan School with the main campus.

79 Tang Center for Management Education
Sloan School of Management
70 Memorial Drive
Ellenzweig Associates, 1995

:: The glass-walled east façade reveals the auditorium and student lounges. Jackie Ferrara's slate floor puts the art underfoot.

80 Eastgate Married Student Housing
Building E 55, Kendall Square at Wadsworth Street
Eduardo Catalano, 1967

:: The thirty-story Eastgate tower marks the east end of the MIT campus and balances the Tang tower on the west end. Adjacent is another Catalano design, the Hermann Building (1965). Picasso's concrete sculpture *Figure*

Bench by Scott Burton

Model of Media Arts and Sciences Building by Maki and Associates intended for advanced laboratories adjacent to the Weisner Building © Kitajima Toshiharu

Tang Center for Management Education

Picasso's *Figure découpée* (1958, 1963)

découpée (*Cut-Out Figure*, 1963) was originally done in oil paint on wood. It was enlarged and cast by Carl Nesjar, a Norwegian artist who developed the technique called *betongravure* used in this work.

81 Kendall Square MBTA Station
Renovation: Ellenzweig Associates, Inc., 1987
Sculpture: Paul Matisse, 1987, 1988

:: Not found in any other city are *Pythagorus* and *Kepler,* two delightful interactive sound sculptures suspended between the tracks. Levers on both platforms allow curious subway users to set them in motion. Graphic panels along the platforms depict the history of Cambridge on one side and a time line of major technological achievements at MIT on the other side.

82 Genzyme Center 𝗂𝗂𝗂
500 Kendall Street
Behnisch Architects, 2003

:: Genzyme set a national standard for green office buildings in its twelve-story headquarters. Solar conservation went beyond operable windows, shading devices, solar panels, and double-skinned façades. Heliostatic harvesting

Sonic sculpture in Kendall Square MBTA Station © Steve Rosenthal

Kendall Boiler and Tank Company,
Binney Street

of daylight provides most of the task
lighting. Water conservation includes
efficient fixtures, waterless urinals, and
a green roof using captured rainwater.
By-product steam and an efficiently
shaped envelope contribute to its platinum green certification. In addition to
the use of recycled and locally sourced
construction materials and components,
construction waste was recycled and
sustainable furnishings were selected.

Genzyme Center

83 675 West Kendall Street

Steven Ehrlich Architects with Symmes
Maini & McKee Associates, 2003
Landscape: Michael Van Valkenburgh
Associates

:: As one site of Cambridge's burgeon-
ing biotech industry, the disengaged
end wall's varying terra-cotta panels
represent the gels of DNA molecules:
adenine, thymine, guanine, and cyto-
sine. The bulk of the building is broken
down into contrasting forms articulated
through different materials, creating a
complex group rather than a big box.
Balconies and terraces appear ran-
domly scattered. A projecting canopy
shades the roof garden facing Boston.
On the ground plane are pedestrian
walkways, an outdoor skating area,
a piazza, and a small boat facility on
the Broad Canal that flows to the
Charles River.

Heliostatic daylight harvesting, Genzyme
Center © Roland Halbe

Like its neighbor at number 500,
675 was built on a former brownfield.
The process of toxic remediation required deep excavation, which resulted
in sites pre-dug for underground parking.

675 West Kendall Street © Peter Vanderwarker

American Academy of Arts and Sciences © Steve Rosenthal

Other Cambridge Sites

84 American Academy of Arts and Sciences 🏛
136 Irving Street
Kallmann, McKinnell, and Wood,
1979–1981
Landscape: Carol R. Johnson and
Associates
Program: Lawrence B. Anderson

:: The highly specific program called
for intimate, comfortable spaces suited
to conversation and reflection. Concrete, the architect's usual material,
was specifically prohibited. Edwin
Land, one of the academy's influential
members, insisted that emphasis
should be on the individual rather than
on groups.

The deep-eaved hip roofs, set on
substantial brick piers, are unintimidat-
ing in the five-and-a-half-acre wooded
setting. The entrance focuses on a
skylit staircase and hearth area and
leads through tall Honduras mahogany
doors into a labyrinth of rooms of varied
sizes, some with provocative mantels
and others with bookcases, seating
nooks, or French doors opening onto

the garden. Materials and detailing are
impeccable, and the furnishings of varied styles and eras are unremarkable
but comfortable in their settings. It is a
building that does not shriek but speaks
with quiet authority.

85 Cambridgeside Galleria
160 Cambridgeside Place
Arrowstreet, Inc., 1990

86 Thomas Graves Landing
Edwin H. Land Boulevard at Monsignor
O'Brien Highway
Unihab, 1989

87 Lechmere Canal Park
Carol R. Johnson and Associates, Inc.,
1988

:: The Cambridgeside Galleria urban
mall rejected several mall myths to cre-

Cambridgeside Galleria

ate 1,000,000 square feet of new retail space in a lively and intimate style near the old discount shopping area of Lechmere. It avoids the vast mall wastelands that have plagued the country since Victor Gruen's 1950s model shopping centers. The animated façade curves around a lagoon with cafés and paddleboat rentals. No fence or wall is needed to keep people out of the lagoon, despite its continuous pedestrian edge; a minimal 6-inch granite curb and nautical bollards are sufficient definition. Inside, the Tinker Toy brutalism is warmed with hanging plants under skylights bringing natural light into the narrow linear space. Despite the hotel-style glass elevators, the nineteenth-century European arcade reference predominates.

Across the lagoon of Old Lechmere Canal is Thomas Graves Landing, named for Cambridge's first settler. For several centuries before the Charles River was dammed, a popular oystering spot was off the landing. The canal inspired a nautical theme of pipe balconies on the eight-story condominium building. Its roofline alternates sheet metal mansards with pronounced red brick gables.

88 Albert House
136 Fifth Street
Albert, Righter & Tittman Architects, 1993

∷ With full-blown swags, fluted square columns, and checker work, this 1,200-square-foot house has tongue-in-cheek pretensions belied by its tacky materials. The deft use of vinyl siding and asphalt shingles charms even as it acts the jester to architectural icons. Not incidentally, it relates well to its neighborhood.

89 Tittman House
29 R C Kelley Street
Albert, Righter & Tittman Architects, 1998

Albert House © Jacob Albert; Albert, Righter, Tittmann Architects

∷ Pulling back the entrance to the middle side of the house in the manner but not the style of side-entry colonial houses allowed a plan of symmetrical major rooms off a central hall. The restrained Greek revival street façade with pilasters and pediment is contradicted by the windows biting into the frieze. The set-back entrance porch is under a domed projection that combines with the front façade and chimney to suggest a church baptistery and campanile composition. The work of this firm is rife with historical architectural quotations.

90 Bulfinch Square
47 Thorndike Street between Second and Third Streets

91 Middlesex County Courthouse
Attributed to Charles Bulfinch, 1814
Additions: Ammi Young, 1848
Renovation: Graham Gund Architects, 1984
National Register of Historic Places

∷ A group of six Middlesex County buildings once threatened with demolition was restored and renovated for

Bulfinch Square © Steve Rosenthal

public and private offices. Beside the 1814 Middlesex County Courthouse, the Old Superior Courthouse (now Clerk of Courts Building), and the Registry of Deeds, there are merchants' brick row houses from the 1830s. One courtroom was restored for use as a theater, and a former parking lot was transformed into a landscaped courtyard and park.

SPECIAL INTEREST TOURS

Six tours have been designed according to particular themes rather than by the topographic system used elsewhere in this guide.

Tour A: Charles Bulfinch

The first special interest tour is for enthusiasts of Charles Bulfinch and includes all of his Boston and Cambridge buildings. Most of these will be found on Beacon Hill and are treated in detail elsewhere in the guide.

Beacon Hill

- Third Harrison Gray Otis house, 45 Beacon Street
- John Phillips house, 1 Walnut Street at Beacon Street (altered)
- Amory-Ticknor house, 9 Park Street at Beacon Street (altered)
- State House, Beacon Street
- Beacon Hill Memorial Column, behind State House
- 49–57 Mount Vernon Street

- Second Harrison Gray Otis house, 85 Mount Vernon Street
- 87 Mount Vernon Street
- 29A Chestnut Street
- Swan houses, 13, 15, and 17 Chestnut Street, and stables at 50–60 Mount Vernon Street
- Charles Paine houses, 6–8 Chestnut Street
- First Harrison Gray Otis house, 141 Cambridge Street
- Massachusetts General Hospital (Bulfinch Pavilion and Ether Dome), off Cambridge Street

Faneuil Hall and North End

- Faneuil Hall (enlargement by Bulfinch)
- St. Stephen's Church, Hanover Street

Wharves and Seaport/Custom House District

- Central Wharf, 146–176 Milk Street, and several buildings on Broad Street (5, 7–9, 63–65, 64–66, 67–73, 68–70, 72, and 102)

Harvard University

- Stoughton Hall, Harvard Yard
- University Hall, Harvard Yard

Tour B: Henry Hobson Richardson

The complete existing work in central Boston and Cambridge of another significant Boston architect, Henry Hobson Richardson, is covered in Tour B.

Back Bay

- Trinity Church, Copley Square
- Trinity Rectory, Clarendon Street at Newbury Street
- First Baptist Church, Clarendon Street at Commonwealth Avenue
- Crowninshield house, 164 Marlborough Street

The Royal Mile/Theater District

- Hayden Building, 681 Washington Street

Fenway

- Stone bridge, Boylston Street, Back Bay Fens

Harvard University

- Sever Hall, Harvard Yard
- Austin Hall, north of Harvard Yard
- Stoughton house, 90 Brattle Street

Tour C: Ralph Adams Cram

Tour C treats the work of Ralph Adams Cram, a less well known but very influential Boston architect, writer, and teacher whose work is found throughout the country. Cram was a leader in the Gothic revival movement and is best known for his religious buildings. Although he was the son of a Unitarian minister, Cram converted to the Anglican church under the influence of the Oxford Movement. He never attended college but apprenticed in architecture in the office of Rotch and Tilden, wrote two dozen books and many articles, and was head of the MIT School of Architecture for several years. Examples of his work can be found in Boston and several surrounding communities.

Central Boston

- Church of the Advent, Lady Chapel interior, Mount Vernon Street at Brimmer Street, Beacon Hill
- Post Office, Post Office Square, financial district
- Telephone Building, 185 Franklin Street, financial district
- John Hancock Tower, 180 Berkeley Street, Back Bay
- The New England (originally New England Mutual Life Insurance Company), 501 Boylston Street, Back Bay
- Ruggles Street Church, Audubon Circle, Beacon Street at Park Drive
- Boston University Chapel, 735 Commonwealth Avenue

Dorchester

- All Saints' Church, 209 Ashmont Street

Hyde Park

- Christ Church, 1220 River Street

Brookline

- All Saints' Church, 1773 Beacon Street
- Richmond Court Apartments, 1213 Beacon Street

Cambridge

- Conventual Church of Saints Mary and John and Monastery of the Order of St. John the Evangelist, 980 Memorial Drive

Arlington

- St. Anne's Convent Chapel, 14 Claremont Avenue

Somerville

- First Unitarian Church, 125 Highland Avenue

West Newton

- First Unitarian Church, 1326 Washington Street

Milton

- St. Michael's Church, 112 Randolph Avenue

Sudbury

- St. Elizabeth's Church, Concord Road

Tour D: Contemporary Landmarks

Outstanding works of contemporary architecture, beginning with examples of modernism in central Boston and Cambridge, are offered in Tour D. While the "landmark" status of some of these might be debated, many of the sites are now classics of modern architecture. The Walter Gropius residence in Lincoln, built in 1937 and co-designed with Marcel Breuer, was the first "modern" house within 100 miles. Its boxy shape, vertical siding, flat roof, and large windows were a curiosity and attracted throngs of sightseers. Gropius built the house in the first year after he came to America, and with it proclaimed many of the Bauhaus design principles.

Central Boston

- New England Holocaust Memorial, Congress Street; Stanley Saitowitz
- Nashua Street Park, Nashua Street at Charles River; Halvorson Design Partnership
- Charles F. Hurley Building, Cambridge Street; Paul Rudolph et al.
- City Hall, City Hall Plaza; Kallmann, McKinnell, and Knowles, et al.
- Post Office Square Park, Congress Street; The Halvorson Company
- John Hancock Tower, 200 Clarendon Street; I. M. Pei and Partners
- Boston University Buildings, off Commonwealth Avenue; Sert, Jackson and Gourley et al.

Charlestown

- Leonard P. Zakim Bunker Hill Bridge; Christian Menn
- City Square; Halvorson Design Partnership
- Charlestown Navy Yard Row Houses, First Avenue at Thirteenth Street; William Rawn Associates

Walter Gropius House © Robert Damora

Seaport District

- Artists for Humanity EpiCenter, 100 West Second Street; Arrowstreet
- Institute of Contemporary Art, 100 Northern Avenue; Diller Scofidio + Renfro
- Boston Convention and Exhibition Center, 415 Summer Street; Rafael Vinoly et al.
- Kennedy Library, Columbia Point; I. M. Pei and Partners

Harvard University

- Carpenter Center for the Visual Arts, Quincy Street; Le Corbusier
- Fogg Museum Addition, Quincy Street; James Stirling, Michael Wilford, and Associates
- Gund Hall, Quincy Street; John Andrews, Anderson and Baldwin
- Tanner Fountain, in front of Science Center, Harvard University; Joan Brigham, Peter Walker, and the SWA Group
- Harkness Commons and Graduate Center, north of Harvard Yard; Walter Gropius and The Architects Collaborative
- Design Research Building (now Crate and Barrel), 48 Brattle Street; Benjamin Thompson and Associates
- Peabody Terrace, 900 Memorial Drive; Sert, Jackson and Gourley

Massachusetts Institute of Technology

- Simmons Hall, 229 Vassar Street; Stephen Holl
- Ray and Maria Stata Center, 32 Vassar Street; Frank Gehry
- Brain and Cognitive Sciences Complex, Vassar and Main Streets; Charles Correa et al.
- Genzyme Center, 500 Kendall Street; Behnisch Architects
- Baker House, Memorial Drive, West Campus; Alvar Aalto
- Chapel and Kresge Auditorium, West Campus; Eero Saarinen
- Library of Art, Architecture, and Planning addition; Schwartz & Silver
- Green, Dreyfus, Landau, and Wiesner Buildings, East Campus; I. M. Pei and Partners
- Academy of Arts and Sciences, 136 Irving Street; Kallmann, McKinnell, and Wood

Lincoln

- Walter Gropius residence, Bridge Road; Walter Gropius and Marcel Breuer

Tour E: Boston Urban Design

Tour E deals with design at the large scale—urban and landscape design. Areas of both historic and contemporary development where outstanding quality has been achieved are included. These are excellent study areas for learning about urban design and planning. Each of these districts has a special character and form uniquely expressive of Boston. Although many of the areas have historic roots, through thoughtful and creative urban design they have been adapted to meet the needs of contemporary users without losing important connections with the past. Some areas, however, have been stressed to their limits by development pressures, especially the Financial District and Broad Street.

- Wharves and Seaport, HarborWalk
- Rose Kennedy Greenway
- Fort Point Channel District
- Financial District, focusing on Post Office Square, Liberty Square, Winthrop Square, and Church Green
- Faneuil Hall District
- Blackstone Block and Government Center
- Bay Village
- Beacon Hill
- South End, garden squares and Washington Street restoration
- Back Bay, especially Commonwealth Avenue

- Charlestown Navy Yard
- Emerald Necklace, from the Boston Common to Franklin Park
- New and renovated MBTA stations, especially on the Orange and Red Lines

Tour F: Lowell Urban National Cultural Park

Lowell, Massachusetts, 25 miles north of Boston on the Merrimack River, is a city rich in history and ethnic culture. Founded by Francis Cabot Lowell in 1823, it was the first planned industrial city in America.

Although Lowell began as an experimental mill city and flourished for a period as a model industrial community, the flight of the textile industry to the South after the Civil War left it in a depressed state. The authors' 1970 plan for the Lowell Discovery Network incorporated more than one hundred scattered but significant sites of the early Industrial Revolution in America into a linear educational/recreational park along the banks of Lowell's canal system. Through the network the entire community became an educational and recreational focus for development.

Based upon the plan, in 1974 Lowell became the first Urban National Park in the country outside of Washington, D.C., and has been the model for many later state and federal urban heritage parks. Many sites have been restored, including the historic mills, gates, locks, and more than 5 miles of man-made canals that were built to power the mills.

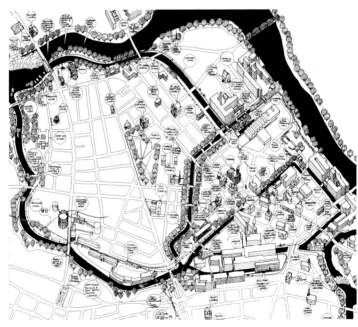

Lowell Urban National Cultural Park conceptual plan © Michael & Susan Southworth

GLOSSARY

acanthus. An ornamental form derived from the broad, curling leaf of the acanthus plant. It is always found on Corinthian and composite column capitals.

acroterion. A small pedestal, often of stone, located at the three corners of a pediment to support a figure or ornament.

anthemion. A classical decorative pattern based on alternating lotus and palmette with scrolls, creating a continuous design. It is a favorite decorative device in Greek revival architecture.

apse. The semicircular or multifaceted conclusion of the chancel (the altar area) in a church.

arcade. A row of arches supported by posts and columns.

arch. A curved opening created by wedge-shaped blocks of brick or stone. The curve may assume a variety of shapes, from nearly flat to pointed lancet arches, multicurved trefoil arches, or ogee arches (pointed arches with reverse curves near their apexes).

architrave. The lower or supporting section of an entablature. Above it are the frieze and then the cornice. Architraves are sometimes found above doorways.

art deco. A style of the early twentieth century characterized by bold geometric and stylized figural and floral forms applied as surface decoration. Typical motifs include chevrons, spraying fountains, deer, sunbursts, and bows and arrows. Its name was abbreviated long after the 1925 Paris *Exposition Internationale des Arts Décoratifs et Industriels Modernes* popularized it. Hollywood movies and U.S. department stores soon took up the style.

ashlar. Squared stones laid in regular courses with narrow joints to produce a smooth wall.

balusters. The regularly spaced vertical elements of a fence or stair rail. Small columns are often used to support the railing.

balustrade. A series of balusters supporting a railing.

banded column. A column where horizontal bands of rustication alternate with smooth or fluted bands.

baroque. Usually refers to the style derived from seventeenth-century architecture, painting, and sculpture associated with Rome and to some extent other cities in Italy. The style is characterized by extravagant ornamentation and dramatic spatial effects.

barrel vault. A ceiling or roof arched in a continuous half-cylinder form.

bartizan. A turret projected out from a wall on a supporting corbel.

bas-relief. A sculpture that projects only slightly from a background plane.

bay window. A projection from the façade of a building containing windows and beginning on the ground, either square or polygonal in plan (see **bow window** and **oriel window**).

berm. Earth mound for weather protection, barrier, or landscape decoration.

blind arcade. A series of arches attached directly to a wall and thus serving a purely decorative purpose. Characteristic of Romanesque architecture.

bow window. Similar to a bay window except that it is curved in plan.

broach spire. One of the most complex of spire forms, it was originally developed in wood but has since been copied in stone. An eight-sided spire is mounted on top of a square tower, producing four odd spaces that are filled in with small half-pyramids. Broach spires are often further adorned with windows topped with gablets.

brutalism. A modernist style popularized by Le Corbusier that used bold, aggressive forms and materials such as rough poured or precast concrete.

bull's-eye window. A round or oval window with circular center and radiating panes.

buttress. A structural mass of stone, brick or concrete to reinforce a wall, particularly when an arch or vault is exerting outward pressure on the wall. Two buttresses at right angles to each other at a corner are **angle buttresses. Setback buttresses** are similar to angle buttresses but are set back from the corner.

campanile. A freestanding tower built to hold a bell.

cantilever. A structural element that projects beyond the wall beneath it.

capital. The decorative focus at the top of a column or pilaster.

cartouche. An ornamental frame often enclosing an inscription or symbol.

castellated. Featuring castle architectural forms such as crenellation in a building that is not, in fact, a castle.

chamfered. Beveled or cut at an oblique angle.

classical. A style derived from the architecture of ancient Greece and Rome.

clerestory. An upper story projecting above the mass of a building and having frequent windows to bring light into the interior.

coffered. Having a regular pattern of recessed panels: an ornamental ceiling treatment.

colonial. The style of architecture in the American colonies in the seventeenth and eighteenth centuries, derived mainly from English traditions.

colonnade. A series of columns supporting an entablature.

colonnette. A small column.

console. A scroll bracket used to support an element such as a mantel or lintel.

contextual, contextualism. An approach to design that emphasizes how a building or object relates to and fits into its surroundings rather than treating it as a pure form in a vacuum.

corbelling. Stone or brickwork that steps out from the face of a wall to support a projecting element.

Corinthian. The late Greek architectural order that is more elaborate than the Doric and Ionic styles. Corinthian capitals combine eight volutes (scroll-shaped ornaments) with acanthus leaves. Below the elaborate capital is a fluted shaft.

cornice. The projecting top of an entablature in classical architecture, or the top of the façade of a building or of a door or window.

crenellation. A series of openings along a parapet for fortification.

cresting. A decorative topping on a roof or wall, such as the ornamental iron cresting often found on the rooflines of Victorian houses.

crocket. A Gothic ornament usually based on the leaf, used to decorate the ridges of spires, gables, and other elements.

cyma reversa. A molding with a double curve in which the upper curve is convex and the lower, concave.

dentils. The row of rectangular blocks arranged like teeth on the lower edge of a cornice.

diaper. A repetitive pattern of small carved or painted ornament on a wall.

donjon. In medieval castle architecture, the large central tower, the most protected area of the complex.

Doric. The earliest and simplest of the classical Greek orders.

dormer. A window projection added to a sloping roof.

egg-and-dart molding. Alternating ovals and double-pointed spears in high relief; sometimes called egg-and-tongue or egg-and-anchor.

engaged column. A column that appears to be partially built into a wall, but retains its roundness, unlike a pilaster, which is flat.

entablature. In classical architecture, the entire assembly that is supported by columns and includes the architrave, frieze, and cornice.

entasis. A slight increase in the circumference of a column toward the center. This was created in Greek architecture to fulfill the Greek ideal of beauty and perfection by correcting the natural optical illusion that makes a straight column appear smaller in the center.

exedra. A large recess in a wall, usually semicircular in plan.

façade. An exterior vertical plane of a building; often used to refer to the front elevation.

fanlight. The semicircular or fan-shaped window above a door that provides light into a hallway or other room.

Federal. An American architectural style beginning with the Revolution and continuing until the rise of the Greek revival in the early nineteenth century. It was largely a continuation of Georgian stylistic ideas, but more restrained and simplified. It is characterized by simple flat façades with little ornament. Window sizes usually graduated from the large ground-floor windows to small third-floor windows, except some architects continued to place the tallest windows on the second floor in the Georgian manner.

finial. The decorative top of a spire, gable, pediment, or other element.

Flemish bond. A brickwork pattern in which the headers (short end) and stretchers (long side) alternate in each course to form a pattern that is decorative.

frieze. The central part of the entablature between the cornice and the architrave; it is often decorated.

gable. The triangular end of a wall under a roof formed of two sloping planes.

gablet. A small gable, generally decorative, although it may contain a lucarne to admit light or air.

gallery. A long room or hallway extending the length of a house, or an upper level in a church or theater.

gambrel. A roofline with two different slopes, the upper being flatter and the lower being steeper.

Georgian. The architectural style named for the period of the reign of the four Georges on the throne of England (1714–1830) but more truly neo-Palladian. It is an elegant symmetrical style with a large ornamental vocabulary developed by Andrea Palladio. Features include pilasters at corners, a portico or central pavilion with pediment and pilasters, fanlights, and Palladian windows.

Gibbs surround. A lively checkered pattern of stone blocks around the jamb of a door or window under a triple key-stone head; James Gibbs is credited with popularizing the device.

Gothic. A medieval style of architecture developed in France and found primarily in northern Europe, characterized by pointed arches, vaults, and flying buttresses. The Gothic revival reached the United States in the nineteenth century with romantic notions about reviving the ornament and atmosphere of medieval times.

Greek revival. A style developed in America between 1825 and the 1850s based on classical Greek architecture, with bold simple forms. The elements of the Greek temple front—pediments and columns—are key components of Greek revival, which represented a strong break from Georgian and Federal styles.

header. A brick that is laid so that only the short end is visible in a wall.

hipped or hip roof. A roof form without gable ends, in which four planes slope up to the ridge.

"historic skirt." An approach that hides the lower floors of a new high-rise building behind a historic building or group of buildings to maintain the traditional streetscape while vastly increasing the density of use on the site. The approach was developed as a compromise between those who wanted to retain old low-rise buildings and those who wanted large-scale new development. It differs from the "façade wrap" in that the new development is set back a significant distance behind the historic façades, with a roofline that looks authentic.

hood mold. Developed in medieval architecture, it is a projecting molding over a door, window, or archway to protect the opening from dripping rain.

in antis. Recessed into the face of a building, as a portico *in antis*.

infill. Structures built to fill gaps in an existing architectural context.

international style. A style developed in the 1920s and later that attempted to eliminate historical and cultural references from architecture and to begin anew with simple forms and materials suited to contemporary technology and human needs. Le Corbusier, Walter Gropius, Mies van der Rohe, and Marcel Breuer were among the leaders of the movement.

Ionic. In classical architecture, a fluted column shaft is mounted on an Attic base and surmounted by a capital composed of two large scrolls (volutes) topped by a dentil cornice.

jetty. A projection on the exterior of a building caused by an upper floor overhanging a lower floor.

lancet window. A tall, narrow Gothic-style window.

lintel. A horizontal supporting member that spans an opening.

lucarne. A small window projecting from a roof and often surmounted by a gablet; particularly associated with Gothic architecture.

lunette. A half-moon-shaped window or wall panel.

machicolation. A picturesque parapet developed in medieval castles for defense. Stone or brick corbels support arched openings in the floor through which the enemy could be attacked from above. The form is purely decorative and the openings are omitted in nineteenth- and twentieth-century architecture.

mansard roof. A steep, almost vertical roof, usually with dormer windows, enclosing the top floor, as in most Back Bay houses. The style came from Paris, where it was associated with the designs of the seventeenth-century architect Francois Mansart.

marquetry. An inlaid pattern of stone, wood, or other materials.

modernism. A twentieth-century design movement that rejected traditional styles and ornament and emphasized function, technology, and pure form, independent of place and culture. It emerged in Europe early in the century and by mid-century had global impact.

modillion. Ornamental brackets within the cornice of Corinthian and composite orders. Modillions are arranged in uninterrupted rows above the dentils but are more widely spaced.

mullion. The major vertical member used like a rail to create large subdivisions of a window or door.

muntins. The bars that subdivide window sash into small panes and hold the glass.

nave. The major space of a church between the entrance and the chancel.

neoclassical. A style of architecture developed in Europe in the later eighteenth century based on the rediscovery of the architecture of ancient Greece and Rome.

neomodernism. Reemergence of modernist expression, but without the philosophy behind it, late in the twentieth century in response to the indulgences of postmodernism.

oculus. A round or oval window or opening.

oriel window. Similar to a bay window, except that it is not supported from the ground but is projected from the wall, usually of an upper floor. Oriels are found throughout the Back Bay but are less common than the bay window.

Palladian window. A window composition with a central arch supported on columns flanked by shorter side lights. The motif was popularized by the Italian architect Andrea Palladio.

panel brick. A style of elaborate brickwork mixing brick types, colors, sizes, and shapes in three-dimensional patterns

parapet. A low wall, often at the edge of a roof.

patera. A round or oval low-relief decoration on a wall.

pediment. A triangular expression of a gable roof, as in the Greek temple front; often used above doors and windows. A **broken pediment** eliminates most of the base of the triangle, while an **open pediment** is open on top, with center point missing.

piano nobile. In Renaissance architecture, the principal floor with the most important formal rooms, one level above the ground floor. The term was adopted in later European architecture.

pilaster. A flattened column attached to a wall for decoration.

pinnacle. A miniature spire that is purely ornamental, often used on top of a buttress or gable.

porte cochere. A roofed extension of an entrance that accommodates carriages to allow passengers to enter the building protected from inclement weather.

postmodern. An eclectic style developed in the United States beginning in the 1960s, in reaction to the sterility of the international style. Elements from a variety of architectural vocabularies are used decoratively, often with great exaggeration.

putti. Cherublike babies, often with wings, favored in Italian baroque ceiling designs.

quatrefoil. Gothic window tracery divided into four circular parts.

quoins. The prominent stones at the corner of a masonry building.

reconstruction. A room or building that is rebuilt to look like the original.

recycling. Drastic adaptation to new uses of a building once serving a different purpose.

renovation. Alteration and repair of a building, retaining many of its original features but adapting them to new uses.

restoration. A process of retaining all original materials and features in an old building and using historically correct methods in repairs to return it to a state as much like its original condition as possible. Little is adapted or altered in restoration.

retro-deco. Design of a contemporary building to look vaguely art deco in style with mannered surface decoration. Motifs are typically geometric, but they may also be stylized figural or floral forms; in any case, they are clearly surface applied rather than integrated with the structure.

roll molding. A round molding of at least a half-circle in section.

Romanesque. A pre-Gothic European style of architecture particularly associated with Italy. Its round arches and vaults were much appreciated by H. H. Richardson and incorporated into his own style.

roundel. A circular ornament that differs from a patera in that it has no relief decoration. A roundel may be completely blank.

rustication. A treatment of stone that emphasizes the joints.

segmental arch. An arch composed of a circular segment of less than a semicircle centered on a point beneath the spring line.

spandrel. The triangular area between two adjacent arches.

stela, stelae. A vertical slab or pillar with incised inscription or decoration.

stilted arch. An arch that appears vertically elongated because it is sprung from a point above the supporting posts or columns.

stretcher. In brickwork, a brick laid so the long side is exposed.

stringcourse. A prominent horizontal band of masonry on a façade which sometimes projects.

superblock. A large parcel of developed land in which several blocks are joined by the elimination of streets. A superblock avoids through-circulation to create a protected enclave.

swag. An ornament that resembles draped fabric.

trabeated. Constructed by the post-and-lintel system.

tracery. The ornamental branched mullions particularly associated with Gothic churches.

transept. The crosswise arm of a cruciform church.

trefoil. Gothic tracery dividing an arch into three curved parts.

trompe l'oeil. A painted or low-relief view intended to fool the eye and create a sense of distance or perspective grander than reality. The device was developed and perfected by baroque architects and painters.

Tudor. A picturesque style that originated in fifteenth-century England, characterized by half-timbered stucco or brick with half-hipped roof and leaded windows.

turret. A small tower projecting above the roofline and derived from medieval castle architecture.

tympanum. The triangular surface within a pediment.

vermiculated. Having a mossy, worm-eaten, or spongelike appearance; a finish given to stone.

Victorian. The long eclectic period of architecture more or less during the reign of Queen Victoria (1837–1901).

Vitruvian. Any architectural ornament associated with the Roman architect Vitruvius. The Vitruvian scroll is a series of wavelike forms.

voussoir. A wedge-shaped stone used in forming an arch; the center stone is called a keystone.

SELECTED REFERENCES

Amory, Cleveland. *The Proper Bostonians.* New York: E. P. Dutton, 1947.

Boston Landmarks Commission. *Building and Streetscape Preservation Survey for Boston's Theater District.* Boston Landmarks Commission, monograph, 1979.

——————. *Central Business District Preservation Study.* Boston Landmarks Commission, monograph, 1980.

Boston Society of Architects. *Architecture Boston.* Barre, Mass.: Barre Publishing, 1976.

Bunting, Bainbridge. *Houses of Boston's Back Bay: An Architectural History, 1840–1917.* Cambridge, Mass.: Harvard University Press, 1967.

Bunting, Bainbridge, and Robert H. Nylander. *Report Four: Old Cambridge.* Cambridge, Mass.: Cambridge Historical Commission, 1973

Committee on the Visual Arts. *Art and Architecture at M.I.T.: A Walking Tour of the Campus.* Cambridge, Mass.: Committee on the Visual Arts, 1982.

Cushing, George M., Jr., and Ross Urquhart. *Great Buildings of Boston: A Photographic Guide.* New York: Dover Publications, 1982.

Drake, Samuel Adams. *Old Landmarks and Historic Personages of Boston.* Boston: Little, Brown, 1906.

Fein, Albert. *Frederick Law Olmsted and the American Environmental Tradition.* New York: Braziller, 1972.

Frothingham, Richard. *History of Charlestown, Massachusetts.* Boston: Little and Brown, 1845.

Grover, Kathryn, and Janine V. da Silva. *Historic Resource Study: Boston African American National Historic Site, 31 December 2002.* Boston: National Park Service, 2002.

Harris, John. *The Boston Globe Historic Walks in Old Boston.* Chester, Conn.: The Globe Pequot Press, 1982.

Hitchcock, Henry-Russell, Jr. *The Architecture of H. H. Richardson and His Time.* New York: Museum of Modern Art, 1936.

Hunnewell, James F. *A Century of Town Life: A History of Charlestown, Massachusetts 1775–1887*. Boston: Little, Brown, 1888.

King, Moses. *King's Handbook of Boston*. Cambridge, Mass.: Moses King, 1878.

Kirker, Harold. *The Architecture of Charles Bulfinch*. Cambridge, Mass.: Harvard University Press, 1969.

Kirker, Harold, and James. *Bulfinch's Boston 1787–1817*. New York: Oxford University Press, 1964.

McIntyre, Alexander McVoy. *Beacon Hill: A Walking Tour*. Boston: Little, Brown, 1975.

Miller, Naomi, and Keith Morgan. *Boston Architecture 1975–1990*. Munich: Prestel-Verlag, 1990.

Morison, Samuel Eliot. *One Boy's Boston 1887–1901*. Boston: Houghton Mifflin, 1962.

Newton, Norman Thomas. *Design on the Land: The Development of Landscape Architecture*. Cambridge, Mass.: Belknap Press of Harvard University Press, 1971.

Rettig, Robert Bell. *Guide to Cambridge Architecture: Ten Walking Tours*. Cambridge, Mass.: M.I.T. Press, 1969.

Sawyer, Timothy Thompson. *Old Charlestown*. Boston: J. H. West, 1902.

Southworth, Michael and Susan. *Topographic Histories of Boston Neighborhoods* (12 volume monograph). Boston: Boston 200 Corporation, 1973–74.

—————. *Ornamental Ironwork: An Illustrated Guide to Its Design, History, and Use in American Architecture*. New York: McGraw-Hill, 1991.

Stebbins, Theodore E., Jr. "Richardson and Trinity Church: The Evolution of a Building." *Journal of the Society of Architectural Historians,* December 1968, vol. 27, no. 4.

Tucci, Douglas Shand. *Built in Boston: City and Suburb 1800–1950*. Boston: New York Graphic Society Books, 1978.

Van Rensselaer, Mariana Griswold. *Henry Hobson Richardson and His Works*. New York: Dover Publications, 1969.

Victorian Boston Today: Ten Walking Tours. Boston: New England Chapter of the Victorian Society in America, 1975.

Weston, George F. *Boston Ways: High, By, and Folk*. Boston: Beacon Press, 1957.

Whitehill, Walter Muir. *Boston: A Topographical History*. Cambridge, Mass.: Harvard University Press, 1963.

—————. *Boston Statues*. Barre, Mass.: Barre Publishing, 1970.

INDEX

Joy, Benjamin, 18, 21
Joy, John, 19, 23
Joy Street, 19, 40–44, *41*
Joy Street Horse Stables, 40–41, *41*
Julius Adams Stratton Building Student
    Center, 299
Jung/Brannen Associates, 81, 91, 120, 122,
    130

K

K. M. DeVos and Company, 238
Kallmann, McKinnel, and Knowles, 52
Kallmann, McKinnel, and Wood Architects,
    58, 216, 217, 309
Kallmann and McKinnell, 56, 101
Kalman, Max, 45
Kaneko, Jun, 76
Kariotis Hall, 231–32, *232*
Keeley, Patrick C., 146, 155, 241
Kelley, S. D., 182
Kelley Street, 310
Kellogg, Harold Field, 238
Kellogg, Henry, 82
Kendall Boiler and Tank Company, *308*
Kendall Square, 274, 306
Kendall Square MBTA Station, 307, *307*
Kendall Street, 307
Kenmore Square, 228
Kent Street, 236
Kepes, Gyorgy, 34, 296
Kerr Hall, 228
Kessler, S. J., 171
Keyes, Henry F., 96
Kiley, Tyndall, Walker, 97
Kilham & Hopkins, 228
Killian Court, 297, 298, *298*
King's Chapel, 103–5, *104*
King's Chapel Burying Ground, 227
King's Chapel Parish House and Rectory,
    11, 11–12
Kingston Street, 85
Kirby, Charles K., 145
Kirkland Street, 282
Kirstein Business Branch, *102*, 102–3
Kneeland Street, 133
Knoll International, 199
Koch, Carl, 71
Kohn Pederson Fox, 118, 124
Kresge Auditorium, 298–99, *299*
Kubitz and Pepi, 219

L

Laboratory Buildings, 261
Laconia Lofts, 154, *155*
Lady Chapel, 29
La Farge, John, 182, 211
La Grange Street, 133
Lajas Heder & Associates, 234
Lamb, Thomas, 106, 131
Lampoon Castle, 287, *287*–88
Landau Chemical Engineering Building,
    302–3, *303*
Landmarks, contemporary, 315–16
Langham Court, *159*, 159–60
Langham Hotel, 122
Larkin, John, 247
Larz Anderson Bridge, 289
Law and Education Tower, 206, *206*
Lawrence, Amos and William, 237
Lawrence Model Lodging Houses, 145, *145*
Lawrence Street, 142, *143*
LDA Architects, 68
Leather and Garment district, *87*, 87–88
Lechmere Canal Park, 309–10
Le Corbusier, 275, 280
Leers Weinzapfel Associates, 119, 285
Lemoulnier, Charles, 156
Leonard P. Zakim Bunker Hill Bridge,
    240, *240*
Leslie Lindsey Memorial Chapel, *198*,
    198–99, 205, 226
Levi Newcomb and Son, 131
Lewis, W. Whitney, 188, 198
Lewis Wharf, 71–72, *72*
Liberty Square, *121*, 121–22
Liberty Tree Block, 126
Library of Art, Architecture, and Planning,
    301–2, *302*
Lillie, Lloyd, 55
Lincoln, 315, 316
Lincoln Street, 87, 88
Lincoln Street Garage, 88, *88*
Lincoln Wharf Condominiums, 79, *79*
Lindsey, Mr. and Mrs. William, 199,
    205, *206*
Lindsey Memorial Chapel, *198*, 199,
    205, 226
Littauer Center, 290, *291*
Little, Arthur, 205
Little and Browne, 106, 169, 172, 188,
    193, 205

Maps

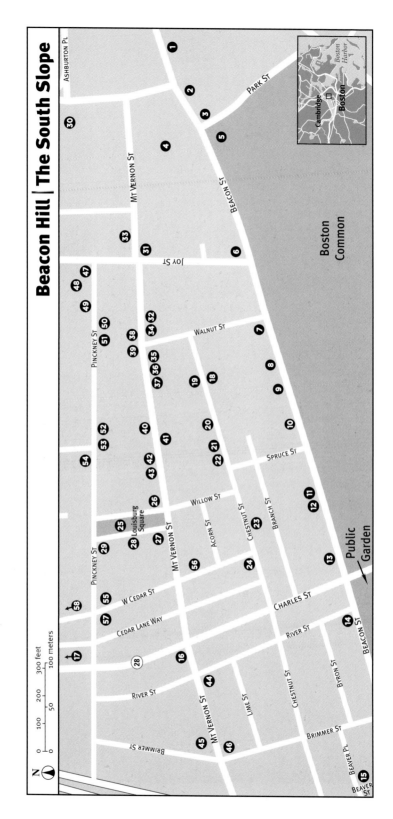

Beacon Hill | The South Slope

N

0	100	200	300 feet	
0	50		100 meters	

Ashburton Pl

Park St

Mt Vernon St

Beacon St

Boston Common

Joy St

Walnut St

Pinckney St

Louisburg Square

Spruce St

Willow St

Chestnut St

Branch St

Acorn St

Mt Vernon St

Public Garden

Pinckney St

W Cedar St

Charles St

Cedar Lane Way

River St

Beacon St

River St

Byron St

Chestnut St

Lime St

Brimmer St

Mt Vernon St

Brimmer St

Beaver Pl

Beaver St

Boston Harbor

Cambridge

Boston

Beacon Hill/The South Slope

1. Boston Athenaeum
2. Chester Harding House
3. Amory-Ticknor House
4. State House
5. Shaw Memorial
6. George Parkman House
7. John Phillips House
8. Appleton-Parker Houses
9. Somerset Club
10. Third Harrison Gray Otis House
11. William Hickling Prescott House
12. 56–57 Beacon Street
13. King's Chapel Parish House and Rectory
14. 70–75 Beacon Street
15. Deutsch House
16. Charles Street Meeting House
17. 121, 125–135 Charles Street
18. Charles Paine Houses
19. The Swan Houses
20. 23–25 Chestnut Street

21. 27 Chestnut Street
22. 29A Chestnut Street
23. Francis Parkman House
24. Harvard Musical Association
25. Louisburg Square
26. 1 and 3 Louisburg Square
27. 4 and 6 Louisburg Square
28. Louisa May Alcott House
29. 14–20 Louisburg Square
30. Beacon Hill Memorial Column
31. Lyman-Paine House
32. 28, 30, 32, and 34 Mount Vernon Street
33. 37 Mount Vernon Street
34. John Callender House
35. 40–42 Mount Vernon Street
36. 44, 46, and 48 Mount Vernon Street
37. Swan Stables
38. Mason Houses
39. 59 Mount Vernon Street

40. 67–83 Mount Vernon Street
41. 70–72 Mount Vernon Street
42. Second Harrison Gray Otis House
43. Stephen Higginson House
44. "Sunflower House"
45. Church of the Advent
46. Samuel Eliot Morison House
47. Middleton-Glapion House
48. Hidden Houses
49. 17–19 Pinckney Street
50. 20 Pinckney Street
51. "House of Odd Windows"
52. Pie-Shaped House
53. House with Hidden Chamber for Fugitive Slaves
54. Boston English High School
55. 86 Pinckney Street
56. 7, 9, and 11 West Cedar Street
57. 36 West Cedar Street
58. 61–63 West Cedar Street

Beacon Hill | The North Slope

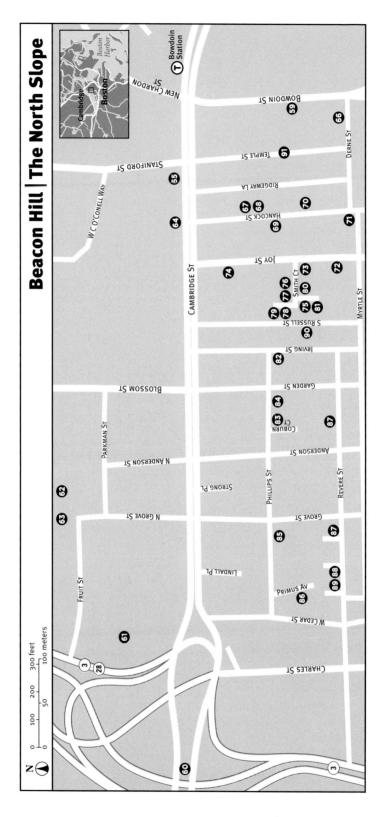

Beacon Hill/North Slope

59 Mission Church of St. John the Evangelist
60 Longfellow Bridge
61 Suffolk County Jail
62 George R. White Memorial Building
63 Bulfinch Pavilion and Ether Dome
64 First Harrison Gray Otis House
65 Old West Church
66 2–6 Derne Street
67 Home of Charles Sumner
68 22 Hancock Street
69 31–37 Hancock Street

70 32–34 Hancock Street
71 57 Hancock Street
72 Joy Street Horse Stables
73 Abiel Smith School
74 74 Joy Street
75 Joseph Scarlett House
76 James Scott House
77 5 Smith Court
78 7 Smith Court
79 Holmes Alley House
80 African Meeting House

81 Holmes Alley
82 John P. Coburn Houses
83 3 Coburn Court
84 The Vilna Shul
85 66 Phillips Street
86 Primus Avenue and "Flower Lane"
87 Rollins Place and Goodwin Place
88 Sentry Hill Place
89 Bellingham Place
90 Joseph Ditson House
91 Temple Walk

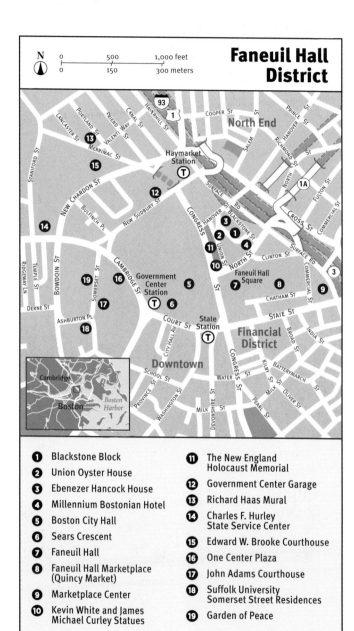

Faneuil Hall District

N

| 0 | 500 | 1,000 feet |
| 0 | 150 | 300 meters |

- **1** Blackstone Block
- **2** Union Oyster House
- **3** Ebenezer Hancock House
- **4** Millennium Bostonian Hotel
- **5** Boston City Hall
- **6** Sears Crescent
- **7** Faneuil Hall
- **8** Faneuil Hall Marketplace (Quincy Market)
- **9** Marketplace Center
- **10** Kevin White and James Michael Curley Statues
- **11** The New England Holocaust Memorial
- **12** Government Center Garage
- **13** Richard Haas Mural
- **14** Charles F. Hurley State Service Center
- **15** Edward W. Brooke Courthouse
- **16** One Center Plaza
- **17** John Adams Courthouse
- **18** Suffolk University Somerset Street Residences
- **19** Garden of Peace

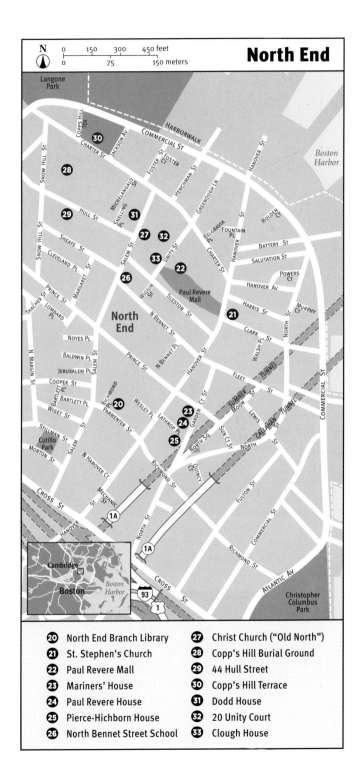

North End

N

| | 0 | 150 | 300 | 450 feet |
| 0 | | 75 | | 150 meters |

Langone Park

HARBORWALK

COMMERCIAL ST

Boston Harbor

COPPS HILL TER
CHARTER ST
JACKSON AV
SNOW HILL ST
FOSTER ST
FOSTER CT
HENCHMAN ST
GREENOUGH LN
HANOVER ST

30

28

MICHELANGELO ST
HULL ST
SNELLING PL

29

31

SHEAFE ST
CLEVELAND PL
MARGARET ST
SALEM ST

27 **32**

33 UNITY ST

BELGRAVIA PL
FOUNTAIN PL
HANOVER
CHARTER ST
HOLDEN CT
BATTERY ST
SALUTATION ST
POWERS CT
HANOVER AV

26

22

WIGGIN ST
TILESTON ST
Paul Revere Mall

HARRIS ST
MURPHY CT
NORTH ST

21

North End

THACHER ST
PRINCE ST
LOMBARD PL
NOYES PL
BALDWIN PL
JERUSALEM PL
N MARGIN ST
SALEM ST
PRINCE ST
N BENNET ST
N BENNET PL
HANOVER ST
WALSH PL
CLARK ST

FLEET ST
TUNNEL
SUMNER ST
MOON ST
LEWIS ST
CALLAHAN TUNNEL

COMMERCIAL ST

COOPER ST
BARTLETT PL
BARTLETT PL
WIGET ST
RICHMOND
WESLEY PL
PARMENTER ST
LATHROP PL
GARDEN CT ST

20

23
24
25

STILLMAN ST
Cutillo Park
MORTON ST
SALEM ST
N HANOVER CT
MECHANIC ST
HANOVER
CROSS ST

NORTH SQ
SUN CT ST
NORTH
QUINCY CT
RICHMOND ST
FULTON ST
COMMERCIAL ST
RICHMOND ST

1A

1A

Cambridge
Boston
Boston Harbor

93
1
CROSS ST
ATLANTIC AV
Christopher Columbus Park

20	North End Branch Library	**27**	Christ Church ("Old North")
21	St. Stephen's Church	**28**	Copp's Hill Burial Ground
22	Paul Revere Mall	**29**	44 Hull Street
23	Mariners' House	**30**	Copp's Hill Terrace
24	Paul Revere House	**31**	Dodd House
25	Pierce-Hichborn House	**32**	20 Unity Court
26	North Bennet Street School	**33**	Clough House

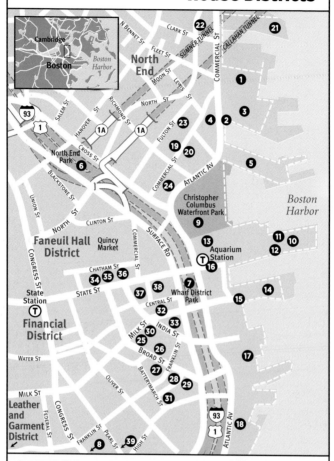

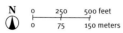

Cambridge

Boston

Boston Harbor

North End

Faneuil Hall District

Quincy Market

State Station

Financial District

Leather and Garment District

Christopher Columbus Waterfront Park

Aquarium Station

Wharf District Park

Boston Harbor

North End Park

Wharf District

① Pilot House
② One Lewis Wharf
③ Lewis Wharf
④ Prince Building
⑤ Commercial Wharf
⑥ North End Park
⑦ Wharf District Park
⑧ Chinatown Park
⑨ Christopher Columbus Waterfront Park
⑩ Long Wharf
⑪ Custom House Block
⑫ Chart House Restaurant
⑬ Marriott Long Wharf Hotel

⑭ New England Aquarium and Central Wharf
⑮ IMAX Theater
⑯ Aquarium Station
⑰ Harbor Towers
⑱ Rowe's Wharf
⑲ Commercial Block
⑳ Christopher Columbus Plaza
㉑ Union Wharf
㉒ Lincoln Wharf Condominiums
㉓ McLaughlin Building
㉔ Mercantile Wharf

Custom House District

㉕ The Architects Building
㉖ 72 Broad Street

㉗ Batterymarch Building
㉘ 99–105 Broad Street
㉙ 109–139 Broad Street
㉚ 20 and 21 Custom House Street
㉛ Chadwick Lead Works
㉜ Central Wharf Buildings
㉝ Grain and Flour Exchange Building
㉞ Richards Building
㉟ Cunard Building
㊱ MBTA Traction Power Station
㊲ Custom House
㊳ State Street Block
㊴ Lincoln Street Garage

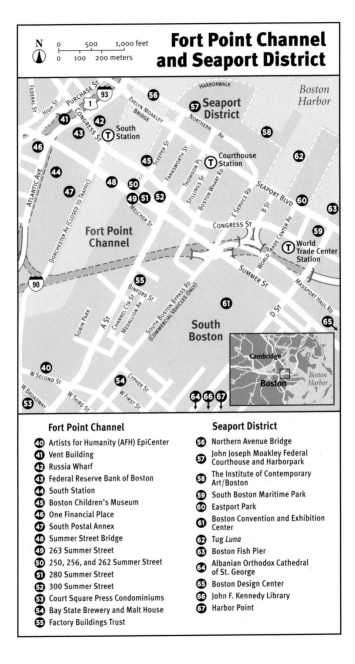

Fort Point Channel and Seaport District

N

0   500   1,000 feet
0   100   200 meters

FEDERAL ST
HARBORWALK
Boston Harbor

High St
PURCHASE ST
93
EVELYN MOAKLEY BRIDGE

1
56
Seaport District

57
NORTHERN AV
58

41
CONGRESS ST
42
South Station

43
T

46

45
SLEEPER ST
FARNSWORTH ST
THOMSON PL
STILLINGS ST
BOSTON WHARF RD
Courthouse Station
T
62

ATLANTIC AV
44
48
50

47
SEAPORT BLVD
E SERVICE RD
B ST
60
63

DORCHESTER AV (CLOSED TO TRAFFIC)
49 51 52
MELCHER ST

Fort Point Channel
CONGRESS ST
59
World Trade Center Station
T
WORLD TRADE CENTER AV

90
55
BINFORD ST
SUMMER ST
MASSPORT HAUL RD

SOBIN PARK
A ST
CHANNEL CTR ST
MEDALLION AV
SOUTH BOSTON BYPASS RD (COMMERCIAL VEHICLES ONLY)
61
D ST
65

South Boston

Cambridge

40
W SECOND ST
54
CYPHER ST
Boston
Boston Harbor

53
W BROADWAY
W THIRD ST
W FIRST ST
64 66 67

Fort Point Channel

- **40** Artists for Humanity (AFH) EpiCenter
- **41** Vent Building
- **42** Russia Wharf
- **43** Federal Reserve Bank of Boston
- **44** South Station
- **45** Boston Children's Museum
- **46** One Financial Place
- **47** South Postal Annex
- **48** Summer Street Bridge
- **49** 263 Summer Street
- **50** 250, 256, and 262 Summer Street
- **51** 280 Summer Street
- **52** 300 Summer Street
- **53** Court Square Press Condominiums
- **54** Bay State Brewery and Malt House
- **55** Factory Buildings Trust

Seaport District

- **56** Northern Avenue Bridge
- **57** John Joseph Moakley Federal Courthouse and Harborpark
- **58** The Institute of Contemporary Art/Boston
- **59** South Boston Maritime Park
- **60** Eastport Park
- **61** Boston Convention and Exhibition Center
- **62** Tug *Luna*
- **63** Boston Fish Pier
- **64** Albanian Orthodox Cathedral of St. George
- **65** Boston Design Center
- **66** John F. Kennedy Library
- **67** Harbor Point

Downtown and Financial District

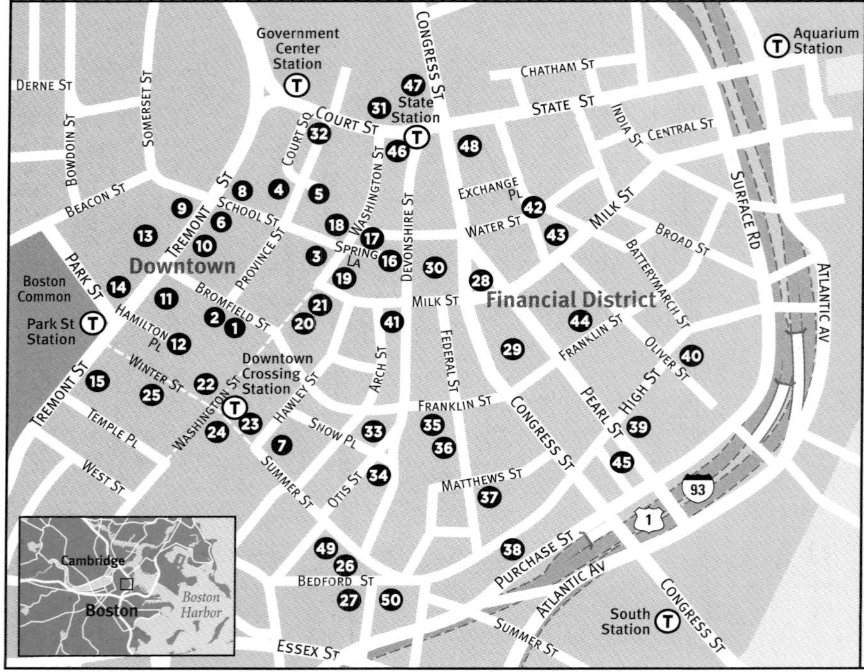

Downtown

1. 28–30 Bromfield Street
2. Wesleyan Association Building
3. 10 School Street
4. Old City Hall
5. Kirstein Business Branch
6. Parker House
7. 26–38 Summer Street
8. King's Chapel
9. 73 Tremont Street
10. Tremont Temple
11. David J. Sargent Hall, Suffolk University Law School
12. Orpheum Theater
13. Old Granary Burial Ground
14. Park Street Church
15. Cathedral Church of St. Paul
16. Spring Lane
17. Winthrop Building
18. Old Corner Bookstore
19. Old South Meeting House
20. Boston Post Building
21. Boston Transcript Building
22. Washington Street Downtown Crossing
23. 426 Washington Street
24. 450 Washington Street
25. Locke-Ober Café

Financial District

26. Church Green Building
27. Bedford Building
28. Angell Memorial Park
29. Post Office Square Park
30. Post Office
31. Ames Building
32. 26 Court Street
33. Wigglesworth Building
34. New England Press Building
35. State Street Trust Building
36. 101 Federal Street
37. United Shoe Machinery Building
38. MBTA Operations Control Center
39. 125 High Street
40. International Place
41. International Trust Company Building
42. Liberty Square
43. Appleton Building
44. Langham Hotel
45. Richardson Block
46. Old State House
47. 28 State Street
48. Stock Exchange Building and Exchange Place
49. 99 Summer Street
50. 125 Summer Street

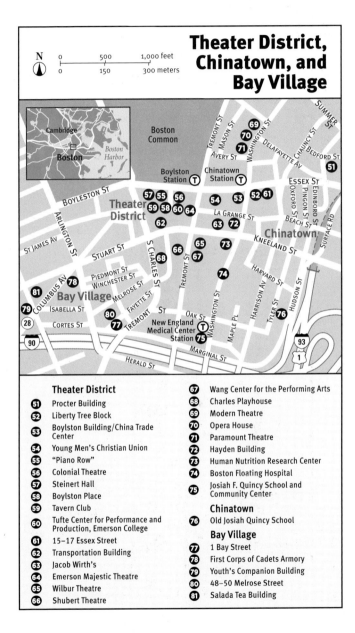

Theater District, Chinatown, and Bay Village

N

| 0 | 500 | 1,000 feet |
| 0 | 150 | 300 meters |

Cambridge

Boston Harbor

Boston

Boston Common

TREMONT ST
MASON ST
WASHINGTON ST
DELAFAYETTE AV
CHAUNCY ST
BEDFORD ST
SUMMER ST

69
70
71

AVERY ST

Boylston Station (T)

Chinatown Station (T)

51

ESSEX ST
EDINBORO ST
PINGON ST
OXFORD ST
BEACH ST
SURFACE RD

BOYLSTON ST

Theater District

57 55 56
59 58 60 64
62

54 53

52 61

LA GRANGE ST

63 72

Chinatown

KNEELAND ST

ARLINGTON ST

ST JAMES AV

STUART ST

65 73
66
67

S CHARLES ST

68

PIEDMONT ST
WINCHESTER ST

TREMONT ST

74

HARVARD ST

HARRISON AV

TYLER ST

HUDSON ST

COLUMBUS AV

78

MELROSE ST

Bay Village

81

79

ISABELLA ST

FAYETTE ST

80

28

CORTES ST

77

TREMONT ST

OAK ST

WASHINGTON ST

MAPLE PL

76

New England Medical Center Station (T)

75

90

HERALD ST

MARGINAL ST

93

1

Theater District

51 Procter Building
52 Liberty Tree Block
53 Boylston Building/China Trade Center
54 Young Men's Christian Union
55 "Piano Row"
56 Colonial Theatre
57 Steinert Hall
58 Boylston Place
59 Tavern Club
60 Tufte Center for Performance and Production, Emerson College
61 15–17 Essex Street
62 Transportation Building
63 Jacob Wirth's
64 Emerson Majestic Theatre
65 Wilbur Theatre
66 Shubert Theatre

67 Wang Center for the Performing Arts
68 Charles Playhouse
69 Modern Theatre
70 Opera House
71 Paramount Theatre
72 Hayden Building
73 Human Nutrition Research Center
74 Boston Floating Hospital
75 Josiah F. Quincy School and Community Center

Chinatown
76 Old Josiah Quincy School

Bay Village
77 1 Bay Street
78 First Corps of Cadets Armory
79 Youth's Companion Building
80 48–50 Melrose Street
81 Salada Tea Building

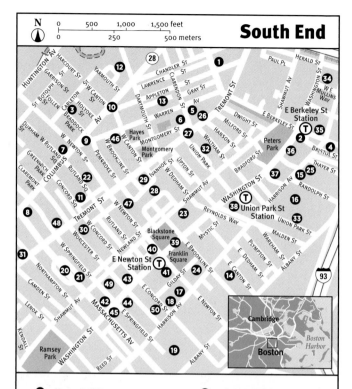

South End

N

| 0 | 500 | 1,000 | 1,500 feet |
| 0 | 250 | | 500 meters |

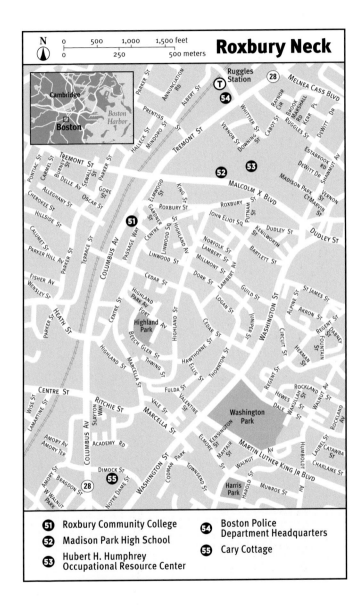

Roxbury Neck

N

| 0 | 500 | 1,000 | 1,500 feet |
| 0 | | 250 | 500 meters |

Cambridge

Boston Harbor

Boston

Ruggles Station

Ⓣ

28

54

MELNEA CASS BLVD

PARKER ST
ANNUNCATION RD
ALBERT ST
PRENTISS
WHITTIER ST
RAYNOR CIR
CABOT ST
BROOK MARSHALL RD
RUGGLES ST
KERR PL
DEWITT DR

HALECK ST
MINDORO ST
TREMONT ST
VERNON ST
DOWNING
ESTABROOK RD
DEWITT DR
SHAWMUT AV
VERNON ST

TREMONT ST
PONTIAC ST
CARMEL ST
BURNETT ST
DELLE AV
SEWALL ST
GORE ST
OSCAR ST
PARKER ST

53

52

MALCOLM X BLVD

MADISON PARK CT
MARVIN ST

ALLEGHANY ST
CHEROKEE ST
HILLSIDE ST

ELMWOOD ST
KING ST
ROXBURY ST
ROXBURY
PUTNAM ST

51

GARDNER ST
CENTRE ST
LINWOOD AV
ST HIGHLAND AV
JOHN ELIOT SQ
DUDLEY ST
KENILWORTH
BARTLETT ST
DUDLEY ST

CALUMET ST
PARKER HILL AV
PARKER ST
TERRACE ST
COLUMBUS AV
PASSAGE WAY
LINWOOD ST
NORFOLK ST
LAMBERT ST
MILLMONT ST
DORR ST
LAMBERT

ST JAMES ST

FISHER AV
WENSLEY ST

CEDAR ST
GUILD ST
LOGAN ST
ALPINE ST
AKRON ST
REGENT ST
DABNEY
FOUNTAIN

PARKER ST
HEATH ST
CENTRE ST
HIGHLAND PARK AV
FORT
HIGHLAND AV
Highland Park
HIGHLAND ST
CEDAR ST
JUNIPER ST
WASHINGTON ST
CIRCUIT ST
HERMAN ST
REGENT ST

HIGHLAND ST
BEECH GLEN ST
THWING ST
HAWTHORNE ST
THORNTON ST
ELLIS ST

CENTRE ST
WISE ST
LAMARTINE ST
MARCELLA ST
FULDA ST
VALE ST
VALENTINE ST

RITCHIE ST
SLAYTON WAY
COLUMBUS AV
ACADEMY RD
MARCELLA ST

Washington Park

ROCKLAND ST
HEWES ST
WAKULLAH ST
DALE ST
WALNUT AV
ROCKLAND AV

AMORY AV
AMORY TER

DIMOCK ST

55

28

AMORY ST
BRAGDON ST
W WALNUT PARK

NOTRE DAME ST
WASHINGTON ST
CODMAN PARK
TOWNSEND ST
ELMORE ST
MAYFAIR ST
KENSINGTON
WALNUT ST

MARTIN LUTHER KING JR BLVD

Harris Park

HAROLD ST
MUNROE ST
HUMBOLDT AV
LAUREL ST
CATAWBA ST
CHARLAME ST

51	Roxbury Community College	54	Boston Police Department Headquarters
52	Madison Park High School	55	Cary Cottage
53	Hubert H. Humphrey Occupational Resource Center		

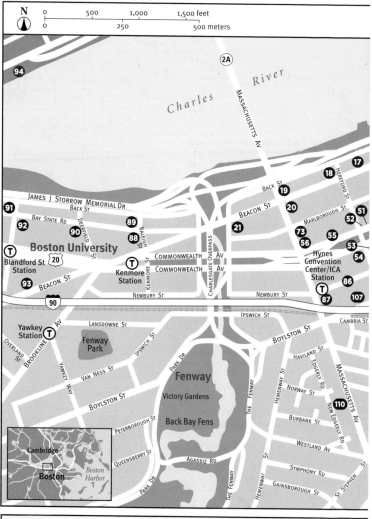

Back Bay

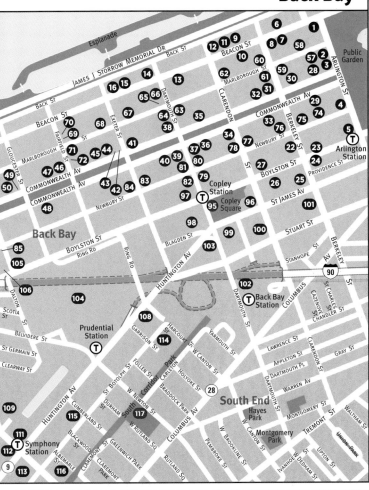

Back Bay (continued)

72 20 Fairfield Street
73 The Marlborough
74 Emmanuel Church
75 37 Newbury Street
76 Church of the Covenant
77 Trinity Church Rectory
78 109 Newbury Street
79 Hotel Victoria
80 Newbury Street at 277 Dartmouth Street
81 Boston Art Club
82 Boston Bicycle Club
83 Newbury Street at 26 Exeter Street
84 Prince School
85 Boston Architectural College
86 Newbury Street Stables
87 360 Newbury Street

Bay State Road & Boston University

88 52 Bay State Road
89 57 Bay State Road
90 112 Bay State Road
91 149 Bay State Road
92 225 Bay State Road
93 Photonics Research Center
94 DeWolfe Boathouse

Copley Square

95 Copley Square Plaza
96 Trinity Church
97 New Old South Church
98 Boston Public Library
99 Copley Plaza Hotel
100 John Hancock Towers
101 200 Berkeley Street
102 Back Bay Station
103 Copley Place

Prudential Center Area

104 Prudential Center Complex
105 Tennis and Racquet Club
106 Engine and Hose House Number 33
107 955 Boylston Street
108 116 Huntington Avenue
109 Christian Science World Headquarters
110 Church Park Apartments and Garage
111 Horticultural Hall
112 Symphony Hall
113 Massachusetts Avenue MBTA Station

St. Botolph District

114 Musicians' Mutual Relief Society Building
115 The School-House Condominiums
116 Albemarle Chambers
117 Southwest Corridor Park

Ventress
Memorial Library

Library Plaza
Marshfield, MA 02050-4998
781-834-5535
www.ventresslibrary.org

Library Hours

MONDAY	10:00 am - 8:00 pm
TUESDAY	10:00 am - 8:00 pm
WEDNESDAY	10:00 am - 8:00 pm
THURSDAY	10:00 am - 8:00 pm
FRIDAY	10:00 am - 4:00 pm
SATURDAY	10:00 am - 4:00 pm
SUNDAY	Closed

A community service from

SCITUATE
FEDERAL SAVINGS

www.ScituateFederal.com

For Better Book Care,
Use This BOOKMARK

Fenway

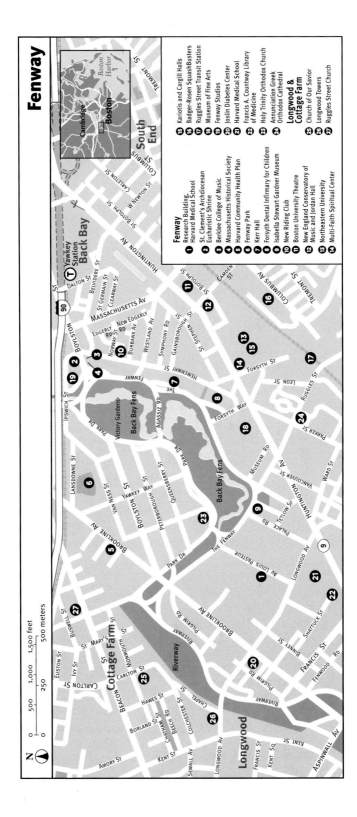

Fenway

1. Research Building, Harvard Medical School
2. St. Clement's Archdiocesan Eucharistic Shrine
3. Berklee College of Music
4. Massachusetts Historical Society
5. Harvard Community Health Plan
6. Fenway Park
7. Kerr Hall
8. Forsyth Dental Infirmary for Children
9. Isabella Stewart Gardner Museum
10. New Riding Club
11. Boston University Theatre
12. New England Conservatory of Music and Jordan Hall
13. Northeastern University
14. Multi-Faith Spiritual Center
15. Kariotis and Cargill Halls
16. Badger-Rosen SquashBusters
17. Ruggles Street Transit Station
18. Museum of Fine Arts
19. Fenway Studios
20. Joslin Diabetes Center
21. Harvard Medical School
22. Francis A. Countway Library of Medicine
23. Holy Trinity Orthodox Church
24. Annunciation Greek Orthodox Cathedral

Longwood & Cottage Farm

25. Church of Our Savior
26. Longwood Towers
27. Ruggles Street Church

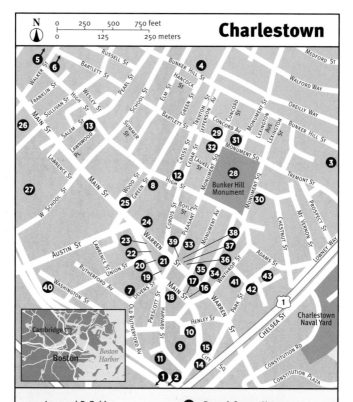

Charchartown

N

| 0 | 250 | 500 | 750 feet |
| 0 | 125 | 250 meters |

1 Leonard P. Zakim Bunker Hill Bridge

2 Paul Revere Park

3 William Kent Elementary School

4 Bunker Hill Burying Ground

5 308 Bunker Hill Street

6 St. Francis de Sales Church

7 St. John's Episcopal Church and Parish House

8 Dexter Mansion

9 John Harvard Mall and Town Hill

10 27 Harvard Square

11 Edward Everett House

12 29–41 High Street

13 Steck House

14 City Square

15 Roughan Hall

16 John Larkin House

17 John Hurd House

18 General Austin's Stone House

19 Warren Tavern

20 Timothy Thompson Sr. House

21 Thompson-Sawyer House

22 Round-Corner House

23 Armstrong Press and Edmands Hall

24 Savings Bank Building

25 Charlestown Branch Library

26 Mishawum Park Housing

27 Phipps Street Burying Ground

28 Bunker Hill Monument

29 Phineas Stone House

30 6–7 Monument Square

31 21–22 Monument Square

32 The Schoolhouse on Monument Square Residences

33 23 Pleasant Street

34 St. Mary's Church

35 Victorian House

36 81 Warren Street

37 81B Warren Street

38 81½ Warren Street

39 83 Warren Street

40 Row Houses

41 Old Training Field School

42 Arnold House

43 Salem Turnpike Hotel

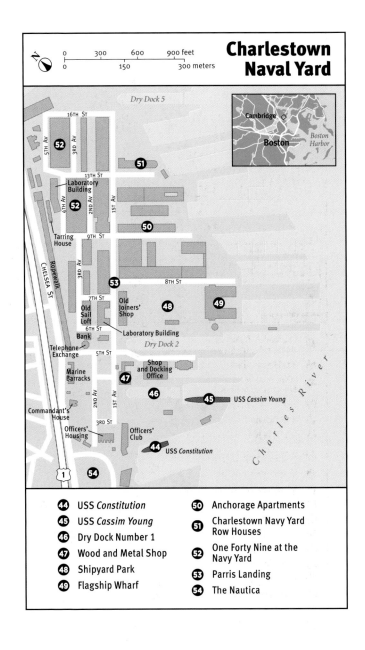

Charlestown Naval Yard

0   300   600   900 feet
0   150   300 meters

Dry Dock 5

16TH ST

Cambridge
Boston
Boston Harbor

5TH AV
3RD AV
52

51

13TH ST

Laboratory Building

4TH AV
2ND AV
1ST AV
52

Tarring House

9TH ST

3RD AV

50

53

8TH ST

7TH ST

Old Joiners' Shop
Old Sail Loft
6TH ST
5TH ST
Bank
Telephone Exchange

48

49

Laboratory Building

Dry Dock 2

Shop and Docking Office

Marine Barracks

2ND AV
1ST AV

47

46

45 USS *Cassim Young*

Commandant's House

3RD ST

Officers' Housing

Officers' Club

44 USS *Constitution*

ROPEWALK
CHELSEA ST

Charles River

1

54

44 USS *Constitution*		**50** Anchorage Apartments	
45 USS *Cassim Young*		**51** Charlestown Navy Yard Row Houses	
46 Dry Dock Number 1		**52** One Forty Nine at the Navy Yard	
47 Wood and Metal Shop			
48 Shipyard Park		**53** Parris Landing	
49 Flagship Wharf		**54** The Nautica	

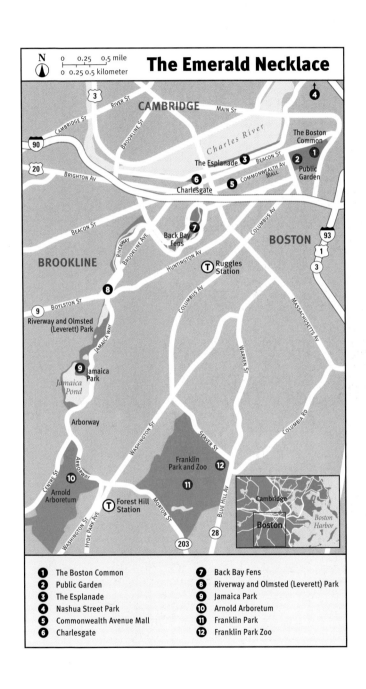

The Emerald Necklace

N

0   0.25   0.5 mile
0 0.25 0.5 kilometer

CAMBRIDGE

RIVER ST
MAIN ST
CAMBRIDGE ST
BROOKLINE ST

Charles River

90

20

BRIGHTON AV

The Esplanade ❸
Beacon St

The Boston Common ❶

❻ ❷
Charlesgate
❺ Public Garden

COMMONWEALTH AV MALL

BEACON ST

RIVERWAY

BROOKLINE AVE

Back Bay Fens ❼

COLUMBUS AV

BOSTON

93

1

3

BROOKLINE

HUNTINGTON AV

Ⓣ Ruggles Station

❽

COLUMBUS AV

MASSACHUSETTS AV

BOYLSTON ST

❾

Riverway and Olmsted (Leverett) Park

JAMAICA WAY

❾ Jamaica Park

WARREN ST

Jamaica Pond

Arborway

WASHINGTON ST

SEAVER ST

Franklin Park and Zoo ❶❷

COLUMBIA RD

❶❶

ARBORWAY

CENTRE ST

❶⓪

Arnold Arboretum

Ⓣ Forest Hill Station

MORTON ST

BLUE HILL AV

Cambridge

Boston

Boston Harbor

WASHINGTON ST

HYDE PARK AVE

203

28

❶ The Boston Common
❷ Public Garden
❸ The Esplanade
❹ Nashua Street Park
❺ Commonwealth Avenue Mall
❻ Charlesgate

❼ Back Bay Fens
❽ Riverway and Olmsted (Leverett) Park
❾ Jamaica Park
❶⓪ Arnold Arboretum
❶❶ Franklin Park
❶❷ Franklin Park Zoo

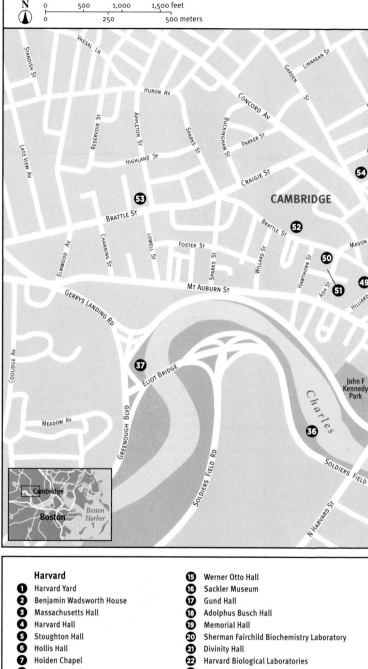

N

0	500	1,000	1,500 feet
0	250		500 meters

VASSAL LN

STANDISH ST

HURON AV

LINNAEAN ST

GARDEN ST

CONCORD AV

RESERVOIR ST

APPLETON ST

SPARKS ST

BUCKINGHAM ST

PARKER ST

LAKE VIEW AV

HIGHLAND ST

CRAIGIE ST

54

CAMBRIDGE

53

BRATTLE ST

BRATTLE ST

52

ELMWOOD AV

CHANNING ST

LOWELL ST

FOSTER ST

SPARKS ST

WILLARD ST

HAWTHORN ST

MASON S

50

ASH ST

51

49

MT AUBURN ST

HILLIARD

GERRYS LANDING RD

COOLIDGE AV

37

ELIOT BRIDGE

John F
Kennedy
Park

Charles

GREENOUGH BLVD

MEADOW AV

36

SOLDIERS FIELD

SOLDIERS FIELD RD

N HARVARD ST

Cambridge

*Boston
Harbor*

Boston

Harvard

1. Harvard Yard
2. Benjamin Wadsworth House
3. Massachusetts Hall
4. Harvard Hall
5. Stoughton Hall
6. Hollis Hall
7. Holden Chapel
8. University Hall
9. Memorial Church
10. Widener Library
11. Sever Hall
12. Warren House
13. Carpenter Center for the Visual Arts
14. Fogg Art Museum
15. Werner Otto Hall
16. Sackler Museum
17. Gund Hall
18. Adolphus Busch Hall
19. Memorial Hall
20. Sherman Fairchild Biochemistry Laboratory
21. Divinity Hall
22. Harvard Biological Laboratories
23. Rockefeller Hall
24. Josep Lluis Sert House
25. Science Center
26. Tanner Fountain
27. Austin Hall
28. Harkness Commons and the Graduate Center
29. Naito Chemistry and Bauer Laboratory Building and Center for Genomic Research

Harvard University

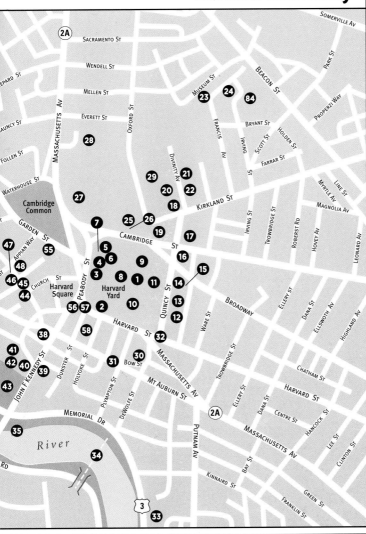

#		#	
30	Apthorp House	43	John Fitzgerald Kennedy Park
31	Lampoon Castle	44	William Brattle House
32	Quincy Square	45	"Architects' Corner"
33	Peabody Terrace	46	Design Research Building
34	John W. Weeks Footbridge	47	Longfellow Chestnut Tree Memorial
35	Weld Boathouse	48	Gutman Library
36	Northeastern University Henderson Boathouse	49	Loeb Drama Center
37	Winsor and Belmont Hill Schools Boathouse	50	Stoughton House
38	Winthrop Square	51	Philip Johnson Courtyard House
39	John Hicks House	52	Vassall-Craigie-Longfellow House
40	Belfer Center for Public Management	53	Hooper-Lee-Nichols House
41	A. Alfred Taubman Building	54	Longy School of Music Concert Hall
42	John F. Kennedy School of Government	55	Christ Church
		56	Farwell-Read Block
		57	Harvard Square Station
		58	Holyoke Center

MIT and Other Cambridge Sites

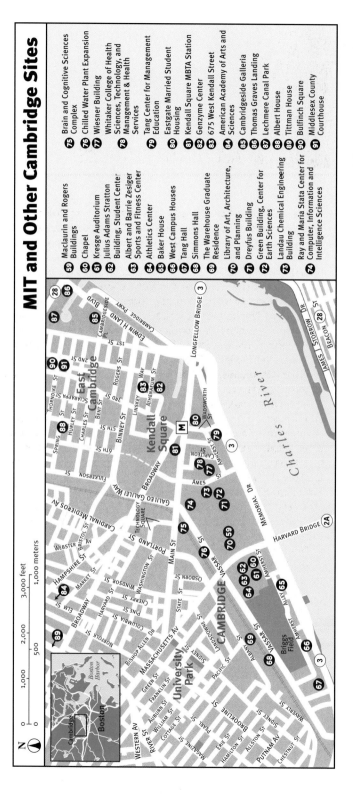

59 Maclaurin and Rogers Buildings
60 Chapel
61 Kresge Auditorium
62 Julius Adams Stratton Building, Student Center
63 Albert and Barrie Zesiger Sports and Fitness Center
64 Athletics Center
65 Baker House
66 West Campus Houses
67 Tang Hall
68 Simmons Hall
69 The Warehouse Graduate Residence
70 Library of Art, Architecture, and Planning
71 Dreyfus Building
72 Green Building, Center for Earth Sciences
73 Landau Chemical Engineering Building
74 Ray and Maria Stata Center for Computer, Information and Intelligence Sciences

75 Brain and Cognitive Sciences Complex
76 Chilled Water Plant Expansion
77 Wiesner Building
78 Whitaker College of Health Sciences, Technology, and Management & Health Services
79 Tang Center for Management Education
80 Eastgate Married Student Housing
81 Kendall Square MBTA Station
82 Genzyme Center
83 675 West Kendall Street
84 American Academy of Arts and Sciences
85 Cambridgeside Galleria
86 Thomas Graves Landing
87 Lechmere Canal Park
88 Albert House
89 Tittman House
90 Bulfinch Square
91 Middlesex County Courthouse